CHINA'S POLITICAL
DEVELOPMENT

CHINA'S POLITICAL DEVELOPMENT

Chinese and American Perspectives

KENNETH LIEBERTHAL
CHENG LI
YU KEPING
editors

BROOKINGS INSTITUTION PRESS
Washington, D.C.

The Brookings Institution is a private nonprofit organization devoted to research, education,
and publication on important issues of domestic and foreign policy. Its principal purpose
is to bring the highest quality independent research and analysis to bear on current and
emerging policy problems. Interpretations or conclusions in Brookings publications
should be understood to be solely those of the authors.

Library of Congress Cataloging-in-Publication data
    China's political development : Chinese and American perspectives / Kenneth Lieberthal,
Cheng Li, and Yu Keping, editors.
        pages   cm
    Includes bibliographical references and index.
    ISBN 978-0-8157-2535-0 (pbk. : alk. paper) 1. China—Politics and government—
21st century. I. Lieberthal, Kenneth, editor of compilation. II. Li, Cheng, 1956– , editor
of compilation. III. Keping, Yu, editor of compilation.
    JQ1510.C489568 2014
    320.951—dc23   2014000169

9 8 7 6 5 4 3 2 1

Printed on acid-free paper

Typeset in Adobe Garamond

Composition by Cynthia Stock
Silver Spring, Maryland

Contents

Acknowledgments   vii

Preface   ix
KENNETH LIEBERTHAL AND CHENG LI

Introduction
Toward Good Governance in China: Perspectives
of Chinese and American Scholars   1
YU KEPING

1   The People's Republic of China's Sixty Years
    of Political Development   39
    YU KEPING
      Comment by Kenneth Lieberthal   62

2   Transition from a Revolutionary Party to a Governing Party   73
    WANG CHANGJIANG
      Comment by Larry Diamond   93

3   The People's Congress System and China's Constitutional
    Development   103
    SHI HEXING
      Comment by Jacques deLisle   121

4   Political Consultation and Consultative Politics in China   136
    LIN SHANGLI
      Comment by Joseph Fewsmith   156

5 The Rise of Civil Society in China   165
   WANG MING
      Comment by Mary Gallagher   183

6 China's Experiments in Social Autonomy
   and Grassroots Democracy   192
   YAN JIRONG
      Comment by Andrew G. Walder   211

7 China's Public Service System   221
   YU JIANXING
      Comment by Tony Saich   244

8 Decentralization and Central-Local Relations
   in Reform-Era China   254
   YANG GUANGBIN
      Comment by Lynn White   270

9 China's Grassroots Democracy   282
   HUANG WEIPING
      Comment by Jean C. Oi   299

10 China's Interest Coordination Mechanism   308
    JING YUEJIN
       Comment by Cheng Li   328

11 Contemporary China's Decisionmaking System   340
    ZHOU GUANGHUI
       Comment by David M. Lampton   359

12 Building a Modern National Integrity System:
    Anticorruption and Checks and Balance of Power in China   366
    HE ZENGKE
       Comment by Melanie Manion   387

Contributors   397

Index   401

Acknowledgments

This volume reflects an unusually wide-ranging collaborative effort, and we are deeply grateful to the many people whose support made it possible and whose determination and understanding have resulted in both Chinese and English editions. We want to express our special appreciation to the following.

The Chinese and American authors of the individual chapters that make up this volume Chinese and American scholars first wrote their pieces for a conference in Beijing in October 2010, then did the editing necessary for publication of the volume in Chinese, and finally again reviewed and worked on additional changes to make the volume more accessible to an English-speaking audience. Some of the authors also participated in a follow-up Brookings conference on this topic in May 2011. The expertise, commitment, patience, and understanding of all the authors have been extraordinary.

The China–United States Exchange Foundation provided financial support to the China Center for Comparative Politics and Economics, directed by Yu Keping, making this entire project possible, including the costs out of this English translation. We want to express our gratitude to the foundation itself and in particular to its chairman, Chee Hwa Tung, for his tireless efforts to improve the depth of understanding between China and the United States.

The Brookings Institution has provided the ideal environment for bringing this project to fruition. Brookings Board Chairman John L. Thornton and President Strobe Talbott have encouraged in every way research, writing, and related activities at Brookings that increase the depth of understanding between Chinese and Americans. We owe a particular debt of gratitude to key leaders in the

Foreign Policy program and John L. Thornton China Center—Martin Indyk, Ted Piccone, Michael O'Hanlon, and Jonathan Pollack—for their encouragement and support. Thornton China Center staff Kevin Foley, Iris An, Teresa Hsu, Jordan Lee, and Robert O'Brien provided excellent logistical support for this project.

Our thanks go to Andrew Marble, John Langdon, and Ryan McElveen for proofreading and editing, and especially Meara Androphy for editing, proofreading, and checking the translation and source citations.

We very much benefitted from the hard work of Professor Yu's research assistants, Yan Jian and He Zhe. Dr. He helped with the initial conference of the Chinese and American scholars in Beijing, and Dr. Yan was exceptionally helpful in coordinating contacts with the Chinese authors and in providing editorial assistance.

Last but by no means least, the terrific team at the Brookings Press has been enormously helpful. We want in particular to thank Valentina Kalk, director; Rebecca Campany, marketing director; Larry Converse, production manager; Janet Walker, managing editor; Susan Woollen, art coordinator; and Katherine Kimball, copy editor.

Preface

KENNETH LIEBERTHAL and CHENG LI

Political science is a relatively new discipline in China. After the founding of the People's Republic of China in 1949, this nascent discipline was first criticized as a pseudoscience, then reorganized along Soviet lines, and ultimately entirely abolished. Only in the wake of the Cultural Revolution was it established anew as one of the consequences of Deng Xiaoping's policy of reform and opening up.

Since the 1980s, political science in China has evolved substantially: from a discipline whose sole emphasis revolved around pedagogy to one promoting both education and research, from being limited to the theories of Marx, Engels, Lenin, Stalin, and Mao Zedong to employing a wide array of conceptual approaches and foreign methodologies, and from basic ideological discourse to indigenously based empirical research. The field of political science has now become firmly established, and prominent Chinese political scientists enjoy broad readership, frequently appear as commentators in the media, sometimes brief top leaders, and actively participate in international forums and dialogues.

The twelve Chinese authors who have contributed to this volume are leading scholars who specialize in analysis of the Chinese political system. Most hold their master's or doctoral degrees in political science from Chinese universities and have years of experience in international academic exchanges and visiting scholar programs. They are both very much a part of the Chinese academy and serious analysts of China's system. Many have perspectives that reflect the critical thinking found among the liberal-minded intellectuals within the Chinese Communist Party itself.

Unique Features of This Volume

Past efforts at publishing collections of papers by Chinese and international political scientists have tended to draw together work on different subjects by different authors and thus have lacked a focused, in-depth discussion among the authors. This book is unique in that it combines the research of Chinese scholars with extensive, substantive comments on each by a counterpart American scholar. The topics include issues involving every part of the political system from the national level to the grass roots, and the chapters explore concerns regarding state structures, norms, and processes as well as those focused on the interaction of the state with its rapidly changing environment. Most of the papers by Chinese authors trace the evolution of the issue under scrutiny over time, identify key contemporary concerns, and, in many instances, provide recommendations for future policies and approaches.

For the twelve participating American scholars, this project presented an important learning opportunity and a chance to discuss their views with influential Chinese academic counterparts. The American commentators are professors at leading U.S. universities and senior fellows at important think tanks; eleven of the twelve have for many years focused their research on Chinese politics and society.[1] This project has encouraged both the Chinese and American political scientists to speak their minds freely. It began with an October 2010 Beijing seminar that brought together all the Chinese and American authors for a thorough discussion of their papers. A follow-up May 2011 Brookings forum on China's governance was attended by a subset of these authors.

The original papers and commentaries were revised and published in China in early 2013.[2] The present English-language volume closely hews to this original Chinese publication, but it is not a direct translation of it. Chinese style encourages scholars to present detailed overviews of all progress made to date, including copious citations of pertinent policies and related comments of top leaders, before providing in-depth explication of existing shortcomings, analysis of key challenges, and recommendations for future actions. This English edition has used editorial discretion to maintain the flavor and core substance of the original Chinese papers while making these papers more accessible to an American audience. Our goal has been to convey both the basic style of analysis employed by each author and the substantive points the author is making.

In its totality, this volume contains an enormously rich set of details on almost every significant aspect of governance in China. Careful reading of the chapters will yield important rewards in terms of details of particular issues and also, especially, insights into the ways these issues are framed and understood in

China. Chinese assumptions about the requisites of good governance differ in many of their particulars from those commonly held in the United States. There also is vigorous debate in China about specific steps the political system should now take. If the two countries are to better understand each other, it is vitally important for Americans to appreciate the thinking of leading Chinese specialists concerning China's own governance and the issues that are now engaging them.

Lagging Political Reform

In recent years China's political reform has not kept up with many of the new realities created by its economic development and social changes, with the consequence that its political system faces increasingly serious challenges. These include a large and growing wealth gap, severe depletion of key natural resources, a deteriorating overall ecological environment, a rapidly aging demographic pyramid, inadequate health and social security systems, food and product safety scandals, rampant corruption, tensions between the central and local governments, ethnic conflicts, and the socially disruptive effects of large-scale urbanization. All these are consequences of the decades-long effort to produce extremely rapid GDP growth, and all now call for more effective steps to improve governance on a major scale.

This is not to say all changes in recent decades have been only economic and social and not political. Significant governance reforms have in fact taken place over the past thirty years, as the papers in this volume detail. For example, lifelong tenure for leading officials has been eliminated, and career paths, decisionmaking processes, qualifications for elite recruitment and promotion, the distribution of authority among various levels of the political system (central, provincial, municipal, county, township), political controls on state-owned enterprises, and many other important aspects of the system have changed consequentially since the outset of the reforms at the end of the 1970s. Even so, as some Chinese leaders and scholars recognize, there is a significant gap between the country's current socioeconomic evolution and its political development. In the words of Wen Jiabao, premier of the People's Republic at the time, the situation has become one of walking with "one long leg and one short leg."[3]

Yu Keping presents a comprehensive introduction to the convergence and divergence of views of the Chinese and American scholars in his opening overview chapter. This chapter also raises a few other important topics that are touched on but not treated in depth in this book. Professor Yu highlights one of the core concerns regarding China's political future: the gap between the pace and content of the country's political development and the speed and consequences of the country's ongoing socioeconomic transformation.

Promoting Democratic Development

The term *democratic development* has been a major trope of China's official political discourse over the past three decades. The efforts at democratic development in China since Mao Zedong's death have focused on many aspects of governance: permitting limited local-level elections; adopting measures to circumscribe the penetration of the society by the state, the domination of the government by the Chinese Communist Party, the privileging of political power over law, and the use of government-developed plans instead of market forces to shape economic outcomes; expanding and improving mechanisms for consultation regarding policymaking, nominations and promotions of people in positions of authority, and development of legislation; and so forth.

The scope of these measures and the seriousness of purpose in developing and implementing them belie common Western stereotypes of the Chinese system. Because these efforts have played such a central role in the country's political development over the past thirty years—and because the type of thinking that has informed them must be better understood if a meaningful dialogue on political development is to become possible with China—this volume treats seriously and systematically the various dimensions of China's "democratic development" efforts to date, including both the thinking behind them and their actual results.

Many countries have put in place different types of democratic systems to meet their distinctive governance needs. Democratic systems at their best mitigate social conflict, increase government legitimacy, and promote economic growth by allowing greater room for creative thinking. Political openness, freedom of expression, and an independent judiciary may help foster technological innovation, which can be especially important for developing countries that are seeking to make the transition from extensive to intensive growth.

The particularities of a country's democratic development are mainly dependent on its historical, social, and political environment, and American scholars do not believe that the distinctive American style of democratic system is wholly suitable for China. Chinese leaders and intellectuals are right in saying that China's democracy will, and indeed should, have its own characteristics. Similarly, the democratic systems of Britain, the United States, India, and Indonesia are different in many important aspects. But there is a serious question as to the attributes a political system must have in order to benefit from the legitimacy and freedom that democratic governance should provide. Both American and Chinese scholars parse this central issue in various ways in their contributions to this volume.

We want, finally, to express our deep appreciation to Professor Yu Keping, who played a major role in both the conception and execution of this project.

We are also deeply indebted to the Chinese and American scholars whose patience, seriousness, and commitment have made this volume—and its Chinese companion volume—possible.

Notes

1. Stanford University professor Larry Diamond, an authority on democracy development and comparative politics, is the only contributor who is not an expert on China.

2. Yu Keping and Kenneth Lieberthal, eds., *Zhongguo de zhengzhi fazhan: Zhong Mei xuezhe de shijiao.* [Chinese political development: Perspectives of Chinese and American scholars) (Beijing: Social Sciences Academic Press, 2013).

3. Wen Jiabao, "Nuli jianshe renmin manyi de zhengfu" [Energetically build a government with which people are satisfied], *Qiushi* [Seek truth], no. 3 (2013), pp. 1–3.

Introduction
Toward Good Governance in China: Perspectives of Chinese and American Scholars

YU KEPING

C hina's continued development over the past three decades since its reform and opening up and its rapid rise on the international stage have generated heated discussion and debate in Chinese and international academic circles, especially regarding political change.[1] Many questions have been raised: How should China's political evolution be viewed? Has China's great economic progress been accompanied by major political progress? What is the political rationale for China's economic success? What changes has China's economic development brought to its governance, and what further changes can be expected? Is there such a thing as Chinese-style democracy? What are the similarities and differences between the political paths of China and Western countries?

These questions have also spurred reflection on some of the general assumptions of political science and have led to even more questions: Is democracy a universally shared human value? Does economic modernization necessarily lead to political democratization? What is the relationship between democracy and social modernization? What are the main sources of political legitimacy in today's world? What are the criteria for democracy and good governance? Can the Western democracy and governance model apply to China?

An in-depth discussion of these questions has direct bearing not only on our understanding of basic political values such as democracy, liberty, equality, human rights, and good governance but also on whether consensus on major real-world political issues can be reached between the Chinese government and public intellectuals or between the People's Republic of China and the international community. The significance of these questions goes far beyond the academic sphere and involves China's political reform and its relationship with the world.

On these issues, Chinese and American scholars can have mutually informative and enlightening discussions and debates. This introductory chapter presents a brief survey of the important works here.

In this volume, twelve prominent Chinese political science scholars and twelve prominent American scholars in political science and sociology—most of whom are experts on China—offer their insights concerning China's political development since the reform and opening-up period that began in 1978, more than thirty years ago. These chapters include analyses and comments on the Chinese Communist Party, the National People's Congress, the political consultation system, government administration, and civil society. They often reflect the authors' views on the basic elements of democracy—such as elections, the rule of law,[2] separation of powers, accountability, decisionmaking, civic engagement, transparency, civil rights, public service, coordination of interests, supervision of power, and societal autonomy. Taken together, these chapters provide an overview of the achievements China has scored on the path to good governance, the paths it chose not to pursue, the challenges it faces, and the direction in which it is heading.

From Revolution to Reform

To understand China's political evolution since the reform and opening-up period and its future political development, it is necessary first to study the political culture and the political system that was put in place after the Chinese Communist Party (CCP) came to power in 1949 and to survey the course of the country's political development since that time. Only in this way can one truly understand the changes the Deng Xiaoping–led reforms made since 1978 to the political mechanisms established by Mao Zedong, how China's political system has evolved over the past three decades, the areas in which China has made political progress since then, and the internal motivations and main themes of these changes.

These questions are the subject of my chapter 1. My basic conclusion is that Chinese society has undergone a comprehensive change since the CCP took power, especially since the reform and opening-up period began in 1978. Overall, the process of reform and opening up has brought not only economic growth but also political and social progress. Economic reform in the absence of political reform is inconceivable. To a certain degree, China's great success in economic modernization is the logical outcome of its political evolution.

In 1949 the CCP overthrew Kuomintang rule and established the People's Republic of China (PRC). This marked the transition of the CCP from a revolutionary party to a ruling party, a substantial change with far-reaching implications for both the CCP and the country. After this, the primary task of the CCP and its government gradually changed from seizing power to consolidating power and from destroying the old state to constructing a new one. The foundation of the party's legitimacy also gradually shifted from revolution to reform and from political campaigns to national law. This process of transition was slow and difficult, and it took thirty years to reach a turning point.

For the CCP, revolution was a formidable weapon with which power was seized and consolidated. *Revolution* was the most bedazzling word in the political vocabulary of the first thirty years of the PRC. Although the communist revolution actively promoted the historical advancement of society, Mao Zedong's theory of "continuous" or "permanent" revolution and the Cultural Revolution it fomented also brought great suffering to Chinese society.

With the convening of the third plenary session of the 11th CCP Central Committee in November 1978, the priorities of both the party and the government changed from class struggle to economic construction, and China again embarked on the road toward modernization. The era of revolution was officially over, and the reform era led by Deng Xiaoping began.

During the next three decades, from 1979 to 2009, *reform* replaced *revolution* as the most highly valued and authoritative word in Chinese politics. As political priorities shifted, China's political culture also changed along five major trajectories: from struggle to harmony, from dictatorship to democracy, from rule of man to rule of law, from authoritarianism to the separation of powers, and from state to society.

Along with the great progress toward political democracy over the past sixty years, the PRC has also faced many problems, including long-standing political corruption, impediments to political participation of citizens, widening income disparities and social inequality, and defective mechanisms of the democratic process of decisionmaking. With the advancement of the market economy and growing political demands from citizens, China's political procession toward democracy has become irreversible. China's political reform in the near term should at least address these primary goals:

—establish a blueprint for China's political democracy from a holistic and long-term perspective

—reform and improve the people's congress system, especially the election of deputies, deliberation, decisionmaking, and supervision, a mechanism for checks and balances, and citizen participation, to strengthen its legislative and supervisory role

—reform and improve the system of the Chinese People's Political Consultative Conference (CPPCC), especially the selection of its members, political consultation, and supervision, to better fulfill its political consultative and supervisory roles at all levels

—advance intraparty democracy, especially with respect to the rights of party members, such as the right to vote, the right to be informed of proceedings, the right to participate, and the right to supervise, in all of which substantial reforms are needed

—advance grassroots democracy, especially democratic elections, democratic decisionmaking, and democratic supervision at the county and township levels, where major reforms are also needed

—make breakthroughs in the key relationships involved in China's democratic development, such as the relationship between the party and the government, supervision of the exercise of power, recommendation and selection of cadres, intraparty elections, grassroots elections, political transparency, and civic engagement

In a word, the success of China's overall modernization will increasingly hinge on its political modernization as judged by its reliance on the rule of law and democracy, and only through substantial political reforms can an advanced level of democracy and rule of law be achieved.

Kenneth Lieberthal, senior fellow in foreign policy at the Brookings Institution, describes my analysis as a comprehensive and clear survey of China's political development in the three decades preceding and the three decades following the 1978 reforms. He notes that my summary and specification of the six major directions of China's political development—from revolution to reform, from struggle to harmony, from authoritarianism to democracy, from rule of man to rule of law, from concentration of powers to separation of powers, and from state to society—and the inherent driving force of the reforms are persuasive. He also observes that the post-Mao reform led by Deng Xiaoping was an all-encompassing social transformation. China has experienced not only a sea change in its economic system but also extensive and profound changes in its political and social systems. The reevaluation of various key issues—such as the party's position and role, the country's economic development pattern, the driving forces of social change, the relationship between the state and society, and the most effective mode of governance—has been driving China's continued political and social transformation.

Lieberthal identifies two major reasons for the success of China's reforms: Deng's political wisdom and exceptional leadership and the strong consensus within the CCP on reforms. He points out that there is never a lack of reformists, but truly successful reformists are historically rare. Deng was a strategic visionary as well as a master of the art of politics. He not only had a clear understanding of the defects of the system left behind by Mao but also was a sharp political strategist who understood how to build momentum behind reforms and how to weaken opposing forces. Additionally, he was ready to compromise on minor issues so as to maintain a basic consensus on the overall policy of reform and opening up.

The disastrous results of the Cultural Revolution, Lieberthal notes, also helped form a consensus within the party that the existing system was in crisis. It was this general consensus, shared by officials and the public alike, that enabled the reformists to overcome both the resistance from vested interests and the fear of the uncertainties inherent in reform.

Lieberthal clearly sees the serious political challenges faced by China, including the growth-oriented entrepreneurship that has penetrated into the core of the political system and the corruption that seems to have become an integral part of the system. However, he recognizes the difficulty in advancing political reforms. First, China currently does not have a strongman reformist of strategic vision like Deng. Second, the existing political and economic systems have led to the formation of vested interest groups whose interests are maximized under the existing system and will be impaired by the reforms. In fact, there already is a strong tendency among local officials to resist reforms. Finally, there is no consensus that China is now in crisis and thus none of the urgency to undertake major reform.

Although China is facing increasing pressures and tension, the achievements brought by the existing system are impressive enough to make many people basically satisfied with the status quo. Noting these factors, Lieberthal suggests that an effective bottom-up approach to reform, rather than top-down reform such as has occurred over the past thirty years, may be of more importance to China's future development.

From a Revolutionary Party to the Ruling Party

Unlike Western countries, which have multiple political parties, China has a single ruling party, the Chinese Communist Party. The party controls the country's core political power, and therefore any change on its part has a direct impact on China's political process. No change in the CCP over the past decades has been greater than its transition from a revolutionary party to a ruling party. In chapter 2, Wang Changjiang has undertaken a systematic review of this transition and its far-reaching ramifications.

Wang points out that the CCP was profoundly influenced by three major legacies: the model of the Communist Party of the Soviet Union, Sun Yat-sen's views on party building, and China's traditional political culture. Under the influence of these factors, the CCP became a highly unified and highly centralized political organization in which subordinates complied with their superiors and the whole party complied with the central committee and, ultimately, with the paramount leader. After coming to power, the CCP further evolved into a totalitarian party, fusing the party and the government into a party-state.

The party leadership led the government through the party's direct participation as an organization in government affairs. As to society, where the party had comprehensive control over state power and all social matters, there were no conditions for the formation of a society relatively independent from the state and the party. Thus the state and the party were one, and society and the state were one.

Such a political party, marked by iron discipline and strict organization, had obvious advantages in seizing political power. However, seizing political power and running the state required completely different approaches. In point of fact, after it came to power the CCP grew disengaged from reality on many major issues, including legitimacy, ideology, governance, and the party's relationship with the state and society. In the face of the problems detailed above, the CCP has actively sought to catch up by embracing a number of reforms and innovations.

First, the present effort at reform has been a process by which the party has increasingly widened reforms, albeit gradually. These reforms were based on its new realization that "the position of the ruling party is neither justified inherently nor inevitably maintained forever once it has been achieved."[3] Second, the reforms came about in response to the expansion of the party's member base. With the adoption of the theory of the Three Represents (三个代表, *san ge dai biao*), the party opened its membership to elites from all circles of life.[4] Third, changes in the way the government is run have sought to promote "democratic rule, scientific rule, and the rule of law" as the basic principles of government. Fourth is a greater emphasis on democracy, intraparty democracy being considered the lifeblood of socialism. Fifth and finally, greater importance has been attached to political consultation with other nonruling parties.

Wang Changjiang sees the CCP's transition from a revolutionary party to a ruling party as a gradual process that has made substantial progress. However, this process is far from complete. The internal reform of the party has entered a deep-water zone where many fundamental problems have yet to be solved.

Intraparty reforms have stayed at superficial levels; substantive steps have yet to be taken. The reforms have tended to avoid the important and dwell on the trivial, with some core issues such as the relationship between the party and the government yet to be determined. There are still many gaps in institutional and organizational arrangements. Although they have increased in number, intra-party requirements, rules, and regulations are often not organically connected and even can contradict one another. Some outdated doctrines remain strongly influential within the party. Intraparty democracy has not progressed evenly. For example, democratic authorization, democratic decisionmaking, partici-patory democracy, and democratic supervision have all lacked comprehensive planning and have faced various bottlenecks. Vested interest groups are pos-ing an increasing threat to the ruling position of the CCP. Obviously, if these underlying problems are not resolved, the CCP's own transformation will not be truly realized.

Larry Diamond, a Stanford University democracy expert with a strong inter-est in China's democratization, has also followed the various reform efforts of the CCP. In his comment on Wang's chapter, he writes that China's leadership is exploring a safer path of political reforms toward a governance system with more accountability, transparency, efficiency, responsiveness, and legitimacy—but has done so without the competitive elections that would put the CCP at risk. Dia-mond enumerates the following reform measures that the CCP has taken: giving more power and authority to the National People's Congress and other legisla-tive organs at the provincial and lower levels; strengthening some independent organs, such as the anticorruption commissions and bureaus and judicial organs, to advance the rule of law and fight corruption; strengthening the professional-ism and independence of civil servants; implementing the separation of pow-ers in economic affairs and gradually delegating political authority; promoting public participation and consultation in decisionmaking; giving more freedom and independence to the media and civil society organizations; and introducing intraparty democracy, especially moving toward more transparency and institu-tionalized power competition.

Although Diamond agrees with Wang that the CCP is no longer a purely rev-olutionary party, he holds distinctive views on other issues. He has some doubt about whether the CCP has completed the transition into a ruling party. What strategies and methods, he asks, should the CCP take to assert its leadership? He holds that the CCP may be drawing on the political model of Singapore, where the ruling party has achieved both economic prosperity and long-term single-party rule. In other words, China's leadership is seeking to build an economically affluent, culturally advanced, and internationally active and confident country and may eventually allow small-scale, low-level competitive elections, while at the same time maintaining permanent leadership in the country. Maybe there will be more political freedom and less suppression, but democracy in the Western sense of the word is not on the agenda.

Diamond notes that in development studies, scholars often ask how a given country can achieve Denmark's level in terms of political, economic, and social development processes. How can a poor or middle-income country approach Denmark's success through structural, institutional, and cultural reforms? Diamond believes that the question the CCP may be asking itself today is instead, "How can China reach the level of Singapore?" He points out that, given the inimitable peculiarity of the Singapore model and the fact that China is a large country undergoing rapid modernization and facing a great amount of social conflict, the political system of Singapore is not a workable model for China to follow.

Finally, Diamond notes that, according to modernization theory, people's conception of authority, political values, and their rights and role in the political system will undergo drastic changes as a country advances its social and economic development. These changes will eventually translate into the pursuit of democracy. Although China's leadership has managed to further economic growth and social stability by relying on various aspects of traditional culture, with the advancement of modernization the Chinese will, especially over the next twenty-five years or so, certainly have a greater demand for deep and comprehensive political reforms. Diamond argues that the partial reforms adopted by the CCP will, in the long run, prove inadequate to solve China's deep-seated problems. With improved education and increasing awareness of the need for political participation, Chinese society will increasingly require that the government reform itself. If the CCP gradually introduces fundamental top-down political reforms—such as separation of party and government, increased freedom of expression and association, restrictions on power, and improved governance—the country's chances of long-term stability and prosperity will be greatly enhanced.

From Dictatorship to Constitutional Government

The Chinese Communist Party describes the state it founded as a dictatorship of the proletariat, a term that has two meanings: that the CCP runs the state exclusively on behalf of the proletariat and that it exercises dictatorship over class enemies and practices democracy among the masses. In the first thirty years of the People's Republic of China, the dictatorship of the proletariat led to, among other outcomes, excessive emphasis on the violent suppression of class enemies and excessive reliance on the party's policies in state governance, with serious neglect of democracy and the rule of law.

This situation began to change after the 1978 reform and opening up, as unprecedented importance was attached to democracy and rule of law. Building a socialist rule-of-law state was formally set as the basic goal of the country's political development, and the notion of "socialist political civilization" with democracy and rule of law at its core was included among the basic tasks of political development.[5] The people's congress system, China's basic government system as set down in the Constitution, began to assume increasing importance. This, the highest organ of state power, has worked toward promoting the country's democratization and rule of law. In chapter 3, Shi Hexing provides a comprehensive analysis of the creation and evolution of the people's congress system from the perspective of constitutional government.

China's Constitution explicitly states that "all power in the People's Republic of China belongs to the people. The National People's Congress and the local people's congresses at various levels are the organs through which the people exercise state power."[6] The local people's congresses at various levels, whose deputies are elected by the citizens, are organizations that represent public opinion as well as the country's legislative and decisionmaking organs. The National People's Congress, as the highest organ of state power mandated by the Constitution, shoulders the important responsibility of maintaining the country's constitutional order.

Shi observes that political order is one of the indispensable foundations of China's constitutional development, while how to handle the relationship among "the Party's leadership, the people as the master of the country, and the rule of law" constitutes an unavoidable question of state governance. China's official stance is that there is an "organic unity among the Party's leadership, the people as the master of the country, and the rule of law."[7] In fact, adhering to this organic unity is the basic organizational principle of China's political development.

Shi holds that the effort to maintain the organic unity of the party, the people, and the rule of law requires that the People's Congress handle well its own relationships with the people, the government, and the ruling party. Furthermore, constitutional government requires that these relationships be defined and clarified based on the Constitution. After the reform and opening up, the Chinese Communist Party and the Chinese government took development of the rule of law as the basic goal of the country's political development. The Chinese leadership explicitly required that all organizations, including the CCP itself, and all individuals make the Constitution the basic standard of conduct and stated that no organization or individual was above the Constitution or the law. This was a monumental step in the history of China's political development.

What is constitutional government? Does China have constitutional government? How should constitutional government be advanced in China? As Shi Hexing observes in his chapter, there have been discussions of these questions throughout China's 100 years of constitutional history. According to Mao Zedong, "Constitutional government is democracy." Zhang Youyu, the founder of the CCP's legal theory, has defined constitutional government as "a political form under which the state's political system, the organization of state power, and the rights and obligations of the government and the citizens are provided for in the Constitution so that the government and the citizens are entitled to their respective rights and bear their respective obligations, and no conduct of any organization or individual in violation of and beyond those provisions is allowed."[8]

Shi fully supports this constitutional government argument and views the people's congress system as the institutional foundation of China's constitutional development. He notes that China's political development thus far has shown that the people's congress system, as an institutional platform of democracy, has provided fundamental support for the country's constitutional development. However, he also notes that China's constitutional development still has a long way to go.

Although according to the Constitution the National People's Congress is China's organ of state power and the people's congress system is its basic political system, for a long period of time the people's congresses at various levels have been described as mere "rubber stamps." Even if the system has undergone positive change, these congresses have still not received much attention. Research on China's people's congress system is sparse in both domestic and international academic circles.

Shi calls for this situation to change. Jacques deLisle, a professor at the University of Pennsylvania, also takes up this issue. His comment on Shi's chapter centers on three aspects of China's congresses: a historical explanation of the expanding and increasing role of the National People's Congress and the people's congress system, the connection between the people's congress system and constitutional order and the role of the People's Congress in strengthening constitutional order, and the connection between the people's congress system and political democracy.

DeLisle writes that since the period of reform and opening up began, the National People's Congress has assumed an increasingly important role. For example, it serves as an institutionalized shelter and power base for the top leadership. DeLisle believes that the people's congress system still faces many obvious difficulties in advancing constitutional government, including the Constitution's intrinsic problem and the fact that the people's congress system is losing "market share" in the face of competition from other institutions. He also has some doubt about Shi Hexing's notion that the people's congress system is at the core of China's constitutional development and democratic governance because, in his opinion, the concepts of constitutional government and democracy are still controversial, confusing, and maybe even unstable. He also calls attention to the fact that the people's congress system has undergone fewer and slower reforms than have other organs and therefore still faces a great risk of losing its market share in the democracy field. Jacques deLisle concludes that prospects for political reform in China are not bright in terms of the expansion of democracy and the strengthening of constitutional restrictions on political power.

From Political Consultation to Deliberative Politics

The CCP explicitly opposed "single-party autocratic rule" in its early struggle with the Kuomintang for political supremacy, but after coming to power the party firmly rejected the Western multiparty electoral system. However, the CCP does not view its own rule as "single-party autocracy" but instead defines it as a "multi-party cooperative and political consultative system under the leadership of the CCP."

In chapter 4, Lin Shangli deems this "party system with Chinese characteristics" to be an important institutional mechanism of popular democracy. Despite its indigenous origin, the system has a strong orientation toward modern democracy in both values and function; and by balancing the relationship between the party, the state, and society, it provides an important institutional foundation for China for maintenance of national solidarity and social stability in its modernization and development process.

Lin explains that China's political consultative system creates a unique political situation in which one-party leadership, multiparty cooperation, and diversified consultation are organically united. In practice, this political ecology is effectively positioned to respond to the two major challenges facing China's political development: the challenge posed by social pluralism to one-party leadership and the challenge posed by economic marketization to the country's existing democratic system.

Owing to historical and practical factors, Lin notes, China eventually put in place a party-state system under which the party's leadership and the state's leadership are organically integrated and combine to determine the country's political life and political development. One of the most important characteristics of the party-state system is that, rather than being the product of the state system, the party shapes the state. The CCP's leadership both provides a political mandate and is itself an integral part of the system and therefore is subject to the constraints and regulations of the system.

Thus leadership, cooperation, and consultation are the party system's political logic, and political consultation—which comprises the four elements of multiparty coexistence, consultative deliberation, mutual supervision, and sharing weal and woe—is its operating mechanism. The CPPCC is the core organization by which multiparty cooperation, political consultation, participation in and deliberation of state affairs, and democratic supervision are achieved.

China's political consultation gradually spread from interactions among parties and between government and society to those taking place among social groups and among citizens in the 1990s. During this time political consultation extended from the top level to the grass roots, from the state to society. The country is working toward the gradual establishment of a democratic consultative system consisting of political consultation and social consultation between the state and society at the state level and among citizens at the social level.

Although the system is still in the process of expansion and improvement, Lin is optimistic that consultation has become an important axis of China's political life. The country's political system is thus developing from one of defined political consultation to one of deliberative politics. Unlike political consultation, where consultation serves narrow political ends, deliberative politics is a system in which deliberation is a basic principle of political life and regulates political relationships, processes, and behavior. Lin predicts that this transition from political consultation to deliberative politics will continue as a key direction of China's political development.

Joseph Fewsmith, a professor at Boston University and an expert on both China's local governance and the CCP, expresses doubts about the concept of consultative democracy, which has become popular among Chinese scholars. He argues that China practices a form of consultative democracy, rather than deliberative democracy, and that there are important differences between the two.

Western discussions view deliberative democracy as a way to make up for the alienation between citizens and the government under a formal democracy. In contrast, Chinese discussions of consultative democracy center on a different premise: that because, under the centralized leadership of the CCP, Chinese society has since the reforms began become increasingly pluralistic, the CCP should use mechanisms like consultative democracy to reduce the tension between its centralized leadership and China's pluralistic society, to enhance the legitimacy of the country's system, and to abate social conflicts. In sum, deliberative democracy is more suitable to addressing problems related to democratic systems, while consultative democracy is more suitable to addressing problems peculiar to China's system.

In recent years, Fewsmith notes, various new attempts at consultative democracy have been made in China, whose content and scope far exceed that outlined in Lin Shangli's chapter. Examples include participatory budgeting, intraparty democracy, direct elections, public hearings on proposed policies, and nongovernmental chambers of commerce—all of which he contends are effective forms of consultative democracy.

Fewsmith agrees with Lin Shangli that the CPPCC holds a unique position in China's political life. However, he also points out that the CPPCC does not have substantive power, including the power to make binding resolutions, and its role has been diminishing ever since the socialist transformation movement and the Great Leap Forward of the 1950s. Although held at the same time as the National People's Congress, the CPPCC usually does not receive much attention and is largely neglected. If the CPPCC has neither power nor authority, it cannot fulfill its role as a consultative organ.

Fewsmith is not optimistic about the prospects for deliberative politics in China, and he believes that two conditions must be satisfied for the CPPCC to become an effective consultative organ: CPPCC organizations at all levels should have their powers explicitly defined and conferred by law, and nonruling democratic parties should play a greater role in the Chinese society. But he feels that both these conditions are unlikely to come about in present-day China.

From Political State to Civil Society

China has maintained a political tradition of "grand unity" for several thousand years. Grand unity means not only a high degree of political centralization but also, in a more profound sense, a high degree both of the integration of politics, economy, and culture and of structural configuration between state and society. China's reform and opening up, in a way, has been a process of segregation of the social structure from the political system. The introduction of the market economy requires the separation between the government and enterprises and gives rise to a relatively independent market system or economic system. Moreover, with the advancement of the market economy, state and society have grown somewhat apart. At the same time the appearance of many nongovernmental organizations has accompanied the formation of a relatively independent civil society, and this is having an increasingly profound impact on China's political life.

In chapter 5, Wang Ming notes that a signboard bearing the words "Civil Society, Grow Together" (公民社会, 共同成长, *gongmin shehui, gongtong chengzhang*) appeared in Shenzhen in 2008. Wang Ming observes that the display of this signboard marked a new trend in China's reform and opening up: the rise of civil society.

According to Wang, the number, quality, structures, and networking systems of nongovernmental organizations (NGOs), as well as the relevant policy environment, are all important aspects of the development of civil society. He presents a survey of the expansion and evolution of civil society in China since the 1980s based on three dimensions: the association activities of citizens, the pursuit of a better society, and the rise of the public sphere. Civil society is mainly made up of various NGOs, or social organizations, as they are referred to in official Chinese documents. According to Wang's statistics, nearly 430,000 foundations, social groups, and private institutions have registered with civil affairs departments at all levels in China, a number that is almost three times what it was ten years ago, four times what it was twenty years ago, and more than forty times what it was in 1979, at the beginning of the country's reform and opening up. According to his estimates, the actual number of active NGOs is eight to ten times the official number, totaling somewhere between 3 million and 4 million organizations. Wang optimistically concludes that as far as association activities are concerned, civil society is booming in China.

China's policies toward civil society have also seen tremendous improvement. The official attitude to NGOs has changed from one of wariness to one of fostering and regulating, as demonstrated by the government's release of a series of policies and regulations on civic organizations. Civic organizations are playing an increasing role in such fields as national policy formulation, civic political engagement, charity and other worthwhile causes, ecological and environmental protection, and civil rights protection. The rescue effort in the wake of the Wenchuan earthquake of 2008, one in which NGOs and the government worked together, ushered in a new era for China's civil society.

Wang also recognizes the serious constraints that hinder the growth of civil society in China, including an outdated regulatory system, rigid ideology, inadequate professionalism, tensions with market mechanisms, and lack of social supervision. Despite these hindrances, Wang affirms that the development of both the market economy and democratic politics means that the rise of civil society in China will continue. He predicts that China's civil society will develop in the following three directions, all of which he feels are different from the paths taken by Western countries: political elite–led and authoritarian-inclined civil society, intellectual elite–led advocacy of democracy, and economic elite–led advancement of wealth.

Mary Gallagher, a professor at the University of Michigan, agrees with Wang's view that China's path toward a vibrant civil society will continue to broaden and is irreversible. She notes the strange phenomenon that civil society is dying out as a topic in Western academic discussion yet is being resurrected in China. She observes that the attention Western academia paid to the growth of civil society in China reached its climax in the 1990s and the early years of the twenty-first century, but with the suppression of the democratic movement in China in 1989 and the predicament of new democracy in Eastern European countries and the former Soviet states, Western academics gradually lost confidence in the growth of civil society in these countries. As a result, although many scholars continue to study state-society relations and controversial social movements, few scholars now use a civil society framework to analyze those issues. Scholars with an interest in NGOs and association activities in China also avoid using the term *civil society* because this concept is closely linked with the expectation of democratic reform. Ironically, Western scholars' increasing neglect has come at a time of constant growth of civil society in China.

While acknowledging the importance of civil society to democratic governance, Gallagher also points out its limitations. On one hand, she admits, civil society is closely linked with social justice, the public interest, and charitable causes. As a powerful means of solving social problems and exercising public power, its essence is the coming together of individuals to improve the social environment by taking collective action. The growth of civil society can thereby increase social capital, improve democratic governance of state and parties, and strengthen corporate social responsibility. On the other hand, Gallagher expresses serious doubt regarding the basic assumption that there is a direct causal relationship between good civic associations and good governance. In her opinion, the experiences in Asia and Europe show that there is no such direct relationship.

Gallagher concludes that there are substantial limits to what civil society can be expected to achieve and that we should therefore lower our expectations and shift the focus of our attention toward the state and market spheres. According to Gallagher, it is more important to reform the legislative and decisionmaking processes, create new political participation models, and promote distributive justice in the market so as to create better conditions for the growth of civil society.

From Government Rule to Societal Autonomy

Less government control, better governance; less governmental direction, more societal autonomy: this is a general trend in political development around the world. Societal autonomy is self-management by the people. It is the most direct form of the people's serving as the masters of the country. It is the foundation and an important characteristic of democratic politics and a practical way of giving power back to the people. The degree of societal autonomy in a country reflects the degree of its political development. A country with a higher degree of societal autonomy usually has more developed democratic politics, a more dynamic social life, and a firmer foundation of social stability.

Societal autonomy has a long history in China, a country whose traditional governance was characterized by "state power stopping at the county level." However, as Yan Jirong notes in chapter 6, with the launch of the socialist transformation movement after the founding of the PRC, the Chinese Communist Party began to reshape the country's social order by putting in place the people's commune system in the countryside, subdistrict office and work-unit systems in cities, and various mass organizations such as trade unions, the Chinese Communist Youth League, and federations of women. "With left-leaning ideology as a guide," these systems facilitated penetration of state power into society and led to a highly centralized, totalitarian government. Only after the reform and opening-up period began, with the transformation to a market-oriented economy, the pursuit of economic growth, and improvements in governance, did China gradually embark on a path toward reduced state power and increased societal autonomy.

Yan holds that following China's economic opening, many people formerly affiliated with the state's unified management system became highly autonomous social members outside the system. This transition led to a certain degree of separation between state and society and the formation of a new social structure, one that has, in turn, created the precondition for societal autonomy.

China's leadership usually considers societal autonomy from the perspective of advancing grassroots democracy and deems the party's grassroots organizations and grassroots governments to be the leading forces of grassroots democracy and societal autonomy. Yan thus points out approvingly that in China the government is the first driver of societal autonomy. It endorses and promotes grassroots societal autonomy through laws and regulations, organizes and implements societal autonomy through the leadership of party organizations and grassroots governments, directs societal autonomy through pilot programs, encourages societal autonomy through incentives, and supervises activities and rectifies malpractices that occur as a result of societal autonomy. Key advances in societal autonomy in China include the autonomy of villagers in the vast rural areas, urban resident and community autonomy, industrial autonomy, and social organization (NGO) autonomy.

While fully acknowledging the great progress China has made in increasing societal autonomy over the past thirty years, Yan also admits that the transparency of government decisionmaking, management, and service provision has significantly lagged behind. Although societal autonomy offers channels for the expression of social interests, the key is achieving openness in governmental decisionmaking, management, and service provision and enabling social topics to turn into issues for public discourse. The government needs to demonstrate more commitment and determination in this regard. Yan argues that progress in China's societal autonomy will in fact depend on how much progress the Chinese government makes in the realms of openness and transparency.

Stanford University professor Andrew Walder highly commends China for its progress toward societal autonomy. In his opinion, high economic growth alone is not enough to ensure social prosperity and political stability. A country's political and social systems must adapt to changes in its social environment and be able to handle new problems. If China fails in this regard, it will face social instability domestically, and its rise on the international stage will be imperiled. Thus the development of societal autonomy is an important step to ensure the sound development of China's political and social systems.

Walder argues that contrary to the fear that local autonomy or societal autonomy will lead to social unrest, China's experience shows that societal autonomy is the prerequisite for lasting political stability. He disagrees, however, with the bottom-up political reform proposed by Yan Jirong. Based on a comparison of the political histories of different countries, Walder concludes that "the changes that will restructure China's state for the twenty-first century must come from the top down."

Societal autonomy, Walder holds, is the road to good governance. As the universal political pursuit of humankind in this age of globalization, good governance has replaced good government to become the ideal political goal. A popular Western view asserts that the Western democratic system, with multiparty competition and representative democracy at its core, is the only path to good governance. Based on a survey of the experience of China and Singapore in good governance, however, Walder has his doubts. In his words, "Many outside observers . . . often assume that only a multiparty political system that enshrines the rule of law can bring good governance." However, we have good reason to doubt this view. In fact, pointing to the many multiparty political systems that are "poorly governed, deeply corrupt, illiberal, violent, and politically unstable," he notes that "it is far from clear that a move to a multiparty system would solve governance problems in China, and it is arguable that it would make them worse."

Nevertheless, Walder also expresses his deep concern about China's political prospects. His main worry is that excessive emphasis on social stability, especially the tendency to maintain social stability at all costs, may ruin the opportunity to enact political reforms and could even lead to a serious political crisis. Many governments have been overthrown because their leaders, for ideological reasons, refused to make political reforms of any kind and resorted to violence to maintain social order and stability. The focus on maintaining stability, in essence, leads to political stagnation; thus when Gorbachev attempted to address the corruption of the Soviet Union's political system, it was already too late. Governments collapsed one by one—Poland, Hungary, East Germany, Czechoslovakia, Bulgaria, Romania, Albania, Yugoslavia, and finally the Soviet Union itself.

Who ended socialism in Eastern Europe? It was not Gorbachev, Walder maintains, but Brezhnev and the country's conservative leadership system, because "on the political side, [the Soviet system] could not imagine anything other than maintaining stability." Walder explicitly expresses what troubles him the most: "My worry about China . . . is that its leaders, trying to avoid the errors of Gorbachev, will gradually take the path of Brezhnev."

From Control to Service

Universal and equal provision of welfare and services for citizens has always been considered an important advantage of socialism. That is why, despite the poor economic conditions that existed at the founding of the PRC, the government still managed to establish a simple and egalitarian public service system under the planned economy. Of course, economic scarcity meant that the public services provided were limited. Given the planned economy and the highly politicized nature of society at the time, the public services provided by the government allowed almost no choice, and citizens' economic, political, and social lives were tightly regulated.

In a way, the process of reform and opening up has been one whereby the government gradually loosens and reduces control over its citizenry and increases and improves public services. With the transition of the CCP from a revolutionary party to a ruling party, the legitimacy of the government that the party runs has also become increasingly dependent on the public services the government provides for society. These public services have a direct bearing on the rights of urban and rural residents and on the country's overall social and political progress.

In chapter 7, Yu Jianxing provides a systematic survey of the development and evolution of China's public service system since 1949, focusing on the social policy, financial support, and supply systems of China's contemporary public services. He points out that China established an egalitarian public service system under its planned economy. Although the government managed to provide universal access to public services despite the scarcity of resources that existed at the time, there still existed such problems as overall inadequacy of public services, low efficiency, and unequal distribution between the urban and rural areas and among different institutions.

In the 1980s and 1990s, the Chinese government began to advance the establishment of a public service system characterized by marketization and achieved the transition from a single supplier to multiple suppliers and from state-funded to fee-based provision of services, bringing a significant improvement in service efficiency and quality. Since 2002, when the government announced its commitment to a "scientific outlook on development" and to building a harmonious society and service-oriented government, public service has become an important part of the government's work at all levels. The Chinese government has now established a preliminary public service system that provides employment security and service, compulsory education, medical security and public health care, old-age security and services, minimum living security and social assistance, and affordable housing.

Yu Jianxing points out that China's existing public service system has played an important role in reducing social conflicts, promoting social justice, advancing national welfare, and satisfying social needs and has become a major contributor to the country's social and political stability. However, this system also faces various problems and shortcomings: the proportion of fiscal expenditure on public services remains low, there is still a significant gap between supply and demand, and the gap between urban and rural areas and among different groups and regions remains prominent.

Yu holds that substantial reform will be required to solve these problems, including such components as advancing the reform of the public administration system to change the functions of government and establish a service-oriented government, building a social policy system that integrates the urban and rural areas to end the duality and segmentation in public services, advancing reform of the public fiscal system to better define the administrative and fiscal powers of the central government and local governments and comprehensively adjust the structure of fiscal expenditures, continuously improving governance and promoting innovation in public services, and establishing and perfecting a mechanism by which the public can express its need for public services and a system to evaluate public service performance.

In the wide-ranging research that Harvard University professor Anthony Saich has conducted on China, public services have been a key subject. In his comment on Yu Jianxing's chapter, Saich calls attention to the nature of public services and the relationship between public services and political development. He notes that China's public service supply system is developing and falling in line with the public service supply systems of other countries in Asia and beyond. In the reform era, policy still gives responsibility for providing public services to the institutions where people work, but in practice it allocates public services by using the market to contract public services to families, privately run service providers, or NGOs, leading effectively to large-scale privatization of the public service sector. This means that, for most people, those they turn to for help are their families, communities, and employers rather than the government. But in fact it is a basic responsibility of the government to provide public services on an equal basis for all citizens. Saich observes correctly that it was only after Hu Jintao and Wen Jiabao took power that China's public service policies began to reflect this view of citizens' rights.

Based on his understanding of the nature of public services, Saich insightfully illuminates the close relationship between public service delivery and political development. Public service reform will influence political development in three main ways: awareness of citizenship, citizens' evaluation of government performance, and diversification of public services, all of which will have influence on societal relations.

Saich holds, for example, that the new social policies announced by the Chinese government in the late 1990s marked a transition toward a citizenship-based welfare system. Measures included the introduction of a basic welfare system covering both urban and rural residents, the extension of the old-age pension system to cover a portion of rural residents, and the inclusion of migrant workers in the local welfare and service systems.

Given China's centralized system, and because the CCP represents the interests of the people, the government is facing increasing pressure to provide public services. The government will increase its commitment to provide public services and will do so in an increasingly transparent manner. And the diversification of public services has the potential to change societal relations in China. Although the government still plays a decisive role in public services, it is often the institution of last resort. Saich makes particular mention of the far-reaching significance of civil social organizations in providing public services: the more developed a civil society, the more committed, transparent, and effective the government's provision of public services.

From Centralization to Decentralization

A high degree of centralization of power has been the Chinese Communist Party's hallmark. Both revolution and dictatorship require the centralization of power. In the process of struggling for political power, the CCP needed revolution and dictatorship and, consequentially, the centralization of power. This centralization of power once provided the party the strength it needed to overthrow the old regime and establish a new regime by way of political mobilization. Excessive centralization, however, strangles individuality and freedom and ultimately hinders social creativity and productivity, economic development, and political progress. That is why a major effort of Deng Xiaoping's reform was to decentralize authority: from the central government to the local governments, from the government to enterprises, and from the state to society.

In chapter 8, Yang Guangbin traces China's centralization and decentralization evolution since the reform and opening-up period from the particular perspective of the relationship between central and local governments. He finds that the reform process has in essence been one of economic decentralization; political centralization has been left largely unchanged.

Yang observes that China has a dual political-economic structure, consisting of "political centralism and economic federalism." Political centralism mainly exhibits itself as the party's monopoly on cadre management and a powerful administrative management system that prevents any substantial reform in vertical leadership. Economic federalism mainly manifests as local governments' relatively independent administrative, legislative, and fiscal powers and the system of tax distribution between local governments and the central government.

Yang holds that with the advancement of reforms, there will be an increasing tension between the unitary political system and the federal economic system. The relationship between the two will become increasingly complicated, which may lead to a series of serious problems such as the fragmentation of state authority, local protectionism, and a fragmented economy.

Yang's distinctive approach leads to several interesting findings. The first is that state authority is becoming fragmented. China's reforms, which sought to decentralize power, did change the country's political structure and process. As noted, the unitary political system, which was based on "the party administering cadres" and the maintenance of a strong government, remained unchanged, thereby guaranteeing social order and security and also strengthening the government's political legitimacy. Nevertheless, the result, according to Yang, has been the fragmentation of state authority owing to interest competition among different departments.

Yang also argues that the economic federalism that has resulted from decentralization has in fact not weakened the central government's fiscal capacity but has actually strengthened it. This reality now provides additional incentives to promote decentralization in other areas.

Finally, Yang finds that reforms to decentralize power have not been allowed to conflict with the country's judicial and administrative enforcement systems. Now that the central government has greater fiscal capacity as a result of decentralization, it should shoulder more responsibility in terms of providing public services. By reducing the share of public services provided by local governments, the central government can check their tendency to blindly pursue GDP growth.

In his comments on Yang Guangbin's chapter, Princeton University professor Lynn White focuses on the significance of decentralization for China. He holds that one of the intrinsic requirements of modern responsible government is function-based decentralization. Which countries, though, are more centralized, and which are more decentralized? These questions are closely related to the issue of political culture. Generally, Asian governments are more centralized, Western governments are more decentralized.

White adds that neither centralization nor decentralization is intrinsically good or bad; the key is which is more beneficial to a country's unity and social development. Based on this differentiation, he makes it clear at the very beginning of his discussion that he agrees with the basic attitude held by Chinese leaders that CCP members should not allow themselves to be influenced by the erroneous Western political views. Whether China should be more centralized or decentralized depends on which is more beneficial to the country's stability and prosperity. Although White acknowledges that it is not for him to say whether centralization is suitable for China, he has questions about whether decentralization is essentially good for China.

Following the above train of thought, White offers an order of priority for China's decentralization efforts: functional decentralization should come first, followed by geographic decentralization and then electoral decentralization. In his opinion, functional decentralization— that is, the presence of clearly demarcated jurisdictional boundaries—has greatest importance. Functional decentralization is an intrinsic requirement of the modern political system because different specialized fields (such as diplomacy, the judiciary, the procuratorate, schools, the military, banks, and enterprises) require specialists of different expertise. In this regard, the Chinese government still has much room for improvement. To strengthen functional decentralization, White argues, is also an important means for the party and the government to deal with social transformations.

White is cautious about geographic decentralization and, in particular, electoral centralization. He explicitly warns that China should follow its own path of political development rather than simply copy the Western democratic model. It would be extremely dangerous for the Chinese economic juggernaut to implement national general elections before firmly establishing functional decentralization.

From Grassroots Democracy to Democracy at the National Level

Putting aside for the moment the persistent debates among scholars as to whether China's political reforms should be from the top down, from the bottom up, or both, what is beyond doubt is that the Chinese government has consistently focused its efforts to enhance democratic development at the grassroots level. As is the case with the roadmap from intraparty democracy to societal democracy, bottom-up advancement is a basic approach of China's overall democratic development. In fact, all the most important breakthroughs in political democracy since China's reform and opening up—such as direct village elections and the "public recommendation, direct election" of township leaders—have taken place at the grassroots level.

Grassroots democracy includes three main aspects: village autonomy based on village committees, urban resident autonomy based on residents' committees, and worker autonomy based on worker congresses. In academic discussions, however, grassroots democracy has a much wider scope. In chapter 9, Huang Weiping asserts that grassroots democracy has two aspects: grassroots society (comprising both the village committee and community committee) and grassroots government (party committees, people's congresses, and governments at the county and township levels). He adds that grassroots democracy has two dimensions—democratic elections and democratic governance—and develops primarily around the process of democratic elections.

Huang holds that China's grassroots democracy has undergone multidimensional changes. It began with village committee elections but then spread from the countryside to the cities, from grassroots society to government at the grass roots, from outside the party to within the party, and from elections to actual governance.

The first major step has been the expansion from village democracy to urban community democracy, mainly in the form of village committee elections and community committee elections. The second has been the expansion from grassroots society to grassroots government, mainly in the form of direct elections of the heads of townships and deputies to the people's congresses at the county and township levels. The third has been the expansion from democracy outside the party to democracy within the party, mainly in the form of the two-ballot system of village party branches and the public recommendation and direct election of members of township and town party committees. Under the two-ballot system, candidates are subject to a primary vote by village representatives and a final vote by party members. Under the "open recommendation, direct election" system (also known as "two recommendations, one election" and "direct recommendation, direct election"), candidates for township and town party committee membership are first subject to recommendation by village representatives, then to review by the party committee at a higher level, and finally to election at the party congress at the township or town level. Fourth, and finally, has been the expansion from democratic election to democratic governance, mainly through democratic decisionmaking, democratic management, and democratic supervision.

Huang provides an in-depth analysis of the driving forces, difficulties, and characteristics of, as well as the prospects for, China's grassroots democracy. In his opinion, the development of grassroots democracy is both inherently driven by and closely linked with the strategic deployments of the party and the central government and by the political innovations of local governments. At present, China's grassroots democracy faces many difficulties, including the country's underdeveloped civil society, inadequate rule of law, lack of electoral tradition, lack of coordination with the macro political environment, anxiety over social and political stability, lack of enthusiasm of local officials for democracy, and the insignificant effects attainable at the moment by grassroots democracy.

Huang believes that the open recommendation, direct election system is the main characteristic of China's grassroots democracy because it is neither mere election nor mere recommendation but rather a combination of the two. He holds that since promoting grassroots democracy is beneficial for strengthening the CCP's ruling position, the system will continue to be supported by the CCP, and there is still great room for the development of grassroots democracy in the existing political environment. Therefore, even though Huang is clearly aware that the development of grassroots democracy in China will be a long tug of war between various political forces, he has considerable optimism for the future.

Stanford University professor Jean C. Oi has a different interpretation of China's grassroots democracy situation. She points out that elections, often seen as the core of the democratic system, are a substantive way to achieve good governance. Evaluations of issues related to elections—such as whether there should be multiple candidates, whether the secret vote should be adopted, whether ballot tallying should be kept transparent, and whether to search out bribery or malpractice is present—are often concentrated at the state level. Even so, she admits that given the country's political reality, the breakthroughs that China has achieved in grassroots democracy have still greatly surprised the Western world. Elections at the village level, for instance, have marked the first time in history that China's citizens have been allowed to vote directly in competitive elections (though these elections are confined to the election of village committee members rather than village-level party organizations). The introduction of these elections was an important step in advancing the country's social progress following the Mao Zedong era. Oi therefore believes that Huang Weiping's discussion of China's grassroots democracy merits serious consideration.

In Oi's opinion the multiparty democratic system and the single-party authoritarian regime represent two ends of the political spectrum, and China is still a single-party state with no national general elections. Against this macro political backdrop, Oi sees the promotion of village elections as a top-down rather than bottom-up process. She holds that village elections are only a tool used by the CCP to resolve rural issues and safeguard and strengthen the party's ruling position. She states that many American scholars continue to doubt whether these village elections will lead to democratic politics at the national level. Based on her reading of Huang Weiping's exposition, she feels that nationwide general elections are still an unattainable goal for the foreseeable future.

Oi is particularly worried about the hollowing of village cadres' power as a result of the reconcentration of rural fiscal and administrative power at the township and town government levels that started in the 1990s, a development that has greatly undermined grassroots democracy. According to her analysis, what matters now is no longer the fact of grassroots elections but how much power the elected officials have and what they can do, how much power township and town cadres have, and what the local people's congresses can do. She sees many challenges in governance faced by China, and she thinks the extent to which China will use elections as the means to solve those challenges is not yet clear.

From Conflicts of Interest to Coordination of Interests

In the words of David Easton, politics is the "authoritative allocation of values for a society."[9] Politics involves decisionmaking on matters of major significance to the public interest and is the institutionalized allocation of important social interests. Reforms of the economic system mainly involve adjusting economic relations for the purpose of promoting productivity and increasing aggregate social wealth, while reforms of the political system mainly involve adjusting the existing interest structure and redistributing economic and political rights and interests among all social groups.

China's reform and opening up, in the final analysis, has been a process of adjusting economic relations and the interest structure. Scientific and technological progress and the establishment of the market system have unleashed huge productivity gains and have greatly increased aggregate social wealth.

A new interest structure is gradually taking shape as the old interest structure has been breaking down. This process has engendered many new conflicts of interest. One of the most important tasks facing the Chinese government now is to provide channels for the expression of these interests, establish a new interest coordination mechanism, reduce conflicts of interest, promote social fairness and justice, and build a harmonious society.

In chapter 10, Jing Yuejin marshals a large amount of data to show that, along with the changes to its social structure, China's interest structure has also undergone great changes since the reform and opening-up period began. The income ratio of urban to rural residents expanded from 2.36 in 1978 to 3.33 in 2009, and the Gini coefficient increased to 0.47 in 2009. The large number of petition cases and mass incidents that have been the greatest headache to the Chinese government have, in fact, been mainly caused by the deprivation of residents' lawful rights and interests, as well as by unfair interest distribution.

Even the government admits that "petition cases and mass incidents reflect internal conflicts among the people regarding interest distribution and are problems arising from the reform and development process."[10] Petitions mainly reflect conflicts between officials and citizens as labor disputes as well. Thus numerous mass incidents, which in essence are public political events, reflect a governance crisis. Conflicts of interest not only give rise to confrontations between labor and management but also to antagonism between the citizens and the government. Such conflicts have become a threat to the social and political order. This, in turn, has significantly increased the pressure on the government to maintain social stability and the costs of doing so, creating an almost unbearable burden.

According to the analysis provided by Jing Yuejin in his chapter, the increasing pressure on the government to maintain social stability stems from the bottlenecks inherent in the existing interest coordination mechanism, which creates huge pressure to transform the whole social and political system. Against this backdrop, establishing an interest coordination mechanism compatible with the market economy and an open social environment has particular importance for China's future social stability and sustainable development.

Jing holds that among the many efforts made by the Chinese government in this respect in recent years, the most meaningful have been in two areas. First are those moves that have sought to optimize the procedure of public policy decisionmaking with increased openness and democracy. These measures have mainly sought to adjust the relationship between citizens and government. Second are efforts to establish a tripartite coordination mechanism among the government, enterprises, and trade unions, with the objective of improving labor relations.

These reforms reflect the commitment of the ruling party to keep up with the changing times, the path dependence of China's reforms, and the imbalance in the country's development. However, Jing has substantial doubts as to whether China's current development model will allow major adjustments to the existing social interest structure, how much room for choice the existing institutionalized system allows, and whether economic pluralism and political centralism can be compatible.

Like Jing, Cheng Li, of the Brookings Institution's John L. Thornton China Center, believes that China's reform and opening up and the development of the market economy have been accompanied by profound social changes, especially social stratification and diversification of interests, which has led to a complicated social interest structure. Various interest groups have appeared and are exerting an increasingly important influence on China's political process. The conflicts between citizens and government and between workers and employers are the concentrated reflection of interest differentiation and conflicts of interests; both are major challenges to the CCP's ruling legitimacy. Therefore, interest groups have great significance for China's social, economic, and political life and will determine China's political direction. In fact, analyzing the influence of interest groups on China's political process has become a key task for those who observe China's politics.

As a scholar who has followed the politics of China's social groups, as well as the politics of China's leadership, very closely for many years, Li has a broad vision. Regarding the two interest groups discussed by Jing Yuejin—the vulnerable in Chinese society and business owners as a group—Li adds that "there are still many other major actors that are not adequately discussed or even mentioned," such as the geographically divided administrative regions, all kinds of bureaucratic organs, the military, the increasingly commercial media, NGOs, and local governments in coastal and inland regions. They are all "political interest groups that exert strong influence in Beijing and work to ensure that the central government adopts policies that advance their regional interests."

Li directs special focus on an emerging interest group: the middle class. He asserts boldly that "the most important interest group that determines China's future politics . . . is neither the black-collar stratum nor blue-collar workers but rather the white-collar members of China's emerging middle class." In his opinion, the increasingly dissatisfied middle class will put increasing pressure on the government. Handling the concerns of the middle class should be a major part of the government's next reforms.

Li points out that, if handled correctly, interest groups can facilitate China's transformation to a more institutionalized, orderly, peaceful, and democratic political system. "In democracies, interest group politics are seen as neither a threat to sociopolitical stability nor a challenge to the legitimacy of the government. Rather, they are regarded as necessary components of democratic governance." Simply adjusting the interest structure at the policy level is far from adequate. What is required is an institutionalized representative democracy system at the political level. Only by establishing such a mechanism to handle conflict among different interest groups, Li argues, can the negative impact of conflicts of interests on social and political stability be eliminated and an institutionalized foundation be laid for lasting social stability and a truly harmonious society.

From Traditional Decisionmaking to Modern Decisionmaking

The decisionmaking system is an important part of any political system, but it is often neglected in political analysis. Sound decisionmaking has a direct bearing on public satisfaction with the government and the government's credibility, and it is also an important factor influencing political stability. The decisionmaking system is of particular importance to China's political development because the CCP's leadership and management of state affairs take the form of concrete policies that are influenced by the policymaking process itself.

Although China's fundamental political system has not undergone substantial changes since reform began, its decisionmaking system has changed greatly. China's major political progress—in terms of democratization, institutionalization, standardization, and scientific soundness—has been prominently reflected in the changes made to its decisionmaking system. This is also why Zhou Guanghui argues, in chapter 11, that China's decisionmaking system is the fulcrum of its political system and a key influence on China's future development.

The decisionmaking system formed after the founding of the PRC was characterized by the CCP's absolute authority in determining the country's fundamental policies and its highly centralized decisionmaking power. The decisionmaking power of the entire state is concentrated in the CCP Central Committee, whose decisionmaking power is concentrated in the top leadership, especially the paramount leader. The decisionmaking power of local governments, in turn, is concentrated in the local CCP committees, especially local party chiefs at various levels.

Zhou argues at some length for the historical justification of that system, but at the same time he explains the shortcomings of the system in its structure, methods, and mechanisms of decisionmaking. Specific problems include the party's acting on the government's behalf; a lack of transparency, openness, democracy, and a reasonable division of labor; arbitrariness; and a low level of institutionalization and specialization. In sum, this was a decisionmaking system based on the individual rather than institutions.

With China's modernization, this system became increasingly outdated and eventually led to serious political crises, most prominently the disastrous Cultural Revolution, a political movement decided on, launched, and led by the paramount leader Mao Zedong. The movement threw China into a massive political, economic, and social crisis for ten long years, but the decisionmaking system at the time did not allow anyone to change the decisions made by Mao Zedong, however erroneous they might have been.

After Mao's death, the CCP, drawing lessons from the past, began to reform the traditional decisionmaking system to establish a modern democratic, scientific, and rational system. The official expression was to achieve the "democratization and scientific soundness of decisionmaking."[11] For this purpose, the CCP reformed many aspects of the original decisionmaking system, including its structure, methods, and mechanisms. For example, policies were introduced to separate the party from the government and the government from enterprises so that the party ceased to control all government affairs, especially staying out of economic affairs and not interfering with enterprise decisionmaking and operation. The new policies emphasized and reinforced collective decisionmaking in party committees and governments and substantially restricted the decisionmaking power of party and government leaders at various levels. A series of modern decisionmaking techniques, including quite a few from Western countries, were gradually adopted and promoted. These included policy hearings, democratic consultation, open government, consultation on decisionmaking, policy evaluation, and administrative accountability.

Zhou points out that although China has made great progress over more than thirty years in reforming its decisionmaking system, the existing system still has major defects at the central level, the division of responsibility between the CCP and various government organs is not clearly provided for, the relationship between the CCP and other democratic parties is not well institutionalized, and, in particular, the role of the National People's Congress and the CPPCC in democratic decisionmaking has not been fully developed. In some fields, decisionmaking power is still excessively centralized and opaque. The decisionmaking process is not well developed, with some hearings and consultation sessions being merely perfunctory and the channels by which citizens participate in public decisionmaking still limited. Finally, the decisionmaking supervision system is poorly developed, lacking a process of judicial review of policy decisions. Zhou also offers suggestions for reforms to establish a decisionmaking system that is led by the CCP, includes the participation of multiple parties in accordance with the law, and uses scientific methods to ensure efficiency and transparency.

David M. Lampton, a professor at Johns Hopkins University and a veteran scholar of decisionmaking in China, notes the importance of the decisionmaking system to a political system. He affirms that China traditionally had highly concentrated decisionmaking, with resulting defects: vulnerability to top leaders' misjudgments, unclear division of power between the party and the state, lack of accountability, lack of coordination among decisionmaking departments, lack of citizen participation in the decisionmaking process, weakness in responding actively to the needs and demands of citizens, nonscientific decisionmaking, ill-informed decisionmaking, lack of restrictive rules and procedures, limited room for expertise and specialized knowledge, lack of feedback channels, and discouragement of innovation. The seriousness of these defects first became evident in 1957 and was at its worst during the Cultural Revolution from 1966 to 1976.

Lampton holds that the most notable reform of China's decisionmaking system was the adoption of a higher degree of "instrumental rationality." Instrumental rationality was introduced by a number of steps: having a clear goal of reform, especially "democratization of decisionmaking," taking into account the interests and needs of a greater number of people, considering public opinion, using scientific data and information for decisionmaking and more clearly defining the roles of the party and the government in decisionmaking, defining the power of public authorities and their interrelationships, emphasizing the rule of law and better ensuring that decisionmaking is in accordance with the law, attaching increasing importance to the role of interest groups in decisionmaking, and undertaking more meaningful consultation with other actors, including the democratic parties.

Lampton also shares his views on the relationship between science and democracy in the decisionmaking process. He states that democracy is both a system and a goal, whereas science is a methodology. Democracy does not merely mean more participation, institutionalization, supervision, and feedback, it also involves the choice of participants, the conferment of decisionmaking power, and the design of the decisionmaking system. The principles of democracy are popular sovereignty and fair competition. Democracy means majority rule, not only in terms of what the majority of people can do but also what they cannot do. Science cannot tell you what you should want normatively, and it cannot give you answers about many basic issues involving social life, such as where to strike the balance between equality and efficiency, between economic growth and environmental protection, and between the collective and the individual. Every government, and every country, must formulate its own answer to those questions.

From Anticorruption to Supervision of Power

The most important aspect of Deng Xiaoping's reforms was the introduction of the socialist market economic system to replace the original socialist planned economic system. This was a gradual process, requiring that the planned economy and the market economy coexist for a period of time. But this dual economic structure created favorable conditions for rent-seeking. And this rent-seeking—coupled with major changes in ideology, belief system, and values and lagging institutional development amid radical social and economic transformations—has made official corruption the most serious political problem in China.

Rampant corruption has not only increased the cost of economic development but has also seriously undermined the CCP's authority and legitimacy. Efforts to establish a cleaner government have become critical tasks of the CCP and the Chinese government. Earlier in the reform period, China's efforts to ensure clean government focused on the political education of cadres and the punishment of corrupt officials. The *sanjiang* (三讲, literally, "the three talks, involving politics, virtues, and learning") campaign and the campaign "to educate party members to preserve their vanguard nature" (先进性教育, *xianjinxing jiaoyu*), for example, were major measures meant to promote clean government.

However, despite a great number of officials having been punished every year, corruption remains prevalent. As a result, the CCP leadership has come to the realization that anticorruption should focus on institutional development. The party is now attaching greater importance to instituting a series of basic systems of supervision and checks on power.

In chapter 12, He Zengke presents a systematic survey of China's anticorruption process since reforms began more than thirty years ago. He explains that the process has unfolded in three stages: from anticorruption campaigns to anticorruption regulations to a national corruption punishment and prevention system. Since reform and opening up began, China has instituted a preliminary corruption punishment and prevention system, which is a goal-oriented, institutionalized system covering both the party and the government.

This anticorruption system has punished a great number of officials. According to statistics, in the period from 1978 to November 2009, the discipline inspection organs registered almost 3 million cases, 90 percent of which resulted in party or government disciplinary sanctions. In twelve years, more than 78,000 cadres at the county or division level or above were punished. From 1978 to late 2009, the procuratorial organs at all levels investigated more than a million cases of embezzlement and bribery cases and punished 667,000 persons. Public satisfaction with the country's anticorruption efforts increased from 60.5 percent in 2005 to 69.2 percent in 2009.

The chapter by He Zengke is a detailed analysis of the effects and limits of China's existing clean-government system and its power supervision system. While fully acknowledging the remarkable achievements in restricting power and curbing corruption, He also points out the defects, particularly in the following five aspects: excessive concentration of power, which makes it difficult to have effective supervision and restrictions on government heads and party chiefs at various levels; placing supervisory organs under the leadership of the organizations to be supervised, which restricts the effectiveness of the supervision system; "integrating deliberation and execution" without the necessary checks and balances between decisionmaking, execution, and supervision; inadequate legal protection of supervision by the press and public opinion; and low levels of the overall development of democracy and the rule of law.

He Zengke is acutely aware that as long as there is still power that is above and beyond supervision, corruption will eventually lead to a political cancer that spells the ruin of the regime. Accordingly, supervision is a key link in effectively preventing and punishing corruption. The core of the many policy suggestions he offers is institution of a rigorous vertical and horizontal accountability system and removal of the barriers to supervision and checks.

Melanie Manion shares with He Zengke a deep understanding of the serious problem corruption poses for China. At present, in her opinion, corruption in China takes its most damaging forms in regard to government appointments, judicial activities, and the legalization of the privileges of leaders and cadres (for example, housing and health care). The corruption of party chiefs and government heads at various levels is particularly serious. She agrees with He's analysis and holds that the ineffectiveness, shortcomings, and imperfections of the supervision and restriction system—especially the lack of effective vertical and horizontal decentralization and accountability mechanisms, a problem that leads to the concentration of power—are the fundamental causes of corruption. The lack of external supervision and accountability turns supervision largely into self-supervision. Manion also mentions the lack of a "structure of incentives . . . that . . . tie the hands of powerful players," a situation that contributes substantially to the country's severe corruption.

Manion seems to lack confidence that serious corruption in China can be eliminated or even effectively contained. On one hand, she affirms He's suggestions regarding how to build a clean government. On the other, she doubts whether those suggestions will be effective, especially whether they will be accepted by officials. She particularly doubts the effectiveness of the efforts to restrict power and create a cleaner government within the establishment. Will those in power embrace a system design that ties their hands? Can we expect such a scheme to be adopted? She questions whether the anticorruption design proposed by He Zengke, were it to be adopted, would become anything more than a "parchment institution."

Manion holds much more faith in He's suggestions regarding various forms of external supervision. Civil society's limitations on state power, the restrictions that elections impose on officials, and supervision of officials by the press will at least lay the necessary foundation for ensuring the accountability of officials, Manion feels, even if they cannot eliminate China's corruption problems at once.

What Does the Dialogue Reveal?

As far as I know, throughout the history of academic exchanges between China and the United States, this volume represents the first high-level direct and comprehensive dialogue focused on contemporary China's political development. Of all the important ideas and insights provided by both the Chinese and American scholars, a number of points are particularly worth noting.

China's political development is receiving increasing attention. This comes as no surprise to Chinese scholars because, given China's historical and cultural traditions, politics plays a much greater role in China than in Western countries in influencing societal development. Judging from the dialogue presented in this volume, it is likely that most American experts in China studies attach great significance to China's political development. In the field of China studies in the United States, research on major political issues has taken an unprecedentedly important position. The focus has shifted, however, from China's foreign policy to its domestic politics—covering such issues as the political system, political values, reform strategies, ideology, democracy and rule of law, local governance, leadership capacity, and ruling party development.

Many scholars who have studied China's history, society, and culture are making more effort to understand the country's political issues. Even some leading academics who have not specialized in China studies per se have begun to pay attention to China's contemporary politics. For example, John Thornton, the chairman of the Brookings Institution, and Larry Diamond, an authority on democracy studies, have paid great attention to the research on China's politics and either directly or indirectly participated in this dialogue.

There are two related reasons why Chinese and American scholars attach such importance to this research. First, they believe that the extent of conflict and cooperation between China and the United States will, to a great degree, depend on China's domestic political development. Second, they think that China's political development will determine China's future.

China has made great strides in political development since its reform and opening up. Since the reform period began in 1979, China has embarked on a unique development path, one that is different from both the traditional Soviet model and the Western model. This new development model has brought a sea change to the Chinese people, creating both an economic miracle and robust social and political progress.

The overwhelming majority of Chinese scholars agree that China has made progress in the political realm since the reform and opening up, especially in such areas as rule of law, civic engagement, grassroots democracy, government responsibility, political transparency, and the provision of public services. Owing to different standards of political evaluation, however, Western scholars usually give high praise to China's tremendous social and economic achievements but are critical of China's political development or the lack thereof. Even so, the American scholars participating in this dialogue acknowledge and generally hold an overall positive attitude regarding China's political progress since the reform period began. These scholars agree that China's political progress since the late 1970s is beyond doubt. Because of the deepening of China's reform and opening up, Western scholars in China studies have had more opportunities to visit China to conduct independent research, gather data, and cooperate more with their Chinese counterparts. Through this process they have gained a deeper and more comprehensive understanding of Chinese politics.

China's political development has taken a unique path. China's course of political development has been markedly different from that of Western countries, as well as from the traditional Soviet model. Through sixty years of development, China has created a model of political development with Chinese characteristics. Its basic political system is one in which the people's congress system, the political consultation system, the regional ethnic autonomy system, and the grassroots residents' autonomy system combine to form a democratic political framework with Chinese characteristics.

In terms of the state power structure, China has not implemented a system of separation of powers among the legislature, the executive, and the judiciary. Instead, China follows a power system that features a combination of legislative and executive powers and a form of "democratic centralism" that at the same time emphasizes the checks and balances among the decisionmaking power, executive power, supervision power, appointment power, and revenue allocations and expenditure responsibilities.

In terms of the political party system, China does not have a multiparty system; rather, under the Chinese system, the CCP, as the only ruling party, cooperates with other democratic parties through political consultation. In terms of state governance, China has a structure in which the party leads the government. The actors involved in China's governance have become diversified—though the most important at all levels are still the various organizations of the CCP. In terms of the approach to political reform, China has adopted a path of incremental development. In terms of the relationship between the central and local governments, a governance structure that "combines horizontal administration and vertical supervision" (条块结合, *tiaokuai jiehe*) has taken shape.

As in the past, China's future political development will not copy the Western political model, and it is not appropriate to interpret China's political development through a simple application of Western theories. Chinese and American scholars participating in the dialogue have reached a remarkable degree of consensus on this core issue.

China's political development faces major challenges. Although both Chinese and American scholars hold an overall positive attitude toward China's political progress and achievements, they have also made it clear that China's political development still faces many pressing problems and challenges. Scholars on both sides have flagged a wide range of issues of common concern, including persistent corruption and official privilege, unfairness in social distribution, declining public confidence in the government, increasing social instability, relative stagnation in the development of democracy and the rule of law, "inadequate basic political identification and consensus" (基本政治认同和政治共识的不足, *jiben zhengzhi rentong he zhengzhi gongshi de buzu*), vested interest groups able to substantially hinder political reform, and the absence of a strategic design and initiative regarding political reforms.

The American contributors to this volume have called particular attention to many other issues. Does the notion of a political development model with Chinese characteristics hold water? Will China eventually embrace Western-style democracy, one with multiparty politics, general elections, and separation of powers at its core? Will China's existing political model continue to ensure China's rapid economic growth and social stability? Will the CCP be able to rise effectively to the existing political challenges and maintain long-term rule? Despite various concerns, most Chinese and American scholars participating in the dialogue hold a cautiously optimistic view on China's political prospects.

Scholarship in the field of Chinese political studies has seen marked improvement. Owing to the sensitivity of political discussion in China and the difficulty in gaining access to first-hand documents, data, and materials, political studies in China, especially studies on China's own politics, are relatively backward and falling behind other fields of philosophy and social sciences. Foreign scholars in Chinese political studies face even greater obstacles because, in addition to the difficulty of accessing first-hand documents and data, they face challenges stemming from their different political and cultural traditions and the constraints imposed by the Chinese side on conducting surveys and field interviews in China. As a result, scholarship in Chinese political studies is not as readily recognized as scholarship in other fields.

The contributions to this volume by the Chinese and American scholars nevertheless demonstrate that most authors have followed internationally recognized academic norms and used scientific methodologies in their research, with a resulting marked improvement in specialization and scholarship. The findings of Chinese scholars received general praise from their American counterparts, and the comments provided by the American scholars were also valued by their Chinese counterparts.

It is particularly noteworthy that American scholars have reached a high level of detail and depth in some fields of Chinese politics and have paid particular attention to the latest developments in Chinese politics, even displaying excellent knowledge of local pilot reforms in China. This change has occurred as the result of two factors. First, with the steady advancement of post-Mao reforms, many fields and materials that used to be considered sensitive are now made available to foreign scholars. And second, with the blossoming of a new information-based society, many materials and data that were kept confidential in the past have become legally accessible.

Academic exchange between China and the United States calls for mutual respect and understanding—agreeing to disagree. Chinese politics has always been a sensitive field of study. In this field, there is not only much misunderstanding and disagreement between Chinese and American scholars, but there has also been a tendency to politicize academic issues, which has led to further estrangement.

Chinese scholars often think that Western scholars lack understanding of China's national conditions and tend to look at Chinese politics through the lens of Western standards and approaches. Because of this, they feel, American scholars fail to grasp the essence of Chinese politics. Chinese academics, therefore, usually do not give much weight to Western scholarship in the field.

In contrast, Western scholars often think that Chinese scholars are not academically rigorous enough in their research and often present politicized arguments in support of China's government. As a result, Western academics often do not attach importance to Chinese scholars' studies either.

In the dialogue that constitutes this volume of scholarship, however, scholars on both sides have shown mutual respect and communicated on an equal footing. The American scholars carefully read the articles penned by the Chinese scholars and wrote critiques on them. The Western commentators expressed full respect for their Chinese counterparts and showed high appreciation of their scholarship. In turn, the Chinese scholars seriously approached the critiques of their American counterparts and drew on these comments when revising their own articles.

There are two reasons for this major change. The first is that alongside China's economic and political rise, Chinese scholarship has also seen a rise in status. The second is that Chinese scholars have made remarkable academic progress and have begun to use internationally recognized methodologies and concepts in analyzing practical issues.

China embarked on a unique path of development after the reform and opening up. True, the process has exhibited various defects and problems. There is even the risk that serious crises could occur if some problems are not handled properly. That being said, however, a series of ongoing political reforms promoting democracy, the rule of law, accountability, openness, fairness, and the provision of public services have put China on track toward good governance. As observed by both the Chinese and American contributors to this volume, there are multiple facets to China's transition—from revolution to reform, from dictatorship to constitutional government, from rule of man to rule of law, from centralization to decentralization, from delivering control to delivering service, from state control to autonomy, and from conflict to reconciliation. These represent some of the most important steps China has taken on the road toward good governance.

Notes

1. This introduction is based on the summary report of the research project China's Political Development: Perspectives of Chinese and American Scholars. This research project involves twenty-four renowned Chinese and American scholars. The author is indebted to the participating scholars for their great articles and insightful comments and especially to Chee Hwa Tung and the China–United States Exchange Foundation (CUSEF) he chairs for the foundation's sponsorship of this research. Responsibility for this article, however, remains solely with the author.

2. Editorial note: Before the late 1990s, when discussing the role of law in China, Chinese authorities often used the phrase "rule by law" (以法制国, to use law to rule the country) rather than "rule of law" (依法治国, to govern the country according to the law). These two phrases are fundamentally different in connotation. The former emphasizes the utility of law from the party perspective, and the latter emphasizes that no individual, group, or party should be above the law. These two terms have exactly the same pronunciation in Chinese but quite different Chinese characters and thus meanings.

3. CCP Central Committee, *Guanyu jiaqiang dang de zhizheng nengli jianshe de jueding* [Resolution on strengthening the governing capacity of the party] (www.gov.cn/test/2008-08/20/content_1075279.htm).

4. Jiang Zemin made a speech at the Central Party School in Beijing on May 31, 2002, in which he argued that the CCP should not only represent the fundamental interests of the majority (that is, the working class) but also should represent two other forces: advanced social productive forces (meaning entrepreneurs and capitalists) and the progressive course of China's advanced culture (meaning cultural elites and intellectuals). This concept became known as the Three Represents.

5. Jiang Zemin, *Quanmian jianshe xiaokang shehui, kaichuang Zhongguo tese shehuizhuyi shiye xin jumian: Zai Zhongguo gongchandang di shiliuci quanguo daibiao dahui shang de baogao* [Build a well-off society in an all-round way and work hard to create a new

situation in building socialism with Chinese characteristics: A report to the 16th CCP National Congress] (news.xinhuanet.com/ziliao/2002-11/17/content_693542.htm).

6. The Constitution of the People's Republic of China (www.gov.cn/gongbao/content/2004/content_62714.htm).

7. Hu Jintao, *Gaoju Zhongguo tese shehuizhuyi weida qizhi wei duoqu quanmian jianshe xiaokang shehui xin shengli er fendou* [Hold high the great banner of socialism with Chinese characteristics and strive for new victories in building a moderately prosperous society in all respects], report to the 17th CCP National Congress (news.xinhuanet.com/newscenter/2007-10/24/content_6938568.htm).

8. Zhang Youyu, *Xianzheng luncong* [On constitutionalism], vol. 1 (Beijing: Qunzhong chubanshe [Qunzhong Publishing House], 1986), p. 100.

9. David Easton, *A Framework for Political Analysis* (Englewood Cliffs, N.J.: Prentice Hall, 1965), p. 96.

10. Zhou Yongkang, "Shenru tuijin shehui maodun huajie, shehui guanli chuangxin, gongzheng lianjie zhifa, wei jingji shehui youhao youkuai fazhan tigong gengjia youli de fazhi baozhang" [Spare no efforts to resolve social disputes, encourage social governance innovation, implement the law justly and unbiasedly, and provide legal guarantee for the sound and rapid development of the economy and society], *Qiushi* [Seek truth], no. 4 (2010).

11. CCP Central Committee, *Zhonggong zhongyang guanyu jiaqiang dang de zhizheng nengli jianshe de jueding* [Resolution on strengthening the governing capacity of the party] (www.gov.cn/test/2008-08/20/content_1075279.htm).

1

The People's Republic of China's Sixty Years of Political Development

YU KEPING

The Chinese Communist Party (CCP) overthrew the rule of the Kuomintang and founded the People's Republic of China (PRC) in 1949, marking the transition of the CCP from a revolutionary party to a ruling party, a substantial change of far-reaching significance for both the CCP and China. Thereafter, the primary task of the party and its government changed from seizing political power to consolidating it, from destroying the old state to building a new one. The foundation of the CCP's legitimacy also gradually changed from revolution to reform and from political movement to law making. This political development advanced down six main paths: from revolution to reform, from struggle to harmony, from dictatorship to democracy, from rule of man to rule of law, from centralization to decentralization, and from state to society. This transition was slow and difficult and did not approach completion until China launched its reform and opening-up program thirty years later. The entirety of political life in the PRC over the past sixty-five years, with all its tragedy and drama, can be explained along these lines of change.

From Revolution to Reform

Revolution is an armed struggle with the aim of overthrowing the existing political order and making a thorough social transformation by means of violence. In the words of Friedrich Engels, "A revolution is the act whereby one part of the population imposes its will upon the other part by means of rifles, bayonets and cannons—authoritarian means."[1] Marxists believe that "revolutions are the loco-motives of history" and a powerful driver of human progress.[2] According to their logic, no reactionary class will depart the stage of history on its own accord; only through violent revolution can a new society be established. The CCP, by applying the Marxist revolutionary theory to China's peculiar conditions to mobilize workers and peasants at the bottom of society and carry out a resolute armed struggle, eventually seized political power. In this sense, the founding of the new socialist state in China also marked the victory of Marxist revolutionary theory.

Revolution was sacred to the Chinese Communist Party and the newly established People's Republic of China. During the thirty years following the founding of the PRC, *revolution* was the shining political term and represented the highest political value and the highest political authority. Revolution was a formidable weapon not only for seizing political power but also for consolidating it. It was the fundamental source of legitimacy for the new government and all its actions. As a result, revolution became the fundamental political criterion dividing right from wrong in China. All thoughts, speeches, behaviors, systems, policies, and guidelines that were approved by the party and government were revolutionary, and thus whatever was opposed or not approved by the party and government was counterrevolutionary or nonrevolutionary.

According to the political logic of the leadership, all counterrevolutionary forces must be resolutely suppressed. During the 1953 Campaign to Suppress Counterrevolutionaries, a total of 1.29 million people were arrested, 1.23 million were disciplined, and 710,000 were executed.[3] Mao Zedong and other leaders also set about transforming every aspect of Chinese society, including ideology and culture, under the name of continuing "permanent revolution" until the fulfillment of communism. Mao Zedong said, "I stand for the theory of permanent revolution. In making revolution one must strike while the iron is hot—one revolution must follow another, the revolution must continually advance."[4] Acting on this theory of continuous revolution, Mao Zedong launched one political campaign after another, from the Anti-Rightist Movement to the Cultural Revolution.

Led by the CCP, the people's revolution fundamentally changed the historical process of China. It not only established the CCP's ruling position but also created for the first time in China a socialist system, including an economic system based on common ownership of the means of production and a basic political system with the people's democratic dictatorship at its core. The socialist revolution greatly advanced China's social and historical progress. First, it substantially increased the country's productivity, leading to rapid economic development within a short time. In 1952 the gross output of industry and agriculture reached RMB 81 billion, up 77.5 percent over 1949 and 20 percent over 1936, the highest level preceding the founding of the PRC. From 1950 to 1980, the gross output of industry and agriculture in China increased more than tenfold, from RMB 57.48 billion to RMB 661.90 billion, representing an average annual growth of 8.5 percent.[5] The large population of peasants and workers who used to be at the bottom of society thus enjoyed significantly improved social and political status, including democratic rights they had never before enjoyed. They became, in effect, the mainstream classes of society. The literacy rate also rapidly increased, and ordinary people began to acquire cultural knowledge. New values such as freedom, equality, and civilization became important components of China's culture. With the founding of the PRC, China also enjoyed enhanced international status and became fully independent from semicolonization for the first time in the modern era.

The fundamental role of revolution, however, is to break up the existing state apparatus and establish a new political order. If revolutionaries continue to make political revolutions even after they have established a new political system, the positive effect of revolutions on historical progress will gradually weaken, leading eventually to negative results. Fundamentally speaking, revolution is a political action that fulfills its role in advancing historical progress by breaking up the existing system and releasing social productivity. But revolution itself is not a productive force: it can promote economic development but absolutely cannot substitute for economic development. Moreover, revolution is an anomaly of the historical process, and it defies any law or regulation. Democracy, a direct goal of the proletarian revolution, is inseparable from rule of law—without the rule of law there can be no democracy. In this sense, revolution is hardly compatible with democracy, as was emphatically proved by what happened in the thirty years following the founding of the PRC, the period in which the theory of continuous revolution was practiced.

The economic growth brought about by the revolution soon slowed down. Less than ten years after the founding of the PRC there occurred the so-called three years of natural disasters, a period in which tens of millions of people starved to death.[6] In reality, "natural disaster" was just another name for economic destitution and fragility. Toward the end of the Cultural Revolution, material privation was so severe that even a box of matches, a bar of soap, a half kilogram of pork, or a foot of cloth had to be bought with coupons, which were of limited supply. The national economy was on the "brink of collapse."[7] In terms of political life, approximately 550,000 intellectuals were branded as "rightists" and were deprived of basic political rights during the Anti-Rightist Movement of 1957–58. The Cultural Revolution was even worse, a political disaster unprecedented in Chinese history: according to one general estimate, more than 100 million people were wrongfully accused, implicated, or persecuted, and several million died in the process, including President Liu Shaoqi and founding marshals Peng Dehuai and He Long. A great number of senior cadre members were accused of being rightists or "persons in power taking the capitalist road" (党内走资派, *dangnei zouzipai*) and persecuted. The revolution eventually turned on itself and began to engulf revolutionaries themselves.

Immediately after the death of paramount leader Mao Zedong in 1976, the leadership of the CCP, in a bid to save the country from even greater chaos, took radical action and arrested the Gang of Four, who were still resolutely implementing Mao Zedong's theory of permanent revolution. This move, in effect, ended the ten-year-long Cultural Revolution. Finally, at the far-reaching and epoch-making third plenary session of the 11th CCP Central Committee, held from December 18 to 22, 1978, the focus of the party and the government was changed from class struggle to economic development. It was at this meeting that China returned to the road of modernization. For the next thirty years, *reform* replaced *revolution* as the dominant political term and the main theme of the new period of China's development.

Whereas the main goal of revolution is to break up an existing order, the main goal of reform is to repair and improve it. Before coming to power, revolutionaries are usually the staunchest opponents of reform; they view all reformers and reformists as reactionary. However, if revolutionaries continue to emphasize revolution even after coming to power, the spearhead of attack will inevitably be directed at its own people. It is the historical responsibility of the successors of founding revolutionaries to shift the focus from revolution to reform and to foster ideology that is supportive of reforms.

The third plenary session of the 11th CCP Central Committee established Deng Xiaoping as the second paramount leader of China. The first obstacle to Deng's reform efforts came from the orthodox ideology, especially its theory of continuous revolution. If the ideological and theoretical issues were not dealt with correctly, any reforms would not have a firm foundation of legitimacy. As the pioneer of reform, Deng led the great debate on the criterion of truth, which marked the beginning of an ideological emancipation movement. Deng advocated emancipation of the mind. What is the criterion of truth—the theory of continuous revolution or the reality of social practice? After heated debate and passionate discussion, the majority of CCP leaders and intellectuals arrived at Deng's intended conclusion, and the party identified social practice as the true foundation of the legitimacy of reform. In early 1992, Deng went even further by summarizing the criteria as the three advances: "advance the development of socialist productive forces, advance the enhancement of China's overall capacity as a socialist state, and advance the improvement of people's living standards."[8]

The reforms led by Deng constituted a wide-ranging social transformation involving politics, economy, culture, and social life. Economically, the reforms started with the people's commune system in the countryside. On January 1, 1982, the CCP Central Committee approved and released the minutes of the National Rural Work Conference. This document changed the rural economic system from one in which the means of production were owned on three levels and the production team was taken as the basic accounting unit (三级所有, 队为基础, *sanji suoyou, duiwei jichu*) to one anchored by the household responsibility system, which was promoted nationwide. This reform, which stimulated farmer incentive to produce and rapidly improved agricultural productivity, soon solved the problem of how to clothe and feed China's 800 million rural people. The CCP leadership then vastly deepened economic reforms by advancing the transition from a planned to a market economy and changing the existing economic system from one of unitary public ownership to a mixed ownership system based on public ownership. Another important component of the economic reforms was the opening-up movement, including opening up the domestic market for foreign investment, introducing advanced corporate management experience and practices and advanced technologies, joining the World Trade Organization, and participating extensively in international economic competition.

The thirty year period that followed the third plenary session of the 11th CCP Central Committee was an era of reform in every way. With the transition of the country's basic economic system from a socialist planned economy to a market economy, a full range of components of the economic system were overhauled, including ownership, business operation, employment, allocation, foreign trade, circulation, finance, and compensation, to name only a few. In addition to economic reforms, there were also major changes in many other systems such as the political, education, cultural, public health, welfare, and insurance systems as well as other important social and political administration systems. Reform became the embodiment of justice and reason during this period: all beautiful things, all good systems, and all eminent persons were identified with reform.

The Deng reforms brought a sea change to Chinese society. In terms of the challenges the Chinese people faced and the extent to which they advanced socially, nothing less than a revolution occurred. The greatest change of all was a miracle of economic growth unprecedented in human history. In the thirty years from 1978 to 2008, China's GDP soared from RMB 364.5 billion to RMB 30.1 trillion, with per capita GDP, urban per capita disposable income, and rural per capita disposable income increasing from RMB 381 to RMB 22,600, from RMB 343 to RMB 15,781, and from RMB 134 to RMB 4,761, respectively. The telephone usage rate increased from less than 1 phone per 10,000 residents to 74.3 phones. The number of college students increased from 860,000 to more than 20 million. The ratio of urban to rural population changed from 18:82 to 46:54. And the country's foreign reserves increased from USD 170 million to USD 2 trillion. The reforms were far more than a process of economic development: they were also a process of overall social progress. With rapid economic development and substantially improved living standards, China's social, political, and cultural life also underwent marked changes.

The reforms both transformed China's history and saved the socialist cause of the CCP. In this sense, it can be said that in spite of the seeming confrontation with and deviation from revolution, from the perspective of the ultimate goal of the CCP and China's socialist revolution the reforms were actually a continuation of the revolutionary cause.

From Struggle to Harmony

Maintaining a revolutionary environment inevitably leads to the prioritization of class struggle because revolution is a means of struggle and the highest form of class struggle. According to classic Marxist theory, private ownership and the division of labor appeared after humanity became civilized, and this in turn led to the creation of different classes. The history of society is the history of class struggle.[9] Since the emergence of a class structure, society as a whole has split into two fundamentally hostile camps. The first ruling class is the exploitative class, which is in possession of the means of production. The ruled class is the exploited class, which is not in possession of the means of production. The former has been the minority while the latter the overwhelming majority. Owing to their fundamental antagonism, the two classes have fought fiercely against each other. When the ruling class is unable to rule as usual, class struggle turns into revolution. Class struggle has many forms, but violent revolution is its highest form.

The CCP not only accepted all the above Marxist doctrines on classes and class struggle; after the founding of the PRC, it pushed the theory of class struggle to the extreme. According to Mao, the historical process starting with the coming to power of the proletariat and ending with the realization of communism is a long one. This process is always accompanied by classes and class struggle, even fierce class struggle at times. Mao also held that after the CCP came to power, class division and class struggle had developed within the party, leading to the emergence of two antagonistic camps. He warned, "You are making the socialist revolution, and yet you do not know where the bourgeoisie is. It is right in the Communist Party—those in power taking the capitalist road. The capitalist-roaders are still on the capitalist road."[10] He admonished the Chinese people to "never forget class struggle." "Class struggle," he said, "must be held in mind every year, every month, and every day."[11]

In the thirty years after the founding of the PRC, class struggle was a current that ran through every aspect of society. In the economic field, the slogan was "Socialist weeds are better than capitalist seedlings." Politically, "Who are our enemies and who are our friends?" became the foremost question in revolution and was used to make political classifications of social groups. Landlords, rich peasants, counterrevolutionaries, bad elements, and rightists (地富反坏右, *di fu fan huai you*), the so-called Five Black Categories (黑五类, *heiwulei*), were classified as class enemies and were deprived of basic civil rights. Across society, the theory of class origin (出身论, *chushenlun,* or 成份论, *chengfenlun*) was widely adopted, positioning persons according to their family backgrounds and social relationships. Only those born into poor working or peasant families were considered the successors to the revolution, and all the rest were subjected to political education and political testing. Ideologically, the people were required to examine the bourgeois elements of their own thoughts and exercise self-criticism, combat selfishness and repudiate revisionism (斗私批修, *dousipixiu*), and combat selfishness as soon as it flashes in their brain.

In socialist theory, the ideal state to be achieved by class struggle is the gradual narrowing of class differences and, ultimately, the elimination of classes. The goal is to move toward a more harmonious society where human nature reaches its full potential and every individual enjoys more freedom. In reality, however, class struggle moved in the opposite direction, so that class differences were constantly strengthened, human nature was increasingly suppressed, and only one way of thinking was allowed throughout the nation. Ironically, of the 550,000 people who were persecuted in the Anti-Rightist Movement, fewer than 100 were not eventually rehabilitated. The Cultural Revolution evolved into an all-encompassing armed internal struggle in which each force claimed to represent "the Great Leader Chairman Mao" and "attacked with reason and defended with force" (文攻武卫, *wengongwuwei*). During this armed struggle in which more than a million people lost their lives, many couples became enemies, fathers and sons disowned each other, and comrades became foes. The Cultural Revolution, triggered by class struggle, was a huge disaster for the Chinese nation and "brought catastrophe to the Party, the state and the whole people."[12]

It is an invariable rule that without social stability and harmony there will be no social progress and development. It is an anomaly for revolution to advance historical progress, and it is the norm for stability to promote social development. Mao did not, and indeed could not, bring order to China because his ambitious belief that "great disorder across the land leads to great order"[13] defied the law of historical development. As a result, Mao became increasingly estranged from the overwhelming majority of his revolutionary comrades. No sooner had he died than his successors took resolute action to put an end to the class struggle and permanent revolution that he had vehemently advocated, and they instead placed emphasis on the solidarity and cooperation of different social classes. As proclaimed in the communiqué of the third plenary session of the 11th CCP Central Committee, "The large-scale nationwide mass movement to expose and criticize Lin Biao and the 'Gang of Four' has been completed victoriously," and "the stress of the Party's work should shift to socialist modernization as of 1979."[14] Soon afterward, the CCP Central Committee announced that the system of exploitation of man by man had been eliminated, exploiters no longer existed as a class unto themselves, and class struggle no longer constituted the principal contradiction within Chinese society.[15] The transition from "taking class struggle as the key link" to "pursuing economic development as the top priority"[16] was a difficult change. Because it merely deemphasized and essentially avoided the issue of class struggle, however, it was only the first step toward greater change. Another step, equally difficult but also important, was to explicitly put forward the goal of building a socialist "harmonious society." Although harmony is an important element in traditional Chinese thought as well as an important characteristic of communist society as envisaged by Karl Marx, there was no attempt within the CCP to associate harmony with socialism before the beginning of the twenty-first century, owing to the long-standing emphasis on class struggle and the severe criticism of the theory of class harmony that appeared following the founding of the PRC.

This situation derived in part from the Resolution on Certain Questions in the History of Our Party since the Founding of the PRC, which states explicitly that "it is necessary to oppose both the view that the scope of class struggle must be enlarged and the view that it has died out"; to advocate social harmony was still thought of as advocating the theory of "the dying out of class struggle."[17] In reality, however, the political purpose of negating class confrontation and class struggle is to promote social solidarity and harmony. This did not begin to occur until the beginning of the twenty-first century when, at the CCP's 16th National Congress in 2002, the mission of promoting social harmony was advanced along with China's long-term goal of building a moderately prosperous society in all respects. At the fourth plenary session of the 16th CCP Central Committee in 2004, the goal of building a harmonious socialist society was explicitly proposed.

In 2005, at a CCP Central Party School meeting, Hu Jintao emphasized the commitment to building a society of "democracy and order, fairness and justice, honesty and friendliness, and a harmonious relationship between man and nature."[18] At the sixth plenary session of the 16th CCP Central Committee in 2006, it was put forward for the first time that "social harmony is an essential attribute of socialism with Chinese characteristics."[19]

The transition from class struggle to a harmonious socialist society as the essential mission of Chinese socialism has far-reaching theoretical and practical significance. First, it represents a change in the CCP's understanding of the essential attributes of socialism. In contrast to Mao's theory, which holds that class struggle is an essential attribute of socialism, harmony is now considered an essential attribute of socialism. Second, it enriches the strategic goal set by the CCP for China's modernization: shifting from building a strong, prosperous, democratic, and culturally advanced country to building a strong, prosperous, democratic, culturally advanced, and harmonious country. Finally, it lays a solid foundation of legitimacy for social stability. There is no development without stability. Pursuit of a harmonious socialist society means that all institutional designs, policies, and laws and regulations will have social solidarity and harmony as their ultimate goal.

From Dictatorship to Democracy

Class struggle inevitably leads to the dictatorship of the proletariat, and emphasizing class struggle of the proletariat inevitably leads to emphasizing dictatorship of the proletariat. This is an important aspect of classic Marxist theory. According to Lenin, the recognition of class struggle, especially of the dictatorship of the proletariat, is the touchstone for judging whether a person is a true Marxist. In the first thirty years of the PRC, party and state leaders, focusing on class struggle, naturally put the dictatorship of the proletariat in a prominent overriding position. "Never forget class struggle" and "Strengthen the dictatorship of the proletariat" were the resounding political slogans in the thirty years before the reform and opening up began.

The idea of the dictatorship of the proletariat was first put forward by Karl Marx: "Between capitalist and communist society lies the period of the revolutionary transformation of the one into the other. Corresponding to this is also a political transition period in which the state can be nothing but the revolutionary dictatorship of the proletariat."[20] A dictatorship is a system in which an individual or a small group has absolute power or authority over its subjects. By this definition, Marx's dictatorship of the proletariat means that the proletariat has exclusive control of state power or absolute power. Lenin extended Marx's thought on the dictatorship of the proletariat. In Lenin's theory, the dictatorship of the proletariat meant not only that the proletariat would gain exclusive control of state power but also that it would violently suppress its enemies.[21]

The CCP accepted Lenin's formulation. Mao said, "All the experience the Chinese people have accumulated over several decades teaches us to enforce the people's democratic dictatorship, that is, to deprive the reactionaries of the right to speak and let the people alone have that right. The combination of these two aspects, democracy for the people and dictatorship over the reactionaries, is the people's democratic dictatorship."[22]

Placing excessive emphasis on violent suppression of reactionary classes, even long after the founding of the socialist state, led to a dilemma in the theoretical realm and disaster in actual practice. Theoretically, if the main content of the dictatorship of the proletariat is the suppression of the reactionary classes, then why is it necessary to maintain the dictatorship of the proletariat after reactionaries have been eliminated as a class? If the dictatorship of the proletariat simply means that the proletariat exercises exclusive control of state power, then its practical implication is the exclusive leadership of the Communist Party. This is because, according to classic Marxist writers, the proletariat exercises its control of the state through its vanguard, the Communist Party. If the dictatorship of the proletariat means the suppression of law-breaking elements, this function is found in any state system and is not confined to the dictatorship of the proletariat. In practice, if the emphasis is still placed on exercising a dictatorship over the bourgeoisie even after the elimination of the exploiters as a class, then the only result will be the suppression of many ordinary citizens, revolutionary cadres, and dissidents as class enemies.

The only way out of this dilemma in both theory and practice is to give prominence to the "democracy" element of the dictatorship of the proletariat. This was exactly the path chosen by the party and state after the reform and opening-up period began. After he regained leadership, Deng emphasized the need to adhere to the Four Cardinal Principles[23] including the dictatorship of the proletariat. In his explanation of the twofold meaning of the dictatorship of the proletariat—democracy among the people and dictatorship over enemies—he placed more emphasis on democracy. Some of his most famous statements, including "Without democracy there can be no socialism and no socialist modernization" and "The more socialism develops, the more must democracy develop," were introduced in his talk on upholding the Four Cardinal Principles. In subsequent major laws and policy documents of the party and state, the term *proletarian dictatorship* was largely replaced by the term *the people's democratic dictatorship,* which was advanced by Mao in the early period.

The work reports delivered at the CCP national congresses of the reform and opening-up period put greater emphasis on developing socialist democracy because "the reform and opening up has endowed the Four Cardinal Principles with new meanings as our time advances."[24] "The people's democracy" and "socialist democracy" gradually became the loudest, the most enduring, and the most convincing political slogans in the thirty years of the reform and opening up.[25] The 16th CCP National Congress formally stated that "intraparty democracy is the lifeblood of the Party," and the 17th congress stated that "the people's democracy is the lifeblood of socialism." With the transition from proletarian dictatorship to socialist democracy at the level of theory, the political system on a practical level also underwent major changes. The basic framework of China's democratic politics—the people's congress system, the political consultation system, the village committee system, and the community committee system—was restored and improved. The CCP also substantially changed how it governed: scientific, democratic, and law-based governance became a basic requirement. As the rule of law became the basic principle of governance, the suppression of hostile forces no longer relied on proletarian dictatorship but was instead to be handled in accordance with the law. Mention of counterrevolution, which had been targeted as a serious crime by the proletariat's coercive apparatus, quietly disappeared from the CCP constitution and from the criminal code.

From Rule of Man to Rule of Law

Proletarian dictatorship operates beyond the constraints of law. The emphasis of dictatorship inevitably leads to defiance of law, which in turn leads to the rule of man, as shown in the supremacy of power over law, party organizations' disregard for the law, the absolute power of the paramount leader, and political campaigns that go beyond the law, to name a few.

Although a legal system that comprised many laws and regulations was in place for the first thirty years of the People's Republic, the rule prevailing in this period was fundamentally the rule of man, not the rule of law. This can be understood from three aspects. First, efforts to build the legal system, considered to be of prime importance in the first several years of the PRC, were soon disrupted by political movements. The National People's Congress (NPC), the country's law-making body, was unable to operate normally beginning in 1957. The second and third sessions of the 2nd National People's Congress were separated by as long as twenty-eight months. From July 1966 to January 1975, the NPC was in a state of stagnation, failing to convene a single meeting or enact a single law. As a result, many urgently needed basic laws could not be promulgated and were substituted for by numerous party and government regulations.

Second, existing laws were wantonly trampled on, and the basic constitution-ally guaranteed rights of citizens were no longer protected. Arrests, detention, convictions, and punishments were imposed according to various provisionally endorsed policies rather than laws. Third, some individuals and organizations wielded power beyond the law. In particular, the paramount leader of the party and authorities at various levels enjoyed power not limited by the law and could decide the fate, including the life and death, of others. The speeches and actions of Mao were deemed supreme directives that were higher than any law, allowing them to become authority-conferring tools used by various political groups to justify their actions. A wide variety of task forces, revolutionary committees, and "courts of the masses" wielded power beyond the law.

The rule of man led to a succession of tragedies. This included the arrest, detention, imprisonment, property confiscation, interrogation, forced confes-sion, reeducation through labor, sentencing, and even execution of an untold number of people, from the president of the country to ordinary workers, peas-ants, and intellectuals. Other cruel tortures and serious physical and mental suf-ferings were imposed on an even greater number of people. One of the most painful lessons from the first thirty years of the PRC, especially the decade of the Cultural Revolution, is that the rule of man must give way to the rule of law.

The disastrous consequences of the rule of man awakened the entire party and the people. After the end of the Cultural Revolution, most party leaders and intellectuals emphasized the importance of strengthening the rule of law. After the reform and opening-up period began, the party and government began to place an even greater emphasis on governing the country according to law, and the rule of law and democracy were often mentioned and emphasized together. Deng emphasized development of the rule of law in almost every important talk. In 1978 he stated that "to ensure people's democracy, we must strengthen our legal system. Democracy has to be institutionalized and written into law, so as to make sure that institutions and laws do not change whenever the leadership changes, or whenever the leaders change their views or shift the focus of their attention. The trouble is that our legal system is incomplete, with many laws yet to be enacted."[26] At the third plenary session of the 11th CCP Central Commit-tee, many older-generation leaders severely criticized the defects of the rule of man and strongly argued for the importance of building the rule of law.

After the 1980s, many theorists began to advocate for the rule of law. From the very start, the concept of the rule of law received much attention from party and government leaders. The Directive of the CCP Central Committee on Reso-lutely Implementing the Criminal Law and the Criminal Procedural Law not only revoked the system under which cases were subject to the approval of party committees but also for the first time used the term "rule of law."[27] In the early 1980s, the CCP Central Committee reiterated on multiple occasions that all citizens are equal before the Constitution and the law. In the mid-1980s, it was explicitly advanced that the CCP, as the only ruling party, must carry out its activities within the framework of law and that party organizations and leaders do not have any power beyond the law.[28] After the 1990s, establishing the rule of law became a long-term goal of China's political development, with the major milestone event being the 15th CCP National Congress convened in 1997. The political report to that congress explicitly stated the goal of "building a socialist country under the rule of law,"[29] and soon thereafter the goal was written into China's Constitution, making it not only the CCP's but also the country's political aspiration. After the 16th CCP National Congress, the Chinese government set forth to build a government ruled by law, which not only made the goal more concrete but also indicated that the government would play a leading role in building China into a country governed by law.

The process of the reform and opening up is also a process of building China's socialist legal system. From 1979 to 2005, the NPC and its standing committee adopted 400 laws and law-related decisions, the State Council formulated more than 650 administrative regulations, and local people's congresses and their standing committees enacted more than 7,500 local laws and regulations. The Chinese government's goal was to establish a relatively full-featured legal system by 2010.[30]

From Centralization to Decentralization

Revolution calls for centralization of power, as do dictatorship and, even more so, the rule of man. In its effort to seize political power, the CCP needed revolution, dictatorship, and the rule of man—that is, a high degree of centralism. It had a strict top-down organizational and disciplinary system under which subordinates had to comply with superiors, the minority with the majority, and the party rank and file with the party's central committee. The will and power of the subordinate are centralized at the level of their superiors and ultimately with the party's paramount leader. This centralism gave the party great political mobilization capacity and proved highly effective in overthrowing the old political system.

After the founding of the PRC, this centralism was further strengthened within the party and extended from inside to outside the party, from the political field to the economic and even ideological and cultural fields, thereby allowing the party to control the entire state. In the political and administrative fields, power was highly concentrated within the highest organizations and the major leaders; in the economic field, the power was highly concentrated in the party and the government departments under a planned economic system; and in the ideological and cultural fields, only one sound was heard—that of the party. Mao and other party and government leaders, becoming aware of the possible negative consequence of the centralization of power, attempted to prevent such negative consequences through "democratic centralism," which featured "centralism on the basis of democracy and democracy under centralized leadership,"[31] and by elevating democratic centralism from the party's organizational principle to the basic operating principle of state power. By way of this democratic centralism, Mao aimed to "create a political situation in which we have both centralism and democracy, both discipline and freedom, both unity of will and personal ease of mind and liveliness."[32]

Democratic centralism, however, which in essence is a principle and method of democratic decisionmaking, does not have a decisive effect on the creation and supervision of power and therefore cannot overcome the negative effects of concentrated centralism. Alone, it can neither effectively supervise nor restrict power abuse nor lead to the ideal political state envisaged by Mao. The practice over PRC's first thirty years shows that despite the political reality at the time and despite the positive role it played in maintaining and consolidating the new state, extreme centralism was having increasingly negative effects. It seriously undermined the political enthusiasm of ordinary party members and citizens, greatly dampened the initiative of local governments and party organizations, and in particular fueled arbitrary decisionmaking by key party and government leaders.

With reform and opening up, the leadership of the CCP and the Chinese government began to introduce a large-scale, multifaceted decentralization of power. The focus inside the party and administrative organs was to establish and perfect a collective leadership system that would clearly determine the division of labor among core leadership members, restrict the power of major leaders, and prevent arbitrariness in decisionmaking. Accordingly, many supportive laws and regulations were promulgated for this purpose. The fifth plenary session of the 11th CCP Central Committee, convened in February 1980, adopted Some Norms Concerning Intra-Party Political Life, a far-reaching proposal that defined the party's task as "persisting in collective leadership and opposing individual arbitrariness."

Following this guideline, a series of power decentralization measures were formulated. At the central level, for example, the 12th CCP National Congress in 1982 passed a resolution that dissolved the position of the chairman of the CCP Central Committee and established the CCP Secretariat, implementing a collective leadership system headed by the general secretary. At the local level, the position of first secretary was removed and a standing committee–based deliberation and decisionmaking system was put in place. At the fourth plenary session of the 14th CCP Central Committee, convened in September 1994, a special subsession on strengthening party building was held, at which a series of decisions were made to develop intraparty democracy, improve collective leadership and decentralization, strengthen democratic decisionmaking and its institutionalization, safeguard the democratic rights of party members, and improve the intraparty supervision and elections systems. At the 17th CCP National Congress in 2007, it was decided that decisionmaking power, executive power, and supervisory power should be separated.

In addition to decentralization within the party and government organs, the thirty years after the reform and opening up saw rapid advancement of decentralization in three important areas. The first was the decentralization of political and economic power toward local governments, which began in the mid-1980s. On July 20, 1984, the CCP Secretariat decided to reform the cadre management system. Under this new mechanism, an administrative authority would have control over only the administrative authority immediately subordinate to it. This move substantially expanded local autonomy. In December 1993 the State Council adopted a comprehensive tax-sharing system that greatly increased local government power in economic management.

The second form of decentralization involved enterprises. From the mid-1980s, the CCP Central Committee gradually promoted the separation of enterprises from the government. In November 1993 the third plenary session of the 14th CCP Central Committee adopted the Decision of the CCP Central Committee on Issues Regarding the Establishment of the Socialist Market Economic System, according to which enterprises became independent legal entities and were no longer governed by the state.

The third was the decentralization of power toward society. Under the unitary governance model, all political, economic, and social power is concentrated in the state, and there are neither relatively independent nongovernmental organizations (NGOs) nor substantial social autonomy. Social decentralization came with the emergence of pluralistic governance. The autonomy for villagers and urban residents that was introduced in the late 1980s was an important step toward social decentralization as well as a breakthrough in China's grassroots democracy development. With the implementation of a new round of restructuring of government administration beginning in the 1990s, some government institutions were turned into industry associations. For example, the Ministry of Light Industry became the China Light Industry Association, and the Ministry of Textile Industry became the China Textile Industry Association. Accordingly, some administrative functions that used to belong to the government were transferred to industry management organizations, marking an important step toward industry autonomy. As NGOs mushroomed in the late 1990s, the government began to emphasize their role in social management and allowed their participation in social management while at the same time relegating some state power to specific NGOs in the process.

From State to Society

After coming to power in 1949, the Chinese Communist Party used the state as a platform through which to exercise centralized authority. All power was concentrated in the state and ultimately in the party and its leaders, thus forming a party-state system under which the party and the government and the party and the state were one politically, enterprises were put under the control of the state economically, and all civil organizations were subject to official administration socially, resulting in a further strengthened "grand unity" (大一统, *dayitong*) of state and society.

The socialist economic system in place in the early period of the People's Republic had two pillars: the planned economy, a mechanism by which the government controlled all economic activity, and public ownership, by which all means of production were concentrated in the hands of the state or the collective. At the end of the first quarter of 1956, almost all private industries (99 percent) and private commerce (85 percent) were transformed into joint state-private ownership. After that, the party and government began to set about developing a pure socialist public-ownership economy made up of state-owned enterprises and collective enterprises in cities, towns, and people's communes in the countryside. At the same time, strict restrictions were imposed on the private economy and privately owned enterprises. In 1978, when the reform and opening up was initiated, industries owned by the state and collectively owned industries accounted for 77.6 percent and 22.4 percent, respectively, of the country's gross industrial-output value.[33] Industrial enterprises were 100 percent publicly owned. In addition, all economic activities—including production, operation, allocation, and distribution—were included in the scope of political life, and as a result the economic behavior of enterprises and individuals assumed political significance. Any act that tried to develop the private economy in violation of policies, even if it took the form of simply raising several more pigs or chickens, would be severely punished under the charge of embracing capitalism.

In line with socialist public ownership and the planned economy as well as the unitary leadership in political life, the authorities imposed strict control over

NGOs. After the CCP came to power, almost all NGOs dissolved. Temple fairs, clan associations, ancestral halls, virtuous villagers committees, and civil corps, all of which had been in existence for a long time, disappeared. Only a few special organizations that had helped the CCP in the past, such as the China Democratic League and the Jiu San Society, were retained as democratic parties. Mass organizations established by the party itself—such as trade unions, youth leagues, and women's associations—emerged, but their number and variety were also limited. In the early 1950s, there were only 44 national associations in the entire country. Six years later, there were fewer than 100 national associations and around 6,000 local associations. Even these associations were simple in composition, mainly falling into nine categories of mass organizations, such as trade unions, youth leagues, women's associations, scientific workers' associations, and federations of industry and commerce. These "people's organizations," fostered and led by the party and government, were in essence nothing but disguised forms of party organizations because their budgets were fully funded by the government and their leaders enjoyed the status of state cadres.

In fact, over the first thirty years of the People's Republic, especially during the Cultural Revolution, it was not just industry and commercial enterprises and civil organizations that were politicized; all other aspects of social life were also more or less included in the scope of influence of the party and state and were imbued with political significance. All social activities, from literature, the arts, scholarship, sports, and religion to aspects of everyday life such as clothing, eating, living, and traveling were subject to strong political intervention. This highly nationalized and politicized social system, an abnormal state that arose from special circumstances but turned into a permanent institution, inevitably had serious negative effects. It deprived citizens of their legitimate rights to freedom and autonomy, suppressed people's creativity and initiative, exhausted the vigor of the entire nation, and greatly frustrated the country's social and economic development.

Deng's reforms started with the reform of the country's economic system when he established a socialist market economy. This had two basic elements. The first was the reform of the ownership system, which changed the existing pure public-ownership system into a new system dominated by public ownership but supplemented by multiple other forms of ownership. The second was the reform of the economic system, which changed the planned economy into a market economy. The reform of the economic system, in essence, called for the withdrawal of the party and state from the economic life and the autonomy of enterprises and individuals in how they managed their business affairs. In 2007 the contribution made by state-owned and state-holding industrial enterprises and collectively owned enterprises to the gross industrial output value decreased to 29.5 and 2.5 percent, respectively. In the same year, there were 27.4 million registered small businesses that were privately or individually owned and 5.5 million privately owned enterprises, a growth by a factor of 0.8 and 39.1, respectively, over 1992. Among industrial enterprises above a designated size, 303,000 (90 percent) were non-state-owned enterprises. In terms of output value, in 2007 non-state-owned enterprises above a designated size contributed 68 percent of the gross industrial output value created by all enterprises in that cohort.[34]

With the deepening of reform of the economic and political systems, a relatively independent civil society emerged in China. This civil society, as the third sector along with the market system and the system of government, has mainly consisted of various civil or social organizations. The changes brought by the reform and opening up to China's economic and political environment created the conditions for the rapid growth of civil organizations, especially after the 1980s. In 1989 the number of national social organizations and local social organizations increased to 1,600 and more than 200,000, respectively. After the protests of 1989, the party and the government launched a review and reregistration of civil organizations, resulting in a moderate decrease in the number of these organizations within a short time, so that by 1992 there were 1,200 national social organizations and around 180,000 local social organizations. However, the number of social organizations saw a regrowth soon thereafter. In 1997 there were more than 180,000 social organizations at the county level or above, including 21,404 at the provincial level and 1,848 at the national level.[35] In June 2009 more than 410,000 NGOs were formally registered with civil affairs departments across the country, including 228,000 social organizations, 182,000 privately established nonenterprise organizations, and 1,622 foundations.[36] In addition, there were a great number of other NGOs that were either registered with the industry and commerce authorities or not registered at all, such as clubs, apartment owners committees, and Internet-based social organizations. There are no formal statistics regarding this category of civil organizations, but their number is conservatively estimated at more than 3 million.

This rapid growth of civil society had a major impact on China's political life. The government's social management function became increasingly important, and there soon arose an urgent need for the formulation and revision of relevant policies, laws, and regulations—that is, for the establishment of a sound social management system. As a result, the social management system soon received great attention from the party and government. At the fourth and sixth plenary sessions of the 16th CCP Central Committee, special instructions were given on strengthening social construction and reforming the country's social management system. The two meetings, promoting the enhancement of the party's leadership and the building of a socialist harmonious society, explicitly instructed party committees and governments at various levels to "study the laws of social management, perfect the social management system and related policies and regulations, integrate social management resources, and establish a social management system led by the party, administered by the government, and participated in by the public."[37] The political report made to the 17th CCP National Congress had a special section on making a more active effort to give full scope to the role of social organizations.

Concluding Thoughts

It can be seen from the preceding discussion that the sixty years that followed the founding of the PRC consisted of two markedly different thirty-year periods. These sixty years also saw substantial changes in China's social and political life in the absence of any change of state power and the basic political system, allowing China's political development as a socialist state to enter a new stage. What were the forces behind the great changes before and after the reform and opening up that began in 1978? These changes were in part a result of the transition of the CCP from a revolutionary party to a ruling party, the various crises the party faced in running the state, and the different personalities of Mao and Deng. But if the matter is examined more closely, the decisive factors behind China's political changes over the past thirty years are found to be social and economic changes, the inherent logic of political development, the formation of a new political culture, and the impact of globalization.

After the end of the Cultural Revolution, the CCP leadership found that despite continued economic growth in the thirty years after the founding of the PRC, the gap between China and developed countries had not been quickly narrowed, as previously expected, but rather had expanded steadily, with the majority of workers and peasants still living a hard life. It can be said that China's economic reforms were triggered by the country's political reforms that commenced at the third plenary session of the 13th CCP Central Committee, and the economic reforms, in turn, fundamentally influenced the country's political life. China began to implement a socialist market economy in the 1980s and changed the country's economic system from a structure of unitary public and collective ownership to an all-embracing ownership system covering public ownership, collective ownership, private ownership, individually owned business, Sino-foreign joint ventures, and wholly foreign businesses, which greatly improved productivity and the people's living standards.

Fundamental changes in economic life have been the true driver of China's political development over the past thirty years. Basic requirements of the market economy are that enterprises must be independent legal entities with autonomy in operation, the government must be separated from enterprises, and enterprises must take full responsibility for profits and losses. Under the market economy system and corporate system, the government cannot directly interfere with enterprise operation and production but must instead provide a stable, orderly, fair, and just competitive environment for enterprise operations and economic activities. This requires that the government establish a comprehensive legal system and strengthen market regulation. An efficiency-oriented market economy demands that government strive to reduce administrative costs and improve efficiency. A market economy inevitably leads to the polarization of wealth, which, in turn, calls for the provision of more public services and the establishment of a social security system. Under the new market economy system, various interest groups soon took shape. They needed channels through which to express their interests and influence the government's policies. This has required the government to strengthen democratic politics and social management and foster social organizations that represent different interests. When clothing and food issues are resolved and the people become more affluent, they naturally begin to have more political demands. Accordingly, the government needs to expand the channels of public participation and give citizens more power in democratic management.

Political development has its intrinsic logic, which to a considerable extent determines the direction and outcome of political transformation. At the beginning of reform, China was a large developing country relatively backward in economic development. Boosting the economy was the primary task of the reforms, while social and political stability was the prerequisite of that effort. Therefore, maintaining stability as a top priority became a basic principle of China's political and economic reforms and determined that reforms would be gradual and incremental. Breakthrough measures were introduced now and then in the process of political development, but no radical overall transformation of the political framework was possible.

The Chinese Communist Party is at the core of China's political reforms, and the evolution of the CCP itself has had a decisive influence on China's political advancement. The CCP, having completed the transition from a revolutionary party to a ruling party, has candidly admitted that "the position of the ruling party is neither inherently justified nor has been achieved once and for all."[38] Only by continual reform to strengthen its governance and social management capabilities and to satisfy the increasing material, spiritual, and political demands of the broad masses can the CCP maintain and consolidate its ruling position.

The evolution of political ideology guides China's development. In the final analysis, any political reform represents a political orientation and operates under a political concept. The changes in ideology and political values have a direct impact on China's political development. Since ancient times China has placed an emphasis on ideology, and an ideological change usually heralds political reform. To emancipate the mind, simply speaking, is to free people from the shackles of old doctrines and ideas to embrace new ideas and theories compatible with social progress in the new era and use them to guide social practice.

China's more than twenty years' experience of reform has fully proved that ideological progress has a close connection with social and political progress. To some extent, China's reform and opening up has been a process of clashing between new and old ideologies and concepts and of replacing old ideologies and thoughts with new ones and thereby promoting social progress. Specifically, the greatest theoretical innovation of the CCP since the reform and opening up has been the gradual establishment of a socialist theoretical system with Chinese characteristics, comprising Deng Xiaoping's political and economic policies, the Three Represents, and the scientific outlook on development.

A number of new concepts and values have not only represented a transcendence of traditional political thought but have also directly and profoundly influenced China's social and political life and powerfully boosted China's democratic and political progress. These include human rights, the rule of law, good governance, good government, constitutional government, legitimacy, people orientation, civil society, harmonious society, political civilization, global governance, government innovation, incremental democracy, transparent government, responsible government, service-oriented government, and efficient government.[39] Some of these political concepts existed in the past but were criticized as belonging to capitalist ideology, while others emerged after the reform and opening up. Whether their roots are in traditional Chinese thought, Marxist theory, or Western political thought, they all profoundly embody core human values such as freedom, equality, justice, and harmony.

We are now in the age of globalization. Globalization is an ongoing historical process of world development, its basic characteristic being an inherent, inseparable, and increasingly interrelated world in terms of economic integration. Globalization is first embodied in economic integration, which inevitably has profound influence on all social life, including political and cultural life. Against the backdrop of globalization, reforming China domestically and opening up the country to the outside world are two sides of the same coin. That Deng and other Chinese leaders combined domestic political reform and economic opening up to the outside world as the country's basic national policy from the very start of the new era shows their profound understanding of the times.

China's economic development would not have been possible without the advanced technologies, equipment, managerial experience, capital, resources, energy, and markets of foreign countries, and therefore economic opening up was a necessity. China's participation in the globalization process has been furthered by being a member in such international organizations as the World Trade Organization, hosting the Olympic Games, joining international conventions, and taking part in other global affairs. In doing so, China has had to improve its domestic governance structure to align with international norms. The establishment of special economic zones, for example, was a paradigm shift in China's reform and opening up, reflecting the understanding that domestic governance must adapt to the needs of international capital. As a consequence, foreign management practices, values, concepts, and lifestyles were introduced to China along with the general opening up of the economy. In the process, China not only brought in capital, technologies, and experience but also drew on many concepts and administrative systems used in foreign countries, adapted, of course, to China's own national conditions.

An important purpose of the establishment of the socialist market economy system was to draw on the advantages of the Western economic system. Important concepts such as human rights, the rule of law, good governance, constitutional government, civil society, service-oriented government, and responsible government were first introduced from the West. Many major measures taken in China as part of the effort to build service-oriented government and responsible government—including one-stop service, the administrative accountability system, a service commitment system, and a policy hearing system (a practice for citizen input on policy)—were also introduced from Western countries. A survey of China's political development over the past thirty years shows that all of China's major progress in democratic politics has been closely associated with borrowing, and learning from, advanced political practices of foreign countries.

In the course of its political development since 1949, China has created a political model with distinctively Chinese characteristics. In terms of basic political systems, the National People's Congress, the political consultation system, regional autonomy of ethnic minorities, and grassroots resident autonomy make up the framework of China's unique democratic politics. In terms of state power structure, China, instead of implementing the separation of powers (legislative, executive, and judiciary), implements a democratic centralism that combines the legislative and executive powers and emphasizes checks and balances among the decisionmaking power, executive power, supervisory power, personnel appointment, revenue assignments, and expenditure responsibilities. In terms of the party system, China does not have a multiparty competitive system but implements a system wherein the CCP, as the only ruling party, cooperates with other democratic parties through political consultations. In terms of state governance, China follows a governance structure in which the party leads the government. China's governance actors have become diversified, though the most important, and the core of them, are still CCP organizations at all levels, which are assisted by government organs, enterprises, institutions, and social organizations.

In terms of the approach to political reforms, China has adopted a path of incremental development. China's political reforms are not radical but gradual and incremental. The essence of incremental reform is to maximize incremental interests and enable people to benefit from the reform without jeopardizing or depriving existing interests. Incremental reform emphasizes innovation and transformation, on one hand, and maintains and strengthens the traditional political advantages, on the other, rather than simply severing the present from tradition. It emphasizes the gradualness of the reform process and yet is not without substantial transformations. In terms of the relationship between the central government and local governments, a governance structure that "combines horizontal administration and vertical supervision" (条块结合, *tiaokuai jiehe*) has taken shape. China is a large country implementing a unitary system under which the central government governs the country through both a vertical power system and a horizontal power system. The vertical system consists of state power organizations that are directly under the control of the central government and provincial governments, whereas the horizontal system consists of state power organizations that are under the administration of party and government departments at various levels.

It is the CCP's proclaimed goal to build China into a prosperous, strong, democratic, culturally advanced, and harmonious socialist country. It shows that although maintaining stability and improving efficiency and the rule of law are all important goals of China's political development, its fundamental goal is to develop a people's democracy. In my opinion, China's democratic politics still leaves much to be desired and lags behind the people's demand for democracy and the pace of the country's social and economic development. Long-standing serious political corruption undermines the authority of the party and government. The lack of effective channels by which citizens participate in politics has posed a serious threat to the political stability and lasting peace of China. The increasing income gap and other forms of social injustice also constitute major challenges to socialism's core values of freedom, fairness, and harmony. The lack of consensus between the government and citizens on major political issues is shaking society's political identity. The absence of a comprehensive well-functioning system embracing elections, decisionmaking, supervision, checks and balances, and political participation is increasingly constraining the development of China's unique system of democratic politics. There have not been many breakthroughs in people's democracy or intraparty democracy, leaving a significant gap between the effects and needs of social and economic development and the people's demands.

With the advancement of the market economy and the increasingly vocal political demands of Chinese citizens, China's democratic political process has become irreversible. China's political reform in the near term should address the following main goals:

—providing a blueprint for China's political democracy from an all-encompassing and long-term perspective

—reforming and perfecting the system of the National People's Congress, especially as related to deputy elections, deliberation, decisionmaking, and supervision, to strengthen its legislative and supervisory role

—reforming and perfecting the system of the Chinese People's Political Consultative Conference, especially as related to the selection of its members, political consultation, and supervision, to better fulfill the political consultative and supervisory role of all levels of its organizations

—advancing intraparty democracy, especially as related to the rights of party members, such as the right to vote, the right to know, the right to participate, and the right to supervise, where substantial reforms are needed

—advancing grassroots democracy, especially as related to democratic elections, democratic decisionmaking, and democratic supervision at the county and township levels, all of which call for significant reforms

—making breakthroughs in key links of China's democracy development, such as the relationship between the party and the government, supervision of the exercise of power, recommendation and selection of cadres, intraparty elections, grassroots elections, political transparency, and civic engagement.

The success of China's modernization will increasingly hinge on its political modernization based on the rule of law and democracy, as substantial political reforms are the only way to achieve a strong democracy and the rule of law.

COMMENT
KENNETH LIEBERTHAL

Yu Keping's chapter addresses the major ways in which the first thirty years of communist rule in China produced numerous tragedies and the key directions of reform in the past thirty years that have set the country on a better course. He divides this overview into six major transitions: from revolution to reform, from struggle to harmony, from dictatorship to democracy, from rule of man to rule of law, from concentrated power to dispersed power, and from state to society—and concludes with his reflections on the driving forces of change in China and the areas in which further reform is especially needed.

His chapter highlights the extent to which the Chinese system has changed not only economically but also politically and socially since the era of Mao Zedong. These changes have been driven by major reassessments of numerous factors: the role of the Chinese Communist Party, the best approach to economic development, the driving forces of social change, the nature of the relationship of the state to society, and the most effective techniques of governance.

Yu argues that fundamental errors were made when the CCP leaders failed to recognize that the revolution should have come to an end—and the task of the party should have shifted to effective governance—within a few years of nation-wide victory in 1949. Consequently, Mao dictated that class struggle should continue and intensify, violence should continue to drive change (as violent struggle is integral to revolution itself), all nonpolitical sources of organization and authority should be subsumed under the aegis of the party and the government, and so forth. The internal dynamics of such thinking led naturally to the extraordinary tragedies that befell the system in the last decade of the Mao era.

As Yu makes clear, Deng Xiaoping understood the scope and depth of the problems and began to set the country on a more successful course. Yu does a superb job of providing a broad historical overview of the ensuing basic directions and overall evolution of policy in each of the transitions that frame his argument. His concluding reflections indicate that though China's ultimate goal is to bring about stronger democracy, its reality still falls seriously short. He specifically points to, inter alia, corruption that saps the public's trust, the dearth of effective ways for people to participate in politics, growing income inequality that seriously threatens social order and harmony, and the lack of consensus on some major issues between the government and the population.

Yu concludes that China now needs breakthrough steps to improve intraparty democracy, grassroots democracy, the people's congress system, and the political consultative congress system to meet the needs of the economy and demands of the society. He notes that though the CCP is the core force pushing political change forward, to consolidate its position as a governing party it must pursue unceasing reform, increase its executive and social management capabilities, and satisfy people's increasing spiritual and material needs.

Yu's chapter establishes the case for major additional reform of China's political system and provides an initial basis for considering the types of reforms that are necessary. The considerations involved in launching such reforms and enabling them to achieve their key objectives are, however, implicit rather than explicit in Yu's analysis.

Types of Reform

There are two broad ways of thinking about the types of reforms needed in China and how to realize them: democratic transition and improvement in governance. Although not mutually exclusive, these two approaches differ sufficiently—in both priorities and sequencing—that they warrant individual treatment. Yu's chapter provides fertile ground for a discussion of these alternatives.

Democratic Transition

Many scholars, especially many American scholars, believe that it is important for China's future prosperity, stability, and unity for the People's Republic of China to begin a determined transition to a fundamentally democratic political system. Democracy in this case refers to more than a highly consultative system that increasingly governs in a transparent fashion and uses law to manage society. It includes making the political system and its officials subject to the dictates of the law alongside the rest of China's society, holding competitive elections according to a schedule determined by law, and allowing more than one political party to compete in those elections. Realizing these three democratic imperatives in a meaningful way will, in turn, require adoption and implementation of many additional changes involving transparency, freedom of speech and assembly, and so forth.

The case for starting down the path of determined democratic transition is quite simple: comparative political analysis shows that as populations become wealthier, better educated, more knowledgeable about the world, and more integrated in the global system, it becomes increasingly difficult to maintain a stable one-party political system, even in cases in which that party has long experience in governing and has played a critical role in bringing about these improved conditions. Such transitions, moreover, typically take the governing party by surprise and prove more difficult and less successful than would have been the case had the transition to a fully democratic system begun earlier and been pursued in determined fashion by the governing political party.

In short, the argument runs, China's transition to a fully democratic system, if managed well, would most likely reduce inequality (and possibly corruption) and reflect China's increasing levels of education, wealth, information availability, and degree of globalization. It would also help China address some of its critical pollution problems.

But there is no consensus in China today on the need to shift to a multiparty competitive democratic system, and thus the chances that the leadership will adopt such an approach are miniscule. Even to adopt a more moderate agenda, one that takes significant strides in the directions Yu recommends while doing so under the ongoing leadership of the CCP, will be difficult to initiate, and Yu's chapter implicitly provides a cautionary tale.

Indeed, the chapter's analysis of the conditions under which China undertook its major reforms beginning in the late 1970s calls to mind both the necessity of having a masterful political strategist lead the reform effort and the importance of major prior failure in creating political and social space for fundamental reform. A third consideration is also pertinent: the role of political economy in determining the chances for successful reform.

A Master Political Strategist

Deng Xiaoping was a masterful political tactician as well as a strategic thinker. Yu details the six substantive changes that Deng nurtured and then comments on the importance of Deng's having followed an incremental approach to making these changes. An important aspect that the chapter does not highlight, though, is that Deng exhibited keen sensitivity to how to build capability and support within the system and among the populace to set China onto a new course.

For example, Deng's use of special economic zones limited the opposition of conservatives, buffered the impact of opening to the outside world on a still-dysfunctional domestic political system, and created an example of what a changed approach to international investment and trade could accomplish. By first restoring family farming in the countryside, Deng reformed a relatively uncomplicated sector and achieved major one-off gains as absurdities in the previous system were dismantled. This, in turn, built enormous momentum behind the notion that China's future success could be promoted through structural and policy reforms. And after the events of 1989, the combination of Deng Xiaoping's extraordinary personal authority and his enormous skill in maneuvering within the political system enabled him to put systemic reform back on a viable path forward in 1992.

Deng, in short, not only had keen insight into the fundamental errors of the system that Mao Zedong bequeathed, but he also had a political strategist's sense of how to sequence measures to build momentum and capacity and to undermine the opposition. There have been many reformers of authoritarian systems in various countries in modern times, but few have succeeded in making such major changes in a dictatorial system without in the process bringing down the system itself. The history of the 1970s to the 1990s highlights the importance of having a master political tactician with a strategic vision lead a major reform effort.

As of 2013, however, political power in China no longer resides solely in the hands of a small number of people of enormous prestige at the top. The Politburo Standing Committee and the Politburo as a whole now operate according to a more consensus-driven approach to decisionmaking. In addition, power throughout the system itself has become more dispersed. Overall decisionmaking processes have become more regularized and incorporate more players, and localities have gained substantially increased authority. Corporate and other interests have also become influential. The Chinese system, in short, now faces significant structural obstacles to the emergence of a powerful, dynamic leader capable of initiating and implementing systemic reform.

Prior Catastrophic Failure as a Prerequisite for Major Reform

As Yu details, by the 1977–78 period Deng Xiaoping was able to initiate serious reform because the system itself had entered a stage of acute, system-wide crisis that highlighted the importance of reform and also weakened the political institutions that might otherwise have stood in the way of this effort. This history contains a potentially important lesson for today: it typically takes widespread recognition among both officials and the population that the system is in crisis for reformers to overcome the drag of vested interests and fear of the uncertainties that major reform always entails. While China's performance in recent years has produced widespread recognition of the need for reform, however, there has not been a comparable sense of imminent systemic crisis.

The Importance of Political Economy

A review of China's current political economy highlights a further obstacle to implementing a major reform agenda today. The last three decades of reforms have greatly empowered the leaders in every province, city, county, and township to act in entrepreneurial ways to grow the GDP of their locality every year. They have the flexibility necessary to take initiatives, the power to control a great deal of what occurs within the locality (in the courts and banks as well as in the government and party agencies), and strong incentives to succeed each and every year. In all of this, they must be attentive to the broad priorities of their immediate superiors who appointed them, but the system has a lot of flexibility at every level of the national hierarchy.

If this overview of China's current political economy is accurate, the difficulties of implementing major new reforms are likely to be great. The current system richly rewards local officials who produce desired results and gives those officials great latitude in their efforts. To implement a major new wave of reform in China today would therefore require that top leaders fully agree on the specifics of major reforms, agree to give them top priority, and follow through on rewarding those who implement reforms and punishing those who do not.

Improving Governance

Many Chinese scholars point to a different approach to systemic reforms over the coming years. They recognize the difficulties of launching a democratic transformation, but they also appreciate the importance of making systemic improvements to sustain social stability and enable China to continue down the path to wealth and power. The prescriptions made by these scholars focus on several major provisions: making greater use of law in managing the economy and society, paying more attention to social welfare to reduce inequality and heighten the popular sense of social justice, and increasing the use of democratic techniques within the Chinese Communist Party itself.

The approach referenced here is rule by law, not rule of law. That is, laws will be more carefully crafted and of higher quality. The quality of the legal system will be improved over time. But issues judged to be sufficiently important by the party will be decided on the basis of political criteria, and that can affect the application of the law to officials, too.

Social management will move to the fore, with far more stress on development of a social safety net and of various social organizations and institutions. This will reduce the inequality that is a source of potentially major social instability and will produce greater legitimacy for the system among the population.

Increasingly, democratic practices will be employed within the party. There is fear that, given current levels of inequality, social strain, and general education, introduction of completely free election campaigns might dramatically increase social friction. Therefore, the objective is first to increase democratic practices among the more than 80 million party members, who tend to be the better educated and more publicly engaged members of the population. These democratic practices include greater intraparty consultation, stricter adherence to party rules, and more transparency both internally and toward the populace as a whole. Some such practices will also increasingly apply to the government. For example, citizens' right to information about relevant government practices and decisions is increasingly being recognized.

There are three key obstacles to implementing this improved-governance strategy successfully enough to ensure stability and prosperity over the coming ten to twenty years. First, reforms are driven at the top by overriding national considerations and at the grassroots level by the pressing need to cope with day-to-day problems. But the vast middle reaches of the political system tend to resist reforms that challenge current bureaucratic and other vested interests. Without serious checks and balances—which are extremely difficult to establish without reforms that are closer to those identified in the democratic-transition strategy—the task of truly implementing the improved-governance reforms at the provincial and municipal—and even county—levels can prove daunting.

Second, there are Leninist holdovers in the current political system, such as the principles of democratic centralism and of the party's management of cadres, that will quite likely limit the efficacy of any improved-governance reforms. Each of these includes practices that enable deeply embedded vested interests to mitigate the efficacy of reform initiatives that aim to enhance democratic practices within the party.

Finally, the high level of economic and social inequality that exists now will be difficult to address successfully under these reforms. The 12th Five-Year Plan and its successors will provide impressive resources to enhance the social safety net and extend its coverage. But the current political economy transfers massive wealth to enterprises as a whole and to state-owned enterprises in particular, and it would take fundamental reforms to change this in a major way. Corruption adds to this underlying structural inequality. Without checks and balances, and without placing law above officials, it is difficult to understand how these problems will fundamentally be resolved.

In sum, the improved-governance strategy identifies important areas in which serious efforts will be made, and it reflects an appreciation of the potential for increased social disruption if popular democracy is introduced rapidly. But it risks adopting measures that are inadequate to the task of addressing sufficiently the core problems of inequality, corruption, concentration of power in the hands of individuals at all levels of the system, environmental degradation, and vested interests that cumulatively may produce massive instability in China.

Conclusion

In China, the concentration of political power has greatly diminished, and consensus has now become the accepted style of decisionmaking at a national level. The country is building on a period of unprecedented growth and increased comprehensive national power—a very different situation from that confronting Deng Xiaoping when he sought to launch his post-Mao reforms. The system has evolved to permit an extensive role for various interest groups, including local territorial leaders. In this current situation, how can the kinds of reform that Yu believes are still necessary—those that establish the rule of law, deepen democratic experiments, and create a vibrant and effective civil society—move from ideas to policy to reality on a national level and then be implemented effectively throughout this multi-layered political system? There is no simple, clear-cut answer to this key question.

Notes

1. Friedrich Engels, "Lun quanwei" [On authority], in *Makesi Engesi quanji* [Complete works of Karl Marx and Friedrich Engels], vol. 18 (Beijing: People's Publishing House, 1964), p. 344.

2. Karl Marx, "1848–1850 nian de falanxi jieji douzheng" [The class struggles in France, 1848 to 1850], in *Makesi Engesi quanji*, vol. 7 (Beijing: People's Publishing House, 1959), p. 99.

3. He Li, ed., *Zhonghua renmin gongheguo shi* [History of the People's Republic of China] (Beijing: China Archives Press, 1989), p. 42.

4. Mao Zedong, "Zai zui gao guowu huiyi shang de jianghua" [Speech presented at the Supreme State Conference], in *Jianguo yilai Mao Zedong wengao* [Writings of Mao Zedong since the founding of the PRC], vol. 7 (Beijing: Zhongyang wenxian chubanshe [Central Party Literature Press], 1992), p. 12.

5. Jiang Weigang, "Mao Zedong shidai jingji jianshe de weida chengjiu" [Great achievements in economic construction in the Mao Zedong era], July 13, 2008 (bbs. tiexue.net/post2_2912470_1.html).

6. There are vast discrepancies in the estimates of the number of people who starved to death in the "three years of natural disasters." The most common estimate, however, is around 30 million. Cao Shuji, "1959–1961 nian Zhongguo de renkou siwang ji qi chengyin" [Deaths and causes of death in China from 1959 to 1961], *Zhongguo renkou kexue* [Chinese journal of population science], no. 1 (2005).

7. Li Xiannian, speech presented at the Central Working Meeting, April 5, 1979, in *San zhong quanhui yilai Zhongyao wenxian xuanbian* [Important documents since the third plenary session of the 11th CCP Central Committee], vol. 1, compiled by the Compilation and Translation Bureau of the CCP Central Committee (Beijing: People's Publishing House, 1982), p. 106.

8. Deng Xiaoping, "Zai Wuchang, Shenzhen, Zhuhai, Shanghai deng di de tanhua yaodian" [Key points of talks in Wuchang, Shenzhen, Zhuhai, Shanghai, etc.], in *Deng Xiaoping wenxuan* [Selected works of Deng Xiaoping], vol. 3 (Beijing: People's Publishing House, 1993), p. 372.

9. Karl Marx and Frederick Engels, *Gongchandang xuanyan* [Manifesto of the Communist Party] (Beijing: People's Publishing House, 1992), p. 25.

10. Mao Zedong, "Mao Zhuxi zhongyao zhishi" [Chairman Mao's important instructions], *People's Daily*, May 16, 1976.

11. Mao Zedong, "Zai Zhongguo gongchandang ba jie shi zhong quanhui shang de jianghua" [Speech at the tenth plenary session of the 8th CCP Central Committee], September 1962, *Hongqi* [Red flag], no. 10 (1967).

12. CCP Central Committee, *Guanyu jianguo yilai ruogan lishi wenti de jueyi* [Resolution on certain questions in the history of our party since the founding of the People's Republic of China], June 23, 2008 (www.gov.cn/test/2008-06/23/content_1024934.htm).

13. Mao Zedong, "Mao Zedong gei Jiang Qing de xin" [Mao Zedong's letter to Jiang Qing], July 8, 1966, in *Jianguo yilai Mao Zedong wengao* [Manuscripts of Mao Zedong since the founding of the state], vol. 12: Jan. 1966–Dec. 1968 (Beijing: Zongyang wenxian chubanshe [Central Party Literature Press], 1998), pp. 71–75.

14. "Zhongguo gongchandang di shiyi jie zhongyang weiyuanhui di san ci quanti huiyi gongbao" [Communiqué of the third plenary session of the 11th CCP Central Committee], in *San zhong quanhui yilai Zhongyao wenxian xuanbian,* pp. 1–3.

15. CCP Central Committee, *Guanyu jianguo yilai ruogan lishi wenti de jueyi.*

16. Communiqué of the third plenary session of 11th CCP Central Committee, *People's Daily,* December 24, 1978.

17. Ibid.

18. Hu Jintao, "Zai shengbu ji zhuyao lingdao zhuanti yantaoban shang de jianghua" [A speech on the seminar of major ministerial provincial-level officials] (news.sina.com.cn/c/2005-06-26/21046273948s.shtml).

19. CCP Central Committee, *Guanyu goujian shehuizhuyi hexie shehui ruogan zhongda wenti de jueding* [Resolution on several important issues regarding the construction of socialist harmonious society] (politics.people.com.cn/GB/1026/4932440.html).

20. Karl Marx, "Geda gangling pipan" [Critique of the Gotha program], in *Makesi Engesi xuanji* [Selected works of Karl Marx and Friedrich Engels], vol. 3 (Beijing: People's Publishing House, 1972), p. 21.

21. Vladimir Lenin, *Guojia yu geming* [The state and revolution] (Beijing: People's Publishing House, 1970), p. 32.

22. Mao Zedong, "Lun renmin minzhu zhuanzheng" [On the people's democratic dictatorship], in *Mao Zedong xuanji* [Selected works of Mao Zedong], vol. 4 (Beijing: People's Publishing House, 1991), p. 1475.

23. The Four Cardinal Principles are "keep to the socialist road, . . . uphold the dictatorship of the proletariat, . . . uphold the leadership of the Communist Party, . . . [and] uphold Marxism-Leninism and Mao Zedong thought." Deng Xiaoping, "Jianchi si xiang jiben yuanze" [Uphold the four cardinal principles], *People's Daily* (English online), March 30, 1979 (english.peopledaily.com.cn/dengxp/vol2/text/b1290.htm).

24. Hu Jintao, "Jixu ba gaige kaifang weida shiye tui xiang qian jin" [Continue to advance the great cause of reform and opening up], in *Shenru xuexi shijian kexue fazhanguan huodong lingdao ganbu xuexi wenjian xuanbian* [Cadres' reader: Learning and practicing the scientific outlook on development] (Beijing: Zhongyang wenxian chubanshe [Central Party Literature Press], 2008), p. 347.

25. According to statistics, there have been dramatic changes in the number of times the two terms *democracy* and *dictatorship* were mentioned in the political reports to the

CCP National Congress since 1949: *democracy* and *dictatorship* were mentioned 86 and 29 times, respectively, at the 8th CCP Congress in 1956; 7 and 54 times at the 9th Congress in 1969; 4 and 11 times at the 10th Congress in 1973; 62 and 60 times at the 11th Congress in 1977; 5 times and once at the 12th Congress in 1982; 55 and 5 times at the 13th Congress in 1987; 39 and 5 times at the 14th Congress in 1992; 57 and 3 times at the 15th Congress in 1997; 58 and 2 times at the 16th Congress in 2002; and 67 and 0 times at the 17th Congress in 2007.

26. Deng Xiaoping, "Jiefang sixiang, shishi qiushi, tuanjie yizhi xiang qian kan" [Emancipate the mind, seek truth from facts, and unite as one in looking to the future], in *Deng Xiaoping xuanji* [Selected works of Deng Xiaoping], vol. 2 (Beijing: People's Publishing House, 1994), pp. 146–47.

27. Some view the starting point of the emphasis on the rule of law to be the third plenary session of the 11th CCP Central Committee. Wang Jiafu, "'Yi fa zhi guo' de qidian yingdang shi 1978 nian dang de shiyi jie san zhong quanhui" [The starting point of "rule of law" should be the third plenary session of the 11th CCP Central Committee in 1978], *Wenzhai bao*, April 24, 2008.

28. CCP Central Committee, *Guanyu quan dang bixu jianjue weihu shehuizhuyi fazhi de tongzhi* [Notice on resolutely safeguarding the socialist legal system], July 10, 1986, in *Renmin daibiao dahui wenxian xuanbian* [Selection of National People's Congress documents], compiled by the Research Office of the General Office of the Standing Committee of the NPC (Beijing: Zhongguo minzhu fazhi chubanshe, 1992), p. 166.

29. Jiang Zemin, *Gaoju Deng Xiaoping lilun weida qizhi, ba jianshe you Zhongguo tese shehuizhuyi shiye quanmian tui xiang ershiyi shiji* [Hold high the great banner of Deng Xiaoping theory for an all-around advancement of the cause of building socialism with Chinese characteristics into the twenty-first century], report to the 15th CCP National Congress, *People's Daily*, September 12, 1997.

30. Information Office of the State Council, "Zhongguo de minzhu zhengzhi jianshe" [China's democratic political development], *People's Daily*, October 19, 2005.

31. Deng Xiaoping, "Jianchi si xiang jiben yuanze" [Sticking to the four cardinal principles], in *Deng Xiaoping wenxuan* [Selected works of Deng Xiaoping], vol. 2 (Beijing: People's Publishing House, 1982), p. 175.

32. Mao Zedong, "Yi jiu wu qi nian xia de xingshi" [The situation in the summer of 1957], July 1957, in *Mao Zedong xuanji* [Selected works of Mao Zedong], vol. 5 (Beijing: People's Publishing House, 1977), pp. 456–57.

33. National Bureau of Statistics of China, *Da gaige, da kaifang, da fazhan* [Great reform, great opening up, great development], report prepared in celebration of the thirtieth anniversary of the reform and opening-up policy, October 27, 2008 (news.xinhua net.com/fortune/2008-10/27/content_10259397.htm).

34. Ibid.

35. Ministry of Civil Affairs, *Zhongguo minzheng tongji nianjian, 1999* [China civil affairs statistical yearbook, 1999] (Beijing: China Statistics Press, 1999).

36. Ministry of Civil Affairs, *Minzheng shiye tongji jibao* [Civil affairs statistical quarterly report], 2nd quarter, 2009 (cws.mca.gov.cn).

37. Communiqué of the sixth plenary session of the 16th CCP Central Committee, October 11, 2006, Xinhua News Agency.

38. *Zhonggong zhongyang guanyu jiaqiang dang de zhizheng nengli jianshe de jueding* [Decision of the CCP Central Committee on strengthening the party's governance capability], resolution adopted at the fourth plenary session of the 16th CCP Central Committee on September 19, 2004, *People's Daily,* September 26, 2004.

39. Yu Keping, *Sixiang jiefang yu zhengzhi jinbu* [Ideological emancipation and political progress] (Beijing: Social Sciences Academic Press, 2008), pp. 1–24.

2

Transition from a Revolutionary Party to a Governing Party

WANG CHANGJIANG

The Chinese Communist Party (CCP) is the core actor in China's political system. This premier position is stipulated in the Constitution of the People's Republic of China and is the reality on the ground in today's China. Any change in the CCP will, therefore, inevitably exert deep influence on the country's development. The CCP is now undergoing a transition. On one hand, this transition is a decisive force that is furthering China's reform. On the other, taking place against the background of China's reform and opening-up policy, it is a result of reform. Such complicated interactions between the CCP and reforms are thus bringing the party into the spotlight. Why is the CCP so unique? What kind of rules does it abide by? What is its development trajectory? To answer these questions, this chapter reviews the CCP's developmental path and depicts the party's configuration.

The CCP: A Ruling Party in the Pre-Reform Era

For the Chinese, the idea of a political party is something imported from the West. Before being introduced into China, political parties had been active in Europe and America for more than a century. Political parties in China were thus naturally influenced by the Western political party system in terms of organizational ideas, principles, structures, activities, and the like. The Communist Party of the Soviet Union (CPSU) is a model that decisively influenced the CCP's evolution. This is in part because both the CCP and the CPSU claimed themselves as Marxist parties. Furthermore, Sun Yat-sen (1866-1925), the great precursor of China's revolution, made tremendous efforts to establish party politics in China long before the birth of the CCP; his ideas about party building, therefore, also played a role in the establishment and development of the party. Finally, China's time-honored political culture and traditions are another element that deeply influenced the CCP.

Three Variables That Shaped the CCP

The Communist Party of the Soviet Union was the most important variable that shaped the Chinese Communist Party. The CCP was established as a branch of Communist International (Comintern). Thus it consciously regarded the CPSU (former Bolsheviks) as a prototype to follow. As Chairman Mao put it, "The Chinese Communist Party is a party built and developed on the model of the Communist Party of the Soviet Union."[1]

From its very beginning, the CPSU model was different from its Western European counterparts. In Western Europe, the emergence of political parties closely corresponded to the development of democracy. Modern democratic politics originated from the fight against autocratic theocracy. Democracy is a system under which the people, as the ultimate authority, create (by election), oversee, and assess political power.

This is the rationale of democratic politics. Democratic politics can be categorized into two kinds. In direct democracy, the people directly exercise political power. In practice, however, direct democracy faces insurmountable difficulties, especially large populations, an unqualified citizenry, and high operational costs. As an alternative, people created another kind of democratic politics: indirect democracy.

Indirect democracy is also called representative democracy, a system in which people elect representatives and empower them to exercise public power. Representative democracy calls for the articulation and accumulation of people's interests. Such functions are effectively assumed by the political party, which becomes a major player in representative democracy. Therefore, from its very beginning, the political party emerged in the West as an instrument of democratic politics. To some extent, the political party was justified by its function: to form a bridge between the people and public power. Most Western scholars thus agree that democratic politics is the sine qua non of the political party.[2]

In contrast, the context and purpose of communist parties in Russia and China are completely different. The purpose of the communist party is to change the state rather than to bridge the people and political power. As Karl Marx put it, the communists are destined to destroy the old state apparatus and "bomb the old state power."[3] In other words, the communists aim to seize power by violently overthrowing the old regime. In Russia and China, the political party was cherished for its ability to mobilize the masses and destroy the old system, as expressly stated by Marx, Friedrich Engels, and Vladimir Lenin. In this sense, the political party is a "revolutionary" party. As Mao stated, "If there is to be revolution, there must be a revolutionary party. Without a revolutionary party, without a party built on the Marxist-Leninist revolutionary theory and in the Marxist-Leninist revolutionary style, it is impossible to lead the working class and the broad masses of the people to defeat imperialism and its running dogs."[4] A revolutionary party attempts to delegitimize, sabotage, and destroy the existing state. For example, the CCP was actually a semi-militarized organization for a long period of time. This eventually enabled the party to seize political power and persistently influenced its evolution in the decades to follow.

The second variable that shaped the CCP was Sun Yat-sen's ideas regarding the use of the party in building government. Sun Yat-sen was revered by the CCP as the precursor of the revolution. He was the first to launch a democratic revolution in China, experiencing numerous defeats but never giving up. With an eye toward the democracies in America and other Western countries, Sun was eager to practice democratic politics and party politics in China. He was, however, aware of the impossibility of China's copying Western models. After serious consideration of China's realities, he came up with a set of ideas on China's path of political development, which he called "using the party to build and govern the state."[5]

Reinventing the state through the party was the core of Sun Yat-sen's plan for state building. In his opinion, the purpose of establishing a political party is to launch a revolution rather than to conduct lawful and peaceful competition for political power, as in the West. Sun believed that the party was the embryo of the new state, and a government by the people could only be realized via the party. To translate his ideas into practice, he introduced a quasi-government structure into the party: the leader of the party was the prime minister, under whom three departments responsible respectively for implementation, evaluation, and judicial affairs were established. Having seized political power, the party would become the state, exercising state power on behalf of the people. As he further elaborated, "To govern the state by the party does not mean that China can only be governed if all officials are party members. Rather, it means that China can only be governed if the principles of the party can be honored and practiced by the people. Put simply, it is the principles not the members of the party that actually govern China."[6] In *The General Rules of the Revolutionary Party of China,* Sun divided China's revolution into three phases: military rule (军政, *junzheng*), political tutelage (训政, *xunzheng*), and constitutional government (宪政, *xian-zheng*). During the revolutionary period, "the party members take full responsibility for military and political affairs."[7]

Furthermore, the *General Rules* divided party members into three categories. "Primary members are those who joined the party prior to the uprising of the revolutionary army. Secondary members are those who joined the party prior to the establishment of the revolutionary government. Ordinary members refer to those who joined the party after the establishment of the revolutionary government." Different kinds of party members enjoyed differentiated positions and rights. "As the veteran revolutionaries, primary members enjoy full access to political power. Secondary members, as contributors to the revolution, can enjoy the rights of election and being elected. Ordinary members, as qualified citizens, can enjoy the rights of election." "Nonparty members cannot enjoy citizenship during the revolution. Only after the Constitution is promulgated in the future can they begin to enjoy equal and full citizenship."[8]

As far as the form of the state is concerned, Sun believed China should learn from Russia. As he put it, "Both France and America are old republics while Russia is a new one. We Chinese should pursue this newest form of republic." "Russia is not a representative system but a people's dictatorship system." "Such a people's dictatorship system is much more advanced than the representative system."[9] Sun advocated the restructuring of China as a republic of the people based on the principle of democracy, a new system that would be superior to its Western counterparts.[10]

Although his proposed use of the party to build and govern the state demonstrated Sun's dedication to democratic revolution, his ideas undoubtedly had limitations. In equating a ruling party with the state, Sun failed to recognize the essential distinction between the two. Such a limitation not only deeply influenced the Kuomintang but also made lasting imprints on the Chinese Communist Party. The CCP unswervingly attacked the one-party dictatorship of the Kuomintang. For instance, in a 1941 article Deng Xiaoping harshly criticized the idea of using the party to govern the state. Such a practice, in his view, would enable the party to gain advantages through political power, and the leadership of the party would become the party's supreme authority as well as the party's replacement for government. As he put it, "Using the party to govern the state is an evil legacy of the Kuomintang. It could paralyze, corrupt, and destroy our Party and isolate it from the masses. To unswervingly oppose the one-party dictatorship by the Kuomintang, we must be on high alert against this evil legacy."[11] In practice, however, what the CCP opposed was actually the Kuomintang party building and governing the state. Most people, including the leadership of the

CCP, paid less attention to the issue of the party governing the state and were unaware of the potential hazards related to it.

The third variable that deeply influenced the evolution of the CCP was China's political culture and traditions, which are sharply different from those of the West. In the West, people are wary of state power. They assume that unless constrained, state power will inevitably infringe on the freedom on the individual. The Chinese people believe that politics is related to the virtue of human beings. They envision a country governed by wise persons. The earliest rulers in ancient China—such as Yan, Huang, Yao, Shun, and Yu—all earned their reputation and power on the basis of the deeds and benefits they brought to their people. During the Spring and Autumn period and the Warring States period (722–221 BC), such a tradition was inherited by Confucius. As he claimed, "Politics means the integrity of the ruler."[12] Few Chinese are concerned with constraining state power. Rather, they hope for the state to take care of them as much as possible. In their view, the mightier the state power, the more benefits the people will enjoy. Unlike Westerners, the Chinese seldom keep a watchful eye on those endowed with power. On the contrary, they hope officeholders are virtuous, authoritative, and capable people who will work selflessly for the public interest.

Thus a subject-based political culture emerged in China, one that is entirely different from the citizen-based political culture found in the West. The concept of equality never existed in China's political culture and traditions, which instead centered on hierarchy and differentiation: given their differences, people can be interlinked only by hierarchy, rather than by contract. In China, the basis of such hierarchical order is ethics, which was embodied in Confucianism, the dominant ideology of traditional China. As Lin Yutang noted more than sixty years ago, "Confucianism always imagined itself as a civilizing influence, going about preaching these distinctions and establishing social order. It hoped to bind society together by a moral force, by teaching benevolence in the rulers and submission in the ruled, both kindliness in the elders and respect for old age in the young, and both friendliness in the elder brother and humility in the younger brother."[13]

Such a hierarchical order also penetrated the family. The moral human relations in the family, based on kinship, thus became a bond to regulate individual behavior and maintain social stability. In the opinion of Chinese scholars of the old tradition, the state is nothing but an enlarged (paternalistic) family. So there is no surprise that the Chinese word for "state" is *guojia* (国家, literally, "country family"). Such an interpretation of the state by the Chinese can hardly be understood by Westerners, whose governments do not address the interconnections between state and family. Since the Chinese state was just an enlarged family, the ruler was the parent, and the ruled were the children. As a result, the emperor was the owner of every piece of land and all resources on it and the master of all subjects, as well as the supreme dictator. The gigantic bureaucracy was nothing more than the extension of the topmost imperial power, and all bureaucrats at various levels, by implementing the emperor's orders and ruling the huge population, were merely the servants of the emperor. For the masses themselves, the emperor and his bureaucrats were the parents whose orders must be obeyed. In the end, every individual was incorporated into this patriarchal clan system and hierarchical network.

As a reaction to such political culture and traditions, the CCP strove to accomplish its revolutionary objective by criticizing Confucianism. In so doing, it established its own vocabulary to legitimize its leadership and control over the state and society. Unfortunately, the negative influence of this traditional political culture failed to disappear even after the great Chinese revolution. As Deng exclaimed in his famous article "On the Reform of the System of Party and State Leadership," in 1980, "Although we overthrew reactionary feudalism and feudal land ownership, the task to eradicate the negative influences of rampant feudalism in our minds is far from over."[14]

The Organization and Operation of the CCP

The original configuration of the CCP, which took shape during the revolution, faced pressure to change after the party took power in 1949. One of the forward-thinking leaders of the CCP who saw the need for change was Deng Xiaoping. In his report on revising the party constitution during the 8th CCP National Congress in 1956, Deng stated, "The CCP has turned into a ruling party. . . . The position of ruling party has also engendered some new challenges to our party. . . . To the party organizations and party members, the danger of becoming isolated from reality and alienated from the masses has increased."[15] Several other top party leaders held similar opinions. With the benefit of hindsight, the evolution of the CCP, including its evolution during the Culture Revolution, can be viewed as a part of the CCP's efforts to handle pressure for change. Unfortunately, it turned out that in the end all such efforts failed.

In the CCP's evolution, ideology is the hard core that has been largely immune from change. The party has always claimed itself to be the vanguard of the working class, the most developed organization of the working class, as well as the leader of China's socialism. With Marxism as its official ideology, the CCP has as its ultimate objective the full realization of socialism and communism. To serve the people wholeheartedly is regarded as the core principle of the CCP. These ideological points are still advocated by the party today.

When party ideology is used in different contexts, however, the same political term can denote a different, sometimes opposite, meaning. That is why many foreign observers are baffled and confused by such terms. When the CCP was leading the revolution and implementing the Soviet-style planned economy, these core principles led to centralization of all political power in the CCP. Especially under the planned economy, the party actually commanded all political, economic, and societal activities. This resulted in monolithic leadership and a highly centralized management system. As Deng later explained, "Overconcentration of power means inappropriate and indiscriminate concentration of all power in Party committees in the name of strengthening centralized Party leadership. Moreover, the power of the Party committees themselves is often in the hands of a few secretaries, especially the first secretaries, who direct and decide everything. Thus 'centralized Party leadership' often turns into leadership by individuals."[16] In theory, China is a country governed by the people. In practice, the party governs everything. This has led some to label the CCP a totalitarian party.

Organizationally, the CCP was characterized by a highly centralized, multitiered system. Party organizations and members conducted activities according to principles of subordination of the individual to the organization, subordination of the minority to the majority, subordination of the lower level to the higher level, and subordination of all members to the CCP Central Committee. The network of party organizations was extended to every corner of the state and society, infiltrating and dominating political, economic, military, and cultural organizations. In the revised party constitution passed during the 11th Party Congress, the CCP was defined as "a vigorous vanguard organization made up of the advanced members of the working class, with the task of leading the ruthless revolutionary struggle against the class enemies."[17] Such a definition completely neglected the distinction between a ruling party and a revolutionary party. Even so, party leadership varied in different situations. In some specialized fields, the decisionmaking process was dominated by administrative bureaucrats and the party organizations acted merely as supervisors.

In terms of the relationship between the party and state, the party leadership became the party organizations' direct involvement in government affairs. Like the CPSU, the CCP established its own bureaucratic system paralleling the government system, and the party organizations also exercised state power. This brought about a common challenge for communist countries: how to handle the relationship between the party and government bureaucratic system (referred to as the party-state relationship). To resolve this problem, the usual practice was to formally grant party organizations (with party committees at different levels as the leading government organs) the right to exercise the powers of government. By so doing, the powers of government would be divided into two parts, with important powers appropriated to the party committee while lesser powers were held by the government.

By blurring the boundary between the party and the government and partially replacing government with the party, however, many conflicts were generated. First, the overlapping of party and government negatively affected administrative efficiency. Second, such practices contradicted the PRC Constitution, which stipulated that administrative power should originate from and fall under the jurisdiction of the National People's Congress. In practice, the party committee controlled the most important decisionmaking and administrative power. Third, as mentioned above, the government was endowed with less important administrative powers in practice, which made it de facto subordinate to the party committee.

The government thus was faced with a dilemma. In theory, its power came from the people's congress system and therefore it should be responsible to that system. In practice, though, the government was fully under the leadership of the party committee. As such, the government had only a nominal relationship with the People's Congress. Moreover, even the People's Congress fell under the leadership of the party committee at the same administrative level, which made the former effectively merely an agency of the party.

The party also completely dominated society based on its monopoly of state power. The state was swallowed up by the party, and society, in turn, was swallowed up by the state. The result was the absence of any mechanism that enabled society to articulate its interests. Although various kinds of social organizations (officially labeled mass organizations) existed, they were not interest groups. They were set up not to safeguard the interests of their members but rather to mobilize the masses, implement policies, and fulfill their designated tasks based on directives from the party. Such organizations penetrated every walk of social life. Some organizations were well known—such as the Trade Union Federation, the Chinese Communist Youth League, the Women's Federation, and the All-China Youth Federation. The party also set up some less prominent organizations such as the Writers Association, the Journalists Association, the Business Association, and the Association for the Handicapped. Most of these organizations were officially sponsored to some degree. Their expenditures were dependent on the state, and their leaders enjoyed official ranks and salaries similar to those of government officials.

Another aspect of the relationship between the CCP and society, one that is unique to China, is the CCP's relationship to the so-called democratic parties.

The CCP is not the only political party in mainland China. There are eight other political parties who also play a role in national affairs. Those parties have been called democratic because they fought against the dictatorship of the Kuomintang and pursued democracy along with the CCP in the 1940s. The comradeship between the CCP and the democratic parties evolved into the multiparty cooperation system, which operates under the leadership of the CCP. This is a unique party system, which distinguishes itself from both the multiparty system in the West and the single-party system in the former Soviet Union.

Under the multiparty cooperation system, the CCP enjoys the sole leadership position, which the democratic parties openly accept. The CCP and the democratic parties are in an equal legal position, though they enjoy unequal political power. The CCP keeps its monopoly on political power, an arrangement that is accepted and bolstered by the democratic parties. The essence of the relationship between CCP and the democratic parties is therefore cooperation and consultation rather than competition. Such a party system could have its own advantages, but as it turned out it hardly worked in practice, owing partly to its low level of institutionalization. It completely ceased to function during the Cultural Revolution.

To some extent, the CCP stayed in institutional limbo during the first thirty years of the existence of the People's Republic. Although Western scholars identified the Chinese government as a party-state system, it was neither a finalized form nor a guide to the CCP's future evolution. The weakness of such a system lies in its lack of stability. It is a system rife with internal conflicts and inconsistencies. The People's Republic attempted to accommodate the logic of the party with the logic of the state. However, it failed to do so. In practice, this system was far from mature. It was introduced experimentally, and, based on numerous policies, directives, and tacit rules formed during the revolutionary period, it was barely institutionalized. Thus it could be maintained only by one wave of mass campaigns after another—and, as we have seen, the unreliability and uncontrollability of mass campaigns reached an apex during the Cultural Revolution.

When crisis comes, change is on the horizon. The seeds of crisis had been sown during the planned economy, and they have sprouted during China's transition to a market economy. The party now faces another chance to change. Can the CCP grasp it this time?

Problems and Challenges

When a revolutionary party acquires the power and position to rule, its relationship to state power will change correspondingly. State power will no longer be something that the party should fight against. Rather, the state power along with the party should become an integral part of the political system of a socialist country. That means the revolutionary party should change its role based on its new position as a governing party, and its relations with the state and society need to be redefined as well. Unfortunately, the CCP's adoption of a planned economy failed to bring about these changes. Under the planned economy, the CCP took over all kinds of functions from the state and society and became a totalitarian party in nature. Some CCP members believed that a revolutionary party that can succeed in taking over political power should also be eligible to fulfill the task of constructing a socialist country. This is the theoretical basis for the CCP's retention of revolutionary features during the Mao era.

Reform and opening up and the adoption of the socialist market economy opened the door for the CCP's transition from a revolutionary party to a governing party. With the transition to a market economy, the CCP finally recognized that ideology could not provide the necessary incentives for economic growth. Economic development must be based on the market and on people's motives to pursue their own interests. Although the party and the government can regulate the market, the market economy has its own mechanisms and logic, which are different from those of a planned economy. A market economy is based on the principle of maximizing personal interests, and it is the individual rather than the party and government that makes his or her own economic choices. The party and the government only function to regulate individual behavior, prevent and resolve social conflict, and maintain a stable, healthy, and amicable social environment.

Over time, Chinese society has gained relative independence from the party and the government, and a public sphere has emerged in the market economy. A mature market and a dynamic civil society are the two important components of the public sphere. Under the planned economy, society was overshadowed, swallowed up, and replaced by the state and the party. Under the planned economy, the party needed only to negotiate its relations with the state, but with the emergence of a public sphere it has to handle, simultaneously, relationships between the party and the state, the party and society, and the state and society.

The market economy has intrinsic dynamics that push it to develop beyond national borders. With China's adoption of a market economy and worldwide economic globalization, changes in the international environment have inevitably exerted direct and indirect influence on China and the CCP.

The CCP's transition was clearly articulated in the report of the 16th CCP National Congress in 2002, in which the CCP recognized the differences between a revolutionary and a governing party.

Having gone through the revolution, reconstruction, and reform, our Party has evolved from a party that led the people in fighting for state power to a party that has led the people in exercising power and has long remained in power. It has developed from a party that led national reconstruction under external blockade and a planned economy to a party that is leading national development while the country is opening to the outside world and developing a socialist market economy.[18]

The report also stated that the "Party's historical position" has changed fundamentally.

Faced with such tremendous changes, the CCP is now encountering myriad new difficulties and challenges after thirty years in power.

The Legitimacy of the CCP

The CCP earned its legitimacy through revolution. Its legitimacy stemmed primarily from people's resentment of and resistance to the prerevolution regime. The CCP leadership was supported by the people because of its decisive role in organizing the revolt against the old regime. From this angle, it is safe to say that the party's ruling position, as the choice of history, was based on the consent of the people.

But the legitimacy issue is far from settled. The people choose their government periodically rather than once and for all. The people's choice in the past cannot guarantee acceptance in the future. Over time those who lived through the revolution are replaced by new generations who have no revolutionary experience. The revolutionary spirit and culture can be indoctrinated into younger generations, but revolution itself must inevitably come to an end. With the diminishing political benefits brought about by revolution, it becomes more urgent for the ruling party to establish a new basis for legitimacy.

The basis of legitimacy varies over time. The people supported and participated in the CCP-led revolution because the party promised to construct a society in which the people, as the masters of the country, would enjoy a happy life. The people's support of the ruling party naturally shifts according to the expectations of an evolving society, and the CCP's legitimacy ultimately rests on the fulfillment of its promises.

Economically, the CCP must base its legitimacy on its leading role in achieving economic development. Because the planned economy proved unable to achieve sustained economic development, the market economy was introduced. Politically, the CCP must turn its promise into reality. The party's rule through domination can no longer receive support from the people. Democratic politics implies that public power comes from the people. In a democratic society, the people are the masters of power, and the power exercised by the ruler comes from the people. To this end, a set of rational institutions and mechanisms is needed to correct the relationship between the people and the ruling party. This is the essence of a democratic regime. Logically, only democracy can sustain the legitimacy of the ruling party. How the CCP has ruled China is obviously incompatible with this logic.

The Functions of the CCP

A political party assumes such irreplaceable functions as interest articulation, interest accumulation, political recruitment, and political socialization. All these functions serve to accomplish the objectives of the political party. Since political power stands above all kinds of social interests, a ruling party must attempt to coordinate different social interests and encourage cooperation among different classes. Thus coordination and integration of social interests are the core tasks of a ruling party. In a planned economy, the ruling party can easily and often forcibly achieve the homogeneity of social interests because different sorts of social demands are suppressed and filtered. In a market economy, however, interest differentiation and diversification is accompanied by people's awareness of their interests. With the emergence of today's new media, self-organization of society advances continuously. Even in the West, the position of the political party has been weakened, and its space has been condensed in recent years.[19] The diversification of social interests leads to the diversification of ideas. The boundaries of different ideas become blurred by the interactions among them. Against this backdrop, traditional ideology is losing its purpose and appeal among the people. As a result, the political party can no longer achieve political mobilization and political socialization by promoting its ideology.

The Ruling Style of the CCP

During the revolution and, later, the period of the planned economy, the CCP set specific tasks and objectives that were going to be achieved based on the directives and orders of the party. To accomplish these tasks and objectives, the CCP had to mobilize both resources and the masses. Especially under the planned economy, the party attempted to carry out its policies by forcible commands and directives. Everything changed under the market economy. As noted above, the market economy has its own logic. In addition to the aforementioned restrictions on the ruling party's arbitrary interference in the economy, the market economy brought with it other problems. For instance, the introduction of the household contract responsibility system changed farmer identity from commune member to independent economic actor. The appeal of village-based party branches plummeted under this new system. Under the people's commune system, however, resources such as land, production materials, and circulation channels were actually controlled by the party branches. The peasants were thus heavily dependent on the party branches at that time.

In cities, enterprises became independent entities, and their economic decisions were no longer based on party directives; instead, the market provided direction. The party lost its complete control over enterprises. Correspondingly, social mobility greatly intensified as the relationship between employees and enterprises became contractual. The individual's reliance on the unit (单位, *danwei*) diminished, and the change from unit person (单位人, *danwei ren*) to social person (社会人, *shehui ren*) is now well under way. This change made the unit-based party branches much harder to operate effectively. Undoubtedly, the CCP has incomparable advantages because it still controls a large number of state-owned enterprises and can maneuver huge amounts of resources. Even so, state-owned enterprises are supposed to follow market rules, which makes it impossible for the party to continue ruling according to its old ways. The severity of the situation has been demonstrated by the dysfunction of a large number of party cells at the grassroots level.[20]

The CCP and State Power

The market economy provides the mechanisms to realize people's economic demands. A side effect of the market economy is a desire by the people to participate in democratic politics. Thus equating party rule with people's sovereignty has been challenged under the market economy. Concerning the relationship between the CCP and state power, two issues are now often raised.

First, how will the people, who are the masters of the country, exercise control over state power, especially when a revolutionary party can only provide limited channels for democratic participation? What the general public experiences is the CCP's control over state power. There is no institutional arrangement to guarantee that the CCP carries out its responsibility to understand and implement the people's will. With the awakening of a democratic consciousness among the populace, the old assumptions of the inevitability and indispensability of CCP leadership have become problematic.

Second, will state power as controlled by the party become corrupt? If so, how can the party prevent such corruption? As the vanguard of the working class and the masses, the CCP was supposed to be able to prevent the corruption of political power when it came to power. Based on this assumption, the CCP has always placed great emphasis on training, selecting, and educating its cadres. But the absence of an effective system of checks and balances on political power remains a serious defect of the political system. Consequently, economic development and the surge of national wealth have been accompanied by the pervasive corruption of political power. How then does the party implement effective checks and balances and contain corruption? More concretely, how can the CCP be prevented from becoming a vested interest group based on its ruling position? These tricky issues have perplexed the CCP since it became the ruling party of China.

Furthermore, the worldwide revolution in public management has posed new challenges to the relationship between the CCP and state power. One basic trend of this reform movement is the diversification of political actors and the diffusion of power into society. Public power, no longer exclusively wielded by the government, is now being exercised by more and more citizens. Against such a backdrop, the CCP, as the sole ruling party in China, should assume much greater responsibility. It should play a dominant role in shifting government administration from a model of rule of man to a model of rule of law. On the other hand, it must lead the transformation from a control-oriented government to a service-oriented government. A revolutionary party would naturally have great difficulty effecting these transformations.

The CCP and Society

Social mobilization played a crucial role in the CCP's fight against the Kuomintang. Under the planned economy, mass organizations were, like the party itself, instruments for class struggle. During the Mao era, the hallmark of the CCP's relationship with society was its highly bureaucratized control over the people. But this situation was challenged by the development of the market economy, expansion of democratic participation, and the emergence of civil society. An emerging civil society can be seen in the expansion of civil organizations (民间组织, *minjian zuzhi*). According to the latest statistics, the number of officially registered foundations, social groups (社会团体, *shehui tuanti*), and privately operated nonenterprise units (民办非企业单位, *minban feiqiye danwei*) reached nearly 430,000, while the number of unregistered civil organizations is even more astonishing.

To the Chinese Communist Party, the civil organizations that exist under a market economy are different from the party-led mass organizations that existed during the revolutionary era. Civil organizations, founded for the purpose of safeguarding either the interests of their members or specific public interests, can no longer be manipulated or used by the ruling party or government to serve its will. Faced with an emerging civil society, the CCP is ill prepared both ideologically and tactically. Some believe that an emerging civil society is leading to such negative trends as the alienation of party organizations from the people and even potential threats to the CCP's ruling position. They believe that citizen demands for political participation will weaken the leadership of the party and thus be detrimental to social stability. As a result, there are those who advocate suppressing the development of civil society by imposing all kinds of restrictions. If this argument prevails, the relationship between the CCP and society will only further deteriorate.

CCP Reforms

Faced with the challenges noted above, the CCP has taken active, innovative, and forward-looking measures to reform. The reform is a piecemeal process, one in which the CCP has gradually deepened its understanding and intensified the momentum of reform. The reform started with some minor adjustments in CCP working style but now involves almost every aspect of the party. The following discussion provides an overview of the major CCP reforms.

Changes of Ideology

So far, the term *party reform* (党的改革, *dang de gaige*) has never appeared in official CCP documents. Only when it comes to the specific activities of the CCP are reforms connected with the party. For example, as noted above, Deng called for reforms in the party and state leadership system in 1980. However, the CCP avoided using the term *reform* to describe changes within the party. At the beginning of the reform and opening-up period, the CCP strongly advocated economic and political reform, but party reform was referred to as strengthening and improving party leadership. The expression "strengthening and improving the leadership of the party with the spirit of reform" appeared in 2002 before the 16th CCP National Congress was convened.[21] In the report of the 17th CCP National Congress in 2007, however, the expression was changed to "strengthening party-building with the spirit of reform and creativity," which, it was felt, accentuated the importance of reform.[22] In the Decisions on Some Important Issues to Strengthen and Improve the Leadership of the Party, issued at the fourth plenary session of the 17th CCP Central Committee in 2009, it was clearly stated that party building needed "further reform and innovation," which the CCP regarded as one component of its historical experience with party building.[23]

In fact, this careful wording reflected the CCP's growing sense of risk as a ruling party. More important, this risk further accentuated the necessity to reform the party. At the early stage of reform and opening up, there was no deep understanding within the party of how it should be reformed. To a large number of CCP members, the so-called socialism with Chinese characteristics was seen as nothing more than the combination of a market economy and the political leadership of the CCP. The CPSU actively carried out party reforms in the 1980s but eventually lost its ruling position. This drama greatly shocked both senior leaders and rank-and-file members of the CCP. It seems to have convinced some party members that reforming the party will cause its demise. This view has greatly weakened with the deepening of China's reform and opening up.

Since China has been gradually integrated into the world economy, the CCP has faced unprecedented challenges. Whether the CCP, a vanguard party composed of advanced members of the working class and guided by Marxism, can meet these challenges is not guaranteed. The deeper the reform moves, the stronger the CCP's sense of crisis becomes. In the Decisions on Strengthening the Governing Capacity of the Party, passed by the CCP Central Committee in 2004, the sense of crisis reached its apex: "It is not easy for a proletariat party to seize power. It is even more difficult for the party to keep it. The ruling position of the CCP is neither innate nor everlasting."[24] The decision of the fourth plenary session of the 17th CCP Central Committee further demonstrated the party's sense of crisis: "The party's advancement in the past cannot guarantee its advancement today, and its advancement today cannot guarantee its advancement tomorrow. The party faces some prominent challenges, including governing capacity, reform and opening up, the market economy, and problems posed by the external environment."[25] The growing sense of risk and crisis are the precondition of party reform and the force necessary to produce it.

Broadening the Membership of the Party

In Marxist theory, the political party represents the interests of certain classes or social groups. Based on this argument, the CCP claims to be the vanguard of the Chinese working class and the representative of the fundamental interests of the overwhelming majority of the Chinese people.[26] It is no wonder that "vanguard of the Chinese working class" frequently appears in party documents and in speeches by party leaders. To broaden its membership after 1949, the CCP redefined the concept of the working class by absorbing intellectuals and cadres under its umbrella. With the social stratification and differentiation of social interests that followed reform and opening up, however, such inclusion fell short of accommodating the deep changes in social structure.

To address this issue, the party proposed the theory of Three Represents (三个代表, *sange daibiao*). As stated in the party constitution, "The Chinese Communist Party is the vanguard both of the Chinese working class and of the Chinese people and the Chinese nation. It is the core of leadership for the cause of socialism with Chinese characteristics and represents the development trend of China's advanced productive forces, the orientation of China's advanced culture, and the fundamental interests of the overwhelming majority of the Chinese people."[27] The intention of the Three Represents theory is obvious: to "consolidate the class base and broaden the mass foundation of the party."[28] According to this theory, "Emerging in the process of social change, entrepreneurs and technical personnel employed by non-public scientific and technological enterprises, managerial and technical staff employed by overseas-funded enterprises, the self-employed, private entrepreneurs, employees in intermediate organizations, free-lance professionals and members of other social strata are all builders of socialism with Chinese characteristics."[29] Use of the word "builders" legalized the status of these new classes and at the same time avoided the political sensitivity related to the term "laborers."

The Three Represents theory made it possible for the CCP to include all elites from different social strata. The traditional ideology of the CCP claimed that "private entrepreneurs cannot join the Party because of the existence of an exploitative relationship between them and the workers."[30] Nevertheless, according to this theory, "The CCP should admit into the Party advanced elements of other social strata who accept the Party's program and Constitution, work for the realization of the Party's line and program consciously, and meet the qualifications of Party membership following a long test period, in order to increase the influence and rallying force of the Party in society at large."[31] By breaking with traditional ideology, the debates on whether private entrepreneurs should be admitted into the party was finally brought to an end. Meanwhile, the CCP has retained its distaste for the title "party of the entire people" (全民党, *quanmindang*).

Developing Intraparty Democracy

The establishment of the socialist market economy was accompanied by the people's powerful demand for democratic politics. Against this backdrop, the CCP's understanding of democracy deepened correspondingly. "No democracy, no socialism," a famous statement of Deng Xiaoping's, has been widely accepted in China. It is no wonder that the report of the 17th Party Congress clearly stated that "people's democracy is the lifeblood of socialism."[32] Correspondingly, the issue of developing intraparty democracy has been reiterated and reaffirmed by the party in recent years.

As a matter of fact, though intraparty democracy lags behind development of democracy in society, it has still been accelerated in many aspects, in particular in the use of power within the party. In terms of the delegation of power, for instance, it was clearly stated that the CCP will reform and perfect intra-party electoral institutions, broaden electoral democracy, and enable the CCP

National Congress to play a more active role within the party. In terms of the democratization of decisionmaking, the party attaches great importance to convening meetings of party committees and having them decide issues through voting. In terms of the supervision of power, the CCP has also put the following measures in place: enacting regulations on the supervision of leading party agencies and cadres; requiring the standing committee to report to the entire party committee at the same level; publicizing party affairs; improving intraparty information sharing and reporting systems and a system of soliciting opinions concerning major policy decisions; and having leading cadres report on major matter and declare their incomes. Meanwhile, a property declaration system for public officials has been developed. Intraparty democracy is regarded as the key to orderly democracy. The CCP hopes that intraparty democracy can become a stimulus to democracy in society.

The party units at the local and grassroots levels have had a strong desire to develop intraparty democracy. In recent years, a large number of reforms have been piloted at the local and grassroots levels. For example, to alleviate the conflicts between autonomous organizations of villagers and village party branches, some places introduced a two-ballot system (两票制选举, *liangpiaozhi xuanju*) for the election of a branch party secretary, in which a candidate must be approved by all eligible villagers (that is, the first ballot) before he or she can be nominated by all party members in the village (that is, the second ballot). Some local party units introduced a system of party congresses with regular annual conferences (党代会常任制, *dangdaihui changrenzhi*) so that party deputies can play a more active role in local affairs on a continuing basis (instead of meeting only once every five years), similar to delegates of the people's congresses. Some local party units are even bolder, taking the initiative to elect party leadership at the township level by public recommendation and direct election, in an attempt to solidify the legitimacy of local party cells. It is fair to say that most of these reforms have resulted in positive outcomes. One might wonder, then, why the party cells at the local and grassroots levels are so enthusiastic about party reform. I believe that it is partly because local and grassroots party units and cadres must directly face the social conflicts and challenges that result from social transitions. To handle these challenges, these lower-level officials must be innovative enough to find a way out for themselves.

Transforming the Functions of Grassroots-Level Party Cells

A governing party is different from a revolutionary party partly in that the two assume different responsibilities and thereby require different organizational structures. During the revolutionary period and under the planned economy, the CCP turned itself into a highly centralized and hierarchical organization, incapable of realizing the communications between party and society that the market economy and the information age demand. The demand for pertinent reforms is therefore widespread and pressing.

These types of reforms and innovations have mostly occurred at the local and grassroots levels. In some localities, the focus is to restore the dynamics and vitality of the party. This is largely because the challenges the CCP faces today have surfaced primarily at the local and grassroots levels. The party is aware that without stable and dynamic grassroots party cells its ruling position will be weakened. In the past, the CCP built its cells based on units and regions, and all party cells were designed to command party members and to direct and oversee them as they carry out the directives and policies decided by higher authorities. This obsolete model has become the target of local pilot reforms.

Different models have emerged. Some localities have taken innovative approaches to establishing grassroots party cells. They have eliminated confinement to regions or units and have established party cells based on communities or residential buildings. Joint-party branches (联合支部, *lianhe zhibu*) have appeared among small enterprises in some localities. In some cases, new interconnections among people, mainly derived from the growth of a particular industry, have outstripped the old administrative divisions. Some localities have therefore attempted to establish party cells based on industrial chains. In others, party work has been redefined to serve the large-scale operation of agriculture, and cooperatives and specialized associations have become new platforms for party cells. Some local party cells have oriented their activities to community service, while others have attempted to resolve conflicts of interest in enterprises. All of these reforms, however, are far from final.

To perfect its leadership over state and society, the CCP has in recent years encouraged the government, people's congresses, people's political consultative committees, the democratic parties, and civil organizations to play more active roles. By so doing, the CCP has attempted to harmonize the party's leadership, the people's sovereignty, and the rule of law. Whether such efforts can succeed, however, remains to be seen.

Concluding Thoughts

The CCP has a strong desire to transform itself from a revolutionary party into a governing party. It has also initiated some meaningful reforms in recent years. After more than thirty years of reform and opening up, change is finally reaching new depths. Whether the toughest reforms can be achieved depends to a large extent on how the party reforms itself. The CCP is still facing some fundamental challenges that can only be met by further reforms.

Party reforms so far have been piecemeal and have mainly occurred on the periphery. The tougher reforms have yet to begin. Reforms have succeeded when they have been consistent with CCP traditions, such as requiring the party's standing committee to report to the full party committee, basing decisionmaking on the votes of the party committee as a whole, scheduling party congresses with regular annual conferences, and increasing inspection tours (巡视, *xunshi*). However, reforms to fundamental issues that contradict the CCP's traditions have hardly been able to get off the ground. For example, the relationship between the party and the state, once regarded by Deng Xiaoping as the key to political reform, has almost disappeared from public debate. Reform can easily be derailed under such conditions.

Institution building should be strengthened. Although ever more regulations and stipulations have appeared within the party, they are often inconsistent or even contradictory. Such regulations and stipulations are at best individual elements of institution building, but institution building is far more than the accumulation of various rules. The focus of institution building should be channeled toward building an institutional system. There is a lack of consensus on this point within the party.

Some obsolete ideas still run deep within the party. Such ideas can be categorized into two types. There are ideas that are based on wrong principles. For example, some party members still insist that the basic function of grassroots party cells is to control local residents. The dysfunction of some grassroots party cells is largely a result of the persistence of such outdated ideas. And there are ideas that need to be redefined or upgraded. These include the principle that the party controls cadres (党管干部, *dang guan ganbu*) and the theory of democratic centralism (民主集中制, *minzhu jizhongzhi*). With the deepening of reform, such ideas urgently need to be redefined and updated.

Intraparty democracy calls for serious improvement. The CCP has advocated the orderly development of democracy but has yet to design a grand strategy of democracy. For example, how does one integrate intraparty democracy with democracy in society? How does one make the different aspects of democracy— including elections, participation, decisionmaking, and supervision—compatible and consistent? These issues can hardly be addressed without a grand strategy to achieve democracy. For instance, in some localities, democratic reforms have been suspended or even rolled back owing to this lack of a grand strategy.

Finally, vested interests are posing a real threat to the CCP's ruling position. An unreasonable regime will inevitably result in an unreasonable structure of political power, which will, in turn, provide fertile ground to vested interests. Whether vested interest groups emerge within the party is still an open question, but it is undeniable that some groups and departments are exerting much stronger influence on the political process than others. Without appropriate measures, one of two possible scenarios will emerge: reform stasis owing to obstruction by vested interests, or reform distortion owing to manipulation by vested interests. Neither outcome will be good for the CCP.

COMMENT
LARRY DIAMOND

Wang Changjiang deserves respect and appreciation for the bold perspective and broad historical sweep of his chapter on the Chinese Communist Party (CCP). Of course, to ask where the CCP is headed as a party is really to ask where China is headed as a political system. By way of commenting on this chapter I advance a number of propositions, some of them empirical arguments and some of them theoretical—but certainly all of them debatable. Not being a China specialist, I bring to this discussion the lens of a political scientist who studies continuity and change in the nature of political regimes.

I agree with Wang that the CCP has clearly been in transition from a revolutionary party for some time, though it is not clear to what it is transitioning. A key feature of the evolution of the CCP in the past two decades has been ideological. This may be somewhat underemphasized in the chapter, perhaps because of its particular focus on big institutional and structural issues. But I am struck by the degree to which communist ideology has waned as a factor in China today and even represents a kind of joke among Chinese youth—including those who are busy competing for membership in the CCP for purely instrumental and careerist reasons.

After a period during the 1990s during which far-reaching systemic political change seemed possible, particularly with the expansion of competitive village elections and the prospect that institutionalized electoral competition would rise to higher levels, real political reform in China has since slowed dramatically, if not halted altogether. In terms of the macro question of whether the overall political regime in China is becoming more competitive, open, and accountable, I am struck by how little has changed since the 1990s. The CCP remains hegemonic and shows no sign of risking electoral competition systematically at more consequential levels of political authority than the village.

Although there have been brave, principled, and explicit calls for movement toward multiparty democracy in China—as evidenced in Charter 08—there is no evidence of a large-scale groundswell of mass demand for electoral democracy. Quite the contrary. The survey data from the last two rounds of the Asian Barometer show high levels of popular trust and confidence in the ruling party and government in China, satisfaction with the way democracy is working in China, and belief that China already has a considerable level of democracy.[33] I have lingering reservations about the meaning of these data, but I nevertheless accept that there is not at the moment a widespread public demand for democracy, at least not as it is understood by most of the rest of the world, that is, as multiparty competition for the principal positions of power in regular free, fair, and competitive elections.

As a modernization theorist, I predict that the political expectations and values of the Chinese public will change dramatically in the next generation with continued social and economic development. I have been deeply impressed with the comparative survey evidence from the World Values Survey and many other research endeavors, which demonstrate dramatic change in attitudes and values toward political authority and the proper role and rights of the individual in the political system as people are socialized during periods of greater prosperity.[34] In particular, "Postindustrialization brings emancipation from *both* traditional and secular authority, giving rise to an emancipative ethos."[35] With higher levels of prosperity and education, people generally come to want more power over their own lives and more opportunity to express themselves freely. Much more research is needed to determine exactly when this value transformation occurs along the historical paths of rising per capita income, rising levels of education, increasing exposure to and integration in global networks, rising access to information, and other factors associated with modernization. And it would be facile to assume that there is some rigid rule dictating the democratization of popular attitudes and values at particular levels of development. Nevertheless, there are few countries (and among non-oil-exporting countries, virtually none) that have defied the general trend: eventually, as countries get rich, their people come to want democracy and sooner or later achieve it. In the history of the world, there is only one country that has achieved a high level of per capita income and education ("human development" on the United Nations Development Program scale) without achieving democracy: Singapore.

Some observers have speculated that the goal of CCP leaders is to manage the challenge of keeping political development apace with social and economic development by replicating to a considerable extent the Singapore model. That is, China's leaders will seek to build a rich, educated, internationally dynamic, and self-confident country that is governed indefinitely by a hegemonic ruling party that will eventually accommodate only a thin and superficial veneer of (multiparty) electoral competition. There will be more political space and less repression, but no democracy. Whether or not they have Singapore in mind as a model, I think it is likely that China's current leaders envision a trajectory of political development over the next generation that involves some continued modest growth of civic and political pluralism but without serious multiparty electoral competition.

The CCP has, for more than twenty years now, been determined to keep tight control of the process of reform—especially to ensure that political reform would be extremely incremental and controlled from above. As Wang notes, a major reason for this was the traumatic shock of the collapse of the Communist Party of the Soviet Union as a result of Mikhail Gorbachev's reforms. Chinese Communist Party leaders who were socialized or began their ascent in the party during this period have no intention of repeating Gorbachev's naive mistakes.

Seen in this light, many of the observations in Wang Changjiang's chapter cohere into an interesting larger picture. The CCP has no intention of putting its hegemony to risk in multiparty competitive elections at any level of political authority for the near future. Hence its reforms to date have been, to quote Wang, "piecemeal" and almost entirely focused on internal party issues and structures. If one accepts that a major and genuine transformation in the CCP has been the draining of its ideological content and zeal—the gradual diminution of its character as a revolutionary party—then other changes appear much more modest. What is the significance, in terms of democratic reform, of broadening the base of the party to accept entrepreneurs as members? If the ruling party in a dynamic state capitalist system wants to remain hegemonic indefinitely, it seems a natural and inevitable thing to incorporate big private owners of capital. And, in fact, the implications for democratization may well be negative—by co-opting a powerful and potentially growing source of potential opposition. The theory of the Three Represents is from this perspective not really political reform but a brilliant adaptation for continuing domination. Any ruling party that wants to continue to rule indefinitely should be co-opting all the rising elites from different social strata. This may be inconsistent with becoming a party of the entire people, but it is quite consistent with the goal of ruling the entire people for a long time to come.

There is at least one other important change in the nature of the CCP that I think Wang's chapter neglects and that is consequential for the CCP's adaptation as a party seeking to extend its hegemony deep into the future. That is the institutionalization of term limits, power rotation, and the limitation of the power of individual rulers—one of the hallmark features of political institutionalization. As the CCP now prepares to effect its third iteration of this power rotation since

Deng Xiaoping surrendered formal leadership, the transformation of the CCP (in this sense) into a partial instrument of rule by law seems almost irreversible. That is, it is almost impossible to imagine at this point a general secretary of the CCP and president of the country establishing a personal dictatorship in any way approaching the indefinite and arbitrary rule of Mao.

The above reforms limiting the personal authority of CCP leaders and regularizing leadership rotation—along with the apparent institutionalization of collective decisionmaking processes in the higher ranks of the party and presumably intricate processes of negotiating, logrolling, deliberating, and competing within the senior party ranks—all represent important elements of the maturation of the CCP as an institution. This maturation is not to be confused with democratization, and I argue that in the absence of democratization, it will be not enough to save the party. But it is real change from earlier periods, and I wonder if it is being studied enough.

In a debate in Mexico City in 1990, the Peruvian novelist Mario Vargas Llosa (who recently won the Nobel Prize for literature, but who is at least as gifted a political essayist as a novelist) described Mexico's one-party-dominant authoritarian regime as "the perfect dictatorship." He meant that the long-ruling Revolutionary Institutional Party, the PRI, seemed to have solved a lot of the problems that typically plague and ultimately defeat authoritarian rule. It had managed to develop institutions and conventions to limit the personalization of power while remaining in virtually monolithic control of "almost every aspect of the country's life for sixty years."[36] It did so by limiting the presidency to a single six-year term and accommodating different party factions, while also enabling the ruler essentially to designate his successor. At the same time, it had multiparty competitive elections and claimed that they were democratic, even while it completely controlled the electoral administration, routinely and massively rigged elections, and selectively and usually discreetly used violence and repression to weaken and intimidate troublesome opposition groups in politics and society.

The regime could claim it was a democracy and even convinced many of its people that it was because it had all the appearances. There were opposition parties, elected state and federal governments, and legislatures with some authority. Moreover, opposition parties did win some seats in the Congress and occasionally gained control of one or another state government. But the PRI—also a revolutionary party in its origins, but long drained of serious ideological content—remained utterly hegemonic, and it seemed without the prospect of any serious challenge to its rule. That changed with social and economic development and Mexico's growing integration into global networks, which created rising pressures for real democratic change. Once the PRI president, Ernesto Zedillo, accommodated these pressures by creating a truly independent electoral commission in advance of the 1997 midterm elections, the rest was history. The ruling party suffered serious setbacks in that election and then a humiliating loss of power in the 2000 presidential election. And it lost again in 2006. In short, at its apparent peak moment of hegemony (as observed by Mario Vargas Llosa) in 1990—and at a time when its per capita income was not that much higher in real terms than China's is today or will soon become, and also at a time when a hegemonic ruling party with revolutionary origins had been in power for about sixty years, more or less exactly the amount of time the CCP has so far ruled China—the PRI was just a decade away from losing power.

I do not know whether CCP leaders have studied closely the example of Mexico's long political evolution and ultimate democratic transformation, but they obviously have looked around the world at other examples of regime evolution and change. They know what their goals are: not only to develop China and transform it into a great power but also to remain in power indefinitely. And they know what they want to avoid: the fate of the Communist Party of the Soviet Union, the PRI, the Kuomintang in Taiwan, the Parti Socialiste (PS) in Senegal, the Kenya African National Union (KANU) in Kenya, the postcommunist ruling parties in Serbia, Ukraine, and Georgia, and numerous other examples of one-party hegemonic regimes that liberalized politics, in most cases through at least somewhat competitive, multiparty elections, and then lost power in short order. They are obviously thinking that if there are no competitive multiparty elections then there will be no risk that the CCP will lose power in elections.

During a visit to China in 1998 to observe village elections, I had an interesting exchange with an official who had some involvement with the process at the national level. I asked him when the process of electoral competition might rise up (systematically across the country) from the village level to the more consequential level of authority of the township. He predicted it would happen within five years. Then I asked him when China might have competitive elections for rule at the county level. He said, in another five years. What about the provincial level, I asked? He said, five years after that. Since he was in an open and expansive mood, I asked him, "Well, when could you imagine China having competitive elections for who would rule at the national level?" And he said, five years after that (meaning, 2018). It has been a decade and a half since that conversation, and the first five-year threshold has still not been reached. Nor is there any sign of the systematic introduction of mass-level electoral competition for power at any of these levels. For, in a country as big as China, one could not rise very far up on the ladder of political authority before it would be necessary to organize, at least in de facto terms, competing political parties to render electoral competition sensible and meaningful. The leaders of the CCP have clearly determined that to go down the road of multiparty electoral competition is to court disaster in the same way that the ruling parties in previously one-party hegemonic regimes ultimately experienced it. The CCP seems determined to effect whatever transition it will make from a revolutionary party to a governing party through means other than open electoral competition at the mass level.

Thus CCP leaders are searching now for safe political reforms—institutional changes that can generate more accountability, transparency, and responsiveness, and thus more effective and legitimate governance, without putting the hegemony of the party at risk in competitive elections. A number of reforms might achieve these ends. Here are some possibilities:

—Give more authority to the National People's Congress and other legislative bodies at the national and provincial as well as lower levels.

—Strengthen independent institutions to enforce the rule of law and control corruption, such as countercorruption bodies and the judiciary.

—Strengthen the professionalism and autonomy of the public service, in other words, create a truly Weberian state bureaucracy, which, ironically, could mean going back to the future by establishing an increasingly meritocratic Confucian bureaucracy.

—Decentralize not just economic activity but political authority to lower levels, although this could have perverse effects in giving license to corruption and abuse of rights at lower levels.

—Institute deliberative processes of public participation in decisionmaking, such as through deliberative polling, to enable the public to decide a number of budgetary and practical policy questions and priorities.

—Allow more scope for independent media and organizations in civil society to monitor government policies and performance and pursue some accountability, while drawing clear boundaries that stop the rise of civil society at the border of politics.

—Introduce democracy, in particular greater openness and institutionalized competition for power, within the CCP itself.

Many of these form the subjects of other chapters in this volume, and it is certainly important to assess how far the Chinese leadership is moving the country toward genuine reform along these possible dimensions. Should China make significant progress toward reform on a number of these dimensions simultaneously, it could represent a coherent strategy of producing a more pluralistic and accountable political system without abandoning one-party rule.

The big question in my mind is not really where the CCP leaders intend to take the political system. Obviously, they know the status quo is not viable indefinitely in the midst of rapid social and economic change. I suspect they recognize there are only two viable political regime models for a highly developed economy: some type of adaptive, "rule-by-law," one-party hegemony (probably bearing at least some resemblance to the current system in Singapore), or the competitive, more or less liberal democracy of all the other highly developed economies in the world.[37] I assume most (or all) of the current crop of China's senior political leaders do not have multiparty democracy (liberal or otherwise) as a goal. The alternative, then, is a Confucian-style, more moderate, pluralistic, and benevolent authoritarian regime, what Robert Scalapino terms, referring to Korea and Taiwan before democratization, "authoritarian pluralism."[38]

But the real question is this: Is it possible for an authoritarian pluralistic system to emerge and function for long in a country as large and complex as China? In all other cases (save, for now, the city-state of Singapore) this system has simply been a transitional regime between extremely closed and repressive authoritarianism and democracy.

Is there another alternative—a distinctly Chinese path that ultimately leads to genuine, multiparty democracy? I do not see many signs that the current generation of senior Chinese leaders is asking this question. Although their time horizon is certainly longer than that of leaders in most democracies like the United States, and they are arguably doing a much better job of planning for the future in policy terms, politically their time horizons may not be that much longer. And their political goals are the same: to remain in power, although in this case not democratically. They confront sufficiently daunting policy challenges and political dangers from month to month and year to year that they may not be thinking much about what China's political system is going to look like twenty or thirty years hence. Even limited but genuine political reforms—like real intraparty democracy, genuine grassroots democracy, or systematic separation of the party from government (and especially the judiciary)—seem much too radical and adventurous. Yet if China continues to tread water on the question of genuine political reform (even the kinds of limited reforms that stop well short of electoral democracy), it is hard to see how it can address the deepening problems of governance that are generating growing protest and unease across the country and that threaten to undermine the legitimacy of Communist Party rule in the nation as a whole.

Thus I would pose the dilemma that the CCP faces in much starker terms than are found in Wang's chapter, though I agree with and have greatly benefited from many of his observations. Sooner or later the CCP will find itself on the horns of a profound political dilemma. If it does not embark on a path of genuine political reform—to separate the party from the state (and first and most emphatically from the judiciary at all levels), to increase freedom of expression and organization at least in civil society, and to institutionalize greater means of political accountability (and thus competition) within the Communist Party and outside it—an increasingly educated, participatory, and demanding society will grow increasingly restive and frustrated. Increasingly frozen, detached, and challenged in its legitimacy, the CCP will be at risk of falling suddenly and completely from power in the face of some new economic or political crisis. Such sudden and possibly convulsive political change could be dangerous for China and the world (and thus I do not consider it a desirable path). Yet if the CCP embarks on a serious path of political reform that limits its power and expands the power of independent institutions and civil society, it will (sooner or later) meet the fate of other liberalizing authoritarian regimes, particularly if it gradually introduces electoral competition at higher and more consequential levels of political authority.

It is hard to separate my democratic norms and instincts from purely analytical thinking. Nevertheless—thinking purely analytically as a specialist in comparative politics—I surmise that the CCP would have a longer purchase on rule by gradually introducing from above fundamental political reforms that would refashion its legitimacy, limit its power, and improve the quality of governance than it would by trying to hang on to power indefinitely with excessively cautious, piecemeal, and cosmetic political reforms. Cosmetic reforms will fail to deliver greater freedom, accountability, and participation for China's more sophisticated, more resourceful, and much better educated and informed new generations of citizens. Thus they will fail to solve the looming legitimacy crisis for the CCP.

Perhaps this is another way of saying what Wang says in his chapter: "These issues can hardly be addressed without a grand strategy to achieve democracy." Without that, the CCP will be leading China not to a durable authoritarian pluralism but rather into a situation of great vulnerability, where a regime that appears quite strong and durable on the surface could ultimately prove to be quite brittle.

Notes

1. Mao Zedong, *Quanshijie geming liliang tuanjie qilai, fandui diguozhuyi de qinlü* [Revolutionary forces of the world unite, fight against imperialist aggression!], in *Mao Zedong xuanji* [Selected works of Mao Zedong], vol. 4 (Beijing: People's Publishing House, 1991), p. 1357.

2. On various definitions of political party by Western scholars, see Wang Changjiang, *Zhengdang lun* [On the political party] (Beijing: People's Publishing House, 2009), pp. 41–44.

3. Marx expressed this view in his article "Falanxi neizhan" [The civil war in France], in *Makesi Engesi xuanji* [Selected works of Karl Marx and Friedrich Engels] (Beijing: People's Publishing House, 1972), pp. 324–439. Lenin also cited it on a number of occasions.

4. Mao, *Quanshijie geming liliang tuanjie qilai, fandui diguozhuyi de qinlü*, p. 1357.

5. Sun Yat-sen, *Sun Zhongshan quanji* [Complete works of Sun Yat-sen], vol. 8 (Beijing: Zhonghua Book Company, 1986), p. 282.

6. Ibid.

7. Sun Yat-sen, *Sun Zhongshan quanji*, vol. 3 (Beijing: Zhonghua Book Company, 1984), p. 99.

8. Ibid.

9. Sun Yat-sen, *Sun Zhongshan quanji*, vol. 9 (Beijing: Zhonghua Book Company, 1986), p. 355.

10. Ibid., p. 314.

11. Deng Xiaoping, "Dang yu kangri minzhu zhengquan" [The party and the anti-Japanese democratic government], in *Deng Xiaoping wenxuan* [Selected works of Deng Xiaoping] (Beijing: People's Publishing House, 1994), vol. 1, p. 12.

12. *The Analects of Confucius* (Beijing: Zhonghua Book Company, 2011), p. 177.

13. Lin Yutang, *Zhongguo ren* [My country and my people] (Beijing: Xuelin chubanshe [Xuelin Press], 1994), p. 191.

14. Deng Xiaoping, "Dang he guojia lingdao zhidu de gaige" [On the reform of the system of party and state leadership], in *Deng Xiaoping wenxuan*, vol. 2, p. 335.

15. Deng Xiaoping, "Guanyu xiugai dang de zhangcheng de baogao" [Report on revising the party constitution], in *Deng Xiaoping wenxuan*, vol. 1, p. 215.

16. Deng, "Dang he guojia lingdao zhidu de gaige," pp. 328–29.

17. *Compilation of CCP's Party Constitutions: From the First Party Congress to the Sixteenth Party Congress* (Beijing: Central Party School Press, 2006), p. 90.

18. Report of the 16th CCP National Congress, *Zhongguo gongchandang di shiliu ci quanguo daibiao dahui wenjian huibian* [Compilation of documents on the 16th CCP National Congress] (Beijing: People's Publishing House, 2002), p. 11.

19. Whether the political party is in decline is an open question among political scientists. For recent debates on this issue, see Wang, *Zhengdang lun*, pp. 275–82.

20. Statistics about the dysfunction of grassroots party cells vary with different periods, regions, and statistical methods.

21. Report of the 16th CCP National Congress, p. 10.

22. Report of the 17th CCP National Congress, *Zhongguo gongchandang di shiqi ci quanguo daibiao dahui wenjian huibian* [Compilation of documents on the 17th CCP National Congress] (Beijing: People's Publishing House, 2007), p. 47.

23. CCP Central Committee, *Guanyu jiaqiang he gaijin xin xingshi xia dang de jianshe ruogan zhongda wenti de jueding* [Decisions on some important issues to strengthen and improve the building of the party in the new era] (Beijing: People's Publishing House, 2009).

24. CCP Central Committee, *Guanyu jiaqiang dang de zhizheng nengli jianshe de jueding* [Decisions on strengthening the governing capacity of the party] (Beijing: People's Publishing House, 2004), p. 4.

25. CCP Central Committee, *Guanyu jiaqiang he gaijin xin xingshi xia dang de jianshe ruogan zhongda wenti de jueding* [Decisions on some important issues to strengthen and improve the building of the party in the new era] *People's Daily*, September 18, 2009, pp. 5–6.

26. *Zhongguo gongchandang zhangcheng huibian* [Compilation of the CCP's Party Constitutions], 2006, p. 98.

27. Ibid., p. 163.

28. Report of the 16th CCP National Congress, pp. 51–52.

29. Ibid., pp. 14–15.

30. *Xin shiqi dang de jianshe wenxian xuanbian* [Selected documents on party building in the new era] (Beijing: People's Publishing House, 1991), p. 456.

31. Report of the 16th CCP National Congress, p. 53.

32. Report of the 17th CCP National Congress, p. 27.

33. The Asian Barometer (ABS) is an applied research program on public opinion on political values, democracy, and governance around the region.

34. See, in particular, Ronald Inglehart and Christian Welzel, *Modernization, Cultural Change, and Democracy: The Human Development Sequence* (Cambridge University Press, 2005).

35. Ibid., p. 60.

36. See Leon Krauze, "A Perfect Dictatorship," 2007 (newsweek.washingtonpost. com/postglobal/leon_krauze/2007/02/a_perfect_dictatorship.html).

37. "Rule by law" means here that the law is used in a formal and bureaucratic sense, but the deeper conditions for the rule of law, such as true independence of the judiciary and the equality of all individuals before the law, are far from present

38. Robert A. Scalapino, *The Politics of Development: Perspectives on Twentieth-Century Asia* (Harvard University Press, 1998), p. 127.

3

The People's Congress System and China's Constitutional Development

SHI HEXING

I n contemporary China, the National People's Congress (NPC) is the highest organ of state power, the source of power of all other organs of state power, and the core of the country's political system. The NPC and the local people's congresses together constitute the people's congress system (PCS). The people's congress system was confirmed in the Common Program of the Chinese People's Political Consultative Conference in 1949 and legally established in the first Constitution of the People's Republic of China in 1954. The system was further specified in various articles of the Constitution as amended in 1982. The standard expression is that the people's congress system is China's fundamental political system. One cannot grasp contemporary China's political development and outlook without understanding this fundamental political system. Because the system was introduced along with the Constitution, it is appropriate to study them together.

According to the official website of the NPC and other sources, the PCS, as China's fundamental political system, has five major properties. First, the power of the People's Congress comes from the people. The congress is elected by, accountable to, and subject to the oversight of the people. Second, the power of the People's Congress is exercised collectively, with collective deliberation and decisionmaking and by strict adherence to the principle of democratic centralism. Third, other organs of state power, including the administrative, judicial, and procuratorial organs of the state, are created by the People's Congress, to which they are accountable and by which they are overseen. Fourth, the PCS establishes the corresponding central-local relationship and divides the functions of organs of state power at the central and local levels in accordance with the principle that the central government should have leadership over and give full scope to the initiative of local governments. Fifth, the PCS establishes the relationship between the whole state and minority autonomous regions, in which the regions inhabited by minority ethnic groups implement regional ethnic autonomy on the basis of safeguarding the country's unity.[1] These five features paint a comprehensive picture of China's PCS.

In the past, many people deemed the representative assemblies of socialist states to be merely rubber stamps. This view had some descriptive truth historically but was also more or less an ideological judgment. Today, similar views are largely criticized and corrected by both Chinese and Western scholars. Since the 1990s, legislative organs have played an increasingly important role in socialist states. The view that China's PCS is a rubber stamp is obviously outdated.[2] In fact, despite the influence of the Soviet system, China's PCS had its own unique mechanism from the very start and has since developed along its own unique path.

Although most scholars of Chinese political studies touch on the PCS in their research, for a long period of time the system did not receive special attention or get the focus it deserves.[3] Even some Chinese political scholars have made factual errors in explaining China's political process. Some of these errors were enumerated by Xia Ming, who specializes in the study of China's local people's congresses.[4] That the PCS has been constantly strengthened since the reform and opening-up period has caught the attention of an increasing number of Chinese and foreign scholars, among others. Since the 1990s, scholars of Chinese politics have increasingly come to the realization that the growing independence of the People's Congress has no less significance than both the end of lifelong tenure for leadership positions and the decentralization of power. As a result, there has been an increasing amount of research on the people's congress system.[5]

It was against this backdrop that Kevin O'Brien, Murray Scot Tanner, and others conducted systematic studies of the PCS. O'Brien uses his theories of role conflict and embeddedness to analyze the identities of People's Congress deputies and the relationship between the People's Congress, on one hand, and the party and government, on the other. With the advancement of such studies, Roderick MacFarquhar recommends more scholarship on the system of provincial-level people's congresses. In fact, Xia Ming and other scholars have already begun special research on people's congresses at the provincial and lower levels.[6] This constantly expanding and advancing body of scholarship on the PCS will undoubtedly open a new window through which to understand China's political process.

Compared with the PCS scholarship performed by international academics, Chinese scholars have done an extraordinary amount of research on the subject. A closer look at the literature, however, finds that domestic research on the PCS generally starts out from the design principles and relevant legal provisions concerning the system. These studies often take one of three forms: comprehensive surveys and interpretations of the creation and development of the system, systematic analyses of and suggestions on the running and improvement of specific subsystems, and collections of past cases and literature on the work of the National People's Congress. Such research generally lacks theorization and is not conducted in depth.[7] At the same time, one survey of the recent literature finds that only a limited amount of research approaches the PCS in the light of China's recent and ongoing political development. The focus, rather, has largely been on the primary drivers of China's economic growth, cultural factors in this process, and the favorable and unfavorable aspects of the administrative system rather than on the role of the PCS in China's political, economic, and social development.[8] A full understanding of the PCS requires not only calls for application of political development theories but also a comprehensive look at this fundamental political system in the context of China's historical development.

Constitutionalism: The Establishment of the PCS

In China's historical process of political development, the establishment of the PCS was an event of epochal importance. China's choice of the People's Congress as its fundamental political system was an essential step in establishing its political order.

Thomas Hobbes pointed out the importance of political order, but for a long time theoretical discussions ignored the importance of political order to constitutionalism. As Russell Hardin notes, "Most political theorists and observers tend to think of liberalism, constitutionalism, and democracy as all generally normatively good and they often have little concern with the social scientific understanding of their possibilities."[9] As a result, despite much logical thinking on constitutional democracy, there has not been adequate attention paid to its feasibility or to the political order that serves as the foundation of constitutional democracy. Empirically, if the nationals of a state split into seriously conflicting groups, it will be difficult for them to reach agreement within the framework of constitutionalism.

That Chinese scholars have neglected the foundation of constitutionalism in the study of the PCS is largely ascribed to excessive normative research and logical thinking. Domestic research on China's PCS and constitutional system has traditionally overemphasized popular sovereignty, which has led to more than a few erroneous conclusions.[10] In analyzing the establishment of the PCS, it is a mistake to start out from a value-rationality perspective and make a priori judgments. If full consideration is given to its historical development and reality, it can be seen that the great significance of the establishment of the PCS lies in its role in establishing constitutional order.

In retrospect, China's 100-year search for constitutional government has been a search for a modern political order. The first step in seeking such a political order was to achieve political integration through nation-state building. The greatest worry Sun Yat-sen had about China's reality was disunity. Believing that Chinese society's unity should go beyond family clans to embrace the whole nation, Sun Yat-sen took upon himself the heavy task of building China into a nation-state. The three stages of China's political development envisioned by him—from military rule to political tutelage to constitutional government—reflected both the pursuit of constitutional government and the need for political order.[11] However, as some Chinese scholars have observed, "No country experienced more disasters and hardships than China in the building of constitutional government because China's efforts were made amidst national calamities and wars."[12] With the onset of the Opium Wars in 1840 China was thrown into political disorder. The incessant political struggles that ensued were, in essence, a process of seeking a new political order. The balance among various political forces was not achieved until the promulgation of the Common Program of the Chinese People's Political Consultative Conference in 1949, which marked the formation of the people's democratic united front. "The democratic parties were satisfied with the proportion of their political representation [being] decided through democratic consultation."[13] The founding of the PRC marked the inception of the country's new political order.

The new order represented a reorganization of political forces. After the establishment of the basic political order, the first electoral law of the PRC was promulgated on March 1, 1953. From December 8, 1953, to September 3, 1954, China held an unprecedentedly large-scale general election, which elected a total of 1,226 deputies to the NPC. Party members accounted for 54.48 percent, members of democratic parties 22.35 percent, persons without party affiliation 23.16 percent, and of those, workers 8.16 percent, peasants 5.14 percent, People's Liberation Army soldiers 4.89 percent, and returned overseas Chinese 2.45 percent. The results of the election fulfilled the hope of the CCP for China's new political order: "The government responsible to the People's Congress remained the government representing all ethnic groups, all democratic classes, all democratic parties, and all people's organizations and was in the interest of the people of the whole country."[14] The election, which succeeded in coordinating the interests of different social groups, marked the establishment of the basic social order required for constitutional government in China. As the first general election in Chinese history, it also laid a solid foundation of public opinion for the convening of the first meeting of the National People's Congress on September 15, 1954.

The new political order needed a new political system. The first plenary session of the 1st National People's Congress, on September 20, 1954, adopted the Constitution of the People's Republic of China and the Organic Law of the National People's Congress, and the plenary session on the following day adopted the Organic Law of the Local People's Congresses and Local People's Governments, the Organic Law of the State Council, the Organic Law of the People's Courts, and the Organic Law of the People's Procuratorates.

The adoption of the Constitution and a series of other laws created the basic blueprint for China's political development. According to the Constitution of 1954, "All power in the PRC belongs to the people. The Organs through which the people exercise power are the NPC and the local people's congresses at various levels. . . . [The] NPC and the local people's congresses at various levels are constituted through democratic elections. They are responsible to the people and subject to their supervision." The relevant laws provided in detail for the country's various political systems.[15] The adoption of these laws marked the formal establishment of China as a socialist democratic state and its government system as the people's congress system, the basic framework around which the People's Republic of China was constructed. The establishment of the National People's Congress marked the beginning of the institutionalization of China's political order.

The convening of the NPC in 1954 was the real beginning of the PRC's constitutionalism, and the Constitution of 1954 was the first constitution of the People's Republic. The history of constitutional development in modern China is also a history of facing down crises of legitimacy. Lucian Pye has identified four sources of legitimacy crisis: an inadequate base of authority, excessive power competition, the unacceptability of historical interpretation and future commitment, and ineffective political socialization, all of which have to do with political order as the foundation of constitutionalism.[16] When the Chinese awakened from 100 years of war and chaos, they naturally associated legitimacy with political order and stability. This was the foundation of the PCS's legitimacy in China.

Of course, the establishment of the constitutional order was not completed in one go. The Constitution of 1954 was abandoned during the Cultural Revolution as China's political order deviated from the normal path. The constitutions of 1975 and 1978 were also aborted because of the lack of a corresponding foundation of political order. Against this backdrop, it was no wonder that Deng Xiaoping, the architect of China's reform and opening up, repeatedly emphasized maintaining stability. Thanks to strong political stability, the Constitution of 1982 has shown tremendous vigor, and the PCS has also been continuously improved.

Regulatory Governance: Optimization of the PCS

The establishment of the constitutional order does not imply the achievement of constitutional government, which calls for an optimized administrative relationship and a governance structure within the boundaries of the Constitution. In other words, constitutional government can only be gradually achieved through the rule of the Constitution, which itself requires the presence of a constitutional order. Having undergone a difficult and tortuous process of political development, the Chinese people had become increasingly aware of the great significance of the rule of law. At the beginning of the reform and opening-up period, Deng explicitly stated that "in the post-Liberation years we did not consciously draw up systematic rules and regulations to safeguard the people's democratic rights. Our legal system is far from perfect and has not received anywhere near the attention it deserves."[17]

The primary driver of the development of China's legal system has been the need to address various problems arising from the process of the country's own development. More than half a century after the founding of the PRC, one of the most important issues regarding state governance is the relationship among political parties, democracy, and the rule of law—something that cannot be avoided in contemporary China's constitutional development. The issue, to express it in the Chinese way, revolves around the organic unity of the party's leadership, the people as the master of the country, and the rule of law, which must be based on the platform of the PCS. Accordingly, the People's Congress has to handle well its relationships with the people, other state organs, and the ruling party.

Development of the PCS

The Constitution of 1982 laid a solid legal foundation for the development of the PCS, and the People's Congress then promulgated a series of laws regarding the legal system. On December 10, 1982, the fifth session of the 5th National People's Congress adopted the Organic Law of the National People's Congress of the People's Republic of China, which provided especially for the sessions, standing committee, and special committees of the NPC and the deputies to the

NPC. In 1979, after the launching of reform and opening up, the second and current Electoral Law was promulgated. The Constitution of 1982 was amended multiple times—in 1982, 1986, 1995, 2004, and 2009. In 1992 the fifth session of the 7th National People's Congress adopted the Law of the People's Republic of China on Deputies to the National People's Congress and Deputies to Local People's Congresses. The Organic Law of the Local People's Congresses and Local People's Governments promulgated in 1979 was also amended multiple times—in 1982, 1986, 1995, and 2004. In 2000 the third session of the 9th National People's Congress adopted the Legislation Law, a key effort in advancing the rule of law. In 2006 the Law on the Supervision of Standing Committees of People's Congresses at Various Levels was promulgated. This promulgation and implementation of a series of laws has provided legal protection and the basis for people's congresses at various levels to more effectively exercise the power granted them by the Constitution and more effectively play their role as state organs. It has also greatly promoted the development of the people's congress system.

An important move in strengthening the PCS was to increase the power of the NPC Standing Committee. In 1979 standing committees of people's congresses at the county level and above were established, underscoring their increasing importance. From the 9th National People's Congress onward, any legislative bill placed on the agenda of a meeting of the standing committee would be subject to three deliberations, rather than two as in the past, before being put to a vote. The increasing professionalization of the standing committees has been another major aspect of strengthening their function. Since the 1980s, NPC standing committees have no longer been responsible for administrative, trial, and inspection duties. In 2003 a new mechanism was introduced to professionalize the standing committees. A 159-member standing committee was constituted at the 10th National People's Congress, which included 19 academically accomplished members who were in the prime of their lives, marking a major change in the personnel composition of the standing committee.

Another important aspect of strengthening the PCS has been the improvement of the rules of procedure. In the 1980s the rules of procedure for the NPC, its standing committee, and local people's congresses were formulated in succession, with special provisions for the convening, bill submission, deliberation, questioning, speaking, and voting concerning the congresses. The updated rules of procedure were adopted at the 7th National People's Congress. The rules of procedure for the NPC Standing Committee and the Council of Chairmen were formulated before 1988. The Rules of Procedure for the National People's Congress were adopted at the second session of that congress. Implementation of the 2002

Legislative Law further strengthened the rules of procedure and advanced the legal institutionalization of the National People's Congress and its standing committee.

Yet another important aspect of strengthening the PCS has been the establishment of special committees, which are known as standing committees and described in some countries as the parliament in action. Peng Zhen, the inaugural head of the CCP Central Political and Legislative Committee, emphasized the great importance of the special committees on many occasions. Wan Li, chair of the NPC in the late 1980s, also emphasized the great importance. In "Doing Well in the Work of the Special Committees of the People's Congress," he said that "it is our responsibility to help the government make correct and more scientific decisions and reduce the occurrence of mistakes" and that "engaging some specialists and professors as researchers or advisors should be considered."[18] Since the promulgation of the Constitution of 1982, efforts have been made to strengthen special committees, of which six were already established under the NPC. Since 1998 the NPC has maintained nine special committees, which have played an increasing role in improving the PCS and strengthening the People's Congress. In 2005 the General Office of the NPC Standing Committee issued Several Opinions on Giving Full Scope to the Role of Special Committees, which further strengthened the role of the special committees via a specific work system and set of procedures.

The last important aspect of strengthening the PCS has been the development of local people's congresses. On July 1, 1979, the second session of the 5th National People's Congress decided to establish standing committees of people's congresses at the county level and above as the organs for exercising the power of these people's congresses when they are not in session, which marked the beginning of strengthening the function of local people's congresses. Since then, local people's congresses have scored great achievements. One study on the subject by scholars outside of China have found that "the local people's congresses are playing a more active role than imagined and, in many places, are closer to the power center than the NPC in Beijing."[19]

People's Congress and the People

The relationship between the People's Congress and the people is provided for in article 2 of chapter 1 of the Constitution of 1982: "All power in the PRC belongs to the people." "The NPC and the local people's congresses at various levels are the organs through which the people exercise state power."[20] However, it is not enough for the power of the people to be demonstrated in substantive provisions; it should also be guaranteed procedurally. From the perspective of procedural democracy, the people must above all have their basic rights as citizens fully guaranteed; otherwise, that the people are the masters of the country is nothing more than an empty slogan. There is also the question of how the people exercise their rights, that is, how to fulfill substantive democracy through procedural democracy. Since the promulgation of the Constitution of 1982, China has made unprecedented progress on these issues.

The Constitution of 1982, enacted after the disastrous Cultural Revolution, was designed to overcome the legitimacy crisis, particularly by bringing to prominence the constitutional rights and duties of citizens. That enumeration of the fundamental rights and duties of citizens is presented in a separate chapter and placed immediately after the section on general principles is enough to show the great importance attached to the rights of citizens. The amendment to the Constitution adopted at the second session of the 10th National People's Congress proclaims that "the state respects and protects human rights" and establishes those rights as part of the country's fundamental law. According to an analysis by Chinese jurists, "This marked a major development of China's socialist constitutionalism and symbolizes that China's efforts to advance the socialist democracy and rule of law have reached a new level."[21]

The inclusion of human rights in the Constitution has had the effect of guiding the legislative work of the People's Congress toward a greater balance between state power and the rights of citizens, strengthening the defenses against abuse of power, and further emphasizing the development of humanistic concerns in state governance. Of almost equal importance has been the protected right of citizens to own lawful property. This amendment stipulates that "the lawful private property of citizens may not be encroached upon," according to article 13 in chapter 1.[22] The protection of private property is a cornerstone of the constitutional order and a major source of political legitimacy. The elevation of the rights and position of citizens—from being more focused on an individual's harmonious relationship to society, to writing human rights into the Constitution, to heightened concern about the people's livelihood—shows the increasing fulfillment of the principle of people as the masters of the country and has increased the political legitimacy of the party and the government. This is the basis of substantial changes in the relationship between the National People's Congress and the people in recent years.

The Constitution of 1982 provided guidance on how people could exercise their rights, describing a multilayered relationship between the People's Congress and the people involving systems regarding election, representation, accountability, supervision, participation, and the like. In-depth discussion on the representation and supervision systems is discussed elsewhere in this volume. Here, a discussion of the electoral and participation systems suffices to show how the changes in this relationship have had positive effects on the development of the PCS itself.

The electoral system is the organizational foundation of the People's Congress. In article 34, chapter 2, the Constitution stipulates that "all citizens of the PRC who have reached the age of 18 have the right to vote and stand for election, regardless of ethnic status, race, sex, occupation, family background, religious belief, education, property status, or length of residence."[23] In 1953 the Electoral Law of the People's Republic of China for the National People's Congress and Local People's Congresses was promulgated, which established China's electoral system. From the promulgation of the second Electoral Law in 1979 to the enactment of the Law of the People's Republic of China on Deputies to the National People's Congress and to the Local People's Congresses at Various Levels to the amendment to the Electoral Law in 2009, China carried out a series of reforms of its electoral system, further developing and improving it.

The result of these reforms has been the expansion of the right to vote, improvement of electoral procedures, and increased standardization of the methods of election.[24] The nomination of candidates by joint recommendation of ten voters or more and multicandidate elections have given the voters a wider scope of choice, and the realization of "equal votes, equal rights" in the rural and urban areas ensures a truly equal right to vote for all Chinese. Overall, the development of the electoral system is reflected in the expansion of the scope of both general and direct elections, the implementation of multicandidate elections, the division of electoral districts, and improvement of candidate nomination methods. These practices may be commonplace in countries with developed electoral systems, but given China's complicated path toward constitutionalism over the past 100 years, the significance of this progress can only be felt by people with a good understanding of this history. "Equal votes, equal rights" for urban and rural dwellers, in particular, put an end to the "one-fourth clause" of the previous Electoral Law, under which the vote of a rural dweller was equal to one-quarter the vote of an urban dweller. This revision not only constituted major progress in China's electoral system but also had monumental significance for constitutional democracy in general.

Although not prominent in traditional constitutional democracy, the participatory system has extraordinary significance in modern democratic governance in general and in the history of China's political development in particular. Political participation related to the PCS primarily means participation in legislation. The formulation of the Constitution of 1954 underwent a three-month nationwide discussion, and the draft of the Constitution of 1982 also experienced four months of similar discussion. As China moved into the twenty-first century, new forms of political participation were introduced. In 2008 Wu Bangguo, the chairman of the NPC Standing Committee, expressed a commitment to "advancing scientific and democratic legislation and expanding public participation in the legislative process."[25]

On December 7, 2009, the Legal Development Committee of the NPC Standing Committee published in the *People's Daily* a signed article entitled "Expand Public Participation in Legislation," advocating that while giving full scope to the role of People's Congress deputies in legislation, efforts should also be made to expand public participation in legislation. Such measures of expansion included adhering to and improving the mechanism for the announcement of legislative bills, strengthening the effects of legislation symposiums, holding meetings and hearings on issues of general concern to the public, listening to the opinion of people from all circles (especially ordinary citizens), improving legislative bills, and keeping the public informed in appropriate ways of the adoption of the suggestions proposed. That the NPC also employs technology to expand public participation merits special attention. For example, a special column, entitled "Netizens' Suggestions," has been added to the official website of the *People's Daily*, through which the public can participate in the sessions of the NPC, thereby constituting a new form of democracy.

China's political participation as related to the PCS emphasizes orderliness. This has to do with the great tragedies caused by the explosion of participation during the ten years of the Cultural Revolution. Therefore, the third session of the 5th National People's Congress in 1980 cancelled article 45 of the Constitution of 1978 concerning "the [people's] right to 'speak out freely, air their views fully, hold great debates, and write big-character posters.'"[26] This was an early effort to ensure orderly political participation. With the emergence of various social movements, including mass incidents, after the 1990s, advocacy for orderly participation has become a strategy in handling the relationship between the citizens and the state.

People's Congress and Other State Organs

Speaking about the PCS, the former president Jiang Zemin once said, "The PCS both reflects our state's nature and is in accord with our national conditions. On the one hand, it ensures uniform exercise of state power by the people and mobilizes their enthusiasm and initiative as the master of the country, and on the other hand, it is instrumental for the division of labor and cooperation among the organs of state power and for the coordination of efforts in socialist construction."[27] Reference to the division of labor and cooperation reflects the general relationship between the People's Congress and other state organs. The term *coordination* expresses a unique feature of the PCS and is also a reflection of the concept of political order in the relationships among state organs. Of course, the characteristics of the division of labor and coordination are formed over a long period of exploration. With respect to the overall relationship between the People's Congress and other state organs, division of labor and coordination are at the core of the rule of law in China.

Governance according to law entails the upholding of the authority of the Constitution and law in the country's political life. According to the Constitution, the NPC is the highest organ of state power and is responsible for the uniform exercise of state power and the creation of the government, the court, and the procuratorate, which are both responsible to and subject to the supervision of the People's Congress. In chapter 3 of the Constitution, titled "The Structure of the State," there are detailed provisions regarding the relationship between the People's Congress and other state organs. Since the promulgation of the Constitution of 1982, the basic framework of the system has been firmly established. This framework is described as a vertical triangle: the People's Congress is at the top of the power structure at both the central and local levels, and it creates and has supervision over the government, the court, and the procuratorate. In contrast, the image of a horizontal triangle is used to describe the constitutional framework and institutional arrangement whereby the three branches of government—the legislature, the executive, and the judiciary—interact on the same plane.[28] This metaphor offers a vivid representation of the characteristics of the relationship between the People's Congress and other state organs in the PCS.

Both the horizontal triangle and the vertical triangle are the result of the Constitution's arrangement of the country's state system. For the state system to run effectively, efforts must be made to implement governance according to the Constitution and the rule of law. China's leadership is clearly aware of this: "The first step in implementing the basic principle of governance according to law is to ensure the all-round enforcement of the Constitution."[29] Since the establishment of the PCS in 1949, the PRC has promulgated four constitutions as well as four amendments to the 1982 Constitution.

Governance according to law dictates that state organs operate within the boundaries of law, which requires a complete legal system. In line with the constant advancement of the reform and opening up and ensuring all-around social and economic development, the Chinese government announced in the late 1990s the goal of "establishing a socialist legal system with Chinese characteristics by 2010."[30] At the NPC in early 2010, top legislator Wu Bangguo announced the commitment to "ensuring that China's unique socialist legal system will take shape as scheduled." One year later, Wu Bangguo announced on March 10, 2011, that a socialist system of laws with Chinese characteristics has been established "on schedule" in China, hailing it as a "major milestone" in the history of the development of China's socialist democratic legal system.[31]

Supervision over administrative, adjudicative, and procuratorial organs is one of the major responsibilities granted to the NPC by the Constitution. The 6th National People's Congress placed great emphasis on its supervisory role and made great effort in that regard. At the suggestion of Peng Zhen, the congress began to deal with its supervisory function. On this basis, the 7th National People's Congress continued to "research and formulate specific rules and procedures of supervision, clarify the scope and methods of supervision, and strengthen the institutionalization and legalization of the supervision."[32] In 2007 the Law of the People's Republic of China on the Supervision of Standing Committees of People's Congresses at Various Levels came into effect, marking the beginning of the People's Congress's supervisory function.

People's Congress and the CCP

The relationship between the Chinese Communist Party, on one hand, and the People's Congress and other state organs, on the other, mainly concerns the CCP's leadership and its methods of governance. Today, this is in essence the question of governance according to law that is also in accord with the rule of law. Although the leadership role of the party in the People's Congress was established at the beginning of the PRC and has been constantly strengthened, the party's governance according to law in the people's congress system has undergone a long and difficult process of development.

There were indeed misconceptions about the relationship between the Chinese Communist Party and the National People's Congress. The Constitution of 1975 contained the provision that "the NPC is the highest organ of state power under the leadership of the CCP," which was changed to "the NPC is the highest organ of state power" in the Constitution of 1982, marking a historic progression in the conception of the issue. During the reform and opening-up period, Deng repeatedly emphasized the need for the proper handling of the relationship between the party and the government, which also covered the relationship between the party and the People's Congress. Wan Li, then chairman of the NPC Standing Committee, who consistently advocated for democracy in decisionmaking, remarked that "the people's congresses and their standing committees are important organs through which the Party's positions are turned into state policies, and to ensure their correctness, decisions must be made democratically and scientifically."[33]

When speaking of the reforms of the political system in 2001, Jiang Zemin, who was president at the time, summarized the three major achievements since the reform and opening up: "Intraparty democracy and the people's democracy have been restored and developed and lifelong tenure of leadership positions has been put to an end. . . . A lot of progress has been made in rectifying the Party's interference with government functions. . . .The PCS has been adhered to and improved, which is playing an increasingly important role in the country's political life." This shows that with the deepening of the reform and opening up and the optimization of the relationship between the party and the government, the relationship between the PCS and the CCP has been increasingly institutionalized within a comprehensive legal framework.

The changes in the relationship between the ruling party and the PCS can be analyzed from two perspectives: institutional design and policy. In terms of institutional design, at the state level, the position of the chairman of the NPC Standing Committee has been held by a Politburo Standing Committee member since the 9th National People's Congress in 1989. Since the 1990s, party chiefs of provinces and autonomous regions have generally held the position of chairman of the people's congress at their respective levels; this has become the prevailing practice and has been gradually institutionalized and extended down to municipal and county levels, especially since the 16th National Congress of the CCP, where members decided to change the method of governance. According to statistics, as of 2008 the party chiefs of twenty-four provinces and autonomous regions also held the position of chairman of the standing committee of their corresponding people's congresses.[34] This was a major adjustment to the relationship between the ruling party and the People's Congress for the purpose of strengthening the de facto as well as de jure authority of the People's Congress, advancing the people's congress system, enhancing the leadership of the ruling party over the PCS, and improving the legitimacy base of the CCP under the PCS.

From the perspective of the policy process, the relationship between the people's congress system and the ruling party involves the relationship between law and policy. Traditional view holds that law has supremacy over policy, and accordingly, the elevated position of law means the demoted position of policy. This obviously reflects a zero-sum thinking that pits law and policy against each other. But in terms of actual politics, law is an instrument of policy, which is true in all systems of representative democracy.

Without doubt, "in all political order, the source of law is the state."[35] However, there is a complicated relationship between law and policy. Although law has supremacy over policy in the political order, "policy has precedence over law in the dynamics of politics. Only after public policy has been determined are lawyers called in to draft a statute and construct a set of administrative regulations for implementation."[36] The formation of public policy is a multivariate process that is inseparable from the center of political power, the only difference being that the political structures of countries have different power centers.

Murray Scot Tanner has proposed a "garbage can model" of decisionmaking to characterize the role of the People's Congress in China's policy formation process. He concludes that the Chinese legislative system is increasingly not subject to clear leadership, often deviating from its coordinating role.[37] If a reflection is made on the dynamics between law and policy in integrating the direction of policy formation of the party and the deliberations on issues at the legislature, then Tanner's conclusion may be revised, and the leadership of the CCP over the People's Congress also becomes more readily understandable. It reflects the unique political order of China's political process.

The Three Represents concept advanced by the CCP at the beginning of the twenty-first century not only solved the issue of political legitimacy but also largely solved the issues concerning the consistency and coordination between policy orientation and law enactment. It changed the political process involving the traditional sense of interest representation and coordination, which often placed legislative interest above the party policy. An understanding of Three Represents is essential to understanding the relationship between the PCS and the party in the decisionmaking process. In contemporary China, before policy is turned into law, not only should the principle of the Three Represents be followed, but democratic consultation with participating parties is also required. This is closely associated with the characteristic of consultation of China's political democracy. The provocative question here is how to approach the relationship between the representation mechanisms of the party and the representative body.

The Foundation of Constitutionalism: Reform and Development of the PCS

Whether the Chinese government is a constitutional government has been the subject of great debate in academic circles in recent years. In fact, this debate is not recent. It has accompanied China's search for constitutional government over the past century. In the 1990s constitutional government again became a hot topic. Mao Zedong, in the 1940s, offered the following definition: "What is constitutional government? It is political democracy."[38] The recent debate questions whether defining constitutional government as democracy is too narrow a view and suggests that the rule of law and human rights should also be taken as integral elements of constitutional government.

Zhang Youyu, a legal scholar and official of the same generation and from the same political camp as Mao Zedong, has aired a similar view. Having stated that constitutional government is political democracy, Zhang Youyu immediately added, "Constitutional government means a form of politics under which the state's political system, organization of state power, and the rights and obligations of the government and the citizens are provided for in the constitution so that the government and the citizens are entitled to their respective rights and bear their respective obligations, and no conduct of any organization or individual in violation of and beyond those provisions is allowed."[39] This statement acknowledges the importance of human rights and the rule of law and thereby represents a complete definition of constitutional government as political democracy. Zhang has no intention of debating the concept of constitutional government and agrees that the basic concept of constitutional government has two major aspects: establishing and safeguarding the rights of citizens and having effective allocation of and strong constraints over state power.[40] If the issue is understood from this perspective, then the important questions are whether China has the conditions to implement constitutional government and whether China's politics can make progress in safeguarding the rights of citizens and in checking state power. China's political development to date shows that the people's congress system provides strong fundamental support for the development of China's constitutional development and constitutes an excellent institutional platform to advance China's constitutional democracy. Nevertheless, in comparison with public demands for social and political development, the PCS still has a long way to go.

The development of the PCS still hinges on a stable political order, which is one of the preconditions for constitutional government. Indeed, the Constitution of 1954 and the Constitution of 1982 were both based on their respective stable political orders. Successful constitutional orders fall into three categories: those that arose spontaneously in democratic countries, as represented by the United States and the United Kingdom; the executive orders of later advanced countries, as represented by Germany and Japan; and reconciling orders, such as China's ongoing governance structure and political order.[41] As China has moved into the twenty-first century, its political development has assumed a trend of interaction between political order and constitutional development. On one hand, the stable political order has provided an important precondition for the development of constitutional government. On the other, the advancement of the constitutional cause has also become a major foundation for social and political stability.

According to Lucian Pye, "The essence of political stability is the ability to realize purposeful change."[42] Many transitional countries with a hybrid regime that combines traits of authoritarianism and democracy are entangled in the tension between the need for democracy and state institutionalization.[43] A failed state cannot have a developed economy and ensure social justice. As one scholar observes, "You cannot expect people suffering unemployment, inequality and social insecurity to applaud political transition with a starved stomach."[44]

Similarly, a country facing conflicts and social instability cannot take the risk of constitutional reform. Constitutional democracy cannot be achieved in a chaotic social and political environment. The history of political development has repeatedly validated Russell Hardin's observation that the successful running of a constitutional democratic system is dependent on a stable political and economic order as well as the ability to coordinate different interest groups and promote their reciprocal relationship.[45] In this sense, China's lasting peace and stability needs the support of a strong constitutional order.

The relationship among political parties, democracy, and the rule of law remains the core issue of political development. Institutionally, the fundamental question regarding the successful running of constitutional democracy in China is how to better handle these relationships. China's democratic development is characterized by three features: the democracy of the National People's Congress, based on the PCS and in relation to the exercise of the state power; intra-party democracy of the ruling party; and societal democracy based on political consultation, multiparty cooperation, and grassroots autonomy, which does not involve the exercise of state power.[46] If these three elements are properly placed in the framework of constitutional democracy, the question of supremacy of one over another will dissolve. In all these dimensions, the democracy of the People's Congress can best represent the constitutional order and is in best accord with the path of China's constitutional development and should therefore be given due attention. Bernard Manin summarizes three ideal types of representative government: parliamentarism, party democracy, and communicative democracy. These not only represent different paths of modern democracy but also demonstrate the relevant dimensions and different aspects of representative democracy.[47] Although China's democratic development cannot copy any of these patterns, their democratic connotations deserve our serious attention.

The Chinese Communist Party's leadership, the people as masters of their country, and governance according to law all concern the question of how to handle the relationship between the party, democracy, and the rule of law. The core of this question is the position and role of the party in the governance structure. Under a government characterized by the rule of law, the ruling party's positions are brought to the fore and influence what laws are passed; these laws then become the will of the state, thus gaining their legitimacy. Candidates recommended by the ruling party are subject to the approval of the electorate. The reestablishment of the relationship among parties, the people, and the rule of law shows China's advancement toward constitutional democracy as well as the optimization of a democratic legal system under the PCS. The unification of these relationships under the PCS represents the blueprint of China's constitutional democracy development, whereby the party and state organs perform their respective functions within the boundaries of the law, the people exercise their protected rights under the rule of law, and the rule of law is advanced steadily in a sound constitutional and democratic order.

China's Constitution states that "no organization or individual is privileged to be above the Constitution or the law," and the leadership has since moved to establish a relatively comprehensive legal system. Although the supremacy of law may be commonplace in countries with a developed legal system, it has extraordinary significance for China, given that the country has lacked the tradition of rule of law. In the words of a veteran Chinese statesman, rule of law "will determine China's political landscape in the 21st century."[48]

The constant improvement of the PCS is the foundation of China's constitutional development. The PCS is the institutional platform of China's constitutional development, and the National People's Congress is the core structure of that system. China's constitutional development cannot be separated from the constant improvement of the PCS. Much attention has been paid, both in academic studies and in practice, to the future of the PCS. Sun Zhe has systematically studied this issue. He proposes three criteria of China's constitutional development: "advancement of both stability and reform," "equal emphasis on speed and quality," and "unity of concept and benefit." He envisages an NPC that is stronger, more independent, more confident, and able to bring new rules and order to China's political life and to better coordinate diversified social interests.[49]

Nevertheless, in practice, the improvement of the People's Congress must be carried out within the overall framework of the PCS. In this regard, efforts should be made in the following seven directions. First, the people's right to vote and the deputies' right of representation must be guaranteed. Special effort should be made to ensure the voting rights of the transient population. This does not just concern the method of election but also calls for the further improvement of the electoral system. Second, the question of inadequate public participation must be addressed. Legislative techniques need to be enriched, and a series of systems including the legislation system should be further strengthened to ensure public participation both substantively and procedurally. Third, deputies to the People's Congress must meet appropriate qualifications, and conflicts of interest should be avoided. Fourth, in view of the short duration of the People's Congress sessions and the diversity of issues on the agenda, effort should be made to further increase and strengthen special committees, including strengthening the institutionalization of those committees, granting them substantial power, and legally providing for their composition and authority. Fifth, a modern public budgeting and fiscal system should be established to strengthen and improve the supervisory function of the People's Congress, especially in relation to the review of and supervision over the government budget, making budget supervision a driver of China's constitutional development. Sixth, a constitutional review system should be put in place.

Finally, the social foundation of the people's congress system should be continuously strengthened to advance China's constitutional development. The world history of political development shows that in the development of the constitutional system, the representative system plays an intermediary role in the interaction between state and society. In terms of the relationship between state and society, a democratic system cannot succeed without good social capital.[50] As shown by the history of political development around the globe, the establishment of a constitutional democratic system alone is no guarantee that the system will run effectively in all time periods and across all geographic regions. This point is illustrated by Carl Schmidt, in his analysis of the Weimar Republic, and by Robert Putnam, who undertook comparative research on democratic operations in the southern and northern regions of Italy.[51] The research of these and other scholars shows that a well-developed civil society provides strong social capital for constitutional democracy.

In China's case, the PCS and the building of civil society need to be organically integrated to increase the social capital required for constitutional development. In China, there is a lack of optimism for increasing the social capital of political development, the primary reason being that China retains a deep-rooted tradition of the rule of man and lacks the soil for the growth of the rule of law. Zhao Baoxu notes that the rule of man thrives under two conditions: the presence of an undisputed figure of absolute political authority and a lack of awareness and political participation among the population. "In present-day China, however, these two conditions indispensable to the rule of man do not exist."[52] Nevertheless, excessive pessimism about the social capital of China's constitutional development is not warranted. The growth of civil society in contemporary China along with the county's progress in the rule of law gives reason to hope that as long as the PCS is put into full and effective operation, China's constitutional development will have bright and broad prospects.

COMMENT
JACQUES DELISLE

Shi Hexing provides a comprehensive, detailed overview of China's people's congresses. He focuses mostly on the National People's Congress (NPC), but his concerns are broader and deeper: the people's congress system (PCS), including the NPC and provincial and lower-level people's congresses that comprise China's legislative and representative bodies, and their place in China's governance, constitutional development, and possible democratization.

Shi's project is positive (examining the changing roles of people's congresses) and normative (articulating the roles that people's congresses must or should play for China to achieve more robust constitutionalism and progress toward more meaningful, if distinctively Chinese, democracy). This commentary addresses three themes that emerge from Shi's chapter, focusing on the reform era: explanations for the expansion in roles and importance of the NPC and the PCS, the connection between the NPC and PCS and China's problematic constitutional order, and the relationship between the PCS and still-unsettled questions of democracy and democratic change in China.

Rise of the NPC and the PCS in the Reform Era

Shi's chapter offers several explanations for the increasing importance of the NPC and the PCS. These explanations have differing implications for the NPC's and PCS's prospects for fulfilling the more robust roles that Shi envisions. The first is based on a leader-centered model.[53] It suggests that the NPC and the PCS rose in influence because the NPC functioned as an institutional home and power base for members of the top leadership. The rise of these institutions reflects post-Mao shifts toward pluralistic or collective leadership and greater political institutionalization. Repeatedly, a member of the uppermost elite became chairman of the NPC and thus had self-interested reasons to strengthen both the National People's Congress and the people's congress system. One means for the NPC head to enhance his power within the collective leadership was to pursue a greater role in politics and governance for activities undertaken by the people's congress. Thus at the beginning of the reform era, Peng Zhen became the face of the socialist legality project centered on the National People's Congress, made a high-visibility pronouncement of seven basic laws (including key laws on the PCS and other organs of government) passed by the NPC in 1979, advocated for the prerogatives of the legislature, and pushed for the Village Elections Law, which resonated with the (limited) democracy norm that was a basis of PCS legitimacy. Tellingly, Premier Zhao Ziyang reportedly worried that the growing strength of the NPC could impede the party's control and the government's ability to pursue reform policies.

A decade later, with Tiananmen protests headed for crisis, NPC chairman Wan Li became the focus of speculation regarding whether he would lead the NPC to exercise its constitutional powers to remove Premier Li Peng, overturn

Li's martial law declaration, or address claims that martial law had been declared through procedures that violated the spirit and perhaps the letter of constitutional provisions (which gave the NPC Standing Committee sole authority to declare martial law for an entire provincial-level unit such as Beijing). Wan also stressed the benefits for the party-state of open policy discussion and debate within the NPC, thereby asserting the NPC's value and supporting a greater role for the institution. Later NPC heads, including Qiao Shi, Li Peng, and Wu Bangguo, variously became closely associated with NPC perspectives (including a more cautious approach to economic reform) and enhancement of NPC functions (including adopting legislation to play a larger role in governing)—despite these leaders' previous lack of affinity for lawmaking.

A leader-centered model is consistent with three prominent instances of apparently high levels of NPC influence. The NPC made the initial Enterprise Bankruptcy Law less tough and market-oriented and delayed its more capitalist-leaning successor for many years. It greatly delayed and modestly limited the reformist content of the Property Law amid arguments that the law strayed too far from socialist values. And it altered proposed legislation on criminal procedure and emergency powers in ways that marginally limited the powers of executive entities.

These examples may reflect a leader-centered pattern in three ways. Some may reflect the preferences of NPC chairmen who have often (including at the time of the debates over bankruptcy and property law) but not always held relatively "conservative" policy views. They may reflect the comparative advantage of the NPC, which lies mostly in its power to delay and revise legislation or express disapproval of government work, and which relatively often has meant tapping the brakes on reforms or checking enhancements or poor exercises of power by the State Council, its agencies, and other government organs. Finally, they may show the growing validity of the maxim "Where you sit determines where you stand": leaders of legislative organs adopt preferences consistent with those organs' institutional interests and with the preferences of quasi-constituencies that were, early on, threatened by reform or, more recently, concerned about negative side effects of reform. Parallel patterns can be found among subnational people's congresses.

A second model emphasizes bureaucratic politics or institutional competition or, more specifically, bureaucratic pluralism or fragmented authoritarianism.[54] In this model, the NPC and the PCS gained influence by behaving like other participants in political processes characterized by relatively strong institutions with weakly institutionalized mechanisms for resolving conflicts. Facing hollow constitutional promises of legislative supremacy, the NPC and the PCS have engaged in bargaining and conflict with other institutional actors and have sought to exploit areas of comparative advantage and gain a larger political market share for the special functions (including lawmaking) of legislative institutions.

In this model, the NPC and the PCS might seem at a disadvantage, given their lack of clear institutional missions or interests analogous to those of functionally differentiated ministries or provincial entities. But the challenge is not insurmountable. Expanding the market share for PCS functions in Chinese politics enhances the PCS's relative power in a manner familiar in bureaucratic politics. The NPC and the PCS also may have institutional missions reflecting connections to quasi-constituencies that include less prosperous regions and state-sector workers (especially early in the reform era), reformist intellectuals and economic "winners" (especially recently, under the Three Represents policy), and a broader citizenry increasingly critical of shortcomings in governance.[55]

A third model is functionalist: the NPC and the PCS have grown more influential because of their utility in performing vital systemic functions, many of which Shi details.[56] One such function is making rules that establish frameworks for market-oriented, internationally open economic reform. Laws are singularly suited to providing the clarity of rules, the promise of predictability, and bounded freedom that economic markets or foreign investors (and, increasingly, Chinese firms) demand. Under an economic reform strategy that has embraced or tolerated decentralization and diversity (as adaptation to local circumstances or as "test points" for potential national rules), lawmaking by subnational people's congresses (and national laws authorizing it) has played a vital role. The NPC, and the PCS at lower levels, has adeptly increased capacity by expanding legislative staff and resources, establishing specialized committees, strengthening the less-unwieldy standing committees and the chairmen's groups, rationalizing internal rules of procedure, and drawing on expertise from legal scholars, economic experts, and others. These moves helped level the playing field in shaping economics-related law that had been skewed toward the State Council and subordinate entities. This enhanced the NPC's and the PCS's value and claim to power.

Other functions include lawmaking more broadly and legislative oversight still more broadly.[57] The leadership has emphasized ruling the country by law and putting policies in legal form. That was the message of a sixteen-character statement in the communiqué of the third plenary session of the 11th CCP Central Committee, Jiang Zemin–era commitments to the rule of law, amendments formally constitutionalizing a rule-of-law state, Hu Jintao's emphasis on the Constitution and prolific references to law in his 17th National Party Congress report, Wen Jiabao's endorsement of rule-of-law government, and early Xi

Jinping–era calls to firmly establish the authority of the Constitution and laws and to strengthen rule-of-law guarantees. Because the NPC and the PCS are lawmakers, law interpreters, and supervisors of law implementation, they benefit from this emphasis on law. Their existing and at least potentially significant law-related powers include the following:

—pressing for the effective supremacy of the Constitution and legislation after the Law on Legislation and other reforms clarified the formal hierarchy of sources of law

—exercising greater control and supervision over makers of other law-like rules, including through the filing and examination (备案审查, *beian shencha*) system for administrative and local regulations and through responding to questions from, and developments among, lower-level legislatures and nonlegislative state organs

—enhancing and deploying the PCS's increased capacity, including in-house staff, streamlined and enhanced internal structures, and outside expertise, to craft more detailed and effective legislation

—writing organic laws for government organs and substantive laws that such organs administer in ways that maintain or enhance PCS influence and authority

—exercising more energetically the PCS's powers of oversight, including powers to critique and reject work reports from the government, procuracy, and courts, to supervise and override judicial decisions, and to investigate the implementation of legislation

Expanded opportunities for the public to make its views known in the law-making process and expressions of such views via people's congress representatives have opened channels for legislative oversight and input. Partly legitimated by ideological and formal connections between the PCS and democracy, the PCS has taken on some roles akin to a tribune of the plebeians. This has become relatively important in addressing governance problems (such as corruption, unresponsiveness of local officials to central laws and policies, and abuses of citizens' legal rights) that can threaten growth and feed discontent. For the leadership and in the system's own terms, PCS bodies are relatively acceptable, unthreatening means for promoting accountability, at least compared with such alternatives as empowered courts or electoral democracy.[58]

The functionalist model is consistent with both a top-down account and a bottom-up account. The NPC and the PCS have performed roles that the reform-era leadership has wanted and that advance its chosen strategy. They also have competed effectively in China's political marketplace to perform functions necessary for the stability and viability of the system, such as accommodating and mediating pressures from below.

Finally, a model of democratic legitimacy may contribute to explaining the rise of the NPC and the PCS, attributing it partly to their significance as symbols of democracy and mechanisms of (limited) democratic representation.[59] The PCS has been relatively democratic among China's political institutions. Representatives sometimes challenge, criticize, delay, amend, and even scuttle government and party-backed legislation or appointments. Such actions sometimes reflect interests and preferences of social groups that would be strongly represented in a democratic system. Opposition or unofficial candidates occasionally make modest (if, for themselves, costly) headway in direct elections for local-level people's congresses. Some democratic input occurs through public comment and debate on draft laws (including via the Internet) and hearings under the Law on Legislation and in PCS practice. A formal mechanism authorizes citizen petitions to challenge consistency of lower-level laws with higher laws and the Constitution. Other procedural and electoral (or, more accurately, "selectoral") mechanisms have made the NPC and the PCS somewhat open to diverse citizen input.

These are, to be sure, limited elements of democracy, but the point is the PCS's relatively democratic stature, compared with other institutions. This feature matters for ideological and functional reasons. Shi rightly takes seriously issues of legitimacy (and democratic legitimacy specifically). In his discussion of Lucian Pye and others, he shows that he grasps the complexity of these issues. Few regimes can fully eschew claims to democracy, especially after democratization in East Asia and the former Soviet world during the 1980s and 1990s (and notwithstanding recent partial retrenchment). A claimed commitment to democracy matters abroad and, increasingly, at home for China's regime. The NPC and the PCS are by legal mandate and formal structure the principal institutional locus of democratic legitimacy, as Shi emphasizes. Their marginalization or transparently rubber-stamp status would undermine efforts to build, or tap, democratic legitimacy. Their comparatively democratic roles may help preempt, or deflect, calls for more radically democratic change. Their openness to some popular input and social-elite input (given that people's congress deputies come disproportionately from the well educated and the well off and given that outsiders' opportunities to participate in people's congresses' law-drafting activities fall mostly to intellectuals and major stakeholders) can relieve pressures for greater democratization and co-opt potentially disgruntled, politically salient groups.

The PCS, the Constitution, and Constitutionalism

Shi places the people's congress system at the center of China's constitutional order, as a normative and, perhaps, positive claim.[60] Full implementation of the formal constitution would give the NPC a huge role: interpreter and maker of the Constitution and laws that apply broadly—even to the CCP, top organ of state power, appointer and remover or top officials, and so on.⁶¹ Less idealistically, the recent rhetorical or policy emphasis on the Constitution and constitutionalism enhances, at least marginally, the NPC and the PCS in light of their status as institutions central to the constitutional order. Construed as advocacy, Shi's chapter is an extended argument for advancing these trends and doing more to implement these promises.

But such changes in legislative bodies' roles will require significant, difficult reforms, many of which Shi addresses. First, creating a constitution-centered order or making the formal powers of the PCS real requires that China's constitutional unevenness be addressed. Some constitutional provisions reflect serious commitments (including those concerning state and collective property, the market economy, the leading role of the Communist Party, and territorial integrity and sovereignty). Other articles have been mostly empty pledges (including those setting forth liberal and democratic rights). Provisions on state structure typically lie somewhere in between. High-profile amendments (including 2004 changes on states of emergency, private property, and human rights) pose more complicated issues of interpretation and implementation. More broadly, there are no effective mechanisms for enforcing the Constitution. In principle, its provisions depend on legislative implementation. In practice the NPC's powers of constitutional interpretation have been dormant. Invoking the Constitution or constitutionalism will not suffice (or have significant impact) so long as the Constitution has such an uneven relationship to political reality and a fragile stature standing.

Second, the NPC (and the PCS) is at risk of losing market share in Chinese constitutionalism. Striking—although very limited—examples of constitutionalism come from courts, not the NPC. In the Qi Yuling case, the Supreme People's Court famously (if only briefly, until its reply was withdrawn in December 2008) approved direct applicability and judicial enforceability of constitutional rights (specifically, the right to education) without implementing legislation by the NPC. In the Henan Seeds case, Judge Li Huijuan refused to apply a local ordinance found to be incompatible with a higher-level law. This arguably usurped (although without lasting effect) the NPC's exclusive but fallow power to enforce a Chinese parallel to the U.S. Constitution's supremacy clause. Other courts have relied directly on constitutional provisions (without legislative implementation), albeit as "gap fillers" and without much formal interpretation.⁶²

The three supremes (三个至上, *sange zhishang*)—associated with Hu-era Supreme People's Court president Wang Shengjun—also threatened to erode the powers of legislative organs. Calling on courts to follow CCP policy and public opinion as well as the Constitution and laws, this imperative reduced the dominant status that law—the output of the PCS—had enjoyed under Wang's predecessor, Xiao Yang. The logic of the Three Supremes is that acts of the NPC and the PCS merely stand alongside norms from nonlegal sources in governing the vast range of social, economic, and governmental behavior that now reaches the courts. The replacement of Wang by Zhou Qiang and other early Xi-era changes are more favorable omens for the agenda Shi envisions.

The NPC has forgone opportunities to expand the Constitution's impact when it has failed to use constitutional review powers, despite rising calls to do so. A key example is the Sun Zhigang incident, in which reformist legal scholars pressed the standing committee of the NPC to declare unconstitutional the Custody and Repatriation Regulations (收容遣送, *shourong qiansong*) under which Sun, a student mistaken for an illegal migrant, was detained (with fatal results). Instead of facing constitutional review by the NPC Standing Committee, the regulations were withdrawn and replaced by the entity that had issued them, the State Council. This outcome is especially striking because one of the principal criticisms was that the regulations were unconstitutional in that they sought to achieve by mere executive regulation something that the Constitution required be done by legislation.[63]

More broadly, the NPC has not been aggressive, or effective, in using powers under the Constitution and the Law on Legislation to assert primacy of its legislation over other sources of law (or normative documents and party decisions that create many operationally relevant rules) or to reject acts by other state organs that exceed those organs' legal powers. The NPC and the PCS are far from the robust legislative and constitutional institutions that some observers argue are necessary for effective constitutionalism and rule of law.[64]

The PCS and Democracy with Chinese Characteristics

Shi also places the NPC and the PCS at the center of prospects for democratization and a constitutional order that is democratic, protects civil and human rights, and integrates increasingly diverse interest groups. Such people's congress democracy is an understandable focus for reasons already noted, including the PCS's uniquely democratic pedigree, its role in China's formal constitutional system, the sprouts of quasi-democracy in the practice of people's congresses, and the endorsement of potentially PCS-centered and arguably democratic norms in the Hu Jintao and Xi Jinping leaderships' rhetorical emphasis on governing in the interests of ordinary people and upholding the Constitution. Shi recognizes significant impediments to the big changes that he believes are necessary and that democratization would require. It is worth noting two points that are less central to Shi's account and that parallel the foregoing discussion of constitutionalism.

First, democracy, constitutional democracy, and democratic constitutionalism in China remain contested, ambiguous, and perhaps unstable. As Shi notes, some version of democracy (with Chinese characteristics) is officially endorsed, but its meaning is far from settled. Liberal electoral democracy with separation of powers remains off the table, given the fate of the Charter 08 manifesto and statements from top leaders consistently rejecting Western-style models. Shi's position seems consistent with the relativist approaches of many Chinese sources, favoring PCS-centered democracy and a constitutional order that differs from ostensibly universal but arguably Western patterns urged by foreign critics and more radical reformers. But there is little consensus in political or intellectual circles in China about what China's order should look like.

Second, the people's congress system risks losing market share in China's democratization even as some accounts see the PCS as a foundation for limited pro-democratic change.[65] There are some modest elements of PCS-centered, arguably democratic progress, including serial reforms to electoral laws promising more open contests for direct elections to local people's congresses, changes to the system of selecting higher-level congress deputies, representation in the legislatures of more diverse interest groups and segments of society, redress of severe imbalances in urban and rural representation in the National People's Congress, and expanded opportunities for citizens to have input into legislation and press people's congresses to use their powers to address citizens' concerns.[66]

With such limited gains and poor prospects for further expansion, the role played by the NPC and the PCS in democratization may be shrinking. This bodes ill for PCS-centered democracy but not necessarily for China's democratization. Electoral democracy has made its greatest (if limited) inroads outside the PCS. Local people's congress elections have been, by conventional measures, less democratic than village elections. Although the Law on Legislation and related reforms opened channels for popular input, and despite long, ongoing delays in creating an administrative procedure law, many rule-making institutions (outside the PCS) have established hearings and other procedures for popular participation and engagement. Less formal processes for enhancing government accountability and triggering reform of rules that govern citizens flow from the public through non-PCS channels. These include letters and visits to local governments, ministry organs, and courts; local experiments with consultative democracy, including semi-structured meetings between citizens and officials to discuss government budgets and other governance issues; mass protests, which elicit responses—including accommodation and redress—from state and party organs; and informal rule making among nongovernmental groups, such as homeowner associations. Intraparty democratization is another much-discussed, if murky, non-PCS-centered democratization, of a sort.

Conclusion: The Road Ahead?

Shi expresses bounded optimism for gradual progress toward a more constitutional and law-governed order with greater accommodation of democratic elements. Three features of Shi's analysis offer plausible—if not, for the relatively skeptical, convincing—support for this view. First, relativism: around the world, successful constitutional orders vary greatly, in part reflecting local circumstances. Shi's prescriptions for incremental reform and development of democracy and constitutionalism prescribe adaptation to current Chinese conditions and recent history. Second, an emphasis on stability: Shi stresses the central role played by concerns with stability in mass and elite Chinese thinking. The established foundations for future developments, and the reforms that Shi endorses, are consistent with this priority of stability. Although possibly realistic, this approach seems resigned to relatively dim prospects for much-expanded democracy, robust constitutional constraints on political power, and vesting institutionalized authority to make policy in a body that might more radically change the political status quo. Third, weakened underpinnings for the rule of man: Shi argues that unchallenged political authority of leaders and absence of strong demand for popular participation no longer characterize politics in China. If Shi is correct, China may have no viable alternative to pursuing the difficult and lengthy path toward rule of law and constitutional governance that Shi envisions. Shi also points to scattered but potentially significant protodemocratic antecedents in earlier periods as a foundation for such a pursuit, as well as to incipient developments in contemporary Chinese political institutions that accommodate the increasing diversity of interests and preferences in Chinese society. One must be wary of asserting that necessary or functional changes will occur or that potential progress will be achieved. And the will and capacity of the Chinese Communist Party to undertake fundamental constitutionalist or democratic reforms remain at best uncertain. Nonetheless, the accomplishments and resilience of the reform-era regime and the many developments Shi catalogues weigh against dismissing lightly the prospects for successful adaptation that Shi foresees.

Notes

1. Zhang Chunsheng and Chen Sixi, "'Xiangpi tuzhang' zenme bian ying: Tan renmin daibiao dahui zhidu de gaige yu wanshan" [How to harden the "rubber stamp": Reform and optimization of the people's congress system], in *Xianzheng jiangtan* [Lectures on constitutional government], edited by Cai Dingjian, 1st ed. (Beijing: Law Press China, 2010), pp. 207–08.

2. Robert A. Dahl, ed., *Regimes and Oppositions* (Yale University Press, 1973), p. 96.

3. Roderick MacFarquhar, *The Politics of China: The Eras of Mao and Deng,* 2nd ed. (Cambridge University Press, 1997); Kenneth Lieberthal, *Governing China* (New York: W. W. Norton, 1995); Tony Saich, *Governance and Politics of China* (New York: Palgrave Macmillan, 2004).

4. Xia Ming, *The People's Congresses and Governance in China* (New York: Routledge, 2008), p. 2.

5. Roderick MacFarquhar, "Feijingji yinsu yu Zhongguo gaige" [Noneconomic factors and China's reform], translated by Zhang Minjie, in *Zhongguo de di er ci geming* [China's second revolution], edited by Zhang Minjie, 1st ed. (Shanghai: Commercial Press, 2001), pp. 191–92.

6. Ibid., p. 192; Kevin J. O'Brien, "Chinese People's Congress and Legislative Embeddedness: Understanding Early Organizational Development," *Comparative Political Studies,* no. 1 (1994); Murray Scot Tanner, *Politics of Lawmaking in Post-Mao China: Institutions, Processes, and Democratic Prospects* (Oxford University Press, 1999); Xia, *The People's Congresses and Governance in China;* Cho Young Nam, *Local People's Congress in China* (Cambridge University Press, 2010).

7. Sun Ying, "Jianping Zhong wai renda yanjiu xianzhuang" [Brief review of current Chinese and foreign scholarship on the people's congress system], *Renda yanjiu* [People's Congress studies], no. 3 (2009), p. 10–11.

8. Yu Keping and others, *Zhongguo moshi yu "Beijing gongshi": Chaoyue "Huashengdun gongshi"* [The China model and the Beijing consensus: Beyond the Washington consensus] (Beijing: Social Sciences Academic Press, 2006).

9. Russell Hardin, *Ziyouzhuyi, xianfazhuyi he minzhu* [Liberalism, constitutionalism, and democracy], translated by Wang Huan and Shen Mingmin (Shanghai: Commercial Press, 2009), pp. 1–2 (preface to the Chinese edition); see also preface, p. 22.

10. Li Jingpeng, "Lun shehuizhuyi minzhu de yunxing jizhi he lilun jichu" [Movements of socialist democracy: Mechanism and theoretical basis], *Zhengzhixue yanjiu* [Political studies], no. 3 (1988); Zhu Xueqin, *Daode lixiangguo de fumie: Cong Lusuo dao Luosipi'er* [Downfall of the moral republic: From Rousseau to Robespierre] (Shanghai: Shanghai Joint Publishing Company, 1994); Yang Guangbin and Yi Donghua, "Wo guo renmin daibiao dahui zhidu de minzhu lilun jichu" [Theoretical basis of the democracy of the people's congress system], *Zhongguo Renmin Daxue xuebao* [Journal of Renmin University of China], no. 6 (2008).

11. Sun Yat-sen, *Sun Zhongshan quanji* [Complete works of Sun Yat-sen] (Beijing: Zhonghua Book Company, 1981), pp. 297–98.

12. Zhou Yezhong and Dai Jitao, *Gonghezhuyi zhi xianzheng jiedu* [Interpreting communist constitutionalism] (Beijing: People's Publishing House, 2005), p. 195.

13. Peng Youjin, ed., *Dangdai Zhongguo de renmin zhengxie* [Chinese People's Political Consultative Conference in contemporary China] (Beijing: Contemporary China Publishing House, 1993), p. 44.

14. Mu Zhaoyong, ed., *Di yi jie quanguo renmin daibiao dahui shilu* [Facts about the 1st National People's Congress] (Guangzhou: Guangdong People's Publishing House, 2006), p. 76.

15. See chapter 1, article 2 of the Constitution of the People's Republic of China (1954). For the application of the governing principle, see Yi Zhongqing, ed., *Quanguo renmin daibiao dahui ji qi changwu weiyuanhui dashi ji* [Milestone events of the National People's Congress and its standing committee, 1954–2004] (Beijing: Zhongguo minzhu fazhi chubanshe [China Democratic Legal System Press], 2005), pp. 39–45.

16. Lucian W. Pye, *Zhengzhi fazhan mianmian guan* [Aspects of political development], translated by Ren Xiao and Wang Yuan (Tianjin: Tianjin People's Publishing House, 2009), pp. 223–26.

17. Deng Xiaoping, "On the Reform of the System of Party and State Leadership," in *Deng Xiaoping wenxuan* [Selected works of Deng Xiaoping], vol. 2 (Beijing: People's Publishing House, 1982), p. 332.

18. Peng Zhen, "Jin yi bu shishi xianfa, yange anzhao xianfa ban shi" [Implementing the Constitution further, acting according to the Constitution], speech, delivered on December 3, 1983, in *Peng Zhen wenxuan* [Selected works of Peng Zhen] (Beijing: People's Publishing House, 1991), p. 488; Cai Dingjian, *Zhongguo renda zhidu* [China's people's congress system] (Beijing: Social Sciences Academic Press China, 2003), p. 244; Wan Li, "Zuohao renda zhuanmen weiyuanhui de gongzuo" [Doing well in the work of the special committees of the People's Congress], in *Wan Li wenxuan* [Selected works of Wan Li] (Beijing: People's Publishing House, 1995), p. 591.

19. Xia, *The People's Congresses and Governance in China*, p. 250; Cho Young-Nam, *Local People's Congress in China* (Cambridge University Press, 2010), p. 163; Melanie Manion, "When Communist Party Candidates Can Lose, Who Wins? Assessing the Role of Local People's Congresses in the Selection of Leaders in China," *China Quarterly*, no. 195 (2008).

20. Constitution of the People's Republic of China (1982), chapter 1, article 2.

21. Xin Chunying, "Guojia zunzhong he baozhang renquan: guanyu renquan ruxian de lishi yiyi" [The state respects and protects human rights: The historic significance of the writing of human rights into the Constitution], *Qiushi* [Seek truth], no. 9 (2004), p. 36.

22. See the Constitution of the People's Republic of China (1982), chapter 1, article 13.

23. Ibid., chapter 2, article 34.

24. Cai, *Zhongguo renda zhidu*, p. 244; Sun Zhe, *Quanguo renda zhidu yanjiu 1979–2000* [Studies on the national people's congress system, 1979–2000], translated by He Lingzhi and Zhao Kejin (Beijing: Law Press China, 2004), pp. 223–68.

25. Wu Bangguo, "Report on the Work of the 10th NPC Standing Committee" (news.xinhuanet.com/misc/2008-03/08/content_7746340.htm).

26. See Constitution of the People's Republic of China (1978), chapter 3, article 45.

27. Jiang Zemin, *Lun you Zhongguo tese shehuizhuyi* [On socialism with Chinese characteristics] (Beijing: Zhongyang wenxian chubanshe [Central Party Literature Press], 2002), p. 305.

28. Ji Weimin, "Renda wushi nian san ren tan" [Dialogues on the fifty years of development of the people's congress system], *Zhejiang renda* [Zhejiang People's Congress Magazine], no. 10 (2004), p. 21.

29. Hu Jintao, "Zai shoudu ge jie jinian Zhonghua Renmin Gongheguo xianfa fenbu shixing ershi zhounian dahui shang de jianghua" [Speech in the capital commemorating the twentieth anniversary of the promulgation and implementation of the Constitution], *People's Daily,* December 5, 2002, p. 1.

30. Jiang Zemin, *Quanmian jianshe xiaokang shehui, kaichuang Zhongguo tese shehuizhuyi shiye xin jumian* [Build a well-off society in an all-round way and work hard to create a new situation in building socialism with Chinese characteristics], in *Jiang Zemin wenxuan* [Selected works of Jiang Zemin] (Beijing: People's Publishing House, 2006), pp. 30, 555.

31. Wu Bangguo, "China to Ensure Socialist Legal System Shaped This Year" (www. npc.gov.cn/englishnpc/news/2010-03/09/content_1557574.htm); "Socialist System of Laws with Chinese Characteristics Enriches World's Legislative" (www.npc.gov.cn/pc/11_4/2011-03/11/content_1642244.htm).

32. Wan Li, "Zuohao renda zhuanmen weiyuanhui de gongzuo" [Doing well in the work of the special committees of the People's Congress], in *Wan Li wenxuan,* pp. 584–85.

33. Ibid., p. 598.

34. Guo Dingping, "Dangdai Zhongguo zhengdang yu guojia guanxi moshi de chonggou: Bijiao de shiye" [Reconstruction of the relationship between the political party and state in contemporary China: A comparative perspective], *Shehuikexue yanjiu* [Social science research], no. 1 (2009).

35. Scott Gordon, *Kongzhi guojia* [Controlling the state: Constitutionalism from ancient Athens to today], translated by Ying Qi and others (Nanjing: Jiangsu People's Publishing House, 2005), p. 4. See also Scott Gordon, *Controlling the State: Constitutionalism from Ancient Athens to Today* (Harvard University Press, 1999), p. 4.

36. Ibid.

37. Tanner, *Politics of Lawmaking in Post-Mao China,* pp. 13–35.

38. Quoted in Lin Laifan and Zhu Chenke, "Zhongguo shi 'xianzheng' de gainian fazhan shi" [History of the concept of "Chinese-style" constitutionalism], in *Zhengfa luntan* [Political and legal forum], no. 3 (2009), p. 38–49.

39. Zhang Youyu, *Zhang Youyu xueshu jinghualu* [The best academic works of Zhang Youyu] (Beijing: Beijing Normal University Press, 1988), p. 7.

40. Jiang Ping and others, "Market Economic Reform and Constitutionalism," in *Xianzheng jiangtang* [Distinguished lectures on constitutionalism], edited by Cai, p. 78.

41. Xia, *The People's Congresses and Governance in China,* pp. 9–24.

42. Pye, *Aspects of Political Development,* p. 93.

43. Verena Fritz and Alina Rocha Menocal, "Developmental States in the New Millennium: Concepts and Challenges for a New Aid Agenda," *Development Policy Review,* no. 5 (2007).

44. François Polet, "The Dynamism and Challenges of the Social Movements in the South," in *Globalization of Resistances,* edited by Liu Jianzhi (Beijing: People's Literature Publishing House, 2009), p. 18.

45. Hardin, *Liberalism, Constitutionalism, and Democracy,* p. 22.

46. Pu Xingzu, "Yi renda minzhu wei zhongdian, jixu tuijin Zhongguo minzhu zhengzhi fazhan" [Advance China's democratic political development with the focus on the democracy of the People's Congress], *Journal of Fudan University* (Social science edition), no. 5 (2005).

47. Bernard Manin, *The Principles of Representative Government* (Cambridge University Press, 1997), pp. 193–235.

48. Zhao Baoxu, *Zhengzhixue yu hexie shehui* [Political science and harmonious society] (Beijing: Peking University Press, 2009), p. 117.

49. Sun, *Quanguo renda zhidu yanjiu 1979–2000*, pp. 11, 13, 326–44.

50. Shi Hexing, *Guanxi, xiandu, zhidu* [Relationships, limits, and institutions] (Beijing: Peking University Press, 1996), pp. 249–51.

51. Robert Putnam, *Making Democracy Work: Civic Traditions in Modern Italy* (Princeton University Press, 1993); Carl Schmidt, *Xianfa xueshuo* [Constitutional theory], translated by Liu Feng (Shanghai: Shanghai People's Publishing House, 2005); *Xianfa de shouhuzhe* [Guards of the Constitution], translated by Li Juntao and Su Huijie (Beijing: Commercial Press, 2008).

52. Zhao, *Zhengzhixue yu hexie shehui*, p. 116.

53. Examples of this type of model include Pitman B. Potter, *From Leninist Discipline to Socialist Legalism: Peng Zhen on Law and Political Authority in the PRC* (Stanford University Press, 2003); and Xia, *The People's Congresses and Governance in China*, chap. 2.

54. For examples of models of this type, see Kenneth G. Lieberthal and David M. Lampton, eds., *Bureaucracy, Politics, and Decision Making in Post-Mao China* (University of California Press, 1992).

55. A variant on the bureaucratic politics model gives the NPC and the PCS thinner roles, as arenas in which other government, party, and societal actors contend to shape laws and exercise power. See Tanner, *The Politics of Lawmaking in Post-Mao China*. Tanner argues for an arena model, but his analysis often fits NPC participation in weakly institutionalized organizational politics.

56. On some of the functions discussed here, see Xia, *The People's Congresses and Governance in China;* Jacques deLisle, "Law and the China Development Model," in *In Search of China's Development Model,* edited by S. Philip Hsu, Yu-Shan Wu, and Suisheng Zhao (New York: Routledge, 2011); Susan L. Shirk, *The Political Logic of Economic Reform in China* (University of California Press, 1993).

57. Analyses of the NPC often find a link between the turn to law and the rise of the NPC, including Kevin J. O'Brien, *Reform without Liberalization: China's National People's Congress and the Politics of Institutional Change* (Cambridge University Press, 1990); Michael W. Dowdle, "Of Parliaments, Pragmatism, and the Dynamics of Constitutional Development: The Curious Case of China," *NYU Journal of International Law and Politics* 25, no. 1 (2002), p. 1; Randall P. Peerenboom, *China's Long March toward the Rule of Law* (Cambridge University Press, 2002).

58. Jacques deLisle, "Legalization without Democratization in China under Hu Jintao," in *China's Changing Political Landscape: Prospects for Democracy,* edited by Cheng Li (Brookings Press, 2008); Tanner, *Politics of Lawmaking,* chaps. 1, 10.

59. Many studies address potentially democratic NPC and PCS features, including Xia, *The People's Congresses and Governance in China;* O'Brien, *Reform without Liberalization;* Tanner, *Politics of Lawmaking;* Dowdle, "Of Parliaments, Pragmatism, and the Dynamics of Constitutional Development"; and Jiang Jinsong, *The National People's Congress of China* (Beijing: Foreign Languages Press, 2003).

60. Shi finds deep and somewhat surprising roots here, pointing to Mao's crabbed, substantive, anti-institutionalist notions of the constitution as a basic law that "fixes" certain principles, provides the people with a "clear and correct road to follow," and can be reduced to "democratic politics" (in Mao's illiberal, nonelectoral sense).

61. Shi recognizes limits to implementation of principles of ruling through—or in accordance with—law (以法執政, *yifa zhizheng*) and the complexity of relations between the CCP and the PCS and between policy and law, but he emphasizes progress from earlier, low baselines.

62. Shen Kui, "Is It the Beginning of the Era of the Rule of the Constitution? Reinterpreting China's 'First Constitutional Case,'" *Pacific Rim Law and Policy Journal* 12, no. 1 (2003), p. 199; Cai Dingjian, "The Development of Constitutionalism in the Transition of Chinese Society," *Columbia Journal of Asian Law* 19, no. 1 (2005), p. 1; Mo Jihong, "The Constitutional Law of the People's Republic of China and Its Development," *Columbia Journal of Asian Law* 23, no. 1 (2009), p. 137.

63. Keith J. Hand, "Using Law for a Righteous Purpose: The Sun Zhigang Incident and Evolving Forms of Citizen Action in the People's Republic of China," *Columbia Journal of Transnational Law* 45, no. 1 (2007), p. 114; Zhu Guobin, "Constitutional Review in China: An Unaccomplished Project or a Mirage?," *Suffolk University Law Review* 43, no. 3 (2010), p. 625.

64. Peerenboom, *China's Long March,* chap. 6; Minxin Pei, *China's Trapped Transition: The Limits of Developmental Autocracy* (Harvard University Press, 2006), chap. 2; and Cai Dingjian, "Constitutional Supervision and Interpretation in the People's Republic of China," *Journal of Chinese Law* 19, no. 2 (1995), p. 219.

65. Tanner, *Politics of Law Making,* chaps. 2, 10 ("inadvertent transitions" and democratic prospects); Dowdle, "Of Parliaments, Pragmatism, and the Dynamics of Constitutional Development," pp. 174–94 (NPC as a mechanism for "pluralism" if not full-fledged democracy); and Pei, *China's Trapped Transition,* pp. 72-80 (skeptical view of democratic prospects).

66. Jacques deLisle, "What's Happened to Democracy in China? Elections, Law, and Political Reform" (www.fpri.org/enotes/201004.delisle.democracyinchina.html (2010); Jiang, *National People's Congress,* chap. 7.

4

Political Consultation and Consultative Politics in China

LIN SHANGLI

Modern politics is structured around two spheres: the individuals and the state. On one hand, it stresses the rights and free development of individuals, and on the other, it emphasizes the holistic integration of the state, which provides the space for the development of individuals and ensures their safety. There is an inherent tension between the two spheres: the free development of individuals requires the protection of the state but also attempts to break through the constraints imposed by the state; the holistic integration of the state recognizes the diverse development of individuals but also requires individuals to have a common identification with the political system. The basic way to balance this tension is to develop a democratic system.

Every country has its own history and culture and thus its own development plan as formed in light of its own national conditions. Countries have different starting points in balancing this tension. Some may start out from the rights of the individual, and others may begin with state construction, thus resulting in different democratic development strategies and democratic systems.

China's political consultative system, a system of multiparty cooperation and political consultation led by the Chinese Communist Party (CCP), is a party system with Chinese characteristics. It is an important institutional establishment that was formed as the CCP was leading its revolution and founding the People's Republic of China (PRC). Although of indigenous origin, the system is highly modern and democratic in both value orientation and function. It balances the relationship among political parties, the state, and society and provides an important institutional infrastructure for ensuring solidarity and stability in the process of China's modernization and development.

People's Republic: Political Foundation of China's Political Consultation System

China's political consultation system is the name given to the system of multi-party cooperation and political consultation led by the CCP; political consultation is both the foundation and the core purpose of the system. It was on this basis that the CCP achieved multiparty cooperation, established the Chinese People's Political Consultative Conference (CPPCC), and, ultimately, founded the PRC. The political consultation system performs the function of cementing social solidarity and national integration. Our understanding of China's political consultation system must be based on the historical context and inherent political logic of that system; that is, it should start with the creation and development of China's party system.

The revolution of 1911 put an end to the imperial rule that had existed in China for several thousand years and led to the establishment of the republican era in China. It marked the beginning of China's modern party system development, which, however, was interrupted by failed attempts to create both a multiparty system and the Kuomintang's one-party autocracy. China now has a system of multiparty cooperation and political consultation, which is led by the CCP and was created by the CCP during the creation of the People's Republic and which coexists with the People's Republic.

"The party building the state" (党建国家, *dang jian guojia*) was the slogan and political logic of China's modernization. It was first practiced by the Kuomintang and then by the CCP. This political logic was the inevitable choice for China's modernization. It emphasized that to achieve democratic republicanism in China, a modern state must be established on the ruins of the Chinese empire, which had existed for several thousand years, and that the task of building the modern state rested on the shoulders of the ruling party. Both the Kuomintang and the CCP were founded to fulfill this historical mission. Eventually the CCP was chosen via revolution and by the Chinese people to lead China's modernization.

Soon after it came to power, the CCP set about building the new state apparatus and became the ruling party in 1949. In line with the guideline of establishing an all-around and deep-rooted connection with the Communist Party of Russia in ideology, theory, and organization, the CCP established the Chinese Soviet Republic in 1931 in Jiangxi; this association ended, however, soon after the CCP left Jiangxi and started the legendary 25,000-kilometer Long March northward in response to the campaigns of the Kuomintang. After the Long March and in the face of changed international and domestic situations, the CCP made an important adjustment to its revolutionary strategy. The party began to take as its historical mission repelling the Japanese invasion and saving the Chinese nation. Accordingly, the party changed its original conception of state power building and explicitly announced its intention to build a people's republic, not a republic of workers and peasants. Within the framework of the people's republic, the government would not just unite the working class, the peasantry, and the urban petite bourgeoisie; rather, it would embrace all elements, regardless of class backgrounds, that were willing to take part in the national revolution. For this purpose, the CCP advanced the goal of establishing a broad-based national united front to form a strong revolutionary force by joining all forces that could be mobilized. It was through this process that the history of CCP cooperation with other democratic parties began.

According to Mao Zedong, the Chinese Communist Party was able to win the Chinese revolution thanks to three principal factors: the united front, armed struggle, and party building. In fact, the united front has been at the core of the CCP's survival and development and is key to its leadership of China's modernization process. It was understood that to win the revolution, the working class had to establish a broad-based alliance of revolution with the peasantry and the petite bourgeoisie. In the beginning, the united front was merely a strategy and tactic used by the CCP to promote the alliance of the working class and the peasantry, a process by which the CCP constantly strengthened itself by mobilizing all kinds of forces and also weakened the enemy. However, with the formation of a new vision to build a people's republic, the united front evolved into an important political mechanism in building that republic.

The CCP states that in designing and building the people's republic it was neither borrowing the Western modern capitalist republic nor replicating the Soviet proletarian dictatorship but was instead creating a state power structure formed in light of China's actual conditions. According to Mao, the architect of the People's Republic, the numerous types of state systems in the world can be reduced to three basic kinds, according to the class character of their political power: republics under bourgeois dictatorship, republics under the dictatorship of the proletariat, and republics under the joint dictatorship of several revolutionary classes.[1] He believed that China, unlike the Soviet Union, was a semifeudal and semicolonial state and thus could only adopt the third state system, that is, become a republic under the joint dictatorship of several revolutionary classes. These classes, in his opinion, constituted the people of the state. Although he did not approve of indiscriminately imitating the Soviet model and establishing a republic under the dictatorship of a unitary class, basic Marxist and Leninist principles were adopted in the organization of the new regime. Accordingly, what was established was not the Western parliamentary system but rather a system of democratic centralism, the people's congress system (PCS), wherein state power belonged to the people. The result of Mao's design was a state with distinctively Chinese characteristics, a state system marked by the joint dictatorship of several revolutionary classes and a democratic centralist form of government.

The organic unity of the CCP allowed it to lead the revolution and build the united front and also to construct the people's republic. Mao once described the new democratic republic, designed during the period of the Anti-Japanese War, as a "republic of a united front against the Japanese invasion."[2] This unity was achieved because the strategy of the united front and the conception of the people's republic had a common foundation: China's social structure. China's social structure had two main characteristics. First, Chinese society, traditionally ordered according to kinship ties, constituted a high degree of intrinsic dispersion. With the dissolution of the imperial system, society became even more dispersed. That was why Sun Yat-sen famously said that Chinese society was like a plate of loose sand: a poor and weak state where the people are not closely bound together.

Second, because of China's agricultural tradition, social modernization in the country lacked modern class forces, meaning that to take on the task of the country's modernization, any single class or social force had to form an alliance with other classes through social mobilization and integration. In such a social structure, mobilization, solidarity, and integration were the preconditions for any attempt at revolution and modernization; without them, efforts would be doomed to failure. Therefore, the CCP built a close cooperative relationship with other democratic parties formed in the process of revolution and introduced the multiparty cooperation and political consultation system to unite all social forces in the effort to achieve social integration within a unified state system. When summarizing the basic experience of the Chinese revolution on the eve of the founding of the PRC, Mao said that the first stage had served to arouse the masses. The underlying logic of this statement is that it was the united front that made it possible to establish a real people's republic.

Political Orientation of China's Political Consultation System

Stemming from the party's building of the state and the logic of politics, the state system eventually put in place in China was a party-state system (党国体制, *dangguo tizhi*).[3] Under this system the party's leadership and the state's leadership were organically integrated, working in tandem to determine China's political life and development. China's political system is essentially a reformed and improved party-state system. In his article "On the Reform of the System of Party and State Leadership," a programmatic description of China's political reforms, Deng Xiaoping combined party leadership and state leadership in his planning of China's political reforms.[4] On the surface, the party-state system is the institutional result of the CCP's leadership in the Chinese revolution and state construction, but in essence, it is a historically inevitable representation of China's transition from a traditional empire to a modern state because it is a practical necessity. Under the party-state system, China's political structure is not merely two-dimensional, made up of the state and society. Rather it is three-dimensional, made up of the party, the state, and society. With such a power structure, the institutional arrangement at the state level is dependent on both society and the Chinese Communist Party. Nevertheless, though the party plays an important role in this system, society remains the critically decisive force because the foundation of CCP legitimacy is the people's democracy, the fundamental requirement of which is that the party and state leadership must guarantee and safeguard the people's fundamental interests.

The people's democracy emphasizes that the state is the people's state, that the government is the people's government, and that the military is the people's military. This political logic was established by the CCP at the beginning of the People's Republic. For the CCP to win leadership and fulfill the historical mission of leading state construction, it must unite the people—the peasantry, the intelligentsia, the working class, and all other social classes. The CCP's leadership cannot lead without the united front. The corollary is that the party-state system, the core of the CCP's leadership, must be based on the united front. In other words, the united front is both the leadership strategy of the CCP and the inherent mechanism of the party-state system.

One of the most important characteristics of the party-state system is that the party, rather than being the product of the running of the state system, shapes the state through its own party building. The CCP not only waged armed struggle but also, and more important, built a united front that gathered political resources and constructed a social foundation to ultimately seize state power. The party also made effective efforts to build and lead the united front to create a new society and state. Through this process the CCP established an extensive cooperative relationship with other parties. Although the alliance with the Kuomintang eventually failed, cooperative relationships with other democratic parties were formed and led to the establishment of the People's Republic of China. It was in the process of working with other parties to build a new state that the CCP established multiparty cooperation and the political consultation system. In this sense, the practice of the party building the state in China was not one party building the state but the building of the state through the leadership of one party and the cooperation of many parties. China's multiparty cooperation was formed not in the running of the state system but in building the state.

At the dawn of modernity in China, two major revolutionary parties appeared: the Kuomintang and the CCP, each with its own theories of state building and its own military forces. Owing to different political ideals, the two disagreed on major questions concerning the future of the Chinese nation, which gave rise to confrontation between them. It was in this political environment that the various minor democratic parties emerged and grew. Other than a very few parties that had their own military forces, most of these parties appeared as political forces whose political stances fell between those of the Kuomintang and the CCP. Therefore they were deemed to be intermediate forces, constituting the coexistence of the CCP, the Kuomintang, and the democratic parties in China's politics. This political situation appeared after the outbreak of the Anti-Japanese War, and the parties together became the key drivers of China's political change after the war ended.

The formal cooperation between the CCP and the democratic parties that began during the Anti-Japanese War was known as the "three-three" (one-third of power held by CCP, one-third by non-CCP left-wing progressives, and one-third by parties between left and right) governance system (三三制, *sansan zhi*). Given the historical conditions at the time, the practice was meant not to build the united front but to show the world that the CCP was pursuing a coalition government based on the alliance of the CCP and other democratic parties, not a one-party dictatorship or a one-party system. The CCP held that the "new democratic state based on an alliance of the democratic classes is different in principle from a socialist state under the dictatorship of the proletariat," like that in the Soviet Union.[5] Not long before the Anti-Japanese War ended, the CCP announced the mission to establish a coalition government rather than a government exclusively controlled by the Kuomintang. To the CCP, multiparty cooperation was both part of its effort to fight the one-party dictatorship of the Kuomintang and an institutional alternative to the Soviet Union's one-class, one-party dictatorship.

In its negotiations with the Kuomintang after the end of the war, the CCP proposed the convening of a multiparty political conference to establish a democratic coalition government. Because the Kuomintang felt that the term *political conference* carried too much political significance, the term *political consultative conference* was used instead. This event marked the beginning of the political consultative system in China. Although this conference generated a series of agreements regarding the peaceful building of a new state, these agreements became but scraps of paper afterward, with the outbreak of the civil war. In a bid to win the civil war, the CCP fought effectively against the Kuomintang while actively uniting and strengthening cooperation with the democratic parties. Following one particularly decisive victory on the battlefield on May 1, 1948, the CCP called for the convening of another political consultative conference attended by the democratic parties, people's organizations, and community leaders to discuss the establishment of a new state and democratic coalition government. One year later, the first meeting of the CPPCC was convened, tasked with establishing a new state. Unlike the previous conference, which was attended by all political forces regardless of political stance, this conference was attended by fourteen political parties and organizations, including the CCP, that had the shared political mission of overthrowing the Chiang Kai-shek regime, ending the Kuomintang's one-party rule, and establishing a democratic coalition government. With the convening of this conference and the establishment of the new government, the cooperative relationship between the CCP and the democratic parties was institutionalized as part of the new state system.

From this historical process it can be seen that neither the CCP nor the democratic parties were political parties in the Western sense; in the words of Zhou Enlai, "they have an indigenous origin in the soil of China."[6] The multiparty cooperative relationship between them was based not on running a democratic system but on the need to construct a democratic state. In other words, all democratic parties that cooperated with the CCP were formally institutionalized with the founding of the People's Republic. After the conference, some democratic parties held that their historical mission had been completed and that there was no need for them to continue to exist. The CCP insisted that the democratic parties continue to exist, however, holding that as long as there are classes there will be political parties, that the state power now in place was a "state power of the people's democratic united front" composed of various revolutionary classes whose foundation was multiparty cooperation, and that this cooperation would be on a long-term basis.[7]

From the beginning, the CCP held that the Chinese People's Political Consultative Conference, rather than being a provisional arrangement, should exist for a long period of time as an organizational and institutional platform to strengthen the united front and practice multiparty cooperation.[8] Thus the existing multiparty cooperation structure was not created from whole cloth but was the result of the historical process of China's revolution and state construction. It was this spirit of cooperation on which the PRC was founded, and the institutional arrangement of this cooperation determined the organization and development of the PRC.

In essence, multiparty cooperation should not be oversimplified as cooperation between one ruling party and eight other parties that participate in government affairs in a leadership-cooperation relationship. Instead, it is the foundation on which the existing state power system can strengthen and develop. The reason, simple yet important and therefore worth being repeated, is that in the political logic of the party building the state in China, multiparty cooperation and political consultation is a unique mechanism that determines that China's one-party system is not a one-party party-state system but a system based on one party's leadership and multiparty cooperation. This party-state system, while underscoring the fact that the state is built by parties and subject to party domination, also shows that the state is led not by a single dominant party but by a multiparty coalition with a core leadership subject to the supervision of the cooperating parties. Judging from the history of the PRC, the political consultative conference was distinctly a constituent assembly. Exercising the function of the National People's Congress, it not only adopted the quasi-constitutional Common Program and the Organic Law of the Central People's Government but also elected members of the central government. This laid a solid political foundation for the establishment of the state system of the PRC and the general progress of state construction. The most important achievement of this conference was that it based the political legitimacy of the PRC on the people's democracy, composed of various classes and political parties. The CCP was the leading, if not decisive, force of this people's democracy, and for it to fulfill that leading role, the CCP had to unite and form a coalition with other democratic parties and strengthen national solidarity. This also explains why the system of multiparty cooperation and political consultation led by the CCP has, since coming into being, been deemed China's basic political system: for the party-state system, it has a bearing on the legitimacy not only of the leadership and governance of the party but also of the state and state power.

Leadership, Cooperation, and Consultation: The Political Logic of China's Political Consultation System

The system of multiparty cooperation and political consultation led by the CCP is both a basic political system in China and a party system with Chinese characteristics. The multiparty cooperation system is a modern party system and in China is a system of multiparty cooperation. The political consultation system is the form of Chinese politics, which emphasizes the unique Chinese characteristics of the system and its actual political functions. Judging from the running of the system, neither multiparty cooperation nor political consultation can succeed without the leadership and governance of the Chinese Communist Party. Thus the system can be categorized as leadership of the ruling CCP with the cooperation of the parties participating in government administration.

As a party system with Chinese characteristics, the system of multiparty cooperation and political consultation organically integrates one-party leadership, multiparty cooperation, and general political consultation, where the leadership of the CCP is both a political precondition and an integral part of the system. Therefore, party leaders are also subject to the constraint and regulation of the system. With this understanding, we can use the logical relationship among leadership, cooperation, and consultation to present the political logic of China's party system. This relationship has two dimensions: the relationship among the actors and the relationship among the actions.

In the sphere of multiparty cooperation, the leadership of the Chinese Communist Party interacts with the democratic parties and the CCP as a whole. In the realm of political consultation the actors are the CCP, the democratic parties, and representatives from all circles of life. These three groups combine to form a stable triangle in China's political system. The number of actors involved in leadership and cooperation are relatively stable. However, the number and relationships of the actors in consultation have been changing and developing because the division of representative social groups in the people's political consultative conference changes along with the social structure. This shows the unique relationship between "one" and "multiple" in Chinese politics, which is mainly reflected in the following two aspects.

First, one-party leadership is involved with multiparty cooperation in a historically formed relationship that is fixed, its foundation being state power based on the coalition of various classes and parties and led by the CCP. According to statistics, there are a total of 32,000 government officials at the county level and above who are either members of democratic parties or personnel with no political affiliation, including 19 holding deputy leadership positions at ministries, commissions, departments, and bureaus directly under the State Council, the Supreme People's Court, and the Supreme People's Procuratorate; 29 deputy provincial governors, deputy chairmen, and deputy mayors in China's 31 provinces, autonomous regions, and municipalities directly under the central government; and 36 deputy mayors in 401 municipal (that is, prefectural, league, and district) people's governments. In 2007 two persons, one from a democratic party and the other with no political affiliation, were appointed as the minister of science and technology and the minister of health, respectively.

In addition, there are 964 counselors at the offices of counselors of the State Council and local governments and 1,665 librarians at the institutes of culture and history at the central and local levels who are either members of democratic parties or lack political affiliation. In addition, there are 87 supervisors, commissioners, and auditors at the Ministries of Education, Supervision, and Land and Resources, the National Auditing Administration, the State Administration of Taxation, the Special Procuratorate under the Supreme People's Procuratorate and 17,000 officials specially appointed by local government departments who are also either members of democratic parties or lack political affiliation.[9] In this regard, the multiparty structure is unchangeable, that is, the number of multiple parties is unchangeable; but what is changeable, and growing, is the number of people from the democratic parties who participate in government administration.

Second, one-party leadership is involved with multifaceted consultation in a developing relationship. The actors participating in multifaceted consultation include not only the eight major democratic parties but also other cross-sector organizations representing different social groups. This relationship is based on the people's democracy, in which all classes and social organizations have the right to participate in the political consultation process to have their voices heard in formulating the country's major policies. As the social structure and interest groups undergo changes as part of the process of general social development, so do the organizations and groups participating in the multifaceted consultation. The CPPCC has always maintained an open attitude toward cross-sector organizations and has constantly adjusted their composition.

The National Committee of the 2nd Chinese People's Political Consultative Conference was mainly composed of political parties, social groups, and specially invited personnel from twenty-nine cross-sector organizations, including democratic parties; personnel with no political affiliation; federations of women, youth, artists and writers, and industry and commerce; cooperatives; trade unions; natural science organizations, social science organizations, educational circles, the press, and the medical and health-care field; organizations committed to promoting friendly and cooperative relationships with foreign countries; social relief and welfare organizations; minority ethnic groups; overseas Chinese; and religious groups. By the end of the eighth meeting, five new groups had been added, bringing the total to thirty-four. With the constant increase of migrant workers across the country and the development of a harmonious society since the beginning of the twenty-first century, the National Committee of the 11th Chinese People's Political Consultative Conference added three seats for migrant workers. Although migrant workers were not introduced as a new cross-sector

Figure 4-1. *Relationship among the Actions Involved in Leadership, Cooperation, and Consultation*

Source: Xia Qi, "Renmin zhengxie jiebie de youlai" [A historical overview of CPPCC cross-sector organizations], *Zhongguo tongyi zhanxian* [China united front], no. 4 (2009), pp. 12–13.

organization, the action was enough to show the open attitude adopted by the CPPCC to changes in the social structure.[10]

Obviously, multiparty cooperation is a closed process, whereas multifaceted consultation is an open one, the former maintaining the stability of China's party-state system and the latter maintaining the system's adaptability and development. This is a major key to China's ability to maintain stability and development in spite of serious challenges from an increasingly pluralistic society.

The second dimension is the relationship among the actions involved in leadership, cooperation, and consultation, illustrated in figure 4-1. Simply speaking, the effectiveness and legitimacy of the CCP's leadership must be based on multiparty cooperation and multifaceted consultation whose stability and orderliness, in turn, are guaranteed by the CCP's leadership. In this sense, this relationship both supports China's party system and impacts the whole process of China's political construction and development. The most typical manifestation is consultation, which, created by and active in China's party system, is developed as an important resource of Chinese political life to create a form of democracy with Chinese characteristics. As a matter of fact, the CCP's self-transformation and construction efforts have also actively proceeded within this relationship to arrange and regulate the CCP's leadership and governance, so that one-party leadership and governance can be fully based on multiparty cooperation and multifaceted consultation, thereby optimizing the organizational system, institutional structure, and behavioral patterns of the CCP's leadership and governance in the process.

According to the political logic of China's party system, the system is not arranged to meet the requirements of the state system for parties but instead is intended to respond to the practical requirements of CCP leadership and the practice of the people's democracy. Therefore, the party system can run as a basic political system side by side with China's fundamental political system—the people's congress system—and develop in the process. This system supports both political parties and the state and thus has an important strategic value to China's political construction and development. Accordingly, since the reform and opening-up period began, the CCP, while constantly strengthening its political position and legal foundation, has made great effort to develop the natural resource of this system: political consultation.

Political Consultation: The Mechanisms of China's Political Consultation System

Political consultation, not imposed from outside but of an endogenous origin, has as its political foundation the CCP's establishment of the united front and founding of the People's Republic. It has four major inherent properties: multiparty coexistence, consultative deliberation, mutual supervision, and sharing weal and woe—all of which are indispensable to a political consultation system with distinctively Chinese characteristics.

The development of political consultation has been directly dependent on the construction and development of the system of multiparty cooperation and political consultation led by the CCP. As a whole, this system was not brought into full play until after the reform and opening up. This was partly owing to the all-around initiation of China's democratic process and partly owing to the need of China's social transformation and development for the support of more political resources.

The Constitution adopted in 1982 defined the nature, position, and role of the CPPCC for the first time, thus giving the system a constitutional basis. In 1989 the CCP formulated a policy on adhering to and improving the system of multiparty cooperation and political consultation led by the CCP. At the first session of the 8th National People's Congress in 1993, the provision that "the system of multiparty cooperation and political consultation led by the CCP will exist and develop for a long time"[11] was formally written into the Constitution, marking the beginning of the system's general institutionalization, standardization, and implementation. In this process, the CCP has become increasingly cognizant of the strategic value of the political consultation dimension of this system to China's democratic development and has taken political consultation and election as two major forms of China's democracy.[12]

Political consultation in China's system occurs in two forms: between the CCP and the democratic parties and within the CPPCC. The former mainly takes the form of democratic consultative meetings, workshops, and symposia. From 1990 to late 2006, more than 230 such consultations were held at the initiative of the CCP Central Committee, the State Council, and other relevant government authorities.[13] Political consultation has not only become more institutionalized, standardized, and procedure based, but it features much wider and more diverse participation.

At the CPPCC level of political consultation, the democratic parties are also an important force. From 1990 to 2006, the democratic parties and their CPPCC members submitted a total of more than 2,400 proposals, including many important ones about state construction and development.[14] Relatively speaking, the main institutional platform of China's political consultation system is the CPPCC. According to the CPPCC constitution as amended in 2004, "The CPPCC is a patriotic united front organization of the Chinese people, serving as a key mechanism for multiparty cooperation and political consultation under the leadership of the Chinese Communist Party and a major manifestation of socialist democracy."[15]

Both the CCP leadership and China's state construction have an urgent need for the CPPCC to generate more solidarity and more democracy. These two inherent themes endow the political consultation of the CPPCC with two basic missions: to create social solidarity and state integration and to create democracy, thereby fulfilling the constitutional right of the people as the masters of the country. The two missions, both based on political consultation, are the two sides of the same coin, where solidarity is created through democratic consultation and effective democratic consultation is built on solidarity.

As the coordination of interests is the foundation of social solidarity and state integration, the purpose of democratic consultation is to express and coordinate the interests of different social strata. In China's political life, the CPPCC is not an organ of state power and does not have a substantial influence on the formulation of policies. As a result, political consultation has only a symbolic meaning and neither fulfills its own mission nor generates substantial political effects easily. To overcome this defect, in recent years the CCP has directly incorporated political consultation as an important feature of the country's political process that exists under the power structure of the party and the state, with the goal of giving the CPPCC substantial influence over the exercise of state power. In 2005 the CCP promulgated the Opinions on Further Strengthening the Building of the System of Multiparty Cooperation and Political Consultation Led by the CCP, which stipulates that "political consultation is an important component of the system of multiparty cooperation and political consultation led by the CCP, an important mechanism for ensuring scientific and democratic decisionmaking, and an important way for the CCP to improve its governance capacity. To incorporate political consultation in the decisionmaking process and subject the decisions on and implementation of matters of major importance to consultation is an important principle of political consultation."[16]

With this institutional arrangement, the CPPCC's functions of democratic supervision and participation in the administration and discussion of state affairs are increasingly being fulfilled through the function of political consultation. Although just begun, this arrangement will provide an important political guarantee and institutional support for the general development of the CPPCC's political resources. Based on this institutional arrangement in the context of China's political system and political process, political consultation resources can be developed from three major dimensions within the CPPCC system and in the field of policy.

Within the CPPCC system, political consultation is mainly shown in participation, discussion, and cooperation. Institutionalized participation is used to ensure that all have equal political rights, thus creating a situation of pluralistic coexistence. As any participation is an expression of interests, the participation itself is a form of political consultation. The purpose of discussion of government affairs is to ensure democratic and scientific decisionmaking in public policies through the expression of opinions, policy consultation, and democratic review. Cooperation is encouraged with the purpose of ensuring the organic unity of governance and participation in governance as well as of consolidating state power through joint research, joint deliberation, and cooperative governance not only among the parties but between the parties and cross-sector organizations and between the parties and the government as well. Political consultation enables the CPPCC to break through the various constraints and barriers among these groups by establishing various mechanisms of contact and communication and various platforms of cooperation.

The formulation of public policy operates in line with the principle of political consultation expressed in the CPPPC constitution: "The decisions on and implementation of matters of major importance must be subject to consultation."[17] The political system absorbs public opinion and expressions of interests, formulates policies and laws, and promotes social governance and development, thus consolidating its legitimacy. This involves the relationships among the parties, the state, and society; between the expression of interests and the allocation of resources; between public opinion and democracy; and between political legitimacy and governance effectiveness. Thus the process has bearing not only on the CPPCC itself but also on the entire political system.

In this dimension, political consultation is seen in integration of interests, oversight of policymaking, and democratic governance. Relevant interests are balanced and reflected in policies through pre-decisionmaking consultation. In policy consultation, the formulation of specific public policies is subjected to an institutionalized process of democratic supervision made up of such mechanisms as reporting, hearings, and consultation. This consultation is mainly meant to ensure that policies are democratic, scientific, and in the public interest. In consultation regarding democratic governance, democratic governance based on multiparty cooperation is achieved through the discussion of government affairs by the parties and through their participation and cooperation in state governance. This consultation mainly centers on multiparty cooperation, governance cooperation, and participation cooperation.

The three dimensions of running the CPPCC and the three dimensions of the CPPCC's contribution to the political process are not interchangeable. The former are based on the logic of the political consultation system, while the latter are mainly based on the political logic of consultation preceding and accompanying decisionmaking. Therefore, the improvement of the former is mainly achieved through the institutional and organizational development of the CPPCC itself, while the improvement of the latter is mainly achieved through the optimization of the decisionmaking and governance processes and mechanisms. This means that the development of political consultation in China is dependent not only on the construction of the CPPCC and the system of multiparty cooperation and political consultation led by the CCP but also on the progress and development of democracy and the rule of law in China's overall political process.

CPPCC: Growing with China's Political Process

The source of legitimacy of the PRC cannot be separated from the CPPCC because the CPPCC served as a constituent assembly that bred the political system of the People's Republic. In China's contemporary politics, the CPPCC is both the organization through which the CCP maintains and builds the united front and an important organization by which the Chinese people exercise their democratic rights, participate in the country's political life, and practice the people's democracy. It is also both the core organ of the system of multiparty cooperation and political consultation led by the CCP and the major organizational mechanism through which China implements and develops consultative democracy. Despite its constitutionally endowed position, the CPPCC is not vested by the Constitution with substantial power. For this reason, the CPPCC has been referred to as nothing but a pretty vase in Chinese politics.

The CPPCC, however, is not at all an insignificant decoration in China's political system. With its unique historical position and multiple functional roles, it is an indispensable and integral component of the system. Before the reform and opening up, it was largely put on the shelf, like other organizations and organs of China's political system, including the People's Congress, the government, the people's courts, the people's procuratorates, and even the CCP leadership during the Cultural Revolution, when the slogan "Kick aside party committees to make revolution" was popular. After the reform and opening-up period and the move toward normalization of China's political system, the CPPCC was also restored and began to function normally.[18] Lacking substantial power, it has not been able to develop as fast as other more powerful organizations and organs and has thus played a less important role. However, this is not to say that it is insignificant. Because the system of multiparty cooperation and political consultation led by the CCP has been written into the Constitution, the CPPCC has experienced substantial development since the reform and opening up began.

The reason the CPPCC has undergone substantial development since the reform and opening up began has to do, of course, with China's embrace of economic marketization and political democratization. More important, though, it is also directly related to the excellent accord between the functions of the CPPCC and the inherent needs of China's actual politics.

The reform and opening up opened China's politics to challenges brought by invigorated political participation, by social pluralism following marketization, and by economic and social development requiring scientific decisionmaking on the part of the government. These three challenges all converged on one core: the multilayer tension between unitary leadership and multifaceted structure. The institutional resource of China's existing political system that is capable of alleviating this tension is the system of multiparty cooperation and political consultation led by the CCP, with its strategic platform being the CPPCC.

A comparison of the different versions of the CPPCC constitution promulgated or amended since 1954 shows that the position of the CPPCC has undergone a process of enrichment. Before the 1980s, the CPPCC was merely defined as a united-front organization. At the fifth session of the 5th CPPCC National Committee in 1982, a new constitution positioned the CPPCC not just as a united-front organization but also as an important platform for developing socialist democracy through multiparty cooperation and political consultation. In 2004 the second session of the 10th CPPCC National Committee adopted the updated version of the constitution, which explicitly defines the CPPCC as a united-front organization, an important organ of multiparty cooperation and political consultation, and an important platform for developing socialist democratic politics. Obviously, with the progress of China's political construction, the CPPCC has gained a stronger political position and has come to play an increasingly important role. Despite limited constitutional powers, the CPPCC will inevitably gain substantial influence on the organs of state power because of its continuous participation in the political process of the party and the state and its continuous influence over national policies.

One important reason why the CPPCC has been able to be integrated with China's political process lies in the construction and development of the CPPCC itself since the reform and opening up. This has occurred mainly as a result of functional enrichment and institutional regulation.

The CPPCC is meant to play multiple roles in China's political life. To fulfill these roles, it must have corresponding power. In early 1989 the Chinese Communist Party made clear its intent to give substance to the functions of the CPPCC. In a reply to a suggestion regarding CCP-led multiparty cooperation early that year, Deng ordered that "a plan on democratic parties participating in the administration and discussion of government affairs be formulated within one year and promulgated the next year."[19] Soon thereafter, on January 27, the fourth session of the 4th CPPCC National Committee adopted the Interim Provisions on Political Consultation and Democratic Supervision, which defined the functions of the CPPCC as political consultation and democratic supervision. In 1994, five years later, the second session of the 8th CPPCC National Committee adopted an amendment to the CPPCC constitution that expanded the functions of the CPPCC to three: political consultation, democratic supervision, and participation in the administration and discussion of government affairs. However, the constitution explicitly defined only the first two functions. It was in the Provisions of the CPPCC National Committee on Political Consultation, Democratic Supervision, and Participation in the Administration and Discussion of Government Affairs, adopted at the 9th CPPCC National Committee in the following year, that the function of "participation in the administration and discussion of government affairs" (参政议政, *can zheng yi zheng*) was explicitly defined. The latest CPPCC constitution, amended at the second session of the

10th CPPCC National Committee in 2004, not only defines the three major functions of the CPPCC but also provides for the content and methods of fulfillment of these three functions.

Institutional regulation, though closely associated with functional enrichment, has a greater influence on the development of the CPPCC because institutional regulation is meant to achieve the institutionalization, normalization, and procedural standardization of the CPPCC. This effort was initiated in the mid-1990s with two missions: to put the performance of duties and the fulfillment of functions of the CPPCC within an institutional, normalized, and procedural framework to ensure the fulfillment of the functions of the CPPCC, and, generally, to improve the organizational soundness, procedural rules, and running of the CPPCC through institutionalization, normalization, and procedural standardization. These changes enabled the CPPCC to become an organization with substantial capabilities for consultation, supervision, and participation in the administration and discussion of government affairs. In 2006, after nearly ten years of exploration and practice, the Central Committee of the Chinese Communist Party promulgated the Opinions on Strengthening the Work of the CPPCC, which expounded the nature, position, and role of the CPPCC and stipulated the working principles as well as the processes and principles of performance of duties of the CPPCC.[20]

Although the relevant documents in 1989 emphasized the important role of the CPPCC in advancing democratic and scientific decisionmaking, they did not emphasize political consultation as an integral part of the decisionmaking process. With the promulgation of the Provisions of the CPPCC National Committee on Political Consultation, Democratic Supervision, and Participation in Administration and Discussion of Government Affairs in 1995, political consultation was made an integral part of the decisionmaking and decision-implementation process. Since then, the CPPCC has become an indispensable link in China's political process. Although the CPPCC still acts as an organization of political consultation rather than an organ of state power, its participation has become a precondition for the legitimacy of policies and decisions. As long as political consultation is an integral part of legitimacy for the policies of the party and the state, the CPPCC will be a substantial force that, though not constitutionally empowered, can influence the political process and check other organs of power in the political process, including the Chinese Communist Party. The party has not only made political consultation an important form of China's democracy, but it also made it an explicit requirement for party committees at various levels when it promulgated the Opinions on Strengthening the Work of the CPPCC in 2006: "Party committees at various levels must attach high importance to the political consultation with the CPPCC by making unified deployments and coordination and conscientiously arranging for its implementation."[21]

Local party committees have made their own exploratory efforts to improve the system and mechanism of political consultation. There are three common practices in this regard. In the first, the party committee works out the political consultation plan for the year and, based on the major tasks of the year or the suggestions of the party group of the CPPCC, reviews and determines the subjects of consultation before undertaking a unified deployment, implementation, and evaluation, thereby strengthening coordination between consultation and the decisionmaking and implementation of policies. A second common practice has been to follow the policy that requires leaders of the party committee, the People's Congress, and the disciplinary inspection commission to participate in political consultation activities and also authorizes leaders and members of the CPPCC to attend the relevant meetings of those groups. The third common practice is the imposition of time limits and other requirements both on party committees that handle suggestions made regarding the CPPCC and on government departments that give feedback in order to give substance to the function of the CPPCC in participating in and influencing the decisionmaking process of the party and the government.[22]

The participation of the CPPCC in China's political process has not only changed the procedure of China's political process and power structure but has also greatly advanced the development of the CPPCC system itself. For example, the CPPCC submitted some 1,500 proposals in the seventeen years before the Cultural Revolution; yet it submitted more than 78,000 proposals in the thirty years following the start of reform and opening up, including more than 5,000 submitted after the formation of the 11th CPPCC National Committee.[23] The inclusion of the CPPCC in China's political process has created a mutually promoting relationship between the CPPCC and the system of multiparty cooperation and political consultation led by the Chinese Communist Party.

Consultative Politics: The Contribution of Political Consultation to China's Political Development

China's political consultation system is characterized by the organic unity among one-party leadership, multiparty cooperation, and multifaceted consultation. This form of political life has effectively responded to the two major challenges facing China's political development: that posed by social pluralism to unitary leadership and that posed by economic marketization to China's existing democratic system. Of course, responding to challenges is not the same thing as solving them, and the key to resolving the problems that result is the development of the CPPCC system itself and its political consultation resources.

Over the past decade, China has made continuous and productive efforts to develop the CPPCC system and its political consultation resources. Both the country's leadership and academia view political consultation as having new potential and providing resources for the development of democratic politics with Chinese characteristics. The Western concept of deliberative democracy was soon endorsed by China's leadership and even equated, by some, with China's political consultation. For a time, the concept of deliberative democracy became widely popular in China.

However, China's political consultation, though indeed a form of democracy, is different from Western deliberative democracy. The latter emerged in response to perceived weaknesses of representative democracy; it allows direct participation of citizens in in the decisionmaking process through direct communication and consultation. Deliberative democracy serves to prevent government decisionmaking from straying from the interests of the citizens. In contrast, the primary purpose of Chinese political consultation is to promote solidarity, alliance, and the balance and coordination of different interests. The relationships such consultation serves to coordinate are those among different social strata, political parties, social groups, and social organizations. What China practices is the people's democracy, with its basic mission being the creation of a political life in which the people, as master of the country, extensively participate in state affairs and jointly manage the state.

Concluding Thoughts

In the studies of Chinese politics, two important subjects are often neglected. The first is the Chinese Communist Party itself. The party is thought to be too colossal, too complicated, and too unique to be meaningfully approached and grasped. This neglect makes it difficult to arrive at an informed understanding of the foundation of China's politics. This difficulty is often experienced by scholars who attempt to explain China's politics solely in a dual state-society framework. Owing to the status of the CCP as China's most powerful establishment, Chinese politics must be approached and explained as a triangular construct comprised of the party, the state, and society (see figure 4-1).

The second is the system of multiparty cooperation and political consultation, specifically the CPPCC. The consultative conference is thought to be too empty of meaning, too China specific, and simply out of place in a modern democracy. This neglect makes it difficult to assess the adaptability and capacity for innovation of the Chinese political system. Although in classic Western political theory it may be found lacking in every way, China's political system has exhibited dynamism and development, not only promoting democracy as a universal value but also maintaining the system's unique political identity. One of the many secrets to the creation of this wonder is China's political consultation system, which provides room for maneuvering and rich political resources for China's political construction and development. Understanding the long-term trend in China's political development requires a similar grasp of the potential development of China's political consultation system.

After only twenty years of substantial construction and development, China's political consultation system is not yet mature. It is one thing to see the great potential of this system and quite another to effectively tap and make use of this potential. The CCP's response to this challenge has mainly focused on elevating the position of the political consultation system and strengthening the institutionalization, procedural standardization, and normalization of political consultation to make this an integral part of China's political process. In future efforts, then, the party should focus on participation in the administration and the discussion of government affairs by generally elevating the political consultation system's political capacity and institutional strength to support multifaceted expression, participation, and cooperation. This is also an inevitable requirement to develop consultative politics. To this end, China's political consultation system remains in need of new concepts, mechanisms, and horizons.

COMMENT
JOSEPH FEWSMITH

Lin Shangli depicts the uniqueness of the Chinese political system as revolving around multiparty cooperation under the leadership of the Chinese Communist Party and a system of political consultation. From the efforts of the CCP to woo the noncommunist, democratic parties in the post–World War II period, unitedfront efforts led to the Common Program, China's first constitution, and to the development of the Chinese People's Political Consultative Conference. Lin recognizes that the CPPCC is widely regarded as empty and ornamental, but he nevertheless argues that it is fundamental to the legitimacy of the political system for historical reasons and that it is key to providing stability and better decision-making in the reform system as a rapidly pluralizing society pulls against the monolithic (一元化, *yiyuanhua*) leadership of the CCP. This system of political consultation (政治协商, *zhengzhi xieshang*) distinguishes the CCP from the Communist Party of the former Soviet Union and from single-party dictatorship.

Lin is well aware that the system of multiparty cooperation did not fare well in the first twenty-nine years of the People's Republic of China, being cast aside in the Great Leap Forward and the Cultural Revolution, but he argues that it is essential to the healthy functioning of the system—and those periods of political extremism certainly did not exemplify a healthy political system. So his case for political consultation, the role of the CPPCC, and the development of various forms of consultative democracy (协商民主, *xieshang minzhu*) rests with the reform era, when, he argues, the CCP has increasingly worked to incorporate diverse interests and wide-ranging expertise into the decisionmaking process.

The idea that there is tension between diversifying societal, economic, and political interests, on one hand, and the CCP, which would prefer central-ized leadership, on the other, is consistent with Kenneth Jowitt's notion that in Leninist systems a period of exclusive leadership, in which the party defines its interests against the diversity of society, gives way in the reform period to inclusivity, which tries to co-opt diverse interests. However, whereas Jowitt sees such inclusivity as eroding and destroying Leninist systems, Lin argues that mul-tiparty cooperation can constrain such tensions and even improve the politi-cal process by incorporating different interests into the decisionmaking process, part of political consultation.[24] Lin's argument draws on recent discussions of *xieshang minzhu,* which is usually translated as "deliberative democracy" but is better understood as consultative democracy. The two concepts differ, and it is useful to clarify the difference. The discourse in the West over the past two decades about deliberative democracy has revolved around a concern that demo-cratic institutions, despite being established for one or two hundred years, are not sufficiently democratic. That is to say, the concern has been that despite elections, freedom of assembly, freedom of speech, and other guarantees of free political competition, this type of formal democracy has led to an estrangement between citizens and government; deliberative democracy seeks ways to close this gap and make democracies more democratic. China's situation is different. China, as Lin says, has a unitary leadership (一元领导, *yiyuan lingdao*) existing in an increasingly pluralistic society. He is looking to consultative democracy to bridge that gap, or, as he puts it, to reduce the tension between these two aspects of contemporary Chinese politics.

It is worth taking a minute to probe the difference between these two situ-ations lest we use a single term to gloss over two situations that are profoundly different. Democratic systems (it really is impossible to call these Western, since Korea, Taiwan, and India, among other countries, are democratic but clearly not Western) accept as a basic premise that the engagement of societal groups will produce a government that reflects the interest of society. It is a matter not of the state versus society but rather of a diverse society generating an effective state. Advocates of deliberative democracy fear that this democratic process has been hijacked by elite interests, including corporations, preventing the pluralism of society from being reflected accurately in the state. Thus they see deliberative mechanisms as a way to reduce the influence of these interests and to close the gap between state and society. But the point is that advocates of deliberative democracy do not see a tension between state and society; on the contrary, strong states are built on a diversity of viewpoints and interests. It is only when certain interests become overly strong that this process is distorted and remedial measures are needed.

Chinese discussions of consultative democracy revolve around a different premise. The CCP is premised on unitary leadership, but society has become increasingly pluralized (多元化, *duoyuanhua*) over the past three decades. There are increasing numbers of societal interests in China, ranging from chambers of commerce to workers' unions to environmental activists to "netizens." So what many people, including Lin, want to do is to find mechanisms, such as consultative democracy and political consultation, that can reduce the tension between the unitary state and the increasingly diverse society, thereby increasing the legitimacy of the state and reducing social conflict. Since the premises of democratic polities and China are different, it seems appropriate to use the term *deliberative democracy* in trying to work through the problems of democratic polities and the term *consultative democracy* when discussing the efforts to work through a different set of problems in China.

Another issue is the institutions to which one is applying the term *consultative democracy*. Lin focuses his discussion on the CPPCC and multiparty cooperation, which raises the issues of legitimacy and the absence of pluralism in the political system but is fairly narrow. In recent years, there have been lots of experiments with various sorts of consultative mechanisms. The most interesting ones have been in the townships of Zeguo and Xinhe, in Wenling, Zhejiang province. Zeguo is the site where He Baogang and James Fishkin have organized regular citizens, chosen randomly, to give their opinions on the priority to be assigned to various public works projects. As their work amply demonstrates, the opinions of these randomly chosen citizens, reflective, it is hoped, of broader public opinion, has differed significantly from the a priori assumptions of town officials. There is nothing binding about the opinions given by this group of citizens; they are advisory (though the township has wisely followed this advice). So this is purely a consultative mechanism.

Xinhe township has carried out the more extensive experiment. It has opened up the township budget to the scrutiny of the local people's congress as well as to local citizens. It is a process that combines democratic consultative meetings (民主恳谈会, *minzhu kentanhui*), another consultative mechanism that has been practiced in Wenling since 1998, with the local people's congress. This is interesting because it combines a consultative mechanism with a legal body. As Lin notes, the CPPCC is not a power organ; it has no authority to make binding decisions. But the people's congress, at least in theory, does. In Xinhe township, after listening to reports from three democratic consultation meetings (covering society, industry, and agriculture), delegates to the congress discuss the budget. They do not have the authority to change the amount of the budget (not even to lower it), but they can make resolutions to move funds from one area of the budget to another. These resolutions are then discussed and voted on. They then become binding, moving them out of the realm of being purely consultative. Nevertheless, given the limited power of local people's congresses, this practice can still be viewed as consultative, and that is the way Chinese researchers describe it.

Another form of consultation involves the many chambers of commerce and trade associations that have grown up in recent years. The development of these trade associations has been best documented in Wenzhou, but they exist in many other places as well (though they seem to be more developed in south China than in the north). As nongovernmental organizations, trade associations have no power to make policy, but they can advocate for policies, and they are frequently consulted when local government draws up new regulations to govern commercial activity.

The reasons for the development of such trade associations, at least in China's more entrepreneurial areas, seem pretty clear. There are two fundamental reasons, one reflecting the interests of the state and the other reflecting the interests of business. In a highly competitive economy such as that of Wenzhou, there was a strong tendency for merchants to undercut other merchants by using ever-cheaper materials. In 1985 the Lucheng District government demonstrated its displeasure by burning some 5,000 pairs of shoes in Hangzhou. The government of the district where Wenzhou's shoe industry was concentrated was worried that Wenzhou's increasing reputation for producing shoddy goods would undermine the economy of the district and, of course, the revenues of the government. So it acted to organize the Lucheng District Shoe Association and to draw up regulations governing standards of production.

In drawing up these regulations, the government consulted closely with representatives of the local shoe industry, which points to the second reason: business is simply more nimble than government. Businesses that are controlled by government in a top-down fashion will be less efficient and competitive. Businesses need, to some extent, to be self-governing. So trade associations provide, to a certain extent, a bottom-up mechanism that can reflect the needs and interests of business while still not being completely free of government. When they work effectively, they maintain a balance between a degree of autonomy, on one hand, and a close proximity to government, on the other.

Of course, businesses do not express their interests simply through such consultative bodies as trade associations; increasingly, entrepreneurs are appointed to the local or national CPPCC or the National People's Congress. Such appointments provide reputational rewards for successful entrepreneurs, but they also provide something very valuable to entrepreneurs: legitimate access. Of course, this inclusion in the CPPCC and the People's Congress allows business people to influence policy, but it also allows for inside dealing.

Another form of consultation that has developed in recent years is hearings (听证会, *tingzhenghui*). These have been less studied because they are still only beginning to develop. The role of hearings is still limited. For instance, there does not yet seem to be an assumption that neighborhood associations might testify before a people's congress on the impact a proposed road construction project will have on their lives. Will it bring in more business? Will it cut neighborhoods apart? Will those forced to relocate be adequately compensated? If one wants to reduce the tension between one-party leadership and an increasingly pluralistic society, as Lin hopes, then it seems a greater role for nongovernmental organizations at all levels of governance is a necessity. Although the CPPCC can play a role, consultation need not be limited to the CPPCC.

It is also important to say something about intraparty democracy. Some people perhaps do not include this as a form of consultation, but others do, so it is worth considering. Intraparty democracy has basically two forms: public recommendation and public election (公推共选, *gongtui gongxuan*) and public recommendation and direct election (公推直选, *gongtui zhixuan*). The difference, simply put, is that in the former, the final decision is made by the local party committee, whereas in the latter, the final selection is made by the whole body of party members in a given locale. In short, the latter is significantly more "democratic" than the former, though both forms expand the number of people participating in the selection of personnel, including the party secretary and other office holders.

There are several reasons why the CCP has adopted these and other forms of intraparty democracy: to break up the personalization of power at local levels, to add checks and balances on the power of the local party secretary, to expand the talent pool considered for promotion, and to involve more party members in party affairs. Both of these systems move beyond what we normally consider consultative because the final decision is given to a larger body. In the case of public recommendation and public election, the selection is made by a type of electoral college (选举团, *xuanjutuan*), which—made up of 100 or 200 people—is significantly larger than the small group of three or four people (and often just the party secretary) who have traditionally made decisions on the selection and promotion of cadres. Public recommendation and direct election expands the pool of electors to all party members and is thus considerably more democratic, though it should be noted that candidate selection is still a tightly held process. Public recommendation and direct election also raise the "danger" that local party leaders will appeal to a local constituency, rather than to their superiors, and thus run the risk of clashing with the traditional organizational principle of "the party controls the cadres" (党管干部, *dang guan ganbu*).

This brief survey of various forms of consultation in contemporary China suggests that consultation has emerged as an important form of political participation in recent years. It has emerged, as Lin suggests, to bridge the gap between a still unitary political leadership system and an increasingly pluralistic society. To the extent that it can do this, it reinforces the legitimacy of the party and "harmonizes" the different interests in society. Yet the single most effective form of consultation looked at above is probably the participatory budget making of Xinhe township in Wenling. Intraparty democracy shows some potential, but it has generally not yet been institutionalized. Both of these types of experiments combine an element of consultation with an organ that has power, either the National People's Congress or the party itself.

This finally leads us back to the CPPCC. The CPPCC has a unique role in Chinese politics, as Lin points out, because it was "present at the creation." The various noncommunist parties that participate in the CPPCC were critical in the CCP's final push for power, and they played an important role in legitimizing the People's Republic by approving the Common Program, which, as noted, acted as the Constitution of the newly established PRC. But, of course, the CPPCC played a lesser role after the what the Chinese call "socialist transformation" and the "high tide of socialism." Many figures in the CPPCC were prominent victims of the Cultural Revolution. It was only after the death of Mao and the launching of reforms that the CPPCC was restored. But its functions have never been broad. It is true, as Lin points out, that the CPPCC at various levels makes large numbers of suggestions, some of which are adopted by the party, but it lacks the power to force the government to adopt its views. Similarly, members of the noncommunist parties have been appointed to various positions, contributing their expertise and prestige. But the CPPCC, in and of itself, is a consultative organ with no power. The question is whether it or similar consultative bodies can bridge the gap between the unitary leadership of the CCP and the increasingly diverse interests of society. Lin's tracing of the efforts to "perfect" multiparty cooperation suggests that this goal remains elusive.

If the CPPCC has little prestige and no power, then it has a difficult time functioning as a consultative body. Would it be possible to enhance the prestige of the CPPCC and thus make it a more effective consultative body? Perhaps, but that seems difficult. To acquire prestige, the CPPCC would need to become an effective consultative body, and the noncommunist parties participating in it would have to have greater roles in Chinese society, which seems unlikely. Ambitious young people generally join the CCP, which is where prestige and power lie. Although there are some capable people in the noncommunist parties, they are not permitted to play the sort of roles in China that would give them real prestige. And without real prestige, neither society nor the CCP will pay much attention to their views.

Lin has limited his discussion to the post-1949 period, but the topic of incorporating diverse interests into an effective political system runs throughout political debates and development of the past century and beyond. As local interests developed their own economic, social, and political interests in the late nineteenth and early twentieth centuries, it seemed possible that China might develop a liberal democratic system, but the force of integrationalist ideology of the long imperial period and the weakness of societal interests in the face of powerful political and military forces doomed that effort. So China followed a revolutionary course of development, first with the Kuomintang and then with the CCP. The Kuomintang faced the same issues that Lin raises and responded to them by developing a corporatist framework. This framework was ultimately not successful because of foreign invasion and domestic revolution, so now the CCP faces the same issues as earlier political regimes. Perhaps Lin is right that consultative mechanisms can somehow reconcile diverse social interests with unitary political leadership, but one suspects that including some socioeconomic interests into these mechanisms still leaves many people out of the system, and that issue will have to be addressed eventually.

Notes

1. Mao Zedong, "Xin minzhuzhuyi lun" [On new democracy], in *Mao Zedong xuanji* [Selected works of Mao Zedong], vol. 2 (Beijing: People's Publishing House, 1991), p. 675.

2. Ibid., p. 676.

3. China's party-state system has its own characteristics because the foundation of its state power is not a single class but the alliance of multiple classes. Therefore, it is not the

same as the term *party-state* as used by Western scholars. For the typical Western view, see the Italian scholar Giovanni Sartori's analysis of the party-state system: Giovanni Sartori, *Zhengdang yu zhengdang tizhi* [Parties and party systems], translated by Wang Mingjin (Shanghai: Commercial Press, 2006), pp. 66–75.

4. Deng Xiaoping, "Dang he guojia lingdao zhidu de gaige" [On the reform of the system of state leadership], in *Deng Xiaoping wenxuan* [Selected works of Deng Xiaoping], vol. 2 (Beijing: People's Publishing House, 1993), pp. 320–43.

5. Mao Zedong, "Lun lianhe zhengfu" [On coalition government], in *Mao Zedong xuanji*, vol. 3 (Beijing: People's Publishing House, 1991).

6. Zhou Enlai, "Fahui renmin minzhu tongyi zhanxian jiji zuoyong de ji ge wenti" [Several questions about giving scope to the active role of the people's democratic united front], in *Renmin zhengxie zhongyao wenxuan xuanbian* [Selection of important CPPCC documents] (Beijing: Zhongyang wenxian chubanshe [Central Party Literature Press], 2009), vol. 1, p. 109.

7. *Zhongguo renmin zhengzhi xieshang huiyi gongtong gangling* [The Common Program of the Chinese People's Political Consultative Conference], in *Renmin zhengxie zhongyao wenxuan xuanbian*, vol. 1, p. 80.

8. Zhou Enlai, "Guanyu renmin zhengxie de ji ge wenti" [Several questions concerning the CPPCC], September 7, 1949, in *Renmin zhengxie zhongyao wenxuan xuanbian* (cpc.people.com.cn/GB/69112/75843/75874/75992/5181293.html), p. 35.

9. Du Qinglin, "Gaige kaifang sanshi nian duo dang hezuo he zhengzhi xieshang zhidu de xin fazhan" [New development of the system of multiparty cooperation and political consultation in the thirty years since the reform and opening up], *People's Daily*, December 8, 2008, p. 7.

10. Xia Qi, "Renmin zhengxie jiebie de youlai" [A historical overview of CPPCC cross-sector organizations], *Zhongguo tongyi zhanxian* [China united front], no. 4 (2009), pp. 12–13.

11. *Zhonghua renmin gongheguo xianfa xiuzheng'an* [Opinions of the CCP Central Committee on strengthening the work of the CPPCC], in *Renmin zhengxie zhongyao wenxuan xuanbian*, vol. 2, p. 531.

12. *Zhonggong zhongyang guanyu jin yi bu jiaqiang renmin zhengxie gongzuo de yijian* [Opinions of the CCP Central Committee on strengthening the work of the CPPCC], in *Renmin zhengxie zhongyao wenxuan xuanbian*, vol. 3, p. 793.

13. State Council Information Office of the PRC, "Zhongguo zhengdang zhidu" [China's party system], white paper (Beijing, 2007).

14. Ibid.

15. *Zhongguo remin zhengzhi xieshang huiyi zhangcheng* [CPPCC Constitution], in *Renmin zhengxie zhongyao wenxuan xuanbian*, vol. 3, p. 692.

16. *Zhonggong zhongyang guanyu jin yi bu jiaqiang Zhongguo gongchandang lingdao de duo dang hezuo he zhengzhi xieshang zhidu jianshe de yijian* [Opinions of the CCP Central Committee on further strengthening the building of the system of multiparty cooperation and political consultation led by the CCP], in *Renmin zhengxie zhongyao wenxuan xuanbian*, vol. 3, p. 762.

17. Ibid.

18. Lin Shangli, *Dangdai Zhongguo zhengzhi xingtai yanjiu* [A study on China's form of politics] (Tianjin: Tianjin People's Publishing House, 2000).

19. Deng Xiaoping, "Guanyu zhiding minzhu dangpai chengyuan canzheng he jiandu zhifu fang'an de pishi" [Reply on formulating a plan for members of the democratic parties to participate in the administration of government affairs and perform their supervisory duties], in *Renmin zhengxie zhongyao wenxuan xuanbian,* vol. 2, p. 464.

20. *Zhonggong zhongyang guanyu jiaqiang renmin zhengzhi xieshang gongzuo de yijian (tiyao)* [Opinions of the CCP Central Committee on strengthening the work of the CPPCC (digest)], in *Renmin zhengxie zhongyao wenxuan xuanbian,* vol. 3, pp. 792–99.

21. Ibid., p. 795.

22. Wang Wenzi, "Lun 'ba zhengzhi xieshang naru juece chengxu'" [On "incorporate the CPPCC in the decisionmaking process"], June 25, 2009 (www.cppcc.gov.cn/2011/11/21/ARTI1321842150578349.shtml).

23. Xiao Yong, "Xin sixing jifa xin huoli, renmin zhengxie puxie zhengzhi wenming xin pianzhang" [New thinking excites new energy, CPPCC composes new chapter on political civilization], February 18, 2009 (cppcc.people.com.cn/GB/34956/8824219.html).

24. Kenneth Jowitt, *Leninist Responses to National Dependency* (Berkeley: University of California, Institute of International Studies, 1978); Jowitt, *New World Disorder: The Leninist Extinction* (University of California Press, 1992).

5

The Rise of Civil Society in China

WANG MING

In 2008 a large signboard bearing the words "Civil Society, Grow Together" appeared in Shenzhen. According to the Publicity Department of the Shenzhen Municipal Party Committee, building "civil society" (公民社会, *gongmin shehui*) is one of the goals of Shenzhen's social and urban development now and for the next several decades, while the term "grow together" expresses the vision of having different social strata, social forces, and the government work together to build a vibrant civil society.[1] This Shenzhen slogan, which epitomizes China's reform and opening up, anticipates a new trend in China's ongoing reform and opening up: the rise of civil society.

Civil Society: Controversy and Definition

The term *civil society* has been used in China for a long time. At first it was translated as "citizens' society" (市民社会, *shimin shehui,* literally, "city residents' society"), leading academics to discuss foreign conceptions of the term and debate its meaning in the Chinese context.[2] The debate had three major characteristics. At the heart of the debate was the meaning of the term as used in classic works on the subject, which were set in the social context of early capitalist Europe and made little reference to China's own social conditions. The debate focused on the general subject of social formation, with the focus on society rather than citizens or the constituent units of society. The debate was between two highly ideologically and politically divided camps, each staunchly defending its own argument.

In the early 1990s the debate on civil society shifted focus to the term's relevance to China's own social development. In his article published in the inaugural issue of *Chinese Social Sciences Quarterly* in November 1992, Deng Zhenglai put forward what he called the "construction of a relationship between the state and civil society completely foreign to China's social and intellectual history."[3] After the publication of Deng's pioneering essay, *Chinese Social Sciences Quarterly* published more than twenty articles on civil society from 1993 to 1994, spurring extensive academic discussion on the subject that attracted wide attention from scholars at home and abroad and generated many insightful ideas. This led to further discussion of civil society in the academic world and the publication of some important papers on the subject.[4]

Discussions on civil society during this period were carried out mainly along two paths. The first was the academic path, where the concept of civil society and its related theories and schools of thought were examined to theoretically inform China's building of civil society.[5] The second was the path of practical application, where "socialist civil society" was explicitly put forward and considered to be "the foundation of the market economy system," "the precondition of political transformation," and "the foothold upon which to research and solve China's various social problems today and in the future," and the concept was called on to foster and develop a "civil society of Chinese characteristics."[6] Although these discussions did not lead to a clear consensus, most participants gradually came to the realization, both theoretically and practically, that with the development of the market economy, reform of the political system, and transition of society, a civil society that was based on the market economy and independent from the state system was taking shape.

As the UN's Fourth World Conference on Women was held in Beijing in 1995, another global nongovernmental organization (NGO) event—the NGO Forum on Women—was held in Huairou in suburban Beijing. The nine-day event consisted of more than 3,000 sessions and was attended by 30,000 representatives of NGOs from around the world. This global event, which brought together civil society actors as its main participants, sent an important message to China: NGOs are the cornerstone of civil society.

In roughly the same period, a number of milestone events took place:

—Grassroots NGOs for human rights and environmental protection emerged.[7]

—NGO-related regulative and administrative system development began to quicken.[8]

— *Citizens' society* gradually became *civil society*.[9]

—Chinese and foreign scholars began to study China's NGO development.[10]

Against this backdrop, actors in China's reform and opening up, including those in the academic community, began to place hope for the development of China's civil society on the development of NGOs.

From ancient Greece to modern times, there has been much disagreement on the definition of *civil society*.[11] In his 2004 book series, *Civil Society*, Michael Edwards presents a systematic survey and comparison of various views on civil society.[12] According to his analysis, there are three types of civil society: civil society as associational life, providing both opportunities for people to act together and an environment in which civic values and skills are developed; civil society as the good society, aiming for social, economic, and political progress; and civil society as the public sphere, a space for argument and deliberation in which citizens can express their different views and negotiate a sense of common interest. In his article "Chinese Civil Society: Concept, Classification, and Institutional Environment," Yu Keping defines civil society as "the sum of all NGOs or civil relationships outside the state/government system and the market/business system" and "the public sphere outside the official political sphere and market sphere."[13]

In this chapter, civil society development is understood as a social phenomenon that comprises the three dimensions summarized by Edwards and has the essential characteristics abstracted by Yu Keping. Specifically, civil society as used here is understood based on its connotation, essence, and extension:

First, in terms of connotation, civil society comprises the following dimensions or elements:

—Civil society is an associational formation based on general and diversified social structure of the autonomous participation of citizens; a rich, sustainable associational ecology; and a system contrasted with the state-government system and the market-enterprise system. In this sense, civil society is what Alexis de Tocqueville and Edwards describe as associational life.[14]

—Civil society represents the pursuit of a good society of citizens who support charitable causes, public welfare, volunteering, and social services as well as the constantly increasing charitable resources and properties that are formed in this process. This is both a reaction to the negative aspects of the market economy, including the "survival of the fittest" mentality, and its consequences and a manifestation of human conscience. In this sense, civil society is what Robert Putnam and John Kenneth Galbraith described as good society.[15]

—Civil society is a process wherein citizens, through autonomous associational activities, become a major force and mainstay of public rights, influencing social consensus, public policies, and social public welfare and driving government reforms and political democratization. This process forms a civil public sphere separate from the political state and the bureaucratic system. In this sense, civil society is what Jürgen Habermas conceptualized as the public sphere.[16]

Second, at the highest level, civil society refers to the sum of all civil social organizations and their social relationships, including their relationships with the government and with enterprises and the various relationships among themselves. At the base of these social relationships is a process by which citizens organize themselves (associational life) to express their shared vision of the future (good society) and take collective action to improve their life as a whole (that is, the public sphere).[17]

Third, by extension, civil society has micro as well as macro structures. At the micro level, civil society equates individual organizations with social organizations, civil organizations, nonprofit organizations, and nongovernmental organizations.[18] Civil society manifests itself as internal governance structures, external associational ecology, and the regulatory environment; as missions, programs, and activities of these organizations; as the constantly expanding public welfare resources; and as the influence, power of discourse, and channels used by these organizations as they participate in public activities in the communal, governmental, and even political fields. From a macro perspective, civil society refers to a social state wherein all kinds of well-developed NGOs that can easily get legitimacy as associations of citizens communicate, engage in dialogue, consult, and negotiate through various channels to express their interests and concerns. In this social state NGOs receive resources from the public sector on the basis of fair competition as organizations through which citizens take part in public affairs. And in this social state the presence of NGOs leads to increased social resources for citizens and citizen groups; greater social responsibility among for-profit organizations such as enterprises; more democracy, efficiency, and accountability on the part of the Chinese Communist Party and government; and increased harmony, inclusiveness, diversity, and tolerance for society as a whole. Such a social state brought on by the full development of NGOs is what we call civil society.

Emerging Civil Society in China

Looking at the realities of China under my particular definition of civil society, as noted above, a dynamic and comprehensive view of the various factors bearing on the development of China's civil society emerges. It can be said that with the advancement of the historical process of reform and opening up, China's path toward civil society has grown increasingly irreversible.

Associational Life

The number, quality, structure, and network system of NGOs and their regulatory system are all important indicators of the development of civil society. Since reform and opening up began, the development of NGOs in China has gone through three stages of development, each spanning roughly ten years.

The first stage was characterized by the rapid development of various learned societies, research societies, rural technology associations, and rural credit cooperatives. Thanks to the favorable political situation after the launch of reform and opening up, the top-down support of party and government leaders, and the lack of regulatory measures, this period saw an unprecedented explosion in associational activity. Judging from the various documents and data I have gathered, in this period the number of civil organizations soared from fewer than 10,000 to around a million. However, owing to the lack of regulatory oversight, these organizations largely developed as they saw fit in such areas as organizational structure, operating management, financial system, internal and external relationships, and legitimacy. This has resulted in many social problems, especially in terms of credibility, which raised the need to develop an NGO regulatory system.

The second stage was characterized by the cleanup and rectification of the mushrooming NGO field and the establishment of a system to regulate NGOs. In this period, the party and the government strengthened political control over and administrative intervention in civil association activities and took a full range of measures in a bid to remove the various negative impacts of the haphazard growth of NGOs.[19] Specifically, a number of administrative regulations were promulgated, and a dual regulatory system (comprised of an NGO registration authority and other authorities in charge of specific affairs) was put in place to strictly control the establishment of NGOs.[20] This dampened the subsequent growth in the number of NGOs and curtailed their capacity and scope of activity. The number of NGOs registered with the civil affairs authority in 1999 was 143,000, down from 185,000 in 1996. According to the data I have collected, the number of NGOs registered in 1999 was roughly one-fifth of the number in 1989 and one-eighth of the number in 2008.[21] On the other hand, it should be noted that as a result of this strengthened legislation and regulation, NGOs have become more institutionalized in such aspects as organizational structure and internal management.

The third and current stage—which marks the maturity of associational life—is characterized by the burgeoning of grassroots organizations, expansion of community-based organizations, growth of market-based civil organizations, and transformation of nongovernmental charity organizations, such as foundations. Thanks to the influence of the World Conference on Women held in Beijing, there have emerged a great number of grassroots organizations within a wide range of fields—including environmental protection, human rights, poverty relief, social welfare, public health, and community development. Those in the fields of environmental protection and AIDS prevention and control, in particular, are the most developed and vibrant. In urban areas, thanks to the advancement of community development programs and administrative reforms launched by governments at various levels, many community-based organizations have come into being. In recent years, the Ministry of Civil Affairs introduced a registration system in some regions such as Nanjing and Qingdao, where community-based organizations that are incorporated in this system number in the tens of thousands, quite likely on par with the number of civil organizations that have been registered.

Another noteworthy phenomenon in this period is that, with the development of the market economy, various market-based civil organizations represented by industry associations have blossomed, including various chambers of commerce, industry associations, industry federations, regional entrepreneurial societies and clubs, and organizations established by various groups of market participants such as organizations that represent the rights of consumers, migrant workers, and transient populations. Some popular organizations, such as the China Disabled Persons Federation, the All-China Women's Federation, the All-China Federation of Trade Unions, the Red Cross Society of China, and the China Association for Science and Technology, have also actively sought to make internal reforms and develop civil organizations within their respective systems. The transformation of foundations has been another milestone during this period. Since the promulgation of a new regulation for the management of foundations by the State Council in 2004, many private foundations founded by entrepreneurs and other wealthy individuals have appeared, growing both in number and in scope (now numbering almost 900, they are almost on par with public foundations). In addition to the abovementioned categories of NGOs, the development of Internet-based groups in this period has also been astounding. There has not yet been established a regulatory system for these groups, which have mushroomed with the advancement of modern communication technology.

In addition, party and government departments at various levels have been making great efforts to reform the NGO regulatory system and put the development of NGOs on their agendas. In some cities, party chiefs and government leaders have led or supervised the reform and innovation of their cities' NGO regulatory systems and introduced various active measures to support NGO participation and public service. This has given rise to many innovative and distinctive models such as the Guangdong model, the Shenzhen model, the Hangzhou model, the Nanjing model, and the Anshan model.[22] At the same time, communication and cooperation among NGOs themselves have also been strengthened, and a series of NGO networks supporting the development of NGOs has appeared. Some newly established private foundations, such as the Narada

Foundation, have also been striving to become grant-making foundations. It is clear, then, that the policy environment for the development of NGOs in China has significantly improved.

Overall, the more than thirty years since the reform and opening up have seen a huge growth in the number of NGOs, including civil organizations and grassroots organizations. There are currently a total of nearly 430,000 foundations, social organizations, and private nonenterprise organizations that are registered with civil affairs departments at various levels. This number is almost three times that of ten years ago, four times that of twenty years ago, and more than forty times that in 1979, at the beginning of the reform and opening up. The actual number of NGOs is estimated to be eight to ten times the number that have registered with the civil affairs authorities. Along with the great growth in the number of organizations has come significant improvement in terms of overall competency, organizational structure, internal management, and standardization of China's NGOs. A network system and structural framework for NGOs have also taken shape. Although the reform of the NGO regulatory system has not been completed, the policy environment for NGO development has gradually improved.

Good Society

The pursuit of charitable causes, public welfare, volunteering, and social service as well as charitable resources and properties is both a reaction to the market economy's negative aspects, including the "survival of the fittest" mentality and its consequences, and a manifestation of human conscience. Since the reform and opening-up period began, social polarization in China has increased along with economic growth. In the process of economic reshuffling, governmental reform, and social transformation, the public management and public services provided by governments at various levels have become seriously inadequate, making it increasingly difficult to ensure fairness, justice, and social equality. The social resources established under the previous planned economic system collapsed, throwing society into a serious crisis of trust. After the dire poverty and economic destitution of the 1970s, China has seen great economic advancement and a significant improvement in people's living standards, but it has also faced a great number of unexpected social problems and serious social crises.

In the face of these problems and crises, citizens have not lost heart in their pursuit of a good society. The development of charitable causes represented by foundations, volunteer actions, and other efforts of philanthropy, civil society organizations, and social entrepreneurship shows that in the profit-driven market economic environment, there is still keen pursuit of a good society.

As mentioned earlier, at the very beginning of the reform and opening-up period foundations emerged as an institutionalized channel by which citizens could make donations to charitable causes. In July 1981 the China Children and Teenagers Foundation, the first foundation in the People's Republic of China, was jointly established by seventeen national social organizations and institutions, including the All-China Women's Federation, All-China Federation of Trade Unions, the Chinese Communist Youth League, Central Committee, and the China Association for Science and Technology. Then, in May 1982 and March 1984, the Song Ching Ling Foundation and the China Welfare Foundation for the Handicapped (later, China Disabled Persons Federation) were established, marking the further development of foundations in China.

As the reform and opening up picked up momentum, many foundations in various fields were established nationwide. According to incomplete statistics released in September 1987, there were 214 formally established foundations nationwide, 33 of which were at the national level and 181 at the local level. In addition, many disaster and poverty relief organizations funded by local governments were established. According to statistics released by the Ministry of Civil Affairs in August 1986, there were as many as 6,275 such organizations. In a bid to regulate the development of foundations, in September 1988 the State Council promulgated the Measures for the Management of Foundations, which called for the cleaning up and rectifying of foundations and authorized the Ministry of Civil Affairs to take charge of the registration of foundations. This put the development of foundations under a unified legal framework.

In the subsequent ten-plus years, owing to the influence of the June 4, 1989, incident in Tiananmen Square, the development of foundations and social organizations was restricted as a whole. The number of foundations in this period did not see remarkable growth. By early 2004, there were roughly 1,200 registered foundations, including more than 80 at the national level. In March 2004 the State Council promulgated the Regulations on Foundation Administration, in which foundations were positioned as nonprofit legal entities and classified as public or private. These regulations outlined aspects such as the conditions for the establishment, organizational structure, and use of properties of foundations, laying the legal foundation for them. In January 2005 the Ministry of Finance promulgated the Accounting Rules for Nonprofit Organizations, which detailed provisions on the accounting system of nonprofit organizations, including foundations, to ensure the standardized development of foundations. In recent years, the Ministry of Civil Affairs has also promulgated a series of rules on information disclosure and the assessment of foundations. In 2007 the ministry launched the first nationwide assessment of foundations. At the same time, the Enterprise

Income Tax Law that took effect in January 2008 made great adjustments in pre-tax deductions on charitable donations and income tax reductions and exemptions for nonprofit organizations.

These measures combined to form a favorable legal and policy environment for the development of foundations and encouraged many entrepreneurs and people in other circles to establish foundations and engage in charitable causes. For the year ending December 31, 2011, according to statistics gathered under the Regulation on Foundation Administration by the Ministry of Civil Affairs, 2,548 foundations with total assets of RMB 50.9 billion were registered. It is worth noting that the number of private foundations, which began being registered in 2005, had reached 1,373 by the end of 2012, accounting for over half of all foundations.[23] Some large enterprises, including both state-owned and private enterprises, also established private foundations and were actively involved in social charitable causes. Charity organizations represented by foundations have played an important and prominent role in relief efforts in major natural disasters such as the devastating earthquake in Wenchuan. In the relief effort that followed, more than RMB 76 billion was raised, marking a milestone in the development of charitable causes in China.

Another important aspect of social charity is philanthropy and corporate social responsibility. Since the beginning of the reform and opening-up period, which was launched with the slogan "Let some people get rich first," China has seen the emergence of "nouveau riche" within a short period. According to the *Hurun Wealth Report* released in April 2010, at the end of 2009 the number of people individually worth at least RMB 10 million had reached 875,000, including 55,000 worth more than RMB 100 million, 1,900 worth more than RMB 1 billion, and 140 worth more than RMB 10 billion.[24] Although this group is small in number, the wealth of people who "got rich first" has surged. According to the data from the Boston Consulting Group, China enjoys the world's fastest growth in both individual and family wealth. Worldwide, 1 percent of families own 35 percent of the world's total wealth, and the super-rich families, accounting for roughly one hundred thousandth of the world's population, control about $21 trillion of wealth, or one-fifth of the world's total wealth.[25]

Half of the donations to the Wenchuan earthquake relief and recovery effort came from wealthy individuals, including private entrepreneurs. According to the 2010 Hurun Rich List in the *Hurun Wealth Report,* the top 100 wealthiest people in China donated a total of RMB 22.94 billion over the previous five years, accounting for 12 percent of all donations in the country during the same period. In the past year alone, the top 50 philanthropists in China's mainland donated a total of RMB 8.7 billion. Among them, private business owners Wang

Jianlin, Lu Zhiqiang, and Cao Dewang each donated more than RMB 100 million to earthquake-stricken Yushu in 2010.

Echoing the philanthropic actions of the wealthy in recent years has been the growing awareness of corporate social responsibility by enterprises in China. These include multinationals, private enterprises, and state-owned enterprises that have not only increased investment in corporate social responsibility programs in environmental protection, laborer protection, and community development but have also mobilized their employees to take part in various volunteer activities. At the same time, a new type of enterprise, called social enterprise, has appeared, committed to promoting public welfare. The social entrepreneurs leading these enterprises are taking direct action, including mobilizing market resources to steer charitable causes in a new direction.

Despite the economic inequality and social polarization in present-day China, Chinese citizens are making active efforts to build a good society. These valued efforts made in the midst of social problems and crises give hope for the development of civil society in China.

Public Sphere

In the public sphere, civil society manifests itself as a process whereby citizens, through autonomous associational activities, become a major force behind and even champion public rights in influencing social consensus, public policies, and social public welfare and driving government reforms and political democratization. Thus a civil public sphere is created in contrast with the political state and the bureaucratic-administrative system. In this public sphere, citizens are playing an increasingly important role in bettering society. What follows are three case studies in different fields.

Wenzhou Lighter Association

The Wenzhou Lighter Association led a collective antidumping action against European Union regulations, a campaign that expanded the public sphere. From 2001 to 2003, the association, on behalf of Wenzhou's lighter manufacturers, who had a combined 70 percent market share of the European lighter market, took joint action against the European Union's ban on the import of non-child-resistant lighters through the methods of collective defense, joint petitioning, lobbying, and pressuring local and central governments.[26] In doing so, it successfully delayed the implementation of the child-resistance law and protected the common interests of Chinese lighter manufacturers. In this case, the Chinese government was unable to respond to EU action owing to its ascension to the World Trade Organization, thus leaving no room for the association to respond directly on behalf of its member enterprises. Although it succeeded only in delaying the implementation of the regulation, the Chinese enterprises gained precious time to make relevant adjustments to comply with the new regulation. To a certain extent, their action also influenced the EU's industrial policies toward China.[27]

Campaign against Nu River Dam

Civil actions have halted a dam-building project on the Nu River, contributing to the development of the public sphere. From 2003 to 2007, efforts by more than thirty NGOs, including the Green Earth Volunteers, halted the controversial project after Premier Wen Jiabao expressed his support twice for putting the project on hold. During this period a heated and prolonged debate on whether the dams should be built took place among NGOs, scholars, relevant enterprises, and local residents via various platforms such as TV, newspapers, the streets, and especially online forums and blogs. Some people's congress deputies and members of the Chinese People's Political Consultative Conference submitted bills and proposals, and relevant government departments had much disagreement on the matter. As a result, the public became engaged in the issue, and the project was eventually halted as a result of the explicit opposition of the premier.

In this case, not only did NGOs take unprecedented joint action, but the cooperation between domestic NGOs and their international peers, close cooperation between NGOs and competent government departments, the use of various communication channels, and the debate among people of different views on the dam-building project were also of great symbolic significance. The handling of this controversy demonstrated the exceptional advocacy skills of domestic NGOs. To a great extent this case influenced China's public-policy decision-making model and accelerated the enactment of laws and regulations regarding public participation in environmental impact assessment.

Privatization of Public Services

Multiple cities explored the possibility of contracting out government services, which widened the space of the public sphere. The purchase of public services by governments from NGOs is a new public service model that Chinese governments at various levels have looked at in recent years. As early as the late 1990s, the Pudong New District government began to explore the possibility of government purchase of pension services, which was later expanded to include comprehensive community services citywide and was funded by an extrabudgetary fund on a regular and institutionalized basis. In Shenzhen, the government purchased social work–related services from NGOs and other social organizations via open tendering for grassroots communities. In July 2010 a total of 250 Beijing-based NGOs covering more than 500 public service items took part in the open tendering for public service purchase launched by the Beijing Municipal Government. More than 300 of these projects were accepted by the government, which secured financial support that ranged from RMB 30,000 to RMB 300,000, with a total sum that exceeded RMB 100 million.[28] Many other cities have also carried out bold efforts in this manner. Through the privatization of public service, the government transfers some of its functions, leading NGOs not only to obtain a certain amount of resources but also to gain the support of the government, thereby allowing them to enter the public service sphere in a legitimate and professional way. This is a new and special opening of the public sphere and an innovative approach by which in-depth cooperation between the government and NGOs can be achieved.

These three cases alone are not enough to present a complete picture of the expansion of the public sphere. Such cases do show, however, that in present-day China, the public sphere can now influence public policies across such fields as the economy, the environment, and health care and is entering the deeper area of public service, thus forming a civil-public sphere that has bearing on the social life of every citizen.

Speaking of the civil-public sphere, the Internet is increasingly becoming a major platform from which people influence public decisionmaking and governance. In some of the most prominent public incidents—including the Nu River dam-building project, anti-Japanese demonstrations in Beijing, the protests against the PX factory in Xiamen, and the protest against the establishment of a waste incinerator in Panyu, the Internet has played an important role. Even government leaders are seeing the importance of directly listening to the opinions of netizens.

Official Attitude toward Civil Society

Echoing these three developments, there has been a remarkable change in how the government views civil society. This is mainly reflected in the expressions that government documents and the mainstream media use to refer to civil society.

In the last half of the 1990s, the term "popular organization" (民间组织, *minjian zuzhi*) was uniformly used by the government to refer to all NGOs, including social groups, private nonenterprise organizations, and foundations. "Popular" (民间, *minjian*), used in contrast to "official," has the connotation of being nonmainstream, unorthodox, and sometimes even unofficial and illegal, the last of which reflecting a distancing, slighting, or even negative attitude on the part of the government toward these organizations. This attitude has changed remarkably in recent years.

In an important political report of the CCP Central Committee issued in 2006, *social organization* (社会组织, *shehui zuzhi*) was used consistently in place of the former *popular organization*. In the Chinese context, social organizations are the third category of organizations, in juxtaposition to political organizations (party and government organs) and economic organizations (enterprises and companies), with meanings closer to that of civil society organization. The term *social organization* was popularized when the focus of China's reform and opening up shifted from economic construction to building a harmonious society, an endeavor in which social organizations were to play a principal role.

In the political report presented at the 17th CCP National Congress in 2007, social organizations were brought to even greater prominence. That was when social organizations were regarded as an important platform for developing grassroots democracy and ensuring the people's more practical democratic rights. This document also attached importance to the development and management of social organizations and the positive role they played in expanding public participation, reflecting people's concerns, and strengthening social autonomy.[29] In the government work report delivered by Premier Wen Jiabao in 2008 and the Opinions on Deepening the Administrative System Reform adopted at the second plenary session of the 17th CCP Central Committee, particular emphasis was placed on bringing into full play the role of social organizations in social management and public service and in promoting the transformation of government functions. That *social organization* was used, rather than *popular organization*, represents a trend toward more fully legitimizing civil society participants, who are becoming an increasingly important force in further deepening China's reform and opening up.

Civil Society Development in China: Constraints and Trends

There is an irreversible path toward civil society in China, one that is becoming wider and brighter. This does not mean, however, that the path will be a smooth one. There are still various factors hindering the development of civil society in China. Given the presence of powerful vested interests formed in the process of China's economic and social development and because of increasing social tension, the ongoing march toward civil society will certainly traverse bumpy territory.

Constraints

Many factors hinder China's civil society development, including exogenous factors such as the regulatory system and ideology as well as endogenous factors such as the lack of professional competency among NGOs themselves. The main four challenges are outlined below.

Outdated Administrative System

China's existing NGO registration system was formed in the late 1980s as an expedient measure to overcome the negative impact of the excessive amount of associational activities in the preceding period. For various reasons, this expedient measure was perpetuated and became the basic system governing China's associational life. The dual administrative system has three major characteristics. First, a strict standard is imposed on the registration of NGOs by making the registration subject to the approval of two different government departments. Second, the two government departments jointly hold political responsibility, and bear the corresponding political risk, for giving legitimacy to the registered NGOs. Third, though they are jointly responsible for the registration and regulation of NGOs, each of the two departments maintains its own scope of authority, thus creating checks and balances. This institutional design imposes a high threshold for the legal registration of NGOs. Many existing NGOs were unable to survive the reregistration process; it also became difficult, if not impossible, for new NGOs to be registered, especially those without a party or government background. The result has been that a great number of NGOs either abandon the effort to register or choose instead to register with the industry and commerce administration to become a legal entity.

Owing to the defects of the system, there have been many calls over the years from academic circles and beyond, including relevant government departments, for reform of the existing NGO registration system. Many local governments have formulated various policies and administrative regulations to replace the dual administrative system. As far as industry associations, agricultural technical societies, and urban grassroots organizations are concerned, there have been some breakthroughs on reforming the dual administrative system. The system as a whole, however, is still difficult to change. This administrative system, in spite of its obvious negative effects on the development of NGOs, is expected to continue to exist for quite some time.

Ideological Restriction

Ideology is another factor that hinders the development of civil society. Owing to the combined influence of a leftist ideology, certain incidents that have occurred, and the complicated international political situation, China's leadership tends to hold a conservative stance toward both civil society and NGOs, thereby hindering the further development of civil society.

As pointed out earlier in the chapter, civil society is not a phenomenon exclusive to capitalism or to the capitalist class. There are extensive discourses on the subject in the works of classic socialist authors such as Karl Marx and Friedrich Engels, which should have served well as the theoretical basis for building civil society today in China. However, there are always some leftist-minded people who claim that civil society is a hostile force, part of the Western world's effort to bring about China's "peaceful evolution" in its unchanged intention to destroy us.[30] These individuals cite isolated views and statements made by classic authors during special historical conditions, isolated cases in which some international hostile forces have engaged in political infiltration under the banner of civil society, statements from internal reports of the U.S. government regarding dissemination of Western values through civil society, cases in Russia and Eastern European countries where some forces have attempted to overthrow their governments in the name of civil society, and so on. The presence of these ideologically conservative forces and their views have affected the attitude of the party and the government toward civil society and have to some extent even slowed civil society–related legislation and institutionalization.

Inadequate Professional Competency

Because of a short history of development, a lack of social resources, and an unfriendly legal and policy environment, China's NGOs generally leave much to be desired in professional competency compared with their peers in other countries and regions. The core competitiveness of NGOs, in both mobilizing resources and providing public services, lies in their professional competency. Many famous NGOs—such as World Vision International, Oxfam International, Amnesty International, and Greenpeace—are staffed with strong professional teams and have their own comprehensive multilayer social mobilization and service networks. In comparison, China's NGOs generally lack professional staffs and have a long way to go in resource mobilization, organization, management, coordination, crisis response, and especially the capacity to provide services in their respective fields.

According to our survey, 90 percent of employees of social organizations and foundations have never received any professional training. Many organizations, unable to afford full-time employees, are maintained by part-timers and volunteers. Only the very few that are qualified to take part in the competitive bidding processes launched by governments are able to do so.

In addition to the lack of professional competency on the part of NGOs, their communication, interaction, and integration with one another and with other market forces, relevant government departments, and the media are also inadequate. In the face of economic development and various accompanying social problems, NGOs and various market forces often represent different interest groups or spaces, and the realization of various social policies and overall social interest is the result of mutual contention, interaction, and compromise. Cases of joint action taken by NGOs, such as the opposition to the proposed Nu River dam, are the exception; most organizations still tend to fight for themselves. In some fields, NGOs will sometimes compete with and attack one another to win projects, and there is even serious internal strife within some NGOs.

Lack of Social Supervision and Encroachment of the Market Mechanism

As they take on public responsibilities, NGOs are traditionally subject to strict social supervision. In China, however, social supervision over NGOs has been largely neglected because the dual NGO regulatory system that emphasizes government administration of NGOs has proved itself either ineffective or insufficient. This has resulted in cases in which people make private gains in the name of charity, which has weakened public support for charitable causes. To reverse this situation, in 2004 the State Council promulgated the Regulations on Foundation Administration, which designed a set of relatively scientific principles and institutional arrangements of social supervision over the operations of NGOs. However, for the hundreds of thousands of social organizations and people-run nonenterprise organizations, especially the great number of NGOs that have not registered or have changed their registration, the problem of social supervision is far from being solved.

In some social organizations, councils have hundreds or even thousands of members, but since their establishment not a single council meeting has been held, leaving decisionmaking power highly centralized in the hands of a few full-time executives. Some private nonenterprise organizations are service entities established and managed by investors, and they do not provide much social service but do charge high and arbitrary fees to maximize their own private gain. Some grassroots organizations that are either not registered or registered with the industry and commerce administration authority are operated in a patriarchal and family-centered fashion, and the resulting haphazardness and inefficiency in management have hindered their sound development. In fact, not a single whistle-blower protection mechanism for charity properties has been established either nationwide or in a specific region. All that concerned citizens can do is turn to the media in hopes of bringing about some, albeit indirect, social supervision.

Owing to the lack of effective regulation and social supervision, many NGOs have become profit driven. Some social organizations make huge profits by holding large-scale exhibitions, fee-based training classes, and commercial lectures; some associations and foundations with government backgrounds charge high fees for various certifications, qualification inspections, and examinations and assessments; some privately run schools, hospitals, and cultural facilities offering high-end commercial services to the rich have become an important force in the market economy; and some foundations and social organizations solicit donations under false pretenses. All these individual transgressions have damaged the reputation of charitable causes as a whole.

Trends

Despite various constraints, China's civil society will continue to grow. In China today, associational life has been so enthusiastically embraced that it has become an indispensable part of the public sphere. No force can stop the historical process of China's development of civil society.

Nevertheless, social transformation, political democratization, and economic marketization are all far from complete, making the prospect of a fully functional civil society in China not very bright. At the same time, different elite groups that are taking shape as the result of social stratification and restructuring are actively influencing and promoting China's social development. Civil society is also subject to their influence, and its development has followed several different trends.

The development of China's civil society may follow one of three trends. The first is a development path led by political elites. An increasing number of political elites will play a leading role in the development of NGOs. Through their full development in various fields of social life, NGOs will strengthen the foundation of the ruling party's legitimacy and help create a new political structure, one in which party organizations at various levels and NGOs constructively interact with, rely on, supervise, and check one another. The political standards of association will be stricter, while social, economic, and cultural standards will be looser. Nongovernmental organizations will most likely become a new category of cross-sector organization in people's congresses and member organizations of the Chinese People's Political Consultative Conference at various levels and gain a legally and institutionally sanctioned capacity to take part in the administration and discussion of government affairs. A comprehensive legal system governing NGOs will be put in place. A unified and strict supervisory system, while ensuring NGO openness and transparency, will to a certain extent restrict their self-governance.

The government procurement service system will become well developed, one in which governments at various levels will contract out most public services to NGOs through a competitive bidding process and a comprehensive evaluation and punishment mechanism. An increasingly sound governance structure will characterize NGOs. More and more political elites will head NGOs and lead their development. Nongovernmental organizations will have access to extensive public resources and have a highly developed public service function, but their advocacy function will remain somewhat underdeveloped. Citizens' economic, social, and public service needs will be satisfied to a considerable degree, but there will be inadequate expression of rights and interests and a lack of independent spirit on the part of citizens. This will be a civil society that is economically prosperous, socially stable and harmonious, culturally inclusive and diversified, and both politically authoritarian and orderly.

The second development path is one of advocacy of democracy led by intellectual elites. Driven by such intellectuals, NGOs will come to more actively expand their presence in the public sphere and promote political democratization. An increasing number of intellectual elites will take part and play a leading role in the development of NGOs. Through their full development in various fields of social life, NGOs will help strengthen public participation and democratic governance and serve as a mechanism to represent and speak for various social classes. This will result in the formation of a new political structure in which NGOs and other political forces compete, interact, supervise, and check one another. The political, social, economic, and cultural standards of association will become looser. A system of comprehensive NGO self-discipline, accountability, and social supervision will be put in place. An institutionalized mechanism of dialogue and communication between party and government departments and NGOs will be established. Some NGOs will take part in the government's service procurement programs, but the majority of NGOs will carry out their activities by soliciting their own funds.

Public foundations will become highly developed, backed by a resource system of public donations and voluntarism. Nongovernmental organizations will come to have a sound democratic governance structure. Many intellectual elites will enter NGOs through competitive elections and lead their development. These organizations will have highly developed advocacy functions, but their public service function may leave something to be desired. Citizens will be able to express their rights and interests fully and have a wide variety of participation channels, greater independence of mind, an enhanced sense of sovereignty, and a significantly improved sense of responsibility for and participation in social and public affairs. This will be a politically democratic, economically diversified, culturally inclusive, and socially pluralistic civil society, one in which citizens' rights, freedom, and liberty are guaranteed to a high degree.

The third and final development path is an advance of wealth led by economic elites. Driven by economic elites, NGOs will have access to richer economic resources and be able to make a greater commitment to social welfare causes, more actively promote economic and political democratization, and, by serving as a mechanism by which different interest groups have their voices heard, play a leading role in social consultation and interaction. With the development of various private foundations, a charity system primarily financed by large foundations and supported by a large number of cooperative organizations that mainly target people in poor areas, disadvantaged groups, and other marginal groups will gradually take shape and bring about an improvement in the whole society's welfare.

The increasing sense of social responsibility on the part of entrepreneurs and the wealthy will play a positive role in narrowing the wealth gap and easing social tension. With adequate resources, NGOs will focus more on charity and expand the scope of coverage from developed areas to poor backward areas and from China to foreign countries and regions. Many entrepreneurs with a strong sense of social responsibility and a good public image will play a pivotal or leading role in NGOs. Economic elites will also promote economic and political democratization through NGOs and, specifically, strengthen not only consultation and dialogue with party and government departments but also both the capacity of NGOs to express their demands and the general mechanisms of social consultation. The charity and social consultation functions of NGOs will become highly developed, but their function of promoting the voices of different social groups may be underdeveloped. This will be a politically democratic, economically prosperous, socially coordinated, and culturally vibrant civil society characterized by highly developed charitable causes.

These three paths for China's potential civil society development are all hypotheses based on existing situations and budding trends. There are factors that both encourage and discourage the country from taking any of these paths. Although we cannot say definitely at the present stage which path will be followed, one thing is certain: the development of NGOs in China has irreversible momentum. Elites in the political, intellectual, and economic realms are all actively involving themselves to promote the development of NGOs. With five thousand years of cultural heritage and a vast territory of 9.6 million square meters, China can accommodate all these possible paths. Of course, in moving toward civil society, we can hope the slogan that guides this effort will not be similar to the earlier "Let some people get rich first" exhortation that was used in the economic marketization process. We can hope the slogan for the future will be one that envisions the prospect of all people sharing the fruits of reform—not unlike the slogan that appeared in Shenzhen: "Civil Society, Grow Together."

COMMENT
MARY GALLAGHER

Wang Ming provides us with a detailed and enlightening analysis of the history, current status, and future possibilities of China's associational life. Focused on civil society (公民社会, *gongmin shehui*), the public sphere (公共领域, *gonggong lingyu*), and associational life (结社生活, *jieshe shenghuo*), Wang's chapter is a vigorous defense and diagnosis of the current state of Chinese civil society, including analysis of its problems and constraints and prescriptions for its future health. Wang finds that China's path to a civil society is increasingly broad, hopeful, and irreversible. I offer readers the Chinese version of these words because over time some of them have been difficult to translate accurately into English; there has also been a not insignificant amount of academic debate about their proper translation, as Wang has noted.

Western scholarly interest in Chinese civil society peaked in the 1990s and the early part of the past decade. Initial optimism and normative faith in the development of civil society waned as the 1989 prodemocracy movement faded into the past, as Eastern Europe and the former Soviet republics struggled with the difficulties of "actually lived democracy," and as China's authoritarian resilience was burnished by rapid economic growth and successful management of economic and social crises, such as the Asian financial crisis, the state enterprise reform of the late 1990s, and most recently the global financial crisis. The use of *civil society* has also been avoided by many Western-educated scholars interested in Chinese NGOs and Chinese associational life because the term seems too closely connected to expectations about democratic political change. The teleological nature of the term was roundly criticized. Western-educated historians helped this decline along by showing that Chinese society in late imperial and republican times seemed to have a cultural proclivity for state-society relations that were less autonomous and more hierarchical than the urban bourgeois societies of Western Europe and North America.[31] Although many scholars continued to study social associations, state-society relations, and contentious social movements, fewer scholars employ the civil society framework.

Given the skepticism in these circles, it is refreshing to find that despite these reservations, Chinese social activists, academics, and some government and party officials have persevered in supporting activities and organizations that allow for the healthy flourishing of groups and networks begun most commonly by the autonomous organization of individuals with a common civic goal (arguably, a relatively precise description of civil society). To be sarcastic, it is gratifying to find that Chinese civil society expands even when Western scholars ignore it!

As Chinese civil society develops further and Chinese society becomes more open to articulating different interests, we may find that our typical focus on civil society against the state is incomplete. If organized interaction and contention between different social interests become more common, more public, and more contentious, it is important to understand how (or whether) China's public sphere can foster civil politics in a rapidly changing society.

Wang first sets out a brief history of the terms and the theoretical debates that have occurred in both China and abroad on the nature of civil society as well as its consequences for social life and politics. As with interpretations of civil society generally, his analysis of civil society is highly normative. That is, civil society is related to the production and realization of normative goals, such as social justice, public interest, and charitable giving. It is the main vehicle to solve social problems and to exercise public power. The key manifestation of civil society is the collective action of individuals to improve social conditions. Civil society as an entity is distinguished from the state and from the market. But realization of civil society contributes to and improves these other dimensions by enhancing social capital, improving democratic governance of the state and the party, and increasing the social responsibility of corporations. It is important to note that his analysis of civil society takes these statements as assumptions rather than as research questions to be tested or explored. His main goal is to evaluate the health and status of Chinese civil society.

Wang also provides a succinct overview of the development of civil society in China's reform era, breaking down the development and trends into three separate stages, each about ten years in duration. The first stage of civil society development has similarities with other economic and political trends of that period of early opening, experimentation, and relative freedom. Increasing from fewer than 10,000 to more than 1,000,000 in a relatively short period of time, Chinese NGOs exploded in number and issue areas. However, this period also brought problems of governance, regulation, and public confidence. The problems of this early flowering led to a more sobering second period of consolidation, increased government oversight and control (especially through the system of sponsorship and registration), and an overall reduction in the number and vibrancy of NGOs. In 1999, for example, only one-fifth of the NGOs that existed in 1989 and one-eighth of those that existed in 2008 were registered. This dip in NGO activity and vibrancy in the 1990s is also related to the political ramifications of the 1989 student movement.

The current period of civil society development is not just a continuation of the early period of relative energy and dynamism. It is also a period of maturation and increased synergy with the market economy. For example, Wang finds that the social organizations of the current period include grassroots organizations, community-based organizations (社区基层组织, *shequ jiceng zuzhi*), business associations, and private foundations linked to corporations or the super rich. On the other side of the market, we also see organizations formed around the rights protection (维权, *weiquan*) of weak actors in the market, such as migrant workers and consumers. The traditional mass organizations of the socialist era have also become more oriented to internal reform and the cultivation of associations that fall under their jurisdiction, including the work of the Women's Federation, the All-China Federation of Trade Unions (ACFTU), and the China Disabled Persons Federation. The Internet has spawned a whole new phenomenon of online organizing and networks of like-minded individuals that can expand beyond the usual boundaries of region, age, class, and so on.

Finally, in the current period local governments have much more actively pursued new styles of governance that encourage and foster, rather than impede and restrain, NGO development. A plethora of different local experiments (in Guangdong, Shenzhen, Nanjing, Hangzhou, among others) have led to new discoveries and innovations. This more lenient, even encouraging, attitude toward NGOs is reflected in the rapid increase of registered NGOs, foundations, and private nonenterprises (民办非企业, *minban feiqiye*). In 2008 there were more than 430,000 registered entities, whereas Wang estimates that the real number of social associations, including those that are registered, unregistered, and registered as commercial entities, is eight to ten times that number (3,440,000 to 4,300,000). These recent developments are related to a number of new developments and breakthroughs in Chinese civil society, including a new era of charitable giving, corporate social responsibility, and foundation work. Activism by social actors has changed government policy and international economic relations. The environmental movement protesting dam building on the Nu River and the Wenzhou Lighter Association protest over EU regulation are two examples. The Internet increasingly serves as a key tool for such activism and, as such, is beginning to constitute an integral part of China's public sphere.

Although China's civil society is currently experiencing a renaissance of sorts after the shrinking and suppression of the 1990s, there are a number of constraints and limitations. The most significant constraint continues to be the sluggish pace of government reform, particularly related to the registration and management of NGOs that lack a party or government background. Related to this delay of effective reform is the tendency for the government to be inherently suspicious of the work of NGOs, particularly after the "color revolutions." The development of NGOs, especially when supported by foreign financial and logistical support, is taken to be an example of peaceful evolution or the work of hostile forces. More pedantically, the civil society sphere struggles with problems of sustainability, professionalization, and the power of the market and market goals over the pursuit of social justice or the public interest.

In commenting on Wang's analysis, I use his conclusion on the future of civil society to question some of our basic assumptions not only about the quality of civil society but also the link between a vibrant civil society and good politics. Wang envisions three potential paths for the future development of China's civil society: paths led by the political elite, the intellectual elite, or the economic elite. Different paths take China's associational life in different directions, obviously, but in all cases these futures are rosy and bright. Vibrant civil societies may be vibrant in different ways; but causally speaking, the effects of this development are beneficial—in pushing forward political reform, in expanding the space and leadership of intellectuals, in enhancing corporate social responsibility and the financial resources of public interest foundations. The future achievements of civil society are impressive, but they also place a considerable amount of responsibility on this one sector.

In 2001 and 2002, for a book on civil society in Asia, I participated in a series of workshops that brought together scholars from India to Japan. In our first meeting we worked on our definitional boundaries and theoretical parameters for a discussion of civil society development in the region. At the second meeting, we were scheduled to make a fuller presentation of our papers and research, dealing with the empirics of each case rather than the general theory or definitions. We were surprised to find that instead of the planned discussion, we almost immediately had to return to the definitional questions and to our foundational theories. What had changed between one workshop and the next? For me, a scholar of China, nothing really. But the terrorist bombings of September 11 and the preparation for a U.S.-led war in Afghanistan significantly affected the analyses of my coauthors writing on Southeast Asian countries with significant Muslim populations. Groups, associations, and networks that had heretofore appeared merely as groups for social welfare and justice, for religious cohesion and education, now appeared differently. It was no longer so clear how one defined civil society. It was also no longer clear that vibrant associational life always leads to good politics and civil behavior.

Skepticism about the effects of civil society is not new. Sheri Berman's examination of Weimar Germany is a seminal work that explores how the energetic associational life of Germans in the Weimar Republic provided an organizational structure that was easily co-opted by the Nazi Party in the interwar period.[32] She also argues that the dynamic development of interwar German civil society was in response to the failure of its political institutions. Like-minded individuals bonded together for common public interests because of their lack of confidence in the government to undertake those responsibilities. "In contrast to what neo-Tocquevillean theories would predict, high levels of associationism, absent strong and responsive national government and political parties, served to fragment rather than unite German society. It was weak political institutionalization rather than a weak civil society that was Germany's main problem during the Wilhelmine and Weimar eras."[33]

Simone Chambers and Jeffrey Kopstein, in the study of what they call bad civil society, also attempt to detach the study of associational life from the assumption that it necessarily leads to good politics and a good society.[34] Examining the decisions of individuals to join such associations, they too acknowledge the importance of political institutions, but they also point to the social and economic prerequisites of civil participation and civil political participation. Habermas's view of the ideal civil society presupposes a laissez-faire state that gets out of the way for civil society's healthy development. Even in the Chinese context, where the state is much stronger and more inclined to intervene, both Western and Chinese scholars assume that the healthy development of civil society is best achieved by removing the state's constraints and its ideological prejudices toward social autonomy.

How do these more skeptical studies of German and American civil societies inform our understanding of China's? We might begin to expect less from civil society and, by lowering our expectations, begin to focus on how reform and changes in other realms (such as the state and the market) can improve the chances for its healthy development. This might include reform of the policy-making and legislative processes to systematically include diverse interests from society, new modes of political participation that incorporate groups (as opposed to the individualistic voting mechanisms used in China's grassroots elections), and reform of markets that enhance the power of weak collectivities against powerful individual interests (for example, enhanced collective bargaining and representation of workers at the workplace).

As Wang clearly recognizes, the development of civil society is intimately connected to these other realms of daily life and participation. It is not possible to disentangle completely the circular relationship between associational life, effective political participation, and distributional and social justice in the marketplace. It is unlikely that any of these will thrive in the absence of the other two.

Notes

1. "Tongwang gongmin shehui" [Toward civil society], *Zhongguo qingnian bao* [China youth daily], December 10, 2008.

2. In her article "Shimin shehui jueding guojia" [On the thought of "civil society shaping the state"], in *Lun 'Heige'er fa zhexue pipan'* [Critique of Hegel's philosophy of right], Li Shuzhen explained for the first time the divisions and contradictions between state and civil society. *Beijing Daxue xuebao, Zhexue shehui kexue ban* [Journal of Peking University (Philosophy and social sciences)] 3, no. 85 (1987), pp. 68–75.

3. Deng Zhenglai, "Shimin shehui yu guojia—xueli shang de fenye yu liang zhong jiagou" [Civil society and the state: Dividing line and two frameworks], in *Guojia yu shehui: Zhongguo shimin shehui yanjiu* [State and society: Research on civil society in China] (Beijing: Peking University Press, 2008) p. 23.

4. Civil society–related papers in this period were mainly published in *Tianjin shehui kexue* [Tianjin social sciences], *Xueshu yuekan* [Academic monthly], *Zhongguo shehui kexue* [Chinese social sciences], *Qiushi* [Seek truth], *Shehui kexue yanjiu* [Social science research], *Shehui kexue* [Social sciences], and *Dangdai shijie yu shehuizhuyi* [Contemporary world and socialism].

5. Xu Yong "Shimin shehui: xiandai zhengzhi wenhua de yuanshengdian" [Civil society: Starting point of modern political culture], *Tianjin shehui kexue* [Tianjin social sciences], no. 4 (1993), pp. 49–52; Qi Heng, "Guanyu 'shimin shehui' ruogan wenti de sikao" [Some thoughts on civil society], *Tianjin shehui kexue* [Tianjin social sciences], no. 5 (1993), pp. 59–69.

6. These terms appear in the following essays: Yu Keping, "Shehuizhuyi shimin shehui: Yi ge xin de yanjiu keti" [Socialist civil society: A new subject of research], *Tianjin shehui kexue* [Tianjin social sciences], no. 4 (1993), pp. 45–48; Jia Dongqiao, "Gongmin shehui: Jianli shichang jingji tizhi de shehui jichu" [Civil society: Social foundation of the market economic system], *Shehui kexue yanjiu* [Social science research], no. 6 (1994), pp. 25–35; Guo Dingping, "Wo guo shimin shehui de fazhan yu zhengzhi zhuanxing" [Civil society development and China's political transformation], *Shehui kexue* [Social sciences], no. 12 (1994), pp. 52–55; Liu Zongtang, "Luelun Zhongguo de shimin shehui yu laonian shiye" [A preliminary study on China's civil society and aging population], *Guiyang shizhuan xuebao, shehui kexue ban* [Journal of Guiyang University (Social sciences)], no. 2 (1994), pp. 14–21; Zhu Baoxin, "Peiyu you Zhongguo tese de shimin shehui chuyi" [Fostering a civil society of Chinese characteristics], *Wen shi zhe* [Journal of literature, history, and philosophy], no. 6 (1994), pp. 63–66.

7. Examples include the Maple Women's Center (1994), Friends of Nature (1994–95), Global Village (1996), Green Earth Volunteer Center (1997), and Green River (1997).

8. In 1998 the State Council set up the NGO Management Bureau under the Ministry of Civil Affairs responsible for the registration and administration of NGOs in China. In October of the same year, two important regulations on NGOs and privately run noncorporate organizations were promulgated.

9. The two terms *gongmin shehui* and *shimin shehui* were distinguished in some works and used interchangeably in others. In Jia Dongqiao's paper "Gongmin shehui," the term *gongmin shehui* is used throughout, and in "Shehuizhuyi shimin shehui," Yu Keping states that "*shimin shehui* is also known as *gongmin shehui*." Therefore, it can be said that *gongmin shehui* became popular in the mid-1990s.

10. Representative works include Wang Ying, She Xiaoye, and Sun Bingyao, *Shehui zhongjian ceng: Gaige yu Zhongguo de shetuan zuzhi* [The middle stratum: Reform and China's social organizations] (Bejing: China Development Press, 1993); Kang Xiaoguang, *Chuangzao xiwang* [Creating hope] (Guilin: Guangxi Lijiang Press, 1997); Kang,

'Xiwang gongcheng' diaocha [Investigation into Project Hope] (Guilin: Guangxi Lijiang Press, 1998); Gordon White and others, *In Search of Civil Society: Market Reform and Social Change in Contemporary China* (Oxford University Press, 1996).

11. Jean L. Cohen and Andrew Arato, *Civil Society and Political Theory* (MIT Press, 1992).

12. *Civil Society* was not published as a single book, only in installments. Michael Edwards, "Civil Society," *China Nonprofit Review*, vol. 2 (July 2008), vol. 3 (December 2008), and vol. 4 (June 2009). The quotation is from vol. 2, p. 110.

13. Yu Keping, "Zhongguo gongmin shehui: Gainian, fenlei yu zhidu huanjing" [Chinese civil society: Concept, classification, and institutional environment], *Zhongguo shehui kexue* [China social sciences], no. 1 (2006), pp. 109–22.

14. Alexis de Tocqueville, *Lun Meiguo de minzhu* [Democracy in America], translated by Dong Guoliang, 2 vols. (Beijing: Commercial Press, 1996); Edwards, "Civil Society," p. 113.

15. Robert Putnam, *Shi minzhu yunzhuan qi lai* [Making democracy work], translated by Wang Lie and Lai Hairong (Nanchang: Jiangxi People's Publishing House, 2001). The term *good society* comes from the book *The Good Society: The Humane Agenda* (Boston: Houghton Mifflin, 1996), in which the American economist John Kenneth Galbraith describes the good society as a "feasible, rather than perfect, society."

16. Jürgen Habermas, *Gonggong lingyu de jiegou zhuanxing* [Structural transformation of the public sphere], translated by Cao Weidong (Shanghai: Xuelin Press, 1999), pp. 28–32.

17. Wang Ming, "Minjian zuzhi de fazhan ji tongxiang gongmin shehui de daolu" [Development of civil organizations and the path toward civil society], in *Zhongguo minjian zuzhi 30 nian—zou xiang gongmin shehui* [Thirty years of civil organizations in China: Toward civil society] (Beijing: Social Sciences Academic Press, 2008), p. 9.

18. Ibid.

19. Three major campaigns were launched in this period to clean up and rectify NGOs. The first was from June 1990 to June 1991, when all NGOs were required to reregister according to new regulatory standards. The second was from April 1997 to October 1999, when measures were taken to strengthen the supervision and administration of social groups and credit unions and to incorporate civil noncorporate organizations in the NGO registration system. The third campaign, which ended in 1999, closed nearly 50,000 rural credit foundations and transferred their combined debts (total RMB 150 billion) to rural credit cooperatives. Ibid., pp. 22–24.

20. The main regulations include the following: the Regulation on Registration and Administration of Social Organizations and Provisional Regulations for the Registration and Administration of People-Run Non-Enterprise Units, both promulgated by the State Council in October 1998, and Interim Measures for Banning Illegal Nongovernmental Organizations, promulgated by the State Council in April 2000.

21. Wang, "Minjian zuzhi de fazhan ji tongxiang gongmin shehui de daolu," pp. 22–24.

22. The Guangdong model, the Shenzhen model, the Hangzhou model, the Nanjing model, and the Anshan model are all practice models developed as local governments

promoted social construction. The Guangdong model is characterized by vigorous government promotion and comprehensive social participation. The Shenzhen model is characterized by active exploration and innovation at the community level. The Hangzhou model is characterized by cooperation and interaction. The Nanjing model is characterized by building a multilayered NGO center. The Anshan model is characterized by vigorously developing social enterprise.

23. Wang Ming, *Shehui zuzhi* [On Chinese NGOs] (Beijing: Social Sciences Academic Press, 2012), p. 206.

24. *Hurun Wealth Report* 2010, released in April (finance.ifeng.com/money/wealth/millionaire/20100401/1999159.shtml).

25. Boston Consulting Group (www.bcg.com.cn/cn/files/publications/reports_pdf/Global_Wealth_ES_Sept_2008.pdf).

26. The Child-Resistant Closure Rule was designed to prevent children from opening lighters. A similar law was enacted in the United States in 1994. The law enacted by the EU has met with resistance from Chinese lighter manufacturers. The law was formally adopted by the EU in February 2006.

27. For details about this case, see Wang Ming and others, "Zhongguo ru shi di yi an" [The first case after China's WTO ascension], in *Zhongguo gonggong guanli tiaolie* [Public policy and management cases in China], vol. 1 (Beijing: Tsinghua University Press, October 2005), p. 114.

28. "Zhengfu chuzi yi yuan goumai gongyi fuwu" [Government spends RMB 100 million to purchase public service], *eBeijing,* July 13, 2010 (www.beijing.gov.cn/szbjxxt/rdgz/t1120711.htm).

29. Hu Jintao, *Gaoju Zhongguo tese shehuizhuyi weida qizhi wei duoqu quanmian jianshe xiaokang shehui xin shengli er fendou* [Hold high the great banner of socialism with Chinese characteristics and strive for new victories in building a moderately prosperous society in all respects], report to the 17th CCP National Congress, October 15, 2007.

30. John Foster Dulles, "Challenge and Response in United States Policy," *Foreign Affairs* 36, no. 1 (1957), pp. 25–43.

31. The scholarly exchange in the journal *Modern China* (1993) on China's civil society was an important part of this debate.

32. See Sherri Berman, "Civil Society and the Collapse of the Weimar Republic," *World Politics,* no. 3 (1997).

33. Ibid., 402.

34. Simone Chambers and Jeffrey Kopstein, "Bad Civil Society," *Political Theory,* no. 6 (2001).

6

China's Experiments in Social Autonomy and Grassroots Democracy

YAN JIRONG

Changes in wealth accumulation, governance, and social life are indispensable indicators of a country's development. Changes of these sorts have taken place in China since the reform and opening-up period began in 1978. These changes can be examined and explained from different perspectives. Indicators can be economic, such as economic growth, the standard of living, the market system, industry structure, and income distribution; they can be political, such as ideology, the political system, and government policy; or they can be societal, such as self-government and social autonomy.

Self-government refers to "a state where an individual or collective entity manages his/its own affairs and is solely responsible for his/its behavior and destiny."[1] Self-government is considered a value goal of social life. In the context of the state, self-government has a twofold meaning. For individuals, it means self-determination and freedom from intervention; for the community, it means participation in the control of economic, social, and political affairs through its representatives. Self-government occurs where the state's highest public power cannot or does not reach.[2] Reasonable self-government is a prerequisite and basic element of good governance. For this reason, social autonomy has always been an important indicator of a state's political development.[3]

China has a long tradition of social autonomy.[4] In traditional China, imperial power stopped at the county level, allowing room for the self-government of rural society. This traditional state governance structure has been summarized by some scholars as a two-layer partition of governance (上下分治, *shangxia fenzhi*), the top layer comprising the central government and its top-down bureaucratic system and the lower layer comprising local governance units controlled by clan heads, local gentry, and local celebrities.[5] The Chinese sociologist Fei Xiaotong (1910-2005) describes this situation as "two-track politics."[6] Based on this same understanding, Huang Zhezhen (1905-92), in his *Outline of Local Autonomy* published in the 1930s, observes that although the term *local autonomy* was introduced to China only in the late Qing dynasty, local autonomy as a phenomenon had existed in China, with various supporting mechanisms, since ancient times.[7]

As part of the socialist transformation following the founding of the People's Republic of China, the Chinese Communist Party (CCP) began to reconstruct the social order by instituting the people's commune system in the countryside, subdistrict office and work-unit systems in cities, and various mass organizations such as trade unions, the Chinese Communist Youth League, and women's federations, thereby strengthening social management and control.[8] With left-leaning ideology as a guide, these systems facilitated the state's penetration of society and led to a highly centralized, totalistic government. It was only after the reform and opening-up period began that China embarked on the path toward reduced state power and expanded social autonomy. (Perhaps, however, this was not out of any design favoring social autonomy on the part of reformist leaders.)

China's reform and opening-up process is often described as one of exploration, or by the Chinese saying "crossing the river by feeling the stones." The development of social autonomy in China over the past thirty years has been driven by three major forces: promotion by the government (which set the development of the country's social autonomy in motion), research by the academy (which intellectually informed the direction of social autonomy), and the practice of civil society (which served as the platform for and the source of the experience of social autonomy). In assessing the development of China's social autonomy over the past thirty years, it is important to to analyze these three forces and how they contributed to China's social autonomy.

Reconstructing State-Society Relations in Chinese Scholarship

The ongoing social autonomy movement in China started in the mid-1980s. This movement had its earliest manifestation in the academic research Chinese scholars undertook on state-society relations and civil society development. As part of their effort to modernize, improve the country's state governance structure, reform the government administration system, and release social creativity from the power and control of the state and government, the Chinese academy began to focus on state-society relations and the double-sided process of state construction and social construction.

The work of Chinese scholars in the late 1980s and early 1990s was directly connected with the prodemocracy movement of the 1980s. Democracy is a long-standing political goal of the Chinese academy and the Chinese citizenry. Following the political disturbance in Beijing in the spring of 1989, the Chinese academy gradually came to the realization that democracy building, as well as being a superstructural transformation, also has to be supported by an appropriate substructure. It cannot be achieved at one stroke through a political movement. Democracy is a political system or political arrangement, but the fulfillment and implementation of democratic politics cover a larger territory than just the political arena. If the establishment of a democratic system is the proper province of political reforms, running a democracy requires support from other systems such as society, the economy, and culture. Democracy building is a systematic project that needs, to use the technology metaphor, not only the corresponding hardware and software but also a compatible operating environment. Building social autonomy and civil society is an integral part of this project.

A survey of China's reform and social development process has found that the research by Chinese academics on state-society relations has progressed through three distinctive stages: the introduction of Western civil society theory, discussion of state-society relations, and summarization of China's experience in social construction and social governance.

Civil Society Theory

Civil society, a term of completely Western origin, has been endowed with rich meaning in its long process of historical evolution. Its introduction into Chinese academic work has a unique background.[9]

As China's political and social systems entered a period of transformation in the 1990s, various social forces were gradually liberated from the previous all-inclusive state system. With deepening market reforms and an increase in social freedom, individual self-awareness began to awaken, and the rigid urban-rural dual registration system began to weaken. By 1992, which marked a new stage of China's economic reforms, there appeared a practical need to rethink and reconfigure state-society relations. With this as a backdrop, the Chinese academy borrowed the concept of civil society as part of a larger effort to draw on the Western experience of modernization with the aim of constructing an ideal framework for modernization and state-society relations in China.

Discussion of civil society in Chinese academia in the early 1990s focused on evaluating civil society theory and borrowing relevant terminology. In that period, discussion took place on the meaning and significance of the term *civil society*, with a general consensus being reached on the following issues:

—Totalitarian politics atomizes society into isolated individuals so as to impose the state's authority directly, and to the greatest extent, on individual social members, and it relies on the existence of a mass society with an extremely low level of organization and institutionalization (that is, made up of isolated individuals).

—Only civil society, with its plural and institutionalized social structure and diversified social interests, can nurture democratic politics.

—Civil society refers to the vast sphere between the state and the individuals in a state or political community, and it is made up of various organizations and groups relatively independent from one another, including family organizations, religious groups, trade unions, chambers of commerce, learned societies, campus groups, community and village groups, entertainment groups and clubs, federations, and associations. Civil society is a spontaneously formed autonomous society outside the state power system and is characterized by independence and institutionalization. Organizing individuals in different social communities according to different forms of association creates a well-organized "citizenry" rather than nondescript "masses."

—Civil society is based on the market economy or even private ownership and supports equal and autonomous contractual relationships, the rule of law, autonomy, and democracy.

—The society that had been in place since the founding of the People's Republic of China was one that integrated politics and society.[10] There was no independent space for society. Every Chinese, from birth to death, was affiliated with the state and his or her work unit. There was no private zone independent from the state. And the development of civil society was promoted by restricting the power of the state and developing democratic politics

Scholarship on State-Society Relations

In the mid-1990s, soon after the introduction in China of the concept of civil society, discussions in the Chinese academic world began to address state-society relations in an attempt to establish an ideal model and argue for the dual task of state construction and social construction, for China's social autonomy and civil society development.

Scholars in China began discussing the Lockean statement that "society precedes and is outside the state"[11] and the Hegelian stance that the state is higher than society. The "strong state, weak society" system put in place in the Mao era, a time when the state overrode and completely controlled society, became the object of reform. In researching the Western experience of civil society, Chinese scholars, rediscovering classic theoretical resources on liberalism, focused on the Lockean theory that society precedes and is outside the state and referenced the theory in their analysis and criticism of China's reality. These discussions lent theoretical support for the state to allow the establishment of nonstate organizations and their social management functions.

With this groundwork laid, Chinese academics had a clearer understanding of state-society relations. This led to the gradual agreement that neither the Hegelian model, in which the state overrides society and commands the complete acquiescence of society, nor the Lockean model, which aligns the state and the society in opposition in a zero-sum game, fit the Chinese circumstance, and that an ideal state-society relationship should be a combination of the two models. Based on this understanding, scholars established a new model of state-society interaction in which state and civil society are interdependent.

The logic is as follows: To remedy the defects of statism, civil society is needed; and to overcome civil society's lack of independence while preventing its collapse requires the presence of the state. There is a process of mutual shaping in effect, in which society makes the state and the state makes society. Each plays an indispensable role in this process because the state making society, unaccompanied by society making the state, will inevitably lead to a strong state with a weak society, resulting in a totalistic state controlling all social fields; and society making the state, unaccompanied by the the state making society, will inevitably lead to a strong society with a weak state, and as a result, every social field will be acting on its own politically. Each case will lead to failure in the development of both state and society. Only a state-society relationship that combines society making the state and the state making society as part of a positive-sum game is desirable.[12]

The interaction between state and society is inherently both tense and harmonious. The unsoundness of the state system is often related to the unsoundness of civil society. In an excessively authoritarian state, for example, civil society tends to be weak or disorderly. The unsoundness or stagnation of civil society often has to do with the great pressure of state power. Socially autonomous organizations can fail to develop as a result of excessive control from the state. For the two to support each other in a benign cycle, efforts must be made to develop both the state and civil society. This means that China's reform needs to be a two-way process.

Constant effort must be made both to regulate state behavior and to strengthen civil society while ensuring a balance between the two. The above analysis offers a clear suggestion: establish a limited-state power structure. In this structure, the functions of the state and government would be explicitly provided for and restricted. This would serve as the basis for adjusting the relationship between the state and nonstate organizations and groups, allowing for the promotion of various social organizations and groups in a way that would put the energy of each social unit to good use within a well-regulated framework.

China's Experience in Social Construction and Social Governance

With deepening discussion on state-society relations and increasing grassroots social autonomy, after the late 1990s China's intelligentsia began to focus on building civil society. Meanwhile, with the rise of research on governance worldwide, the Chinese government's agenda regarding governance reform and institutional innovation entered a new stage by integrating the research on civil society development with that on China's political democratization, social transformation, harmonious society building, and public governance.

As of 2000 an increasing number of scholars have involved themselves in the empirical study of civil society, especially with regard to the demarcation between state and society, the construction of space for social autonomy, and the development of the third sector.[13] The 2009 publication of China's first blue paper on development of civil society in China was regarded by Chinese academics as a landmark achievement in China's civil society research.[14]

The general consensus now among Chinese academics is that what was in place in China before the reform and opening-up period began was a planned economic system and a corresponding system of social control. Under this system, all social resources were centralized in the hands of the government, resulting in a high degree of homogeneity. In cities, people were basically affiliated with the government organ, institution, or enterprise where they worked. In rural areas, people were affiliated with their local people's commune. During that period, state and the society greatly overlapped, with little room for social autonomy.

Since the reform and opening up, great changes have taken place in state-society relations. Not only did the market economy replace the previous planned economic system, but it has also brought about profound changes in the social control system, ways of social life, and the concepts and ideas held by the people. The identity of the people changed: most Chinese, who had been members of people's communes or state-owned enterprises, became independent farmers, workers in enterprises of various ownership systems, private business owners, or other laborers in other categories. This phenomenon marked the collapse of the "unit as castle."[15] A series of other changes also took place in such areas as income distribution, career path, and social security, spelling an end to the petrified social model of unified management and unitary organization. Along with these changes in identity, work, and lifestyle came shifts in people's thinking: the Chinese people became more individualistic and independent. And as a result of these changes, a great number of autonomous self-serving social organizations appeared. As a result of reform and opening up and the resulting economic marketization, many people who had been affiliated with their work units or communes became highly autonomous social members "outside the official system" (体制外, *tizhi wai*), that is, their status changed from a person of the state to a person of society. This led to a certain degree of separation between state and society and the formation of a new social structure, thereby creating the precondition for social autonomy.

Transforming the Governance Model: Government Making the First Move

The most important characteristic of China's thirty years of reform and opening up has been the government's leadership of this movement. The government has played the same role in the development of China's more autonomous society. This leadership role can be seen in two regards: the government has introduced effective policies to reduce the state's intervention in social life, and the government, through self-initiated reforms, has consciously pushed and guided the development of social autonomy.

CCP and Government Efforts toward Social Autonomy

In the report to the 12th CCP National Congress in 1982, the party endorsed the development of grassroots democracy. The report states that "socialist democracy will be expanded to all aspects of political, economic, cultural, and social life, and efforts will be made to promote democracy in the management of institutions and enterprises and the self-governance of citizens in grassroots social life."[16]

On November 23, 1987, at the twenty-third session of the 6th NPC Standing Committee on issues of village committees, committee chairman Peng Zhen noted that "to practice grassroots self-governance of citizens and develop direct grassroots democracy is both the requirement of the Constitution and the policy of the CCP."[17] And at the 14th CCP National Congress in 1992, the CCP announced its commitment to "strengthening grassroots democracy and giving full scope to the role of workers' conferences, neighborhood committees, and villagers' committees."[18] On September 12, 1997, at the 15th CCP National Congress, four democratic developments—democratic elections, democratic decisionmaking, democratic administration, and democratic oversight—for the first time were written into the official report, with the emphasis that

> efforts will be made to expand grassroots democracy, ensure the people's direct exercise of democratic rights and the right to manage their own

affairs and create a happy life of their own in accordance with the law. Governments and mass organizations of self-management at the grassroots level shall improve the grassroots democratic election system, ensure government and financial transparency, and enable the masses to participate in discussion and decisionmaking on grassroots public affairs and charitable causes and to supervise cadres.

On October 14, 2003, at the third session of its 16th National Congress, the CCP adopted the Decision on Several Issues to Improve the Socialist Market Economic System, which required that efforts be made to strengthen "community services and social security in rural areas" and "self-government and self-services in urban and rural communities."[19] On September 19, 2004, at the fourth plenary session of the 16th CCP Central Committee, the Decision of the CCP Central Committee on Strengthening the Party's Governance Capability was adopted, requiring efforts to expand grassroots democracy; improve the democratic management systems of government, mass self-governance organizations, institutions, and enterprises at the grassroots level; improve the transparency of government, enterprises, and villages; and ensure at the grassroots level the rights of the masses to participate in elections, to know facts, to participate in government affairs, and to supervise government in accordance with the law. On October 11, 2006, the Decision of the CCP Central Committee Regarding Several Major Issues on Building a Harmonious Socialist Society instructed that efforts be made to "generally promote community development in urban and rural areas and put in place a new comprehensive community management and service system that features orderly management, provides comprehensive services, and contributes to social harmony."[20] The report to the 17th CCP National Congress on October 15, 2007, stated that efforts would be made to

develop grassroots democracy and ensure that the people enjoy democratic rights in a more extensive and practical way. The most effective and extensive way for the people to exercise their rights as the masters of the country is to manage public affairs and public service programs at the grassroots level; practice self-management, self-service, self-education, and self-oversight; and have democratic oversight over cadres—all as a direct exercise of their democratic rights. Such practices must be emphasized and promoted as the groundwork for developing socialist democracy.[21]

The revised constitution of the CCP adopted at this congress enshrines grassroots democracy as one of the four basic political systems of the People's Republic.[22]

On September 18, 2009, the fourth session of the 17th CCP Central Committee adopted the Decision Regarding Several Major Issues on Strengthening and Improving Party Building in New Situations, which required that efforts be made to promote people's democracy through intraparty democracy, expanding the coverage of democracy, and giving full scope to the role of grassroots organizations in promoting development, serving the masses, consolidating solidarity, and advancing harmony.

This survey of relevant CCP documents demonstrates that China's leadership has considered social autonomy mainly within the context of advancing grassroots democratic politics and has deemed CCP organizations and governments at the grassroots level to be the leading forces of grassroots democracy and social autonomy. To these ends, the CCP has introduced various laws and administrative regulations to implement its policies aimed at putting China's social autonomy on track toward the rule of law and institutionalization. Since the 1980s the party and the state have promulgated a series of laws and regulations on village autonomy and social autonomy. In its efforts to promote social autonomy, the government has set about endorsing and promoting China's grassroots social autonomy through laws and regulations, organizing and implementing social autonomy through the leadership of party organizations and governments at the grassroots level, directing social autonomy through demonstration and pilot programs encouraging social autonomy through awards and commendations, and rectifying malpractices (such as election bribery) through supervision and inspection.

Village Autonomy

China's social autonomy started in the rural areas. Village-based autonomy began following the dissolution of the people's commune system in the early 1980s, when the new household responsibility system began to replace people's communes as the basic production unit. For the sake of convenience of narration, this process toward autonomy is divided into three stages.

Budding and Exploration (1980–87)

After 1978, driven by both the policies of the government and the demands of farmers, rural reform was launched to restore the rural household responsibility system and establish townships in place of people's communes. With the implementation and promotion of the household responsibility system, the people's commune system that integrated government and society was ended. In this new era, who was to take charge of public affairs in the rural areas and how? The farmers came up with the solution: direct election of their leaders.

Just as the household responsibility system, first piloted in Anhui Province, changed the fate of China's rural economy, the first grassroots elections, held in February 1980 in Hezhai Village, in Guangxi Province, changed the landscape of rural local autonomy. Eighty-five villagers representing the households of the six production teams of the Hezhai production brigade selected the first village committee through a secret ballot vote.[23]

In October 1983 the CCP Central Committee and the State Council jointly issued the Circular on Implementing the Separation of Government and Society and Establishing Township Governments, which provided specific requirements for the establishment and running of village committees. The explorative practices at the grassroots level were endorsed by the central government and promoted nationwide through laws and policies. Soon afterward, the village committee system spread across the country. According to statistics, by the end of 1985, a total of 948,618 villager committees had been established.[24]

Piloting and Experimenting (1988–97)

In 1987 the National People's Congress adopted the Organic Law of the Village Committees of the People's Republic of China (for Trial Implementation), which was put into trial implementation on June 1, 1988, providing a legal basis for village autonomy. On February 26, 1988, the Ministry of Civil Affairs announced that pilot village autonomy programs would begin to be implemented, a development that marked a new stage of social autonomy in rural China. By late 1989, the pilot program covered 1,093 of the 2,862 counties across the country.[25]

In February 1994 the Ministry of Civil Affairs issued the Guiding Principles on Conducting Rural Autonomy Demonstrations Nationwide, which updated the existing rural autonomy standards. At the end of 1995, village autonomy had been achieved in 82,266 villages in 63 counties in 29 provinces, autonomous regions, and municipalities.[26] A year later, the elections of the second round of village committees were completed in most regions of China. In Shandong and Liaoning, in particular, there had been five rounds of elections of village committees.

Comprehensive Advancement (1998 to the Present)

The year 1998 had monumental significance in the development of China's village autonomy and the corresponding village committee elections. If the practice of setting up village committees was a temporary experiment, a "quiet revolution," then after October 1998 village autonomy entered a stage of full advancement.[27]

Following almost ten years of experience implementing village autonomy, on November 4, 1998, the National People's Congress revised and formally adopted the Organic Law of the Village Committees of the People's Republic of China. The revised law, with its focus on such issues as candidacy, deliberation, and supervision, added articles and clauses concerning the procedure for direct election of village committee members, the deliberation system of village representatives, and the transparency of village affairs. It also strengthened the provision and procedures of democratic election, decisionmaking, administration, and supervision and established the role of CCP organizations at the grassroots level as the leading nucleus. In addition, provisions were proposed on a wide range of other issues, including the announcement of the list of candidates, the nomination of candidates by villagers, the way village committees would be constituted through village elections, secret-ballot voting, investigation and handling of illegal practices in elections, village representative meetings, transparency of village affairs, and the village autonomy charter. Given such legal endorsement, institutional support, and widespread implementation of direct elections, village autonomy entered a stage of comprehensive institutionalization.

By the end of 2007, according to statistics, 611,234 village committees with a total of 2,411,074 members had been established. Thirty-one provinces had promulgated regulations on village committee elections, twenty-nine had promulgated implementation measures on the organization of village committees, and seven had promulgated regulations on village affairs transparency. General elections had become the norm, with a turnout of approximately 80 percent. Eighty-five percent of villages had established village conferences or conferences of village representatives as the mechanism of democratic decisionmaking, and more than 90 percent of villages had established village finance management groups and village affairs transparency supervisory groups responsible for democratic supervision. Various democratic mechanisms, such as transparency, democratic assessment, democratic deliberation, and hearings had been generally implemented.[28]

Opinions have always differed on the development of social autonomy in rural China. The mainstream view sees its development in a positive light, considering it an experiment of democracy at the grassroots level, an exploration in public governance at the grassroots level, and part of China's larger effort to build a harmonious society. However, many problems and challenges in the development of village autonomy have also appeared. Election problems, such as the issue of the voting eligibility of relocated residents in the process of urbanization, the lack of an explicit definition of election bribery, and lack of specific provisions on withdrawal from elections, have resulted in the absence of a unified standard for addressing problems arising from elections. There has been conflict in the relationship between village committee and the village party branch. And as a result of problems concerning the rights to village autonomy, such as the absence of punitive measures against acts infringing on these rights in the Organic Law of the Village Committees of the People's Republic of China, many illegal election-related acts—such as interfering with vote counting, destroying ballot boxes, tearing ballots, and forcing elections—cannot be rectified. An additional problem is that township government often interferes with village committee elections and the financial affairs of the village.[29]

These problems are merely a byproduct of the development process of village autonomy and cannot be taken as a reason to negate the development of village autonomy. Especially worth noting is that village autonomy is still dependent on the Organic Law of the Village Committees for legitimacy; the law even outlines such details as the precise number range of members on a village committee. Perhaps this is another example of Chinese characteristics in social autonomy.

Village autonomy is indeed an important channel by which to observe China's rural social autonomy and an important basis on which to assess China's social autonomy development. It is not, however, the only basis on which to do so. Village autonomy is reflected not just in these village-based committees and their activities but also in the development of other social organizations in the rural areas.

Grassroots Community in Urban Areas

The development of China's social autonomy has been mainly reflected in the implementation of village autonomy in the rural areas and the fall of the system of work units and rise of the community system in the urban areas. To promote economic development, the government reduced its intervention in the social life of the people and took various measures, described as "breaking the large iron rice bowl" and giving up the government-arranges-all approach, which resulted in laying off a large number of people from state-affiliated institutions. As more and more residents left their state jobs, the responsibilities of public management and social security (such as housing, welfare, relief, and public health) also gradually shifted from the state to society. It is against this backdrop that the autonomy of the neighborhood-based urban community began to be widely promoted.[30]

Evolution of District-Level Governments

After the CCP took over China's major cities in 1949, it announced the abolition of the existing neighborhood administrative system (保甲制度, *baojia zhidu*) and the establishment of district-level governments. After the abolition of the original neighborhood administrative system, various resident organizations—protection brigades, antitheft brigades, and resident groups—were established. Urban grassroots resident organizations were not given the unified name of neighborhood committees, defined as urban resident autonomous organizations, until the promulgation of the Organic Law of Urban Neighborhood Committees in December 1954. After that, the NPC adopted the Organic Law of Urban Subdistrict Offices, which required the establishment of subdistrict offices and neighborhood committees in all regions before the end of 1956.

With the launch of the Cultural Revolution in May 1966, subdistrict offices across the country were seized by so-called rebel groups that renamed them subdistrict revolutionary committees and put them under the unitary leadership of the subdistrict party committees. The subdistrict office system was restored with the adoption of the new constitution in 1978. In January 1980 the State Council reissued the Organic Law of Urban Neighborhood Committees promulgated in 1954, which reaffirmed subdistrict offices as affiliates of their respective municipal or district governments.

Since the beginning of the 1990s, the Chinese government has launched two reforms of its urban administration system. The first was aimed at implementing a new two-level government and three-level administration system. In January 1997 the Standing Committee of the 10th Shanghai People's Congress adopted the Rules of Shanghai Municipality on Subdistrict Offices, which legally established this system. The new system was primarily meant to strengthen the administrative power and functions of governments at the subdistrict level (the third level) and place them in full charge of the social, public, and charitable undertakings within their respective jurisdictions. The Shanghai model was later promoted nationwide as part of the reforms of the subdistrict system.[31]

However, while it strengthened the administrative power and functions of subdistrict offices, this system also strengthened the administration of resident autonomous organizations. In addition, as they were mainly financed by the allocations of subdistrict offices, community services were dominated by subdistrict offices, leaving little room for residents to take part in the decisionmaking process. To address this situation, a second reform was introduced after 2000, the primary purpose of which was to further strengthen the autonomy of neighborhood committees. In the process of this reform, many new models were created across China, in Shenzhen, Beijing (the Lugu neighborhood model), Nanjing, and Qingdao, among other places. Almost all of them involved the abolition of subdistrict offices and communization. This reform strengthened neighborhood management, created neighborhood autonomous organizations, and established the direction of urban neighborhood autonomy in China.

On October 11, 2006, the sixth plenary session of the 16th CCP Central Committee adopted the Decision of the CCP Central Committee on Several Major Issues Regarding the Building of a Harmonious Socialist Society, which declared the goal of building harmonious neighborhoods and required all neighborhoods to improve public services and develop a neighborhood service industry. In October 2009 the National Working Meeting on Harmonious Neighborhood Building was held in Suzhou, Jiangsu Province. The meeting designated 188 national model districts (cities), 253 national model subdistricts, and 500 national model neighborhoods in the pursuit of harmonious neighborhood building. With the reform of the housing system, the past decade has seen the rise of another kind of urban autonomous organization: home owner committees, which have developed from the grass roots, have more initiative and independence, and better reflect the spirit of neighborhood autonomy.

Without a doubt, the neighborhood autonomy movement in urban China has great significance for the development of an autonomous society and the improvement of public administration and services. There are many positive effects of urban autonomy. First, it has promoted the development of neighborhood nongovernmental organizations (NGOs). In the process of neighborhood building, cities across the country have actively sought to foster neighborhood-based service-oriented charitable and mutually supporting nongovernmental organizations and, through such channels as government procurement of services and project management, guide these organizations to take part in the administration and provision of services in such fields as neighborhood culture, sports, education, public health, and senior care. According to statistics, in 2008 Shanghai alone allocated more than RMB 300 million to 10,418 neighborhood-based charity organizations. Tianjin created an NGO registration and regulation system and gave support to 6,506 neighborhood NGOs. Nanjing also introduced measures for the registration of NGOs and gave support to 3,500 neighborhood NGOs.[32]

Second, with its advocacy of volunteerism the neighborhood autonomy movement has promoted the development of neighborhood voluntary services in a more standardized, professional, and institutional direction. In 2008, according to statistics, with the implementation of the neighborhood volunteer registration system nationwide, there were more than 430,000 neighborhood volunteer organizations with more than 20 million registered members who have taken part in more than 30 million voluntary activities.[33]

Third, and finally, neighborhood autonomy has helped expand the coverage of neighborhood-based public services. A statistical report from 2008 shows that nationwide there were 748,000 neighborhood service outlets, 3,515 neighborhood service centers, and 30,021 neighborhood service stations. With 7,223 neighborhood public health service centers and 21,895 neighborhood public health service stations, neighborhood public health service reached 100 percent coverage in cities at the prefectural level and above and more than 90 percent in cities at the county level. There were 67,000 neighborhood labor security work stations. Neighborhood relief organizations were fairly well established, with 7,053 charity stores. There were more than 100,000 neighborhood security service stations and 61,000 neighborhood police offices. Approximately 50,000 neighborhood people's mediation committees and 55,000 legal assistance work stations offered services to local residents. In 2008 alone, more than 1.5 million written agreements were reached among disputing residents via neighborhood people's mediation committees.[34]

Social Capital Investment: Development of Social Organizations and Industry Autonomy

Without a well-developed civil organization system, there cannot be mature social autonomy. Much research has shown that social capital provides the glue for social harmony and is an intangible resource that sets democracy in motion and improves government administration, and that social organizations are a generator of social capital.[35] Since the reform and opening up, social organizations have seen rapid development and are having an increasingly wide and profound influence on China's economic growth, political democratization, ecological protection, cultural development, and social harmony.

In China, NGOs are often called civil organizations, social groups, or the third sector. According to the classification of the Ministry of Civil Affairs, China's civil organizations fall mainly into two categories: social organizations and privately run nonenterprise units. Social organizations are nonprofit organizations that Chinese citizens join on a voluntary basis and that carry out activities according to their articles of association to fulfill the shared mission of their members. Such organizations include associations, learned societies, federations, research societies, foundations, friendship associations, promotion associations, and chambers of commerce. Privately run nonenterprises are social organizations established by enterprises, institutions, social groups, and other social forces with non-state-owned assets for the purpose of engaging in nonprofit social service activities, including all kinds of privately run schools, hospitals, welfare institutions, neighborhood service centers, professional training centers, research institutes, cultural centers, and sports facilities.

According to official statistics, there are currently 431,000 registered social organizations in China, more than 1,800 foundations and hundreds of

Figure 6-1. *Growth of NGOs in China*

Number of NGOs (each unit = 10,000)   Rate (percent)

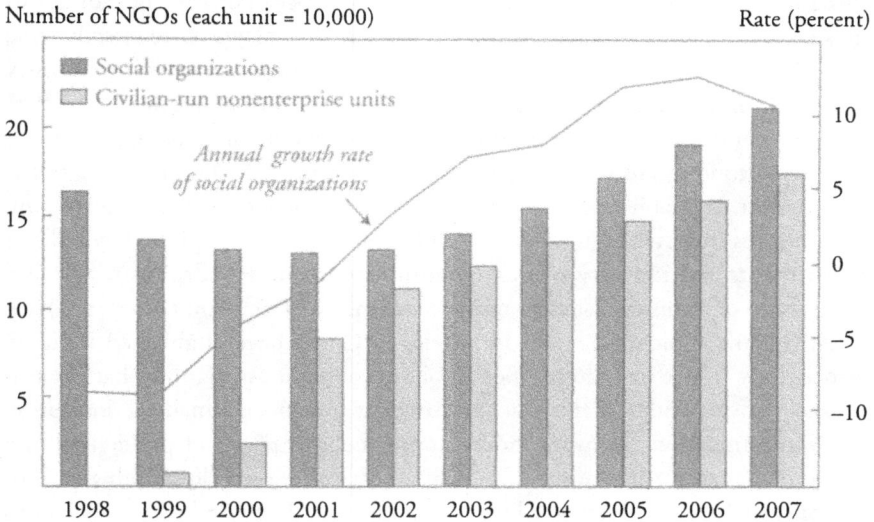

Source: "Minzheng shiye fazhan baogao" [Report on the Development of Chinese Civil Administration] (Beijing: Ministry of Civil Affairs of the People's Republic of China, 2009).

thousands of social groups and civil not-for-profit organizations.[36] These numbers are impressive, but because organizations are sometimes established with great fanfare only to disappear quietly several years later, the figures are debatable. Of course, there are also many social organizations that are not registered at all and therefore not reflected in these numbers.

However, it is certain that the number of social organizations has been expanding rapidly. Since 2000, social organizations have not only seen a rapid growth in number (as shown in figure 6-1), but have also become increasingly diversified, including a wide variety of social organizations such as grassroots organizations and foundations.

Much research has shown that social organizations have become an important social force, method of social organization and mobilization, channel for expression of interests of different social groups, and path of resource concentration in China. Active in various social fields, these nongovernmental organizations have played a major and positive role in helping address social problems in environmental protection, poverty relief, improving the lives of women, social welfare and assistance, civil education, agricultural and business development, social development intelligence support, and so on.

Among the various social organizations, industry associations are arguably those that are most supported by the government because they are thought to make up for the shortcomings of the government and play a more effective role than the government in regulating market competition, maintaining industry order, and improving industry service capacity, all of which are major tasks of industry development and administration. The government's basic policies on industry autonomy are as follows: The government takes the lead in giving financial support to establish industry associations. The government formulates and promulgates industry regulations to guide industry self-discipline. Civil affairs departments and industry regulatory authorities conduct administration and supervision of industry associations in accordance with relevant laws.

At present, almost all major industries in China have established industry associations. These include certified public accountant associations, bar associations, and associations of the tourism, real estate, chemical, financial, insurance, telecommunication, software, home appliance, printing and packaging, and property management industries. In addition there are many local industry associations, such as the Wenzhou Lighter Association. These industry associations have shared regulatory responsibility with the government and promoted industry self-discipline, while also facilitating interest concentration, interest expression, and interest coordination and organizing collective action.[37]

Concluding Thoughts

When it comes to issues in China, the same facts often lead people to different interpretations. This is particularly true of assessments of China's social autonomy development. Starkly different opinions exist on whether China has made real progress in this regard.

Chinese scholars have always focused on social autonomy in the context of China's political democratization based on the firm belief that independent social organizations are an important force in "minimizing government control of social life, ensuring political freedom, and improving people's lives" and that social autonomy is not only the direct outcome of democratization but also the precondition for the successful implementation of democracy.[38] However, the failures of some countries and regions in their democratization process and China's own grassroots democracy exploration since the 1990s have puzzled some people as to whether democratic autonomy can remedy administrative defects or is actually itself a disaster in disguise. Some believe the latter and that to practice democracy is to open a Pandora's box. Some even say that democratic autonomy is the root of instability and a trap set by "hostile Western forces" to overthrow China.

The explorations in social autonomy and democracy at the grassroots level have shown, however, that democratic autonomy, far from being a disaster, can remedy existing administrative defects. Some hold that democratic elections will weaken the control of the party. However, according to some research, the threat to the CCP is not that rural grassroots elections have weakened the political influence of party branches but rather that the problems of party building at the grassroots level that have accumulated over a long period of time have now been exposed in the process of direct and open competition. It is true that elections have challenged the traditional authority of party branches in rural areas, but if the party branches are not actively involved in the elections, they are in effect giving up their political leadership. The elections have called into question the legitimacy of the power of party branches; whether this legitimacy challenge can be solved in rural elections will depend on how the ruling party makes institutional adjustments.[39]

As chapter 5 of this volume shows, the rise of civil society in China has been studied and recognized by many observers. The extraordinary performance of NGOs in the rescue efforts during the Wenchuan earthquake in 2008 offered strong evidence of this. According to an estimate by the Ministry of Civil Affairs, in the months following the May 12 earthquake, more than 3 million volunteers took part in the rescue effort by assisting with medical treatment, food distribution, security, and the like. The assessment report prepared by Sichuan Province showed that a total of 263 NGOs and 63 foundations offered help.

Many China scholars have been concerned with the question of whether the CCP's social control will become stronger or weaker as a result of the the reform and opening-up process and whether economic reforms will lead to the emergence of civil society and thus promote reform of the country's system at a national level. These questions tend to trap the mind in preoccupation with the existence of a state of opposition between the state and society or with the thought of society challenging the state. China's experience in the development of social autonomy seems to give more support to a relationship model in which the state and society are interdependent.[40] In this relationship model, the state creates a large number of social organizations and quasi-administrative organizations for the purpose of managing the nation's increasingly complicated economic and social affairs, leading to a "state-led civil society."[41] Will the state's efforts to promote social autonomy strengthen or weaken the state's capacity? This question can lead to diametrically opposed conclusions.

China's experience in developing social autonomy shows that the state's promotion of social autonomy leads to certain needs for decentralization and social self-management. In the new power structure, all social organizations try to seek operational space by virtue of their own resources. Some of these autonomous social organizations were established at the direction of the government, such as neighborhood autonomy organizations and industry associations; some grew by themselves and were later endorsed and promoted by the government, such as autonomous village organizations; and some were established by social forces and recognized by the government. As Tony Saich, contributor to this volume, notes, judging from the development of social organizations, a complicated interaction and negotiation exists between almost every social organization and the state, a process by which the state controls society by corporatizing social organizations and social organizations elevate their status by taking advantage of policy loopholes.[42] This is a win-win situation that benefits all parties, and therefore it is difficult to make a definitive judgment about the impact of social autonomy on the state's capacity.

Some research holds that given the strict administration of social organizations, what exists presently in China is essentially an approval rather than an authentication system.[43] Indeed, China's social autonomy should to a considerable extent be attributed to the initiation and promotion of the government, and therefore it is primarily the government's means to make up for its own weaknesses in administration. In this sense, autonomous social organizations cannot be equated with typical interest groups. Nevertheless, like growing children, with the passage of time these organizations will become increasingly self-aware and seek to advance their own interests. Examples of this include various demonstrations or petitions used by social groups, such as "taking to the streets" and "tea drinking."

China has seen impressive development in social autonomy over the past thirty years, including village autonomy, neighborhood autonomy, NGOs, and industry autonomy. However, it cannot be denied that there is still a great gap in the "publicness" of government decisionmaking, government administration, and government services. For a country like China, social autonomy is, of course, the first step in its overall development. But the question is, what is the step following social autonomy? Although social autonomy and related organizations have provided the methods and channels by which different interest groups can express their wishes, demands, and will, what is the meaning of these expressions if the government remains deaf and blind to them? The next crucial step is to achieve openness in government decisionmaking, administration, and service to society and to turn public topics into agenda items for public policy decisionmaking. In this regard, the government needs to show more grit and determination. It can be said with good reason that the development of China's social autonomy will only go as far as the Chinese government, through its own efforts toward openness and "publicness," allows it to go.

COMMENT
ANDREW G. WALDER

Yan Jirong has provided us with a highly sophisticated and broad-ranging analysis both of the evolution of grassroots Chinese sociopolitical organization over the past thirty years of market reform and of scholarly discussions, central government policies, and grassroots experiments that have been fostered by efforts to increase citizen participation in local self-governance. I fully agree with Yan's premise that it is not useful to argue about whether new developments in civil society or social autonomy represent a glass that is half empty or half full. Obviously, these nascent developments are still relatively limited. The key issue, as he emphasizes, is whether these reforms lead to improved governance at the grassroots level. As Yan notes, some in China worry that local self-governance is a potential source of political instability, something that may weaken the party-state and open up a Pandora's box of political problems in the future. He argues, in response, that this is an unnecessary zero-sum view of political participation and political control. In fact, he argues, the development of local self-governance can lead to improved governance and can resolve social and political conflicts at the grass roots, which, if left otherwise unattended, might cumulate into more serious threats to political stability.

Yan expresses his concern about the balanced development of China's economy, political institutions, and social institutions. His chapter deals primarily with the last of the three. Although he does not state it directly, I sense that he believes that continued rapid economic growth alone will not suffice to keep China on a path toward prosperity and political stability. Political and social institutions must adapt to new circumstances and problems; if they fail to adapt, China's rise will be put in danger, quite possibly along with its political stability. Yan argues that permitting the full development of societal self-governance is an essential first step in ensuring that China's political and social institutions will continue to develop in a healthy fashion and enhance China's rise instead of serving as a barrier that holds China back.

Yan believes that those who fear that strengthened local self-governance opens the country to potential instability lack confidence in both China's government and in the regime's reservoir of popular support. My own way of stating this idea is that China's leaders should exhibit the same spirit of confident innovation and experimentation in governing Chinese society as they have exhibited over the past thirty years in reorganizing the economy. During the 1980s some Chinese leaders were certain that continued economic reform and opening to the outside world would lead to the collapse of party rule. These fears, of course, proved unfounded, but China was fortunate in the early 1990s to have leaders confident enough to push forward the economic reforms that have enhanced China's prosperity. The broader question raised indirectly by Yan's chapter is whether the political institutions that have guided the economic rise of the past thirty years are adequate to ensure another thirty years of prosperity and stability, or whether they will need to adapt, evolve, and change to fit with the greatly changed economy and society that now exist and that will continue to change rapidly.

I want to make clear that when I say adapt, evolve, and change I do not mean, as so many observers outside China explicitly argue or implicitly assume, an evolution toward a multiparty political system along so-called Western lines or even along the lines of Japan or India. I do mean good governance. What this means is that laws passed by the central government will actually be obeyed by lower levels in the government hierarchy; that officials at the basic level will govern fairly and humanely; that these officials will not take advantage of their positions to enrich themselves, family members, and friends; and that they will not harshly suppress ordinary citizens who speak out about official abuse of power. If this cannot be ensured, and if problems such as these cannot be controlled, China may eventually become a weak and unstable state that lacks the support of its own people, regardless of rates of economic growth.

Many outside observers, and certainly most American observers, often assume that only a multiparty political system that enshrines the rule of law can bring good governance. There are good reasons for doubting this assumption. First, many multiparty political systems are poorly governed, deeply corrupt, illiberal, violent, and politically unstable. Just think of the many postcommunist regimes that were never able to consolidate effective multiparty systems. The long struggles of Russia and Ukraine are well known; even more trying have been the experiences of Georgia, Serbia, Moldova, Belarus, Uzbekistan, and Kyrgyzstan. It is far from clear that a move to a multiparty system would solve governance problems in China, and it is arguable that it would make them worse. The fear of instability, deepening corruption, and political violence is real (although the fear of national dismemberment owing to ethnic nationalism is less real, as I note below).

The second reason is the history of the United States, with which Americans who write about China often appear to have little familiarity. The United States had extensive and deeply rooted political corruption, at both the local and national level, from the 1830s well into the twentieth century. It was not the spread of multiparty democracy that eventually reigned in the most serious abuses, nor was it the establishment of the rule of law. Both of these existed from the establishment of the United States, and the party system and especially the local courts were at the heart of corrupt practices. It was, in fact, the expansion of federal regulation and federal law, and the creation of a professional state admin-istration independent of political parties during the twentieth century—greater regulative capacity of the central government—that finally reduced the level of corruption to reasonable levels.

The same observation holds for the conduct of state and local government throughout the American South starting in the 1880s. Simply put, the central government could not enforce the national constitution in those regions, which created an apartheid regime similar to that of South Africa. This corrupt and oppressive form of rule was reinforced by courts and political parties and backed up by violence and official malfeasance. It was only the continuing strength of central government power that finally, by the 1960s—in response to massive protests in the South and eventually in the North—pushed the central gov-ernment to extend its power into the South and end these practices. America's multiparty system and rule of law were highly unstable throughout the 1840s and 1850s, and this led eventually to a long and bloody civil war. The United States became stable and governable only with the expansion of the powers of the central government, beginning with the wartime administration of Abraham Lincoln and continuing for most of the next century with the New Deal and the further expansion in World War II and the Cold War era.

A third reason for discounting multiparty democracy and rule of law as the only way to generate good governance is the experience of two political jurisdic-tions that have had striking short-run success in rooting out corruption—Hong Kong and Singapore. In both cases an extralegal commission set up by largely unaccountable authorities—the British in Hong Kong and the Lee Kwan Yew administration in Singapore—imprisoned individuals who had assets that could not be explained by their salaries or legal sources of income. Rule of law Amer-ican style would have made this impossible; lawyers would drag out cases in courts, generating enormous fees as the accused hid their assets offshore. Hong Kong and Singapore coupled draconian legal measures—administered by gov-ernment units largely insulated from political manipulation—with increases in the compensation levels for public officials.

My point is not to denigrate multiparty democracy or to justify arguments for delaying further political reform in China. If we take away the equation of political reform with multiparty democracy and Westernization, we take away the excuse not to act in a decisive manner. Good governance demands a con-stant rethinking of organizational forms and administrative techniques—simi-lar to the way the issue of corruption was taken out of the hands of political executives and parties in Hong Kong and Singapore. This involves creating new forms of law and new enforcement mechanisms and a commitment by political leaders to the enforcement of these laws regardless of their consequences. If it is possible to police the Internet and monitor the flow of information within China, surely it is possible to monitor the incomes and behavior of officials and strike hard when malfeasance and abuse of power is detected. Equating political reform with Westernization and multiparty competition prevents effective action of any kind; moreover, it ignores what actually makes multiparty systems stable and effective—a strong central state. The creation of good governance in China should not be viewed simply as a project of democratization—it should be viewed as a project of state building and national self-strengthening. As Yan would probably put it, this is a win for both the people and the state.

Yan's chapter permits me to explore some worries that have nagged at me as I have followed recent political trends in China. Like Yan, I feel that it is essential for China to follow its remarkable record of reforming economic institutions with complementary reform of political and social institutions. I see an excessive concern with ensuring stability at any cost and a fear of instability that prevents strong approaches to problems of corruption and abuse of power at the local levels that are of concern to many Chinese citizens and national leaders alike.

Yan has addressed this problem from a micro perspective—grassroots governance. I would like to shift the view to a macro comparative perspective. What has distinguished China's experience over the past thirty years from those of other socialist economies? What factor has permitted China to escape the severe problems of the former Soviet Union and enjoy a sustained rise in living standards and rapid economic development? I do not think gradual reform versus radical reform is the answer. Radical reforms—a rapid shift to multiparty democracy and a predominantly private economy—have turned out well in many of the small nations on the eastern rim of Europe. Countries such as Poland, Hungary, Slovenia, the Czech Republic, and Slovakia had limited transitional recessions and are now stable, prosperous, open, and free—infinitely better off than they were in the 1980s. With some qualifications the same claims could also be made for Estonia, Lithuania, Latvia, Bulgaria, Mongolia, and even Albania.

Nor do I think political stability is the key element. Radical reform did not create instability in the Soviet Union or in Romania, East Germany, and Yugoslavia. These regimes collapsed because their leaders had postponed or forbidden any manner of political reform for ideological reasons and had relied on repression and demands for discipline and obedience to guarantee the stability necessary for the building of socialism. The problem was that the concern for stability led to political stagnation, so that by the time Mikhail Gorbachev tried to address the accumulated political rottenness of the Soviet system, for example, it was too late. One regime after another came apart at the seams in Eastern

Europe: Poland, Hungary, East Germany, Czechoslovakia, Bulgaria, Romania, Albania, Yugoslavia, and eventually the USSR itself. Who brought down socialism in Eastern Europe? The real culprit was not Gorbachev; in my view, it was Leonid Brezhnev, and the conservative collective leadership over which he presided, which valued stability above all else and was therefore unable to reform its political institutions. Brezhnevism killed the Soviet system because on the political side it could not imagine anything other than maintaining stability, and it could not imagine anything more than improved surveillance, monitoring, censorship, and repression as the answer to internal political problems.

My worry about China at its current juncture is that its leaders, trying to avoid the errors of Gorbachev, will gradually take the path of Brezhnev. If true, this will be unfortunate, because China is in an infinitely better position to think about political restructuring than was the Soviet Union in the 1980s. The economic reforms have worked well. Chinese citizens feel a surge of patriotism and national pride that have followed China's rise. China's university students no longer direct their critical attention to the policies of the central government, as they did in the 1980s. Many are interested in joining the party and holding government jobs, a big change from twenty years ago.

China is not the Soviet Union, certainly not the Soviet Union of the 1980s. It is not realistic to fear that national dismemberment will unfold as it did in the Soviet Union. Only half of the Soviet population was Russian, and the non-Russians were concentrated in fourteen separate republics, only three of which spoke Slavic languages. Unlike Yugoslavia, China is not a federal republic made up of five separate nationalities. China's population is well over 90 percent Han. Soviet-style disintegration is highly unlikely. Soviet-style political stagnation is a greater danger.

The danger of Soviet-style political stagnation is real because China, after all, has one of the few remaining Soviet-style political systems in the world. This system has failed virtually everywhere. The only survivors are Vietnam, North Korea, Cuba, and Laos—not an impressive list. Soviet-style political institutions did not collapse solely because the economy was weak. They failed because they could not provide good governance, and as a result they lost the confidence of both ordinary citizens and large portions of their party members, even top political leaders. To be sure, China has made these institutions work during the first thirty years of its economic reforms. China has prevented the worst problems of Soviet-style rule by ensuring regular rotation of younger and better-trained leaders and by providing strong career incentives for officials. And China is a much more open place today than the Soviet Union in the mid-1980s, permitting its citizens more freedom and access to information. In short, I do not see China's transition as trapped between extensive economic changes and rigid political institutions. But China is at a turning point. If the opportunity to restructure institutions while conditions are favorable is missed, the trap will be sprung, and China's rise will gradually stall.

Soviet-style political institutions were designed to run a centrally planned economy that was inspired by wartime mobilization. They were not designed to rule a nation with a vibrant market-oriented economy, one that is relatively open to the outside world and that competes with more established economic powers on a fairly equal footing. I am sympathetic with arguments that the adoption of a Western-style multiparty system will not solve China's problems, and I also recognize the real dangers of attempting to move in such a direction prematurely (though I cannot define "prematurely"). However, I am certain that it is possible to redesign China's political institutions in a way that does not involve a leap into uncontrolled pluralism. Failure to do so will lead China to suffer the fate of the Brezhnev-era Soviet Union. That day may be much closer than we suspect, and there are worrying signs that the process of political stagnation and decay has already begun.

Finally, I should note that my comments do run counter to Yan's arguments in one important respect. The necessary political changes will not be accomplished from the bottom up unless there are accompanying changes in national political institutions. There is a strong tradition of thought about civil society that views it as an outcome of a certain form of government, not as its creator. That is, a vibrant self-governing society is something that is created by forms of government organization that already enshrine autonomy and political rights. The society observed by Alexis de Toqueville in America in the 1820s was the product of a revolutionary constitution created more than thirty years earlier. It was not a feature of colonial America, and at the time de Toqueville wrote it was not a feature of the mother country of England. The real function of experiments in local self-government in China is educative: it teaches political leaders that there is nothing to fear. Once this fear is overcome, the changes that will restructure China's state for the twenty-first century must come from the top down.

Notes

1. *Bulaikewei'er zhengzhixue baike quanshu* [Blackwell encyclopedia of political thought], translated by Deng Zhenglai and others (Beijing: China University of Political Science and Law Press, 1992), pp. 693–94.

2. Sang Yucheng, *Zizhi zhengzhi* [Autonomous politics] (Hong Kong: Sanlian shudian, 1994), p. 3.

3. There has also been discussion of the relationship between autonomy and other factors affecting political development, such as state capacity, civil rights, and democratic politics. A survey of these discussions can be found in Xu Zengyang's article "Zizhi: Chuantong yu xiandai de bijiao" [A comparison of traditional and modern autonomy], *Jingji shehui tizhi bijiao* [Comparative economic and social systems], no. 1 (2008).

4. Liang Shuming, *Liang Shuming quanji* [Complete works of Liang Shuming], vol. 5 (Jinan: Shandong People's Publishing House, 1992), p. 585.

5. Wang Xianming, *Gentry in Modern China* (Tianjin: Tianjin People's Publishing House, 1997), p. 27. Tsinghua University professor Qin Hui summarizes China's traditional autonomy as a state for which, "because state power did not go down to the county level, all affairs below the county level were determined by clans, all clans were autonomous, autonomy relied on ethics, and ethics relied on the country gentry." Qin Hui, *Chuantong shilun: Bentu shehui de zhidu wenhua yu qi bianqe* [Ten lectures on tradition: Institutional culture of China's indigenous society and its change] (Shanghai: Fudan University Press, 2003), p. 3.

6. Fei Xiaotong, *Zhongguo shenshi* [China's gentry] (Beijing: China Social Sciences Press, 2006), pp. 46–56.

7. Huang Zhezhen, *Difang zizhi gangyao* [Outline of local autonomy] (Beijing: Zhonghua Book Company, 1935), p. 57.

8. Kenneth Lieberthal, *Zhili Zhongguo: Cong geming dao gaige* [Governing China: From revolution through reform], translated by Hu Guocheng and Zhao Mei (Beijing: China Social Sciences Press, 2010), p. 304.

9. The term *civil society* has three slightly different translations in Chinese. See He Zengke, "Introduction to the Research on Civil Society and the Third Sector," *Marxism and Reality*, no. 1 (2000).

10. Deng Zhenglai, "Zhongguo shimin shehui yanjiu de yanjiu" [Research on the research on China's civil society], in *Guojia yu shimin shehui* [State and civil society], edited by Jeffrey C. Alexander and Deng Zhenglai (Shanghai: Century Publishing Group, Shanghai People's Publishing House, 2006).

11. According to John Locke, the "natural state" existed long before the advent of the state, and both the state and government were subject to the preexisting society. See John Locke, *Zhengfu lun* [The second treatise of government], vol. 2 (Beijing: Commercial Press).

12. Gan Yang, "'Minjian shehui' gainian pipan"[Critique of the concept of "civil society"], in *Guojia yu shehui* [State and society], compiled by Zhang Jing (Hangzhou: Zhejiang People's Publishing House, 1998).

13. Wang Qing, "Guanyu fei zhengfu zuzhi yu gongmin shehui" [NGOs and civil society], in *Zhongguo gaoxiao zhexue shehui kexue faz han baogao* [Report on the development of philosophy and social sciences in China's universities, 1978–2008], edited by Wang Puqu and others (Nanning: Guangxi Normal University Press, 2008), pp. 264–69.

14. "Zhongguo gongmin shehui fazhan lanpishu" [Blue paper on China's civil society development], compiled by the Center for Civil Society Studies (Beijing: Peking University Press, 2009).

15. The work unit was a special type of social organization established in China's urban areas by the Chinese Communist Party. Generally speaking, it included government organs, military organizations, enterprises, commercial organizations, schools, and hospitals, among others. The work unit not only paid its employee wages but also provided substantial social benefits to its employees, including low-priced food, commercial goods, medical services, kindergarten, and even primary school. A well-developed work unit could be seen as the modern form of a medieval castle. See Cao Jinqing and others, *Zouchu lixiang "chengbao": Zhongguo danwei xianxiang yanjiu* [Leaving the "ideal castle": Research on China's work units] (Shenzhen: Haitian Publishing House, 1997).

16. See Hu Yaobang, *Quanmian kaichuang shehuizhuyi xiandaihua jianshe de xin jumian: Hu Yaobang zai zhongguo gongchandang di shierci quanguo daibiao dahui shang de baogao* [Hu Yaobang, opening a new chapter in China's socialist modernization drive: A report to the 12th CCP National Congress] (cpc.people.com.cn/GB/64162/64168/645 67/65446/4526308.html).

17. Editing Committee of CCP Documents, *Peng Zhen Wenxuan* [Selected works of Peng Zhen] (Beijing: People's Publishing House, 1991).

18. Jiang Zemin, "Jiakuai gaige kaifang he xiandaihua jianshe bufa, duoqu you zhongguo tese shehuizhuyi shiye de gengda shengli: zai zhongguo gongchandang di shisici quanguo daibiao dahui shang de baogao" [Speed the pace of reform and opening up and modernization drive and make more victories in the course of socialism with Chinese characteristics] (cpc.people.com.cn/GB/64162/64168/64567/65446/4526308.html).

19. *Zhonggong zhongyang guanyu wanshan shehuizhuyi shichang jingji tizhi ruogan wenti de jueding* [Decisions of the CCP's Central Committee on perfecting socialist market economy system] (Beijing: People's Publishing House, 2003).

20. CCP Central Committee, *Zhonggong zhongyang guanyu goujian shehuizhuyi hexie shehui ruogan zhongda wenti de jueding* [Certain major decisions on the construction of a socialist harmonious society], October 18, 2006 (news.xinhuanet.com/politics/2006-10/18/content_5218639.htm).

21. Hu Jintao, *Gaoju Zhongguo tese shehuizhuyi weida qizhi wei duoqu quanmian jianshe xiaokang shehui xin shengli er fendou* [Hold high the great banner of socialism with Chinese characteristics and strive for new victories in building a moderately prosperous society in all respects], report to the 17th CCP National Congress, October 15, 2007 (cpc.people.com.cn/GB/64162/64168/64567/65446/4526308.html).

22. The other three political systems are the people's congress system, the system of multiparty cooperation and political consultation, and the system of regional ethnic autonomy.

23. For a detailed review of the Hezhai Villager Committee and its functions, composition, and elections, see Xu Yong, "Weida de chuangzao cong zheli qibu: Tanfang Zhongguo zui zao de cunweihui de danshengdi" [A great creation started here: The birthplace of China's first villager committee], in *Xiangcun zhili yu Zhongguo zhengzhi* [Rural governance and China politics] (Beijing: China Social Sciences Press, 2003), p. 14.

24. Zhou Luogeng and Wang Zhongtian, "Zhongguo nongcun de jiceng minzhu fazhan yu nongmin de minzhu quanli baozhang" [Democracy in Chinese villages and

protection of the democratic rights of Chinese villagers: The history, reality and future of village autonomy in China], *Shanghai shehui kexueyuan xueshu jikan* [Shanghai social science quarterly], no. 1 (1999).

25. Zhang Xianguo and others, "Cunmin zizhi caogen minzhu tuidong xiang-cun zhili" [Village autonomy and grassroots democracy reshaping rural governance], *Liaowang xinwen zhoukan* [Outlook weekly], October 8, 2008.

26. Hu Yaobang, "Quanmian kaichuang shehuizhuyi xiandaihua jianshe de xin jumian: Hu Yaobang zai zhongguo gongchandang di shier ci quanguo daibiao dahui shang de baogao" [Hu Yaobang, Opening a new chapter in China's socialist moderniza-tion drive: A report to the 12th National Congress of CPC] (cpc.people.com.cn/GB/641 62/64168/64567/65446/4526308.html).

27. Xu, "Weida de chuangzao cong zheli qibu," p. 14.

28. Data are cited from "Cunmin zizhi: Shijie zui da de 'minzhu xunlian ban'" [Vil-lage autonomy: The world's largest "democracy training class"], *Fazhi ribao* [Legal daily], October 12, 2008.

29. Tan Hongjie, "Cunmin zizhi: Xianzhuang yu duice" [Villagers' autonomy: Cur-rent situation and strategies], *Shijie yu Zhongguo yanjiusuo* [World and China Institute], June 6, 2003 (www.world-china.org/newsdetail.asp?newsid=874).

30. According to *Zhongguo tongji nianjian 2009 nian* [China statistical yearbook 2009], at the end of 2008 China had 40,828 township- and town-level administrative divisions, 6,524 subdistrict offices, 19,234 towns, 15,067 townships, 604,285 villager committees, and 83,413 neighborhood committees.

31. Wang Ying, "Shimin zizhi yu shehui guanli fangshi de biange" [Neighborhood autonomy and the change of neighborhood management], in *Zhongguo gongmin shehui de xingqi yu zhili de bianqian* [The rise of civil society and the evolution of governance in China] (Beijing: Social Sciences Academic Press, 2002), pp. 95–96.

32. Data are cited from He Gengxing, "Chengshi shequ jianshe" [Urban neighbor-hood building], in *Jiceng zhengquan he shequ jianshe* [Grassroots government and neigh-borhood building], edited by Zhan Chengfu (Beijing: China Social Press, 2010), pp. 172–77.

33. Ibid.

34. Ibid.

35. Yan Jirong, *Touzi shehui ziben: Zhengzhi fazhan de yi zhong xin weidu* [Investing in social capital: A new dimension of political development] (Beijing: Peking University Press, 2006).

36. *Zhonghua renmin gongheguo 2009 nian minzheng shiye fazhan tongji baogao* [Statis-tical report of PRC civil affairs in 2009] (Beijing: Statistics Press of China, 2010).

37. For example, in some places, various neighborhood organizations such as cyber-café autonomy groups and motor vehicle repair associations are established to strengthen autonomy in their respective fields.

38. Robert Alan Dahl, *Duoyuanzhuyi minzhu de kunjing* [Dilemmas of pluralist democracy], translated by You Zhengming (Beijing: Qiushi Press, 1989), p. 1.

39. Guo Zhenglin, "Zhongguo nongcun quanli jiegou de zhiduhua tiaozheng" [Structural adjustment of China's rural power structure], *Kaifang shidai* [Open times], no. 7 (2001).

40. As some scholars have pointed out, what this model leads to is not a civil society in the Western sense but rather a "quasi-civil" society. He Baogang, *The Democratic Implications of Civil Society in China* (New York: St. Martin's Press, 1997).

41. Michael B. Frolic, "State-Led Civil Society," in *Civil Society in China,* edited by Timothy Brook and and B. Michael Frolic (Armonk, N.Y.: M. E. Sharpe, 1997), pp. 46–67.

42. Tony Saich, "Negotiating the State: The Development of Social Organizations in China," *China Quarterly,* no. 1 (2000), pp. 124–41.

43. Zhao Xiumei, "Zhongguo NGO dui zhengfu de celue: Yi ge chubu kaocha" [Chinese NGOs' government strategies: A preliminary investigation], *Kaifang shidai* [Open times], no. 6 (2004).

7

China's Public Service System

YU JIANXING

With China's great increase in government fiscal revenue over the past three decades of economic reform, there has been far more government spending on public services and a significant improvement of the country's public service system compared with the era of planned economy.[1] In the 1980s and 1990s, however, as economic growth became the core task of government at all levels owing to the influence of developmentalism, the government's public service function and government spending on public services were comparatively neglected, which, coupled with the relative stagnation of public service system reform and construction, led to a serious shortage and uneven supply of public services. Since 2002, with the introduction of a series of progressive concepts and goals—such as the scientific outlook on development, the building of a harmonious society, and the building of service-oriented government—China has entered a new era in which equal importance is given to economic and social development. Public service, in particular, has become an important responsibility at all levels of government. In support of the goal to achieve equal access to basic public services, the Chinese government has used various methods—building a social policy system, reform of the public fiscal system, and innovation of the public service supply—to put in place a preliminary public service system compatible with the level of its economic and social development. This has greatly improved the availability of basic public services and played an important role in easing social conflict, promoting social equality, strengthening social welfare, and satisfying social demands.

Even so, China's existing public service system still faces various problems and shortcomings, including fragmentation, differentiation, inadequately funded

221

localization, a low-level supply model, and structural bottlenecks that result in inadequate and uneven government spending on public services. These problems call for immediate and systematic efforts to make improvements, especially to break through structural constraints and barriers.

Development and Reform of China's Public Service System

The development and reform of China's public service system have undergone roughly four stages: 1949-78, when a Soviet-style public service system was established on the basis of public ownership; 1978-94, when the supply of public services was relatively neglected owing to the priority placed on economic reforms, with the resultant crumbling of the old public service system; 1994-2002, when the government set about building a new social security system as the reform of state-owned enterprises deepened; and 2002 to the present, when the government, guided by the new concepts of being oriented around the people and having a scientific outlook on development, has been committed to building a more inclusive and comprehensive public service system.

In the era of the planned economy, China established a relatively simple, egalitarian government-takes-care-of-all public service system (allocation system) in line with the economic and social systems at that time. This system, with different urban and rural structures, mainly consisted of work-unit welfare in urban areas and collective welfare in rural areas. Under the work-unit welfare system, enterprises and institutions were responsible for providing their employees with various public services such as retirement pay, health care, elementary education, welfare services, and housing. Under the rural collective welfare system—which mainly covered primary education, collective care for the elderly, and a cooperative medical system—the village-based collective economy was the main financing source and provider of public services, and there was little direct financial and other support from the state.

Overall, the public service system in the era of the planned economy achieved universal and equal availability of public services in spite of scarce resources, though there were still some problems. For one, owing to the low level of economic development, public services were generally neither comprehensive nor adequate, and having a centralized supplier and singular supply method resulted in serious inefficiency and wasted resources. For another, public services were mainly available to employed urban residents and workers in heavy industry, while farmers and those in light industry were sidelined. Additionally, the provision of public services in the rural areas was heavily reliant on the local collective economy, and as a result there was a significant gap in public services between villages with different levels of economic development.[2]

The third plenary session of the 11th CCP Central Committee in 1978 saw the establishment of the guiding principle of "focusing on the central task of economic construction." As a result, the basis of the state's political legitimacy largely shifted from the charisma of the paramount leader to economic growth. As GDP growth became a central task of government at all levels, a developmentalist ideology set in, and local governments increasingly became economic development–oriented governments. Actively involving themselves by initiating new investments and projects, maximizing fiscal investment in production projects, and even serving as principal investors themselves, local governments became the major force in driving local economic development.[3] This obsession with economic growth undermined local governments' provision of public services. Although governments at various levels have steadily increased their spending on public services since the reform and opening up, their portion of the total fiscal budget has remained very low.

In the 1980s and 1990s the Chinese government initiated a reform of the public service system characterized by urban-rural duality, socialization, marketization, and localization to accommodate the dual needs of economic and administrative system reform. First, the public service system continued to follow the traditional urban-rural dualistic model. In rural areas, the implementation of the household responsibility system and the dissolution of the rural collective economy led to the disintegration of the traditional public service system. In the 1980s the rural cooperative medical care system became paralyzed in most areas, and the traditional system of family-based senior care also faced a huge challenge as a large number of rural laborers went to work in cities.[4] In 1992 the central government introduced a pilot social pension system in rural areas. Owing to the lack of fiscal support from the government, however, the system offered only minimal support and eventually became financed by personal savings, causing farmers to be unenthusiastic about participating.[5] In 1998 the rural social pension system sank into stagnation nationwide. Rural compulsory education, which was nominally financed by the township and town governments, was in fact financed by farmers themselves in the form of various taxes and fees. It can be said that there was no public service in the rural areas in the 1980s and 1990s.

In cities, the public service system established in the era of the planned economy continued into the early 1990s. But following that, with the deepening of economic system reform, especially the reform of state-owned enterprises, the Chinese government began to explore a new public service system based on the socialization and marketization of public services, rather than on provision by enterprises.

The reform of public service socialization mainly covered urban social security and welfare. In 1992 the goal of establishing a social security system compatible with the socialist market economic system was announced for the first time, appearing in the report to the 14th CCP National Congress. The mission of the social security system reform was to effect the transition from enterprise-based insurance to social insurance (the individual, the employer, and the government holding joint financial responsibility) and to achieve socialization of social insurance financing and management. In the early twenty-first century, an urban social insurance system covering pension insurance, medical insurance, unemployment insurance, work-related injury insurance, and maternity insurance was established.

At the same time, the Chinese government established a social security system that guaranteed a minimum living standard for urban residents in response to the massive urban poverty that had resulted from the reform of state-owned enterprises in the 1990s. However, the system still focused on urban citizens who were formally employed and excluded many people such as part-time workers, private business owners, and migrant workers.[6] In the field of social welfare service, the Ministry of Civil Affairs put forward in the mid-1980s the reform concept of socially based social welfare, whereby social organizations were invited to take part in the social welfare system. The goal of this change was to resolve the problems of the traditional government-dominated welfare system such as overreliance on a single source of financing, low efficiency, and poor service quality. This period saw a rapid growth in social organizations, but owing to a lack of experience, the development of socially based social welfare proceeded relatively slowly, and the main efforts were confined to the exploration of a socially based model of institutional pension service.

The marketization of the provision of public services focused on public health, education, and housing. In housing, the transition from welfare-oriented public housing allocation to commercial housing was effected, and commercial housing became the main source of housing; the housing provident fund system and the affordable housing system, both types of welfare, were preliminarily established. In public health and education, free medical service and free education were gradually canceled, and citizens had to pay for certain public services. Public educational and medical institutions were allowed to operate independently and were made responsible for their own profits and losses, leading to a significant improvement in supply efficiency and service quality. However, in the 1990s a number of factors converged—the increasing industrialization and commercialization of the educational and health sectors, the constantly increasing prices of relevant services, and a serious lack of government spending on these causes—making it difficult and expensive to obtain educational and medical services.

Localization of public service supply was another characteristic of the public service system reform. Arguably, it decisively influenced the overall supply of public services in this period. The focus on decentralization by the administrative and fiscal reforms in the 1980s greatly improved local governments' fiscal strength and their initiative in local governance. On the other hand, it also seriously weakened the central government's fiscal position and its control of local administrative departments. It was against this backdrop that the central government introduced a tax-sharing system with an eye to strengthening fiscal centralization.

The tax-sharing system defined the fiscal power of the central government and local governments, but their duties and responsibilities were not properly divided, and as a result, the central government grabbed more than 50 percent of the fiscal revenue while local governments had to bear responsibility for more than 70 percent of expenditures. As the public services were locally financed and provided, and as the central government's transfer payment system failed to "give adequate support to the local governments in providing these services," the financially stressed local governments found it difficult to provide adequate public services, and some township and town governments were unable to provide even basic public services.[7] The conflict between centralization of fiscal revenue and localization of public service also led to a series of other problems, including extra-budgetary expenditures and illegal charges, among other issues. There was also a remarkable regional gap in the provision of public services: in economically prosperous regions the financially strong local governments could provide relatively ample high-level public services.

To further strengthen control and guidance over local governments, the central government also introduced a promotional "political competition" to evaluate the performance of local governments and officials.[8] This competition, which emphasized the evaluation of such economic indicators as GDP growth, encouraged local governments to perform their duties selectively by actively boosting local economic growth while neglecting their public service functions. In addition, the central government introduced few public service policies and programs in this period, leaving local governments little motivation to make innovative social policies and launch new public services on their own. With the combined effect of the tax-sharing system and the political competition system, even financially strong local governments performed their public service duties selectively. They did not take active measures to step up investment in public services or to improve the quality of public services; and they strictly limited the scope of entitlement to public services by excluding most nonresidents (especially migrant workers) and workers who were not formally employed.[9]

Overall, the reform of the public service system in the 1980s and 1990s brought about the transition from a single supplier to multiple suppliers and from free service to paid service. It also led to a remarkable improvement in supply efficiency and service quality, which fundamentally reversed the shortage of public service supply in the era of the planned economy. However, owing to the influence of developmentalism and inadequately funded localization of public service supply, there was a serious lack of government investment in and supply of public services, leading to a significant decrease in the availability of public services; the exclusion of the majority of disadvantaged groups, rural residents, part-time workers, and migrant workers from the public service system; and a public service gap between urban and rural areas, among different regions, and among different groups. The inadequate supply and uneven distribution of public services further led to the relative imbalance between economic growth and social progress, worsened social inequality, increasing social conflicts, and an increasing amount of unmet social need, posting a serious threat to social stability and future development.

With the introduction of the new "scientific" outlook on development and the goal of building a harmonious society in the early years of the twenty-first century, China has now entered into a new era in which equal importance is attached to both economic growth and social progress. In 2002 the report to the 16th CCP National Congress put forward the explicit goal and requirement to transform government functions. Four basic government functions—economic regulation, market supervision, social management, and public service—were defined for the first time, and particular emphasis was placed on strengthening social management and public service. In his Government Work Report delivered in 2005, Premier Wen Jiabao put forward the requirement to build a service-oriented government. Since then, the building of service-oriented government has become the goal of the administrative system reform. The focus has been to innovate government administration and service, expand public participation in public affairs administration, build a universal public service system, and construct clean, fair, transparent, and accountable governments to improve public service capacity, respond effectively to demand for public services, and provide all citizens with good public services.[10]

Also affecting the provision of public services has been the Outline of the 11th Five-Year Plan, adopted at the fourth session of the 10th National People's Congress, and the Decision of the CCP Central Committee Regarding Several Major Issues on Building a Harmonious Socialist Society, adopted at the sixth plenary session of the 16th CCP Central Committee, both in 2006. These documents put equal access to basic public services on the central government's work agenda in promoting the scientific outlook on development and achieving social harmony. The stated goal was to promote the equality of access to basic public services via three methods: providing equal opportunities, where the protection of the right of all citizens to basic public services is dependent on the building of a public service–related social policy system that, among other things, incorporates urban and rural residents and disadvantaged groups; spending equally on public services, where the equal access of all citizens to public services is dependent on the building of a new public fiscal system that gives more support to rural areas, underdeveloped regions, and disadvantaged groups; and ensuring equal outcomes, where the equality is relative rather than absolute and is dependent on the level of accomplishment of equal opportunities and equal spending. In the report to the 17th CCP National Congress in 2007, an even greater commitment was given to coordinating economic and social development, guaranteeing and improving livelihood, promoting social equality and justice, and "accelerating social construction primarily meant to improve livelihood."

China's Social Policy System Concerning Public Service

In the 1980s and 1990s the Chinese government prioritized economic policies and economic growth and expended little effort on social construction, even tolerating growing social inequality in the name of promoting economic growth. The traditional cradle-to-grave social welfare system was ended, but decision-makers failed to institute a social policy framework to adapt to the country's economic and social transformation. Although the marketization reform brought about a significant improvement in living standards for most people, there was no remarkable improvement in the provision of social welfare; to the contrary, the gap between urban and rural areas continued to grow, and new forms of social inequality emerged.[11]

Since the 16th CCP National Congress, in 2002, the Chinese government has shifted the focus of its public policy from economic policies to social policies. It also released a series of social policies—in such issue areas as employment, compulsory education, medical care, public health, senior security, low-income housing, and social security—that give more support for migrant workers, urban and rural residents, and disadvantaged groups to guarantee and improve their standard of living and promote social equality and justice. On October 28, 2010, the National People's Congress adopted the Social Insurance Law of the People's Republic of China, which became effective on July 1, 2011. This marked a new stage (comprehensive legislation) in the building of China's social policy system.

Employment Security and Service

The labor and employment system reform in the 1980s gradually broke through the planned economy policies of the centralized allocation of labor and full employment. By the mid-1990s, a market-oriented employment and labor contract system had been basically implemented under the employment guideline of "workers keep the initiative in their own hands when choosing jobs, employment is regulated by the market, and the government promotes employment." A bid was made to further expand and promote employment and encourage entrepreneurship, especially to solve the problems of employment and reemployment faced by disadvantaged groups, migrant workers, and unemployed families. The Chinese government has done this since 2002 by constantly increasing government spending on employment-related public services; implementing a series of policies that promote employment through the use of employment agencies, professional training, employment aid, entrepreneurship support, employment subsidies, and the provision of public service jobs; establishing a three-layer employment service platform in the public sector; and forming a relatively comprehensive diversified employment agency and professional training network that is government controlled and invites the participation of society.

In 2007 the Employment Promotion Law and the Labor Contract Law were enacted. The former established the four principles of employment expansion, market-oriented employment, employment nondiscrimination, and integrated employment and explicitly required governments at various levels to establish and strengthen their own employment support system. The latter comprehensively provided safeguards for the rights of workers, especially migrant workers, and included the protection of persons who were not formally employed. These measures have contributed to a fair employment environment, the reduction of inequality in the labor market, and the elimination of all forms of employment and salary discrimination related to the urban-rural dual structure and the household registration system.

Compulsory Education

Compulsory education in China was primarily financed and run by local governments until 1994, when the tax-sharing system was introduced. At that point it became increasingly difficult for local governments in rural areas—especially those with limited financial resources—to finance compulsory education. This resulted in an imbalance in the provision of education between urban and rural areas and among regions, especially in relation to teaching infrastructure and staffing. At the first national work meeting on rural education convened by the State Council in 2003, an important decision was made to accelerate compulsory education in rural areas with a series of subsidy policies for school-age children from poor families. In 2005 a responsibility-sharing mechanism between the central government and local governments on rural compulsory education was established, in which the central government assumed a greater responsibility. In 2006 the National People's Congress adopted the amended Compulsory Education Law, which forbids arbitrary charges related to compulsory education, defines the responsibilities of governments at various levels, and incorporates compulsory education financing within the scope of public fiscal guarantees. At the same time, the Chinese government stepped up investment in primary education infrastructure and staffing in rural areas and underdeveloped regions to narrow the gap between urban and rural areas and among regions and schools. In 2008 free compulsory education was basically achieved in both urban and rural areas, and the educational infrastructure gap between urban and rural areas and between regions was significantly narrowed—though a notable imbalance in faculty strength and educational quality remains. In 2011 the central government began to provide rural students RMB 3 as a lunch subsidy. In 2012, as a response to frequent bus accidents, School Bus Safety Regulations were put forward. However, local governments have not carried out the regulations due to the lack of financial support from the central and provincial governments.

Basic Medical Security and Public Health Service

The SARS (severe acute respiratory syndrome) outbreak in 2003 exposed the fragility of China's grassroots public health system and rural medical care system. After the crisis, a number of goals were put on the agenda: returning medical care to its original welfare function, strengthening the basic medical security and public health service system, promoting equality in health care, and addressing the lack of and expense of medical services. The Chinese government began to increase investment in urban and rural public health infrastructure, leading to a gradual improvement in equal access to public medical services. By 2009 a three-layer county-township-village medical service network had been established nationwide, but there were still prominent problems in the rural areas, such as the lack and instability of medical service personnel.

In 2003 the State Council decided to pilot a new rural medical cooperative scheme to provide basic medical security, integrating personal contributions, collective support, and government subsidies, and focusing on comprehensive arrangements for serious diseases. By 2008 the scheme had been implemented nationwide. In 2007 the State Council, in the spirit of the operating model of the new rural medical cooperative, piloted a similar scheme for urban residents and gradually incorporated unemployed and flexibly employed individuals in the scheme. This marked the establishment of a comprehensive medical care system comprising basic medical insurance for urban employees, a rural medical cooperative, and basic medical insurance for urban residents, to achieve full nationwide coverage. However, the three schemes ran separately and were remarkably different in terms of who contributed what percentage of compensation.

The rural cooperative scheme, in particular, did not reduce the financial burden to farmers as a whole.[12] On April 6, 2009, the State Council promulgated the Opinions on Deepening the Reform of the Medical and Health Care System, which put forward the goal of establishing a medical and health care system with Chinese characteristics and gradually achieving universal access to basic medical and health care services. On August 8 of the same year, the State Council promulgated three documents—the Implementing Opinion on the Establishment of an Essential Drug System, Provisional Regulations on the Administration of a National List of Essential Drugs, and the National List of Essential Drugs (for Primary Healthcare Facilities)—to formally start the construction of a national system for essential drugs. On November 19, 2010, the State Council promulgated Guiding Opinions on Establishing and Standardizing the Essential Drug Procurement Mechanism for Government-Sponsored Medical and Health Institutions at the Grassroots Level. On February 17, 2011, the General Office of the State Council issued the Work Plan on Five Major Issues Concerning the Medical and Health Care System Reform, in which the plan was established to "increase the subsidy standard under the new rural medical cooperative scheme and the urban medical insurance to RMB 200 per person per year and the proportion of government subsidy for hospitalization costs to approximately 70 percent." However, the implementation of the new medical care system reform has been rather slow and ineffective, especially the provision of health services and public hospitals.

Basic Old-Age Security and Senior Services

With respect to providing for the elderly, the government's major work since 2002 has been to consolidate the basic pension system for urban employees, expand insurance coverage for formally employed individuals, and gradually create personal, employer-contributed pension accounts. But most flexibly employed workers, migrant workers, and urban and rural residents have remained outside the basic pension system. In rural areas, the central government has never introduced a new system after the previous rural old-age insurance system was halted for reorganization in 1998. Local governments in some economically developed regions have begun to explore new schemes. In September 2009 the State Council decided to pilot a new rural system for social pension insurance. Under the new system, which uses a fundraising mechanism that combines personal contributions, collective allowance, and government subsidies and a pension model that combines a basic pension account and a personal account, any rural resident over sixty years of age is entitled to a monthly basic pension of RMB 55 from the government. In comparison with the previous rural old-age insurance system, one main benefit of the new system is that it clearly defines the financing responsibilities of government at various levels. It still faces some problems, however, such as the serious inadequacy of the monthly basic pension and the slow rate of the extension of coverage nationwide.

In recent years, some regions such as Beijing, Shanghai, Tianjin, Jiangsu, and Zhejiang have introduced their own pension insurance systems for urban residents with excellent results. The central government has also begun to prepare relevant policies. In 2011 the Chinese government established a social pension insurance system for urban residents imitating the rural system. Since then China's urban and rural areas have achieved full coverage by pension insurance. In addition, the Ministry of Civil Affairs is working actively to build an old-age pension system with a plan to implement an old-age allowance policy nationwide for citizens over eighty years of age.

In this period, China's elderly-services industry has also seen significant development and has broken through the old model of basing service primarily on relevant institutions. In 2006 the State Council promulgated the Opinions on Accelerating the Development of the Elderly Services Industry, which put forward the goal of gradually establishing a pension service system that is based on in-home care, supported by community services, and supplemented by senior-care institutions. Since then, home-based elderly services have been growing quickly across China. However, given the limitations of home-based care services and the increasing needs for specialized nursing care, the Chinese government promulgated the Social Care Service System Building Plan for Old Age (2011–2015) in 2011, focusing the future social care service system on widespread establishment of community day care centers, which would provide more specialized elder care services.

Minimum Living Security and Social Assistance

In the early 1990s, with the acceleration of China's urbanization and industrialization, the issue of urban poverty became increasingly prominent. In response, local governments of a number of economically advanced regions began to establish at their own initiative a social security system that guaranteed a minimum standard of living for urban residents. Soon thereafter the system was rapidly promoted across the country. By the mid-1990s, urban poverty worsened as many people were laid off in the wake of the deepening reform of state-owned enterprises. In response, efforts were undertaken by the central government to set up a national system to provide minimum social security for all urban residents. The promulgation of Regulations on Securing Minimum Living Standards for Urban Residents by the State Council in 1999 marked the formal establishment of the system. After that, further efforts were undertaken in economically prosperous regions along the coast—such as Shanghai, Guangdong, and Zhejiang—to establish such a system for rural residents. By late 2002 ten provinces had established such local regulations for rural residents.

In 2007 the State Council began to set about making the minimum social security system for rural residents accessible nationwide. However, owing to a series of factors—there was no unified national standard, financing responsibility rested on county-level governments, and transfer payments from the central government and provincial governments were inadequate—the overall level of social assistance was low, and there were notable imbalances between urban and rural areas and among different regions. Moreover, positive efforts were made to have the social assistance system cover other forms of relief such as medical care, education, housing, and pensions. Generally speaking, China's social assistance policies are confined to this minimum social security system, and reliance on social assistance is now just beginning to appear.

Low-Income Housing

The market-oriented housing policy reform introduced in the 1990s established commercial housing as the main source of the housing supply (currently accounting for up to 80 percent), which has greatly improved the efficiency and quality of the housing supply but has also contributed to the relative scarcity of low-income housing.[13] After the turn of the twenty-first century, the residential real estate market began to expand rapidly, and housing prices grew beyond the reach of ordinary families and residents. Against this backdrop the central government, while adopting a series of policies controlling housing prices, stepped up the supply of affordable housing for low-income groups.

In 2007 the State Council issued the Several Opinions of the State Council on Solving the Housing Difficulties of Urban Low-Income Families, which for the first time included provision of affordable housing for low-income families within the scope of public services provided by the government. The document also proposed the establishment of a comprehensive housing security system primarily based on low-rent and affordable housing. In 2009 the State Council called for accelerated development of low-income housing and released a timeline and specific goals. On April 17, 2010, the State Council issued the Notice on Resolutely Curbing the Soaring of Housing Prices in Some Cities, which incorporated for the first time the supply of low-income housing within the government's scope of responsibility and accountability, required relevant government departments to fully perform their duties of keeping housing prices stable and ensuring the supply of low-income housing, and set forth the objective of affordable housing supply in 2010.

On October 18 the fifth plenary session of the 17th CCP Central Committee adopted the Proposal on Formulating the 12th Five-Year Plan on National Economic and Social Development, which put forward the goal of building low-income housing primarily based on public rental housing. In 2010 a total of 5.9 million units of low-income housing were under construction, and 3.7 million units were basically completed. In February 2011 the Ministry of Housing and Urban-Rural Development announced the goal of building 10 million units of low-income housing in 2011 and established public rental housing as the main form of public housing supply. China is currently in the process of establishing a national low-income housing system. Whether it will meet the expected goal has yet to be seen.

Overall, China's active efforts since 2002 to build a social policy system have led to the improvement in the supply of basic public services, the achievement of both universal accessibility to basic public services and significant improvement in the fairness and equality of the provision of public services, and particularly the rectification of the serious shortage of basic public services in rural areas. However, these social policies are marked by a serious urban-rural dichotomy. The differentiation in the provision of public services between urban and rural areas and among different groups has not only failed to achieve equality of opportunity but has also seriously limited equality of investment in and access to public services.

China's Fiscal Support System for Public Services

In the 1980s the central government, adhering to the reform concept of decentralization and interest concessions, established a system whereby local authorities take full responsibility for their districts' finances. This effective incentive mechanism greatly stimulated local government initiative and played a positive role in driving economic development. On the other hand, the new mechanism also weakened the central government's financial capacity to the extent that at one time it even became difficult to maintain the normal functioning of central organizations. This was because under this system, the central government's fiscal revenue was dependent on the contribution of tax revenue from local governments, but as the amount of revenue to be contributed by local governments was fixed in advance (usually for a period of five years), sustained and rapid economic development meant that there was a steady fall in the percentage of the newly increased fiscal revenue shared by the central government.[14] Furthermore, the central government retained responsibility for many kinds of fiscal subsidies (such as subsidies for state-owned enterprises that generated losses). As a result, there was an increasing fiscal deficit brought on by the steady decrease of tax revenue.[15] But thanks to rapid economic development and the ensuing growth of local fiscal revenue, local governments not only maintained the normal functioning of the urban public service system from the days of the planned economy but also improved the provision of public services.

In 1994 the State Council launched a tax-sharing reform aimed at fiscal centralization, which redefined the division of fiscal and expenditure powers between the central government and the local governments and preliminarily put in place an intragovernment fiscal system compatible with China's socialist market economy. Taxes were divided into central, local, and shared taxes, and two administrative systems of taxation were established accordingly, the larger part of revenue from the main taxes being allocated to the central government. The central government was mainly responsible for fiscal spending on national defense, major national projects, and administrative and institutional management at the central level. Meanwhile local governments were mainly responsible for fiscal spending on administrative management at the local level: construction of local infrastructure, agricultural development, social security, compulsory education, medical care, and public sanitation. In addition, a tax reimbursement and transfer payment system was established.

The tax-sharing reform greatly strengthened the state's overall fiscal position. Since 1994 China's fiscal revenue growth has always been higher than its economic growth, the proportion of the fiscal revenue to GDP constantly increasing and a substantially increased proportion of the fiscal revenue being captured by the central government (steady at 50–60 percent). However, the tax-sharing reform did not allocate the expenditure responsibilities of the central government and the local governments in proportion to their fiscal powers, which led to a vertical imbalance in intergovernmental fiscal architecture. On the other hand, in spite of the increase in tax refund and transfer payments year to year, the former was overwhelmingly concentrated in economically advanced regions while the latter was relatively small in scale and focused on special transfer payments with little impact on overall transfer payments, resulting in a horizontal imbalance in intergovernmental fiscal architecture. The tax-sharing reform restricted local government capacity and initiative in the provision of public services and caused a serious shortage and uneven distribution of public services.[16] As the World Bank has observed, budgetary weakness at the subnational levels was a key constraint on the implementation of national policies in the education and health sectors in the late 1990s.[17]

Since 2002, in a bid to establish a fiscal support system for equal access to basic public services and reduce the gap in provision of public services between urban and rural areas and among different regions, the Chinese government has advanced "livelihood-oriented" public finance reform, which is mainly concerned with the following four issues:

—*Further adjusting the division of administrative and financial power between the central and local governments.* In 2001 a tax-sharing reform featuring revenue sharing, tax refunds, and change in the division of incremental revenues was implemented, the ratio of sharing between the central and local governments being 50:50 in 2002 and 60:40 in 2003. In 2004 the central government reformed the export tax rebate system that set the ratio by which the central and local governments were to bear the tax rebate at 75:25 and then, in consideration of regional differences, at 92.5:7.5 in 2005. The rebate was returned by the national treasury, the part borne by local governments to be paid to the central government at year's end. In 2005 the central government introduced a "three awards and one subsidy" policy to incentivize local governments to solve fiscal problems at the county and township levels. Furthermore, the central government revoked the agricultural tax altogether in 2006. In terms of administrative power, since 2003 the State Council has revoked many local economic development zones and taken back control of land and mineral resources. The 11th Five-Year Plan formulated in 2006 explicitly identified five major areas that would be supported by investments of the central government: the building of a "new socialist countryside," public services, resources and the environment, independent innovation, and infrastructure.

Overall, the various partial reforms since 2002 have not fundamentally changed the division of administrative and fiscal powers between the central and local governments. Actually, these reforms have further strengthened the central government's fiscal position and to some extent increased the fiscal pressure faced by local governments, especially after the revocation of the agricultural tax. In the period from 2002 to 2012, China's fiscal revenue increased from RMB 1.8 trillion to RMB 11.7 trillion; central fiscal revenue increased at an average growth rate of 18.8 percent, from RMB 1 trillion to RMB 5.6 trillion, accounting for 48–55 percent of the country's total fiscal revenue. In the same period, China's fiscal expenditure increased from RMB 2.2 trillion to RMB 12.5 trillion; the expenditure of local governments accounted for 70-80 percent.[18]

—*Constantly improving the fiscal transfer payment system and increasing general transfer payments.* With the division of administrative and fiscal powers between the central and local governments fundamentally unchanged and the limited and uneven fiscal strength of local governments still prominent, the only option open to the central government was to further improve the transfer payment system and step up the scale of transfer payments to promote equal access to basic public services. Since 2002 the central government has increased the transfer payment for employment, education (especially compulsory education in the rural areas), medical care, and social security. On the other hand, since the tax-sharing reform of 2001, the central government has devoted all revenue from income tax to general transfer payments and established a mechanism to ensure the steady growth of general transfer payments. Since then, the overall scale of transfer payments (which has tilted toward western regions and rural areas) has grown rapidly, with a significant increase in the proportion of general transfer payments to total fiscal transfer payments. In 2007 the central government further improved the transfer payment system with optimized methods of general transfer payment calculation, standardized fund management procedures, and strengthened integration of special transfer payment programs.

From 2002 to 2012, the total amount of central fiscal transfer payments increased from RMB 402.4 billion to RMB 4.02 trillion, representing an average annual growth rate of approximately 25.8 percent, significantly higher than the growth of central fiscal revenue in the same period. Of the total central fiscal transfer payments, the general transfer payment increased from RMB 162.3 billion to RMB 2.14 trillion at an average annual growth rate of approximately 29.4 percent, with its proportion to the total fiscal transfer payment going up from 40 percent to 53 percent; the special transfer payment increased from RMB 240.1 billion to RMB 1.88 trillion at an average growth rate of approximately 22.8 percent. In 2012 the combined amount of general and special transfer payments for employment, education, medical care, and social security reached RMB 1.2 trillion, accounting for 30 percent of the year's total fiscal transfer payment and 27 percent of the year's total national fiscal expenditure in those areas.

—*Actively promoting the "province administering the county" fiscal system reform.* In the administrative restructuring in the 1980s, the Chinese government established a system it called city administering the county (市管县, *shi guan xian*). Although it promoted city-led county-level economic development, the system also seriously restricted the scope of economic development at the county level, owing to the ensuing intense competition between cities and counties. Then came the tax reform that effected the upward allocation of tax revenue and the downward allocation of expenditure responsibilities, further aggravating the financial straits at the county and township levels. As a result, it became difficult for the financially stressed county and township governments to effectively provide basic public services, and there was a widening gap between economic growth and the availability of public services at the county level.

To alleviate the financial difficulties of the county and township governments, since 2002 the central government has advanced a type of fiscal reform it calls "province administering the county" (省管县, *sheng guan xian*). This system had its origin in the "strengthening the county through empowerment" (扩权强县, *kuoquan qiangxian*) reform initiated in Zhejiang Province in 1992, which involved the transfer of some economic and social management powers from cities to economically strong counties, a "province administering the county's finances" (县财省管, *xiancai shengguan*) system, and an increase in the ratio of shared fiscal revenue between city and county governments to promote economic development and improve public services at the county level. Similar reforms were adopted in Guangdong, Liaoning, Hubei, Jiangxi, and Fujian after 2002. In view of the remarkable success of the "strengthening the county through empowerment" reform, the outline of the 11th Five-Year Plan formulated in 2006 took the promotion of the "province administering the county" system in regions with mature conditions as an important part of the effort to advance both equal access to basic public services and the reform of the public finance system. The first policy document of 2009 went one step further, setting the goal of comprehensively promoting the "province administering the county" system.

As far as public services are concerned, this system, which eliminates the management link at the city level, is beneficial for increasing fiscal revenue of county governments and improving the allocation and use of transfer payments from provincial governments and thus to some extent for improving the capacity of county governments in providing public services and narrowing the gap in basic public services among different areas within each province. However, the system has not yet shown any remarkable effect in advancing equal access to basic public services.

—*Adjusting the structure of public fiscal expenditure and systematically increasing fiscal spending on public services.* In comparison with the three reform measures mentioned above, the adjustment of the expenditure structure of public finance has played the most direct and important role in advancing equal access to basic public services. In the 1980s and 1990s the government's fiscal expenditure was mainly concentrated on economic construction and administrative management; basic public services accounted for only a small proportion of expenditures. Since 2002, as part of the drive to build a harmonious society and a service-oriented government, the Chinese government has gradually increased the proportion of fiscal expenditure on basic public services and strictly controlled the growth of expenditure on economic construction (approximately 30 percent) and administrative management (approximately 20 percent). Meanwhile, governments at various levels have begun to explore the establishment of a mechanism to ensure steady growth of fiscal expenditures for public services. Governments at the provincial, city, and county levels in some financially strong regions have announced that they will devote two-thirds of their newly added fiscal revenue to social programs.

From 2002 to 2012 the national fiscal expenditure increased from RMB 2.2 trillion to almost RMB 12.6 trillion, growing at 19 percent annually. The portion covering expenditures on education, medical care, social security, and employment increased from RMB 467 billion to RMB 4.55 trillion, growing at 25.5 percent annually, higher than the fiscal revenue growth in the same period, whose share of the national fiscal expenditure increased from 21.1 percent to 36.1 percent. Since the introduction of mechanisms ensuring funding for rural compulsory education in 2006, in particular, the fiscal expenditure on education has undergone rapid growth, increasing from RMB 264.5 billion in 2002 to RMB 2.12 trillion in 2012. This represents an average annual growth of 23.1 percent; its share of the total fiscal expenditure on education, medical care, social security, and employment stayed at 45–55 percent.

Generally speaking, through livelihood-oriented public finance reforms since 2002, China has established a preliminary fiscal guarantee system for equal access to basic public services, one that has been accompanied by significant growth in fiscal expenditure on public services and remarkable improvement in the provision of and equal access to basic public services. However, the basic public services provided remain at a low level, and there is still substantial room for growth in fiscal expenditures in this regard. Moreover, the structural contradiction between fiscal centralization and localization of public service provision remains fundamentally unresolved. In view of the limited role played by central transfer payments, the level of public services provided remains dependent on the financial strength of local governments. Therefore, the gap in public service expenditures by different local governments, given their different financial strengths, is still a major factor constraining equal access to basic public services across the country. Overall, the economically prosperous eastern regions have done notably better than the central and western regions in providing quality, equal-access public services in urban and rural areas alike.[19]

China's Public Service System: Problems and Prospect

Since 2002 the Chinese government has established a public service system compatible with the level of China's economic development that has played an important role in alleviating social tension, promoting social equity and national welfare, and satisfying social needs. However, China's current public service system still faces various problems. Public service remains of secondary importance compared with economic development and captures a lesser proportion of government expenditures. Expedient policies, unequal urban-rural policies, and other fragmented social policies have greatly constrained equity and equality in public services provision. The contradiction between fiscal centralization and public service localization remains fundamentally unresolved, and the limited financial strength and low level of initiative on the part of local governments remain the major barriers to equal access for basic public services. There is a lack of institutionalized mechanisms for innovating public service provision, the composite mechanism for public service provision having much room for improvement and the planning capacity of local governments needing drastic improvement. The absence of mechanisms to express the kinds of public services needed and to evaluate public services has led to a relative imbalance between supply and demand and low efficiency of input and output.

These problems have seriously constrained the sustainability of China's public service system and must be addressed, especially in terms of overcoming institutional constraints and obstacles. The present system is mixed and fragile. One key to building a harmonious society is to achieve complete equality and accessibility in public service provision through carefully institutionalized arrangements, to strengthen the government's public service capabilities, and to expand the scale of national welfare.[20] The future of China's public service system is dependent on reform and construction in the following five areas.

—*Advancing reform of the administrative system to transform government functions and build a service-oriented government.* How government, especially local governments, positions itself functionally and in which direction it proceeds has a direct bearing on the overall development of the public service system. In present-day China, local government behavior is mainly shaped by the economic development concept of the party and state and the specific evaluation criteria of the work of local governments and officials.[21] The concentration on economic construction in advance of other reforms and the preponderant use of economic indicators such as GDP growth in evaluating officials in the 1980s and 1990s were the main reasons behind the transformation of local governments into development-oriented governments during this period. The behavioral approach of the development-oriented government focused mainly on the keen pursuit of economic growth, and as a consequence local governments neglected and shifted resources away from the fields of public service and social construction.

With the dawn of the twenty-first century, the development concept of the party and state underwent a fundamental shift. The central government has urged local governments to strengthen their public service functions and achieve coordination of economic and social development and livelihood improvement. But for local governments, public service has remained secondary to economic construction. This means that the reform of the administrative system toward a service-oriented government should not only reorganize the government by introducing superministries and the like, in line with the transformation of government functions, but also redesign the criteria for evaluating the performance of local governments and officials by, among other things, establishing an evaluation criteria system that includes, and prioritizes, public service indicators.

—*Building a comprehensive social policy system integrating urban and rural areas that breaks through the institutional urban-rural duality and resulting fragmentation in public service supply.* The social policy system is the institutional foundation of the public service system. Although China has released a succession of active social policies since 2002, it still lacks an overall plan and macroscopic strategy of social policy development. Some important policies have often resulted, at least in part, from emergencies (such as the SARS outbreak), social crises, or pressure from the growing demand of specific social groups and therefore were highly expedient. It is exactly these expedient policies that have led to the duality and fragmentation of China's social policies. This is particularly obvious in the field of basic social security, where policies have differed between urban and rural areas and among different groups and regions, and often there is a great difference in the subsidies and benefits offered. Owing to such inconsistency, the development of the social security system in recent years has increased social inequity and further solidified the urban-rural dual structure.

That is to say, the construction of the social policy system since 2002 has, through fragmentation and differentiated urban-rural coverage, achieved equal opportunity in the sense of universal accessibility in basic public services, but it has not fundamentally achieved equity in investment and actual benefits. Equal access to public services provided by the state is a basic right of the citizenry, and it is a basic obligation of the state to ensure equal access by all people to public services.[22] Therefore, the primary goal of China's construction of a public service system should be to break through the institutionalized urban-rural duality and fragmentation, build a universal social policy system integrating urban and rural areas, implement unified social policies nationwide, and allow local governments to adjust or improve their level of public services in light of their own levels of economic and social development.

—*Advancing the reform of the public finance system for optimal division of fiscal and expenditure responsibilities between the central and local governments and comprehensively adjusting the structure of government expenditure.* The tax-sharing reform has seriously restricted the public service capacity and initiative of local governments. With the expansion of coverage of basic public services since 2002, even financially strong local governments have found it difficult to maintain effective and sustainable functioning of their public service systems. In the effort to establish a public finance system compatible with the goal of achieving equal access to basic public services, the first task is to balance the fiscal and expenditure responsibilities between the central and local governments. If the existing intergovernmental division of labor is not changed, then the ratio of local tax revenue shared by local governments must be adjusted according to the principle of matching expenditure responsibilities to fiscal power so as to increase the tax revenue resources at the disposal of local governments.

If the division of fiscal power between the central and local governments under the existing tax-sharing system is not changed, then the division of responsibilities between them must be redesigned as part of the reform of the administrative system, so that the central government assumes the principal responsibility for public service expenditures. In most developed countries, in fact, it is the central government that is responsible for policy formulation, financing, and centralized management of basic public services, and the national government bears most of the responsibility for expenditures, local governments serving mainly as agencies responsible for the implementation of policies. In consideration of the goal of building a nationally unified social policy system integrating urban and rural areas, it is advisable to redesign the division of responsibilities between the central and local governments but leave the division of fiscal power unchanged.

The establishment of a public finance system oriented toward ensuring the people's livelihood also requires a complete adjustment of the structure of government expenditure by, specifically, improving the proportion of expenditure on public services and introducing an institutionalized flexible mechanism to ensure the steady growth of fiscal public service expenditure. It is clear that the increased resources devoted to public services by governments at various levels since 2002 have mostly come from these governments' incremental revenue. In fact, the low proportion of expenditures on public service and high proportions on economic construction and administrative management have remained largely unchanged.

—*Constantly improving the governance structure to promote innovation of public service supply.* The marketization and socialization of China's public service supply since the reform and opening-up period began has greatly improved the efficiency and quality of public services and fundamentally reversed the overall shortages and low efficiency that existed under the planned economy. International experience shows that marketization and socialization of public services lead to higher quality and greater efficiency. The reform of China's public service system should follow the path of marketization and socialization and constantly improve the governance structure of public service supply. In other words, with the establishment of the leading role of the government in public service supply, efforts also should be made to give full scope to the role of both market and social mechanisms; to constantly deepen and refine the roles and division of responsibilities among all participating parties, especially of the government; to strengthen the government's regulation of the market and service supply partnerships; and to encourage nongovernmental organizations to bring about a public service supply system that features social coordination and public participation and promotes innovation in the supply of public services. In the field of medical care service, in particular, the erroneous concept of "ensuring the welfare nature of public services through government sponsorship" must be discarded.

Innovations in public service supply often begin with pilot programs by local governments. Those with notable success will be followed in other regions before being promoted and introduced nationwide by the central government. This process often takes a long time, and this is one of the major reasons behind the notable gap among regions in provision of public services. Similar problems are also present in social policy innovation concerning public service. The system that ensured a minimum standard of living in rural areas took five years to be introduced nationwide, and during that period various policies and widely varying standards were implemented in different regions, which greatly increased the cost of system unification and integration. How to achieve rapid nationwide promotion of successful local innovations and to achieve close coordination between the central and local governments in system innovation has become a central challenge to be addressed in the construction of China's public service system.

—*Putting in place a sound mechanism for expressing the kinds of public services needed and constantly improving the public service evaluation system.* In spite of the constant expansion of public services and great improvement in public services provision, there is still a sizable shortfall compared with the actual demand for public services. The relative imbalance between supply and demand stems from the slow development of the social policy and public finance systems; it is also closely related to the absence of an effective mechanism for articulating the kinds of public services needed.

Scientific decisionmaking must be based on adequate information. In recent years, the small number of formal channels enabling the public to express its public services needs and the limited effectiveness of existing channels have constrained the transmission of information required for decisionmaking and thus have negatively affected decisionmaking. These problems have also led citizens to attempt to safeguard their interests by resorting to mass incidents. The top-down public decisionmaking model of the Chinese government is thus an important factor behind the discrepancy between the public services supplied and those actually needed. Therefore, the government should increase public participation in decisionmaking regarding both public services and the formulation of the government budget.

Furthermore, China's construction of a public service system has done little to evaluate public services in terms of input-output efficiency. There is neither a mechanism that enables the public to evaluate and express its degree of satisfaction with public services nor a system by which the government evaluates the efficiency of its public services. At present, China's basic public services as a whole are oriented toward input rather than efficiency, and the efficiency of public services remains low in all regions.[23]

In summary, since 2002 the Chinese government has, through reform and construction of the public service system, implemented a relatively comprehensive public services system. This system has, with the steady growth of public spending on public services and the increasing maturity and expansion of the supply mechanism, basically achieved universal availability and accessibility of public services and, in particular, reversed the serious shortage of public services that existed in the rural areas during the 1980s and 1990s, leading to a significant improvement in the level, efficiency, equity, and evenness of supply.

However, owing to a series of factors—including low transformation of government functions, rural-urban duality and fragmentation of social policies, the lagging behind of the public finance system, and the lack of an effective mechanism for expressing the needs for public services and evaluating their provision—the spending on public services in proportion to the government's total expenditures and in proportion to the country's GDP remains low, the imbalance between supply and demand, especially the gap between the public services available and those actually needed (prominently in the social security field), remains a major issue, efficiency remains generally low, and the gap between urban and rural areas and among different groups and regions remains pronounced. The various unsolved problems—segmentation, differentiation, the inadequately funded localization and low level of public service, and structural bottlenecks underlying inadequate input and uneven allocation of resources—have seriously undermined the Chinese government's effort to achieve equal access to basic public services.

To reach the goal of giving every citizen equal access to basic public services, the government needs to make breakthroughs in social policies and institutional mechanisms concerning public services. Specifically, it needs to

—redesign the system for evaluating the performance of local governments and officials to establish the core position of public service in the discharge of local governmental duties,

—accelerate the establishment of a universal social policy system that integrates urban and rural areas to guarantee citizens' equal rights to basic public services,

—restructure the intergovernmental fiscal system and division of responsibilities and comprehensively adjust the structure of government expenditure to improve the availability and equal accessibility of basic public services,

—actively explore mechanisms for institutionalizing and promoting local innovations in public services and comprehensively advance the overall public service supply system to achieve the balance between welfare and efficiency of public service provision, and

—implement effective mechanisms that allow citizens to express their needs for public services and to evaluate existing public services to effectively respond to the needs of the public and improve the efficiency of public services.

It is pleasing to see that the third plenary session of the 18th CCP Central Committee recently passed the Decision on Major Issues Concerning Comprehensively Deepening Reforms, which proposed many significant ideas for public service reform. Firstly, it proposed the systematical and collaborative promotion of economic, social, political, cultural, and ecological construction rather than a lopsided focus on the central task of economic construction and explicitly stated that the basic subject of construction of socialism with Chinese characteristics is to improve common prosperity and people's well-being and for the benefits of development to be more equally shared by all people. GDP is no longer the key indicator to the performance evaluation of local party and government leading cadres and will not be ranked in the future. Secondly, it proposed to deepen fiscal and tax system reform and establish a system in which the government's administrative authority is commensurate with its spending responsibility, while focusing on increasing the administrative authority and spending responsibility of the central government, especially in the area of social security and cross-regional public service. Thirdly, it proposed to continuously promote the equalization of basic public services for achieving social justice, focusing on the central government taking charge of social pension pooling and management, and speeding up the integration and standardization of current fragmental social pensions and health insurance. It is expected that in the near future China's public service system will see significant changes and be further improved and rationalized.

COMMENT
TONY SAICH

In all countries, social policy, which is the real focus of Yu Jianxing's chapter, is an indispensable aspect of rule. Ever since Otto von Bismarck set up the first welfare structures and welfare programs, social policy has been recognized as a key instrument of state building, political rule, social control, social order, efficiency, and regime legitimacy. This notion provides an interesting lens through which to observe political development in China and to assess the potential of its future evolution. Will the Chinese polity evolve through a phase of a developmental welfare state to a more fully developed welfare state, as has happened in South Korea and Taiwan? Or will the polity remain more unchangingly selective in terms of welfare provision, as in Hong Kong, Malaysia, or Singapore? The dominant ideology espoused by the central leadership might suggest movement toward a more inclusive system based on a notion of citizenship. The references to socialism, albeit a socialism with Chinese characteristics, and the stress by General Secretary Hu Jintao and Premier Wen Jiabao on building a harmonious society and "putting people first" seem to suggest a more inclusive system. Current economic practice, however, is less clear and might suggest the latter development of selective provision coupled with inequalities that are reinforced by institutional structures such as the household registration system.

Certainly, China's economic strategy from the early 1990s has forced a significant change in the way welfare services are delivered to its citizens. China's integration into the global production chain rendered obsolete the institutional structures that had endured through the 1980s. The economic restructuring of the state-owned enterprises and the growth of new sectors of the economy that drew in millions of migrant workers from the countryside forced tremendous change on the old residence- and workplace-based system of welfare provision. The nature of dependency relationships that this workplace-based system created is captured well by Andrew Walder under the rubric of "communist neo-traditionalism."[24]

Yu provides a fine description of this system in his chapter, and I agree with his view of how public services were delivered under the planned economy before 1978. However, their distribution was not egalitarian. There was not only the urban-rural dichotomy but also tremendous variation within both urban and rural China that was a major product of a predominantly workplace-based system of public service provision (especially with respect to welfare). While there might be low variation of access and provision within a rural team or a factory, there was enormous variation across rural and urban workplaces. The notion of self-reliance was and remains an important principle for public goods provision in China. Self-reliance was a strategy for consumption as well as production that tailored consumption to local production. This meant that the welfare and public goods that one could access depended not only on whether one was in rural or urban China but also on the strength of the enterprise or commune in which one was working. I was once in a truck driving along a fairly smooth road that suddenly became potholed and bumpy. When I asked what had happened, the reply was that we had crossed from the land of one brigade to another. Self-reliance meant that there was significant intrarural and intraurban variation.

While self-reliance still plays a role in the distribution of welfare, and even more so with a broader array of public goods, policy is now undergoing significant change that could bring potentially profound consequences for political development. A mixture of voluntarism, statutory social insurance, means-tested programs, and the state as both regulator and provider will fundamentally alter citizens' perceptions of the state, their expectations about transparency and accountability, and the general nature of state-society relations. It will be interesting to see whether policy moves further from being strategically selective to more socially inclusive.

Yu's chapter does a good job of highlighting the problems and challenges for future public service provision: the focus on economic growth, the perverse incentives, and the need to generate revenue both to cover local government expenses and to meet mandated obligations from higher levels of government. Yu also highlights the remaining challenges and inequalities in the system. This can be seen, for example, with the payments for the minimum living support scheme (低保, *dibao*). In 2009, while the average assessment for the scheme in urban China was RMB 227.75, Tianjin had the highest assessment, at RMB 430, and Guizhou the lowest, at 170.41 yuan. Note, however, this is not the amount actually paid out to individuals, which nationally averaged RMB 172.[25] In rural areas, the three-month average ranged from a high of RMB 283.32 in Shanghai to a low of RMB 63.53 in Tibet. Yu rightly concludes that social policy is still significantly bipolar and fragmented. In the remainder of this commentary I would like to focus on two issues: the current nature of public service provision as outlined by Yu and the implications future policy direction might have for political development.

The Nature of Public Service Provision

The system for public service provision is shifting to one that shares key features not only with other countries in Asia but also beyond. During China's reform period, public policy has retained the obligation to work, tried to contain costs of any program expansion, and allowed considerable privatization of service provision. Policy has adopted, often unintentionally, the values and methods of the market to allocate public services with the resultant contracting out of services from government and workplace to the family, the private service provider, or nongovernmental organizations. Yu uses the concept of the developmental state to explain why service provision has been subordinate to the demands of economic development, with policy structured to encourage greater participation in the workforce and to reduce the burden of vulnerable populations on the state. This was also the case in the prereform period. Like other countries in East Asia, China has thus spent relatively little on public goods and services and thus the people of China have had high levels of out-of-pocket expenses for education and health.

Underinvestment by the government has reinforced the principle of self-reliance. This has meant that for most people the first port of call is the family, collective, or workplace. This characteristic changed with the policies of General Secretary Hu and Premier Wen. Their policies introduced the glimmers of a rights-based consciousness in assessing access to public goods and services. This is one of the building blocks of citizenship, a point I return to below. During the reform period, the market and alternative suppliers began to play an increasing role in service provision. Yu indicates how public service provision reflects the bias of official ideology that provides preferential treatment for those working in the formal sector in urban China and those in government employ. These key groups were seen as crucial to the industrialization drive and as important constituents of support for the Chinese Communist Party.

The extensive array of benefits through the workplace compensated in part for the low wages paid in the prereform era. This company-based welfare, somewhat resonant with the system in Japan and South Korea, has provided the major challenge to reform policies as benefits have had to be shifted from the enterprise and in some cases rolled back without undermining party support. This corporatist welfare has been more pervasive in China than elsewhere in East Asia and also distinguishes China from other Soviet-style systems.[26] When the mid-1990s reforms began under General Secretary Jiang Zemin and Premier Zhu Rongji to make state-owned enterprises more efficient, the major challenge was to weave the fragmented systems into a more coherent whole by transferring welfare obligations to local state administrative agencies.

Public Service Provision and Political Development

Public service reforms make an impact on political development in three main areas: the emerging notion of citizenship, citizens' evaluation of government performance, and the consequence of the plurality of service delivery for state-society relations. Since the initiatives of Jiang and Zhu from the mid-1990s—but especially with the increasing emphasis under Hu and Wen—policy initiatives have been ambitious attempts, especially for a developing country, to provide basic pension coverage and government-backed minimum income support to those in the rural areas. Such policy initiatives mark the start of a shift from a traditional approach to assistance and alms to a modern welfare state. It remains the case, however, that for most Chinese what you get depends on where you live and whether you work in the formal or the informal sector.

Despite this, policy is moving toward a welfare system based on citizenship. One could argue that this is the case with the broader provision of public service—for example, with the massive investment in rural infrastructure. Future policy design for service delivery and the extension of benefits should be based on a notion of citizenship that breaks down further the barriers between urban and rural China, the informal and formal sectors of the economy, and those employed by the government and those who are not. This does not mean that the government should rush to extend all existing benefits to all citizens. Not only would that be impractical but it would be difficult economically for local governments and might not even enhance social equity. The introduction of the minimum living support scheme for both urban and rural dwellers and the extension of a pension scheme to some rural inhabitants are good examples of policy directions that confirm steps in the direction of a citizen-based approach to public service provision.

The shift in the treatment of migrants is another good example. Policy in the 1980s and the 1990s was dedicated to delinking employment from one's household registration—户口, *hukou*—status; under Hu and Wen, policy has been to delink social services and welfare benefits from *hukou* status. The notion that migrants did not need welfare support because they had land in their home villages as insurance has become untenable. Many migrants and their families are now permanent fixtures in urban areas and may no longer have any land back in their place of registration. While *hukou* reforms of the earlier period until 2002–03 benefited mainly investors and the well-educated (and reflected the more elitist thrust of Jiang and Zhu's policy), the Hu-Wen leadership shifted policy focus to providing training and social welfare coverage to migrant workers. Those who are now long-term inhabitants should, in theory, enjoy better access to urban services. The policy initiatives to incorporate migrants into welfare systems and services in their chosen place of work also offer the potential to develop a welfare system based on citizenship. This would resemble what T. H. Marshall calls, in the context of Western Europe, "social citizenship" that encompasses the right to economic welfare and social security. In China, this process is likely to precede "political citizenship."[27]

This fits with the Chinese Communist Party's preference for economic and social rights over political rights.[28] It also reflects the policy focus of Hu and Wen, the remnant influences of socialist ideology on policy, and the party's claim to speak for all of the nation's people, thereby rejecting the need for any political opposition. Since taking power in 2003-04, Hu and Wen have redirected more resources to those who have not benefited so well from the reforms. This is encapsulated in slogans such as "Building a harmonious society" (by 2020) and "Putting people first." The dependence on socialist ideology has made the leadership vulnerable to criticism from both the old and the new Left who feel that overreliance on the market has created new inequalities while adversely impacting the vulnerable and marginalized populations. This was particularly evident in the criticisms of the inadequacies of the rural health system that Yu notes.

The statist predisposition and Chinese Communist Party's claims that it speaks on behalf of all Chinese citizens place the government under increased pressure to provide satisfactory services. If the local government is required to take on greater responsibility for the provision of public goods and services, especially as China urbanizes, pressure may increase not only for better service provision but also for greater accountability by the local authorities for how public monies are spent. This increased claim for accountability and transparency on behalf of the government is the most likely corollary of an increased awareness of citizenship. As I have shown elsewhere, citizen satisfaction with the performance of government drops significantly as the government becomes closer to the people, and there is also a clear difference between satisfaction levels with urban governance and rural governance.[29] That satisfaction levels are lower at the county, township, and district levels of government is important, as these are the levels of government charged with providing most public services.

The survey is a purposive stratified survey of around 4,000 respondents selected from three administrative levels: city, township and village. It comprises a number of sites selected on the basis of three variables: geographic location, average per capita income and population. Seven cities (eight from 2005) were selected together with seven townships and eight villages. While 95.9 percent of citizens in our survey said that they were relatively or extremely satisfied with the work of the central government in 2009, this number dropped to around 85 percent for the provincial level, 75 percent for the district and county level, and to 62 percent for the township, village, and neighborhood committee level. It is noticeable that satisfaction has risen steadily since Hu and Wen took over leadership. Central government satisfaction has remained high, but significantly, satisfaction with the lowest levels of government has risen from 44 percent in 2003, perhaps reflecting the policy initiatives of Premier Wen Jiabao to improve the lot of those in the rural areas.

However, even in 2009 those extremely satisfied with local government constituted only 7 percent. At the lowest levels of government, satisfaction in 2009 was highest for those living in major cities (72 percent), falling to 66 percent in towns and townships and only 55 percent in the villages. For those living in villages, this was a marked improvement over 2003, when only 37 percent were satisfied with local government. These figures confirm the general impression that the quality of governance is better in larger cities than in rural China, where training opportunities are limited and education levels are low. The services that citizens want their local government to concentrate on include those household-based challenges that have been a result of reforms (pensions, health care, job creation) and those that counteract the negative impacts of reforms (environmental, health, and corruption). They are less interested in local government provision of those services that the state has been traditionally good at providing (road building and water and electricity supply).

The multiple actors engaged in public service provision have the potential to alter significantly state-society relations. While government's role may be crucial with respect to welfare provision, often it is limited to last resort and emergency relief coverage. Despite the new policies, family and extended kinship networks will continue to play a major role in welfare provision in the foreseeable future. This is especially the case for those living in rural China, where government support can only be residual at best.

Old-age security will still be the responsibility of the family in most rural areas, as will major medical expenses, and this will be the case for many in urban China, too. Pooling family resources or establishing lending systems such as the rotating savings and credit associations may be the only ways for many families to cover such expenses. Yet changing demographics mean that reliance on the family in the future will become increasingly problematic. The government will have to allow the intermediary organizations between the state and family to expand their roles or the work of government will have to expand further. Neither markets nor the institutions of civil society are fully playing their role in social welfare provision. Much of the expansion of the market and nongovernmental organizations into service provision has been by default rather than by design. This is part of why services have become too expensive for some, and why those services that are available can be poorly regulated and open to abuse.

In all societies, the state plays a fundamental role in structuring civil society, not only in the regulatory framework but also in norms and assumptions about the respective roles of state and civil society. It is impossible to think of civil society independent of the state. The regulations and practices of the nongovernmental sector reflect the Chinese Communist Party's ambivalence toward its development and the party's desire to regulate it in the same hierarchical manner as other sectors of society. The prevailing view that the party is capable of representing all interests in society imposes severe constraints on the autonomy of civil society organizations in carrying out their activities. The intent of legislation is to mimic the compartmentalization of government departments and limit horizontal linkages.

This regulatory intent notwithstanding, the idea of nongovernmental organizations as service delivery agents has been gaining acceptance, especially in major cities. In the countryside there is often no choice. However, they are still seen by the government as second best. In Shanghai in 1996 the government invited the Shanghai Young Men's Christian Association to manage a community center in the Pudong New District, the first such experiment in China. By the end of 2006, the association was running six such centers, for which the government provided free facilities and sometimes utilities or equipment as well. However, implementation of policy has been inconsistent, and preferential treatment for government agencies persists. Thus each of the six centers in Shanghai must negotiate its own arrangements, and they are vulnerable to the whims of local leaders.

In rural China, community-based organizations are expanding, and it is clear that alternatives are emerging to take over functions that were previously considered the preserve of government. Many of these organizations are based on traditional associations such as temples or social networks, including clans and lineages. Biliang Hu has explored this phenomenon with respect to village trust and the establishment of rotating savings and credit associations in Xiangdong village, in Zhejiang Province.[30] These organizations finance medical expenses and school fees. Lily Tsai shows that in some areas social capital substitutes for governmental performance, and officials allow social institutions to take over the provision of public goods.[31]

None of these institutions are a threat to the rule of the party, but they are important components of political change. A more empowered citizenry that is less reliant on the government to provide its public services may eventually call for more effective service from government itself and push for greater accountability and transparency.

Notes

1. The public services discussed in this chapter are mainly social public services—basic public services in the social policy field. Unless expressly stated otherwise, all data used in this chapter are taken or derived from *Zhongguo tongji nianjian* [China statistical yearbook] (Beijing: China State Statistical Bureau, 2002–09) and official websites of various departments of the central government.

2. Peter Saunders and Xiaoyuan Shang, "Social Security Reform in China's Transition to a Market Economy," *Social Policy and Administration*, no. 3 (2001), pp. 274–89.

3. Joseph Wong, "The Adaptive Developmental State in East Asia," *Journal of East Asian Studies*, no. 4 (2004), pp. 345–62.

4. Mark W. Frazier, "China's Pension Reform and Its Discontents," *China Journal,* no. 51 (2004), pp. 97–114.

5. Shih-Jiunn Shi, "Left to Market and Family—Again? Ideas and the Development of the Rural Pension Policy in China," *Social Policy and Administration,* no. 7 (2006), pp. 791–806.

6. Athar Hussain, "Social Welfare in China in the Context of Three Transitions," in *How Far across the River? Chinese Policy Reform at the Millennium,* edited by Nicholas C. Hope, Dennis Tao Yang, and Mu Yang Li (Stanford University Press, 2003).

7. Christine P. W. Wong and Richard M. Bird, "China's Fiscal System: A Work in Progress," in *China's Great Economic Transformation,* edited by Loren Brandt and Thomas G. Rawski, translated by Fang Ying and Zhao Yang (Shanghai: Shanghai People's Publishing House, 2009), p. 389.

8. Zhou Li'an, "Zhongguo difang guanyuan de jinsheng jinbiaosai moshi yanjiu" [Research on promotion tournament of China's local government officials], in *Wei zengzhang er jingzheng* [Compete for growth], edited by Zhang Jun and Zhou Li'an (Shanghai: Shanghai People's Publishing House, 2008), p. 115.

9. Dorothy J. Solinger, *Contesting Citizenship in Urban China: Peasant Migrants, the State, and the Logic of the Market* (University of California Press, 1999).

10. Yan Jirong, *Fuwuxing zhengfu jianshe: Zhengfu zaizao qi xiang zhanlue* [Service-oriented government building: Seven strategies of government transformation] (Beijing: Renmin University of China Press, 2009).

11. Tony Saich, *Governance and Politics of China* (London: Palgrave Macmillan, 2001), p. 241.

12. Adam Wagstaff and Magnus Lindelow, "Extending Health Insurance to the Rural Population: An Impact Evaluation of China's New Cooperative Medical Scheme," *Journal of Health Economics,* no. 28 (2009), pp. 1–19.

13. Catherine Jones Finer, ed., *Social Policy Reform in China* (Surrey, U.K.: Ashgate, 2003), chaps. 14, 15.

14. Gao Peiyong, ed., *Zhongguo caishui tizhi gaige sanshi nian yanjiu* [Thirty years of China's fiscal and tax reforms] (Beijing: Jingji guanli chubanshe [Economic Management Press], 2008).

15. Zheng Yongnian, *Globalization and State Transformation in China* (Cambridge University Press, 2004), p. 116.

16. Roy Bahl and Jorge Martinez-Vazquez, "Fiscal Federalism and Economic Reform in China," in *Federalism and Economic Reform: International Perspectives,* edited by T. N. Srinivasan and Jessica Seddon Wallack (Cambridge University Press, 2006).

17. World Bank, *China: National Development and Subnational Finance: A Review of Provincial Expenditures* (2002).

18. *Zhongguo tongji nianjian, 2002–09* and official websites of various departments of the central government.

19. Zhongguo (Hainan) gaige fazhan yanjiuyuan [China Institute for Reform and Development (Hainan)], *2007–08 Zhongguo renlei fazhan baogao: Huiji 13 yi ren de jiben*

gonggong fuwu [China Human Development Report, 2007–08: Access for all; Basic public services for 1.3 billion people] (Beijing: China Translation and Publishing Corporation, 2008), pp. 88–89.

20. Tony Saich, *Providing Public Goods in Transitional China* (London: Palgrave Macmillan, 2008), pp. 203–07.

21. Susan H. Whiting, *Power and Wealth in Rural China: The Political Economy of Institutional Change* (Cambridge University Press, 2000), pp. 100–01.

22. T. H. Marshall and others, *Gongmin shenfen yu shehui jieji* [Citizenship and social class], translated by Guo Zhonghua and Liu Xunlian (Nanjing: Jiangsu People's Publishing House, 2008).

23. Chen Changsheng and CaiYuezhou, *Zhongguo gonggong fuwu baogao 2006: Zhongguo zhengfu gonggong fuwu, tizhi bianqian yu jixiao pinggu* [China's Public Services Report 2006: The Chinese government's public services; Institutional evolution and performance evaluation] (Beijing: China Social Sciences Press, 2006), p. xiii.

24. Andrew G. Walder, *Communist Neo-Traditionalism: Work and Authority in Chinese Industry* (University of California Press, 1988).

25. Ministry of Civil Affairs official website (cws.mca.gov.cn/article/tjbg/201006/20100600081422.shtml).

26. See Gosta Esping-Andersen, *The Three Worlds of Welfare Capitalism* (Princeton University Press, 1990).

27. T. H. Marshall, *Citizenship and Social Class, and Other Essays* (Cambridge University Press, 1950); Marshall, *Class, Citizenship, and Social Development* (Garden City, N.Y.: Doubleday, 1964).

28. See Tony Saich, "Globalization, Governance, and the Authoritarian Westphalian State," in *Globalization and Governance,* edited by Joseph Nye and Robert Keohane (Brookings Press, 2001).

29. See, for example, Tony Saich, "Citizens' Perception of Governance in Rural and Urban China," *Journal of Chinese Political Science,* no. 1 (2007); Saich, "Citizens' Perceptions of Adequate Governance: Satisfaction Levels among Rural and Urban Chinese," in *Governance of Life in a Chinese Moral Experience: The Quest for an Adequate Life,* edited by Everett Zhang, Arthur Kleinman, and Tu Weiming (London: Routledge, 2011), pp. 199–214.

30. Biliang Hu, *Informal Institutions and Rural Development in China* (New York: Routledge, 2007).

31. See, for example, Lily Tsai, "Cadres, Temple, and Lineage Institutions, and Governance in Rural China," *China Journal,* no. 48 (2002); Tsai, *Accountability without Democracy: Solidary Groups and Public Goods Provision in Rural China* (Cambridge University Press, 2007).

8

Decentralization and Central-Local Relations in Reform-Era China

YANG GUANGBIN

China's reforms began with decentralization and eventually fundamentally changed the country's political ecology and political process. From the reform of the rural land system in 1978 to the reform of the urban economic system in 1984, China's moves to separate the economy from politics have begun in the rural areas and worked their way to urban areas. An unintended outcome of this change in the political-economic relationship was that the unitary state-society relationship crumbled under the emergence of social autonomy and self-organized society. These changes in both political economy and the relationship between state and society necessitated reforms of the political system. The reforms of the 1980s centered on better delineating the relationship between the Chinese Communist Party and the government, a horizontal change in the power structure. Meanwhile, China's vertical power structure, that is the relationship between central and local governments, also underwent profound changes. According to some foreign scholars, including Lynn White, decentralization has affected not only the vertical central-local relationship but also the separation of power among horizontal government departments and the supervisory role played by professional personnel, such as scholars, lawyers, and journalists, outside the political system. Because the separation of powers among government departments in the Chinese context largely does not fall within the scope of decentralization, this chapter approaches China's decentralization reforms from the perspective of the central-local relationship.

The research on China's central-local state structure conducted by Chinese political and constitutional scholars has mostly fallen within the framework of

254

old institutionalism or legalism. Such works offer legal and institutional descriptions of the central-local relationship mainly as set forth in the Constitution and then draw their conclusions according to the changes of legal provisions by adding different modifiers to the "unitary system" (单一制, *danyizhi*). Given that the state structure is mandated by laws, this legalist research is certainly necessary for a clear understanding of the state structure. Laws are static, however, and there may be a significant discrepancy between written law and the operations of various institutions. We should thus have a good understanding not only of static legal provisions but also of dynamic political processes, especially political-economic interactions.

Comparatively speaking, the research completed by economists on central-local economic relations, especially fiscal relations, is better. Nevertheless, the mission of economists, in the final analysis, is to explore technical arrangements in order to determine the optimal allocation of economic resources; they do not concern themselves much with the macro institutional environment, such as the state power structure, which determines technical arrangements. China's economic transformation has been carried out under the precondition of political stability, and, within the existing political structure, China's economic institutions have undergone revolutionary change. Therefore, understanding China's central-local relationship from a political-economy perspective is key. This chapter proposes the concept of "fiscal federalism under a unitary system" (单一制下的经济联邦主义, *danyizhi xia de jingji lianbang zhuyi*) and analyzes the issues pertinent to this structure.

Unitary Political System

Unitary systems are weakening as the idea of federalism continues to catch on.[1] The case of China, though, is interesting as the country is undergoing a profound transformation in the political-economic evolution of its institutions. While it cannot be viewed simply as a unitary state, China is even less a federal state. Yet from the perspective of political economy, China seems to have both a unitary and federal system.

Whether because of the huge transformations brought by China's economic reforms, the changes brought about by the return of Hong Kong and Macau, or the constitutional provisions concerning regional ethnic autonomy, political and legal scholars have become increasingly dissatisfied with the traditional understanding of China's state structure as a unitary system. They have thus begun to propose various new theories, including the unitary system of democratic centralism, the unitary composite system, the hybrid system, and even the federal political system.[2] In this chapter I argue that the theories that define China's state structure as a unitary system of a peculiar kind address only the political relationship and neglect the importance of the economic; that the hybrid system theory, which refers to the political peculiarity of Hong Kong and Macau, blurs the main nature of China's political system; and that the federal systems theory, which cites the constitutional provisions for regional ethnic autonomy as evidence, reveals a lack of basic knowledge of Chinese politics.

Any real understanding of Chinese politics must begin by recognizing that while its political structure has basically remained intact, China's economic relationship has undergone drastic changes. A second baseline is that the leadership of the Chinese Communist Party (CCP) and the party-government relationship are two basic starting points of research on Chinese politics. In examining China's state structure, an understanding must be developed then of the constitutions of both the People's Republic of China (PRC) and the CCP, the two fundamental documents defining the basic framework of China's political system. A third baseline is that any understanding of China's state structure should be grounded not only in the legal relationship in the structural sense but, more important, also on the factual relationship in the procedural sense—how, for example, the pithy expression found in the PRC Constitution of "upholding the leadership of the Communist Party" is in fact reflected in every aspect of China's political life. Moreover, Chinese politics has always been divided into formal and informal politics, which to a certain extent is reflected in procedural aspects as well.[3]

These three baselines are the starting point for my attempt to understand China's central-local relationship. Article 3 of China's Constitution stipulates that "the state organs of the People's Republic of China apply the principle of democratic centralism."[4] That is to say, the State Council, the Supreme People's Court, and the Supreme People's Procuratorate are elected by and answer to the National People's Congress; the division of functions and powers between the central and local state organs is guided by the principle of giving full scope to the initiative and enthusiasm of the local authorities under the unified leadership of the central authorities. Article 89 of the PRC Constitution requires that the State Council "exercise unified leadership over the work of local organs of state administration at various levels throughout the country, and formulate the detailed division of functions and powers between the Central Government and the organs of state administration of provinces, autonomous regions, and municipalities directly under the Central Government."[5] These two stipulations of democratic centralism in the Chinese context express the unitary nature of the relationship between the people's congress and the government and between central and local governments.

How then does the CCP constitution provide for the party-government relationship? The principle of democratic centralism that every party member learns by heart states that "the lower levels submit to the higher levels and the entire Party submits to the Central Committee."[6] To ensure that the entire party submits to the CCP Central Committee, the party constitution and other documents set forth various mechanisms and principles, including the party committee system, the party group system, the system of sectorial division for management, and the cadre administration system.[7] These systems and arrangements hold as both legal structures and as procedural fact. The principle of democratic centralism in the state constitution provides for the relationship between the National People's Congress (NPC) and the central government; the party constitution, in turn, spells out the relationship between the CCP and the People's Congress and between the party and the government. The political relationships involved in the interaction between the party and the People's Congress are complicated and multifarious, and democratic centralism is best expressed in the cadre administration system and the strong government management system that supports it.

The Party Administering Cadres

According to the List of Official Posts Administered by the CCP Central Committee issued by the CCP Central Committee in 1998, all cadres appointed at the subprovincial level or above are subject to the assessment and management of the Central Committee's Organization Department, while for the appointments to leadership posts at lower levels, the organization department requires only that a list of names be filed.[8] This list requirement is largely a continuation of the cadre management system of the 1980s. In 1984 the central government narrowed its administration of local officials from two levels (the provincial and bureau levels) to one. This consolidated level is responsible only for the assessment, appointment, and dismissal of officials at the subprovincial level or above. As a result, the number of officials directly administered by the central government decreased from about 15,000 to around 3,000. In comparison with the List of Official Posts Administered by the CCP Central Committee issued in 1990, the central government's scope of authority over local officials remained basically unchanged. In the early 1990s, however, as the local governments increasingly became stakeholders, there was a growing tendency toward local protectionism. In some provinces it was not uncommon that the candidates recommended by the central government for some posts were rejected at the level of the local people's congresses in favor of local candidates. Given such a trend, the central government began to find it necessary to maintain and strengthen its authority. The most convenient way to do so was to strengthen its administration of local officials.

In June 1999 the Central Organization Department issued Rules on Official Rotation, which introduced the nonnative principle and the regular rotation system to the administration of local officials. For provincial officials, it emphasized more frequent rotation in the form of transfers to either other provinces or the central government. In the current structure of the provincial leadership group, the provincial party secretary and governor are transferred from other provinces or the central government, while the deputy positions are mainly held by natives. In addition to the traditional principle of avoidance (回避原则, *huibi yuanze*), there is also strict control of tenure for provincial principal officials. Since the late 1990s, there has been a shorter tenure and quicker rotation of local officials.[9]

Since the late 1990s, the central government has greatly strengthened the administration of core provincial officials, the primary purpose being to curb localism and sectarianism, strengthen the authority of the central government, and, ultimately, maintain political unity and stability. In the process of China's economic transformation, the control of core local officials has become a principal means for the central government to restrict the local governments. It is also a core characteristic of the unitary system.

Strong Government Administration System

The unitary system not only is reflected in the administration of officials but also is reliant on a strong government administration system. Although there have been multiple reforms of the government system, the traditional vertical arrangement of government departments has remained fundamentally unchanged or, if anything, even strengthened. China's administrative departments can be divided into several major categories. The first covers a dozen ministries common to other countries, such as the ministries of foreign affairs, justice, education, and civil affairs, as well as macroeconomic regulation departments such as the National Development and Reform Commission, the Ministry of Finance, the central bank, and the Ministry of Commerce. The second category covers special economic management departments in charge of specific products and industries, such as the former ministries of the electricity, petroleum, and chemical industries (all three of which have been restructured into state-owned corporations), the Ministry of Industry and Information Technology, and the Ministry of Water Resources. The third category is government departments with overlapping responsibilities. For example, there are at least four ministerial departments that exercise direct management of transportation, including the Ministry of Transportation, the Ministry of Water Resources, the Civil Aviation Administration, and the Ministry of Public Security. It is rare for a country to have so many government departments with overlapping administration. The fourth and final category covers government departments that are jointly responsible for the administration of the same field yet lack coordination among them, such as the environmental protection departments, agricultural departments, and the water resources departments.

How does this government structure affect the political process? First, the various administrative departments that implement laws are themselves lawmakers. Both the laws adopted by the National People's Congress and the regulations promulgated by the State Council are general legal provisions, and it is within the scope of authority of the administrative organs to interpret and implement those provisions. Put differently, in the process of implementing the laws, the administrative departments are authorized to formulate administrative rules. As a result, it is not only the State Council, the highest administrative organ that has formulated many administrative regulations; the various departments under the State Council have also formulated tens of thousands of industry regulations. Such administrative laws and regulations directly affect all aspects of Chinese society. Since 1979 China has promulgated about 300 laws, more than 800 administrative regulations, and more than 30,000 administrative rules and local regulations. Owing to the vertical organization of government departments, the regulations promulgated by various government departments are parallel in legal status, and in the event of any conflict among them, the court does not know how to adjudicate.

According to the Administrative Procedural Law, an application may be filed with the State Council for interpretation or adjudication. But such applications are subject to a complicated procedure, one in which the accepting court reports the issue to the Supreme People's Court, which then submits the issue to the State Council. This procedure is more costly than most involved persons or major micro-market enterprises can afford. This conflict of interest among different government departments and the segmentation of department interest by regulations, in essence, constitute an erosion and segmentation of the authority of the state. With this consideration in mind, the State Council in its Decree 319 revoked 151 of the more than 800 administrative regulations and ordered the various government departments to revoke many regulations that were in conflict with World Trade Organization rules. Implementing these changes has posed incredible difficulty.

Second, these institutions have discretionary power in policy implementation. According to public choice theory, in the process of implementing policies, the departments that serve as the agents of the central government tend to expand their own authority by taking advantage of the asymmetry of information between principal and the agent. This leads to "bureaucratic discretion whereby the bureaucracies and individuals go beyond their status and functions, and even beyond the control of their overseers, to play a dominant role in the process of public decisionmaking. This political process has been described by Charles Edward Lindblom.[10] Such theories are summarizations of the behavior of ordinary government departments. Unrestricted discretionary power is even more serious in the case of economic administration departments with overlapping responsibilities and interest in the management of specific industries and products. Sometimes this discretionary power is so abused as to become a violation of law. This greatly increases the transaction costs and administration expenses in the market economy, which in essence constitutes a segmentation of the state's authoritative resources.

Third, an inevitable result of the vertical arrangement of government is the departmentalized institutionalization of power.[11] This occurs when departments that enjoy de facto legislative power institutionalize and protect their own powers by adopting regulations in their own interest. That is why institutionalization is easily abused in China. The legislative power of the administrative departments and their discretionary power in the implementation of laws are both the cause of institutionalized power and the result of the departmentalized institutionalization of power. In fact, this is a process whereby administrative departments expand their own powers and interests through regulation formulation, which is protected by general laws. According to article 8 of the Company Law, "Where the establishment of a company is subject to examination and approval as required by the relevant national statutes or administrative regulations, examination and approval procedures must be carried out in accordance with the law prior to its registration." This means that almost all market participants that engage in any economic activities regulated by competent government departments must go through a procedure of examination and approval. Given the huge scope of this procedure and the innumerable items involved, China's economic system may well be said to be an examination and approval economy. Put differently, the market economy endows the various government departments with greater economic interests, and the administrative departments that have de facto legislative power will legalize their own interests.

This control is the corruption of power, also known as the India syndrome. In India, different transactions are associated with different exclusive corruptions of power. This corruption, once institutionalized, can be changed only at a huge cost. In China, the examination and approval system that has resulted from the institutionalization of such powers has had two direct consequences. First, it has significantly increased the cost of market entry, thus increasing the cost of ordinary transactions and reducing the competitiveness of the system. However, the nature of ownership—that is, the dominance of state-owned enterprises under administrative monopoly—determines that the examination and approval–style government system is an inevitable institutional arrangement. Second, it has led to astonishing waste of nonproductive social resources and has also been the main institutional cause of China's corruption problems. The system is a hold-over from the planned economy. This power, when linked with the market, naturally leads to a plethora of corruption cases. There is thus a tendency for highly centralized state power to be dispersed by the state's agents, which leads to the direct consumption of authoritative resources.

Fiscal Federalism

In contrast to the unitary system in the political realm, the proposition of economic federalism is more controversial. Despite decentralization throughout thirty years of economic reforms, the power of the central government and the planned allocation system are still evident in economic life. A few examples are illustrative. The first is the direct management of land resources. The Land Administration Law contains the provision that the State Council has power over the use of land resources. Since 2003 the State Council has canceled many land-use projects launched in the name of creating economic development zones. With respect to mineral resources, the central government has the power of allocation similar to that under the planned economy. In the Xi Mei Dong Song (西煤东送) program, for example, the western part of the country sends 5,000 tons of coal eastward at a subsidy of RMB 10 per ton, with a revenue of RMB 500 million, yet the market value of the same amount of coal is RMB 14 billion, and if used to generate power at a price of RMB 0.23 per kilowatt-hour translates into a revenue of RMB 34 billion. The natural gas in the west of the country is also being transferred to the east, which carries priority.[12] It is hoped that this government-mandated economic arrangement will be replaced by market mechanisms.

Second, the central government has direct management of investment projects. The decision to launch large investment projects, and their ultimate scope, is subject to the approval of the National Development and Reform Commission in order to avoid redundant construction, environmental disruption, or blind decisionmaking. For example, the central government rejected a local government proposal to establish a dam on the Nu River. Local railway projects are also subject to the approval of the commission.

Third, the central government has coercive powers in the realm of macroeconomic control. The main means of macroeconomic control in the 1980s was administrative control. Such control increasingly shifted to the realm of monetary policy in the 1990s. Coercive powers, which are much more abrasive, can always be used to establish control. When monetary policy fails to obtain the desired result, the central government does not hesitate to exercise its coercive powers. The best example has been the Tieben incident in Jiangsu.[13] The powers that the central government has in these cases are not found in typical federal states.

Even so, local governments enjoy almost all local administrative powers, including in education, employment, medical care, urban management, land development, and other economic realms. Correspondingly, local governments have obtained legislative power through the Legislative Law. For example, the provincial people's congresses and governments and especially the governments of the special economic zones, such as the government of the Shenzhen Special Economic Zone, have obtained the power to formulate and interpret local laws and regulations. This represents a fundamental departure from the powers of local governments under the traditional political and economic unitary system.

More important, the fiscal system best reflects the relationship between the central and local governments. The unified revenue and expenditure system under the planned economy gave way to the system of dividing revenue and expenditures between the central and local governments. Under this second system the local governments had more initiative but also took various measures to keep wealth at the local level, thus making a significant dent in fiscal revenue that flowed to the national level.

This situation posed a serious challenge to the central government's macroeconomic control capacity. Under this new system, moreover, the local governments also tended to embrace all kinds of local protectionism, which were a drag on the unified market and the national economy. It was against this backdrop that Zhu Rongji, vice premier at the time, began to promote the tax-sharing reform in some provinces in 1993 and later nationwide. Given the political unitary system, the division between state tax and local tax inevitably tilted in favor of the central government. This tax-sharing reform, as expected, immediately increased the central government's share of fiscal revenue to more than 50 percent, a substantial increase.

The division of fiscal power, especially in regard to the tax-sharing system, had two major effects. First, in terms of the central-local relationship, the central government played a less direct role in the management of the economy but a greater role in terms of macroeconomic control. Second, the local governments also had a greater role to play; in the interplay between politics and the market, the government played a lesser role and the impact of the market was strengthened. The role of local governments changed from agents of the central government to stakeholders in their own right, and the role played by the market changed from supplementary to dominant, making the market a new institutional arrangement. This and other similar arrangements can be called fiscal federalism, promarket federalism, or even economic federalism.

In domestic politics, decentralization is not the same thing as federalism. That is, federalism cannot be understood simply as decentralization. However, decentralization is an important basis of federalism. When local officials are determined through direct election, or when local governments obtain a certain degree of fiscal autonomy and independence through the adoption of local laws and regulations, the relationship between central and local governments is likely to evolve into both contract-based cooperation and a bargaining relationship, which is precisely the essence of federalism. Therefore, there is a positive correlation between federalism and fiscal decentralization and between the decentralization of decisionmaking and political decentralization.[14] In fact, the central-local economic relationship under the tax-sharing system has been generally understood by economists to be fiscal federalism.[15] Some foreign scholars also call it de facto federalism.[16]

The best example of promarket economic federalism was the housing market control policy launched by the Chinese government in April 2010. This control policy drew on features from the planned economy, such as the prohibition keeping non-tax-paying nonresidents who are not covered by social insurance from buying houses in their place of residence. There were problems present in the tax-sharing system. For example, the central government drew heavily from the tax revenues, thereby leaving local governments financially challenged and often having to resort to "land financing," seeking profit from land conversions (see table 8-1). Therefore, macroeconomic control is detrimental not only to real estate developers but also, and even more so, to local governments. In this situation, local governments ally with real estate developers to resist the central government's control through dereliction of duty. How this tripartite contest—between the central government, local governments, and real estate developers—will shake out remains to be seen. This reflects the autonomy of the local governments in economic affairs and the degree of resistance to unfavorable central government policies, which is a typical manifestation of promarket economic federalism.

It is worth pointing out that although economic federalism provides a legal basis for the powers of local governments and strengthens their independence, this does not mean that the central government is correspondingly weakened. To the contrary, the decentralization and power sharing under economic federalism has strengthened the power of the central government and, in some aspects, has increased the obligatory burden of the local governments. For example, the tax

Table 8-1. Land Transfer Revenue as Share of All Local Fiscal Revenue, China, 2001–08

RMB 100 million

Year	Total land transfer revenue nationwide	Total local government revenue	Share (percentage)
2001	1,296	7,803	16.6
2002	2,417	8,515	28.4
2003	5,385	9,850	54.7
2004	5,894	11,893	49.6
2005	5,505	15,101	36.5
2006	7,677	18,304	41.9
2007	11,948	23,573	50.7
2008	9,741	28,650	34.0

Sources: *Zhongguo caizheng nianjian* [Finance yearbook of China] and *Zhongguo guotu ziyuan gongbao* [Bulletin of China land resources], cited from Liu Lingling and Feng Yinan, "Fenshui zhi xia de caizheng tizhi gaige yu defang caili bianhua" [Tax sharing–oriented finance system reform and the change of local fiscal strength], *Shuiwu yanjiu* [Taxation research], no. 4 (2010).

system reform strengthened the central government's fiscal extractive capacity and, at the same time, also relegated more public responsibilities to local governments. The state has not increased the percentage of expenditure on social rights for many years (see figure 8-1).

What this means is that under the tax-sharing system, the central government has substantially increased fiscal revenue and reduced its fiscal burden, thus increasing its discretionary power in regard to where and how to spend money. For example, it has significantly increased national defense expenditures and introduced a RMB 4 trillion package to respond to the financial crisis. Interestingly, a noted Chinese scholar on fiscal administration has claimed that compared with other countries, the central government's share of national revenue is too low and needs to be increased.[17] However, the central government bears only a limited amount of public services responsibilities. Keeping this in mind, the central government's share of national revenue is thus already too high, and local governments remain financially strapped and overburdened with responsibilities. As a result, local governments have been forced to take various measures to increase their fiscal revenue in order to perform their obligatory duties. Under the political unitary system, the amount of fiscal revenue and the way various problems are solved have a direct impact on the career prospects of officials. When the political unitary system and economic federalism are coupled with the excessive obligations placed on local governments, bad things

Figure 8-1. *Social Security Expenditure as Share of Total Financial Expenditure, China, 1991–2005*

Percentage

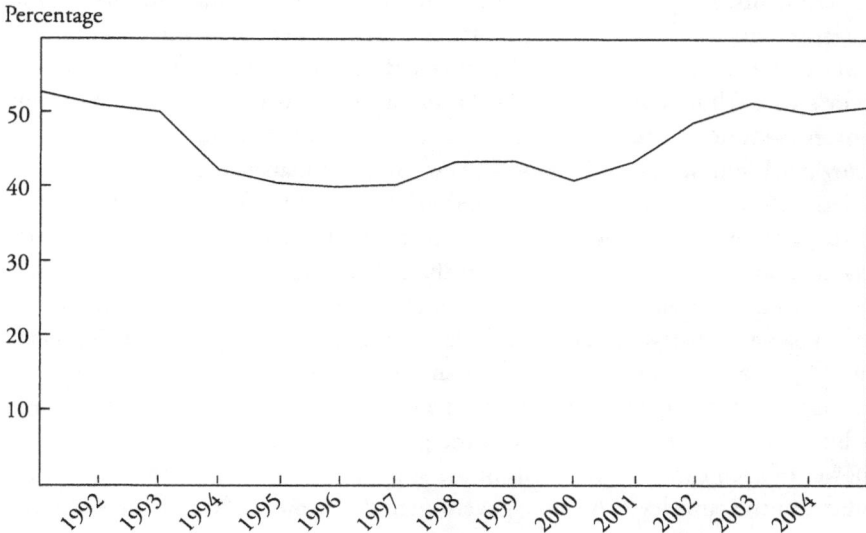

Source: Data from *China Statistical Yearbook* (Beijing: Zhongguo tongji chubanshe [China Statistics Press], 1990–2006).

happen—such as the encroachment on citizens' property rights in the process of economic development.[18]

The Inner Tension of Fiscal Federalism under a Unitary System

The political unitary system—or political centralism and economic federalism, or also economic autonomy and shared economic administrative power—is a typical dual political-economic structure. In economic development, the political unitary system has obvious advantages, including that it helps maintain a unified orderly domestic market and balanced regional development.[19] Even so, this dual structure also faces serious problems. In the market economy, the old vertical arrangement of government departments further strengthens their own interests. While the vertical arrangement of administration has remained unchanged, the horizontal levels have undergone great change, especially the shift in the role of government departments from agents in the unitary economic system to stake-holders in today's economic federalism, a transition that is increasingly segmenting authoritative resources.[20]

The last decade has seen much tension between the old vertical arrangement of administration and the new horizontal arrangement: fiscally federalized local governments. In spite of this change in the role and behavioral patterns of local governments, the traditional quasi-federal arrangement of administration has not experienced any fundamental adjustment. To ensure the enforcement of the state's will, China's unitary system features a vertical correspondence of various government departments with the same functions at the various levels—central, provincial, municipal, and county. There are three management models for the relationship between central and local government departments: departments directly under the management of the central government, such as banks; departments under the joint management of the central and local governments, where the central government is responsible for operations and the local government is responsible for party and personnel affairs; and various departments being managed by local governments. Each department is subject to some sort of multilevel management that requires it to implement the orders of its superior department while implementing the policies of the government at the same level, and the power of each cadre is derived from the superior department or the party committee at the same level. As such, government departments that are subject to the restrictions of different authorities may implement policies with different motivations, leading to a significant reduction in efficiency of administration. This is, again, the much-discussed segmentation of the state's authoritative resources.

There is a more serious problem. In accordance with the principle of correspondence of government departments at various levels, some local governments and judicial departments that have gained significantly strengthened administrative power under economic federalism may become a tool of local protectionism. This would allow them to directly consume the economic resources underlying state power and even allow them to undermine the dignity of laws that reflect the state's will. The debt evasion and rescission phenomenon (逃废债, *tao fei zhai*) is both a new form of local protectionism and the institutional manifestation of the dignity of laws being offset by these new local forces.

One statistical report examined the 62,656 restructured enterprises that have opened accounts with the Industrial and Commercial Bank of China, Agricultural Bank of China, China Construction Bank, and the Bank of Communications, with a total loan amount (inclusive of interest) of RMB 579.2 billion as of the end of 2000. There were 32,140 enterprises or 51.29 percent that evaded or repudiated a total of RMB 185.1 billion (inclusive of interest), or 31.96 percent of the total loan amount. Of the enterprises evading or revoking the debts, 22,296 were state-owned enterprises (69.37 percent), with a total loan amount evaded or revoked (inclusive of interest) of RMB 127.3 billion

(68.77 percent); 9,844 were non-state-owned enterprises (30.63 percent), with a total loan amount evaded or revoked of RMB 57.8 billion (inclusive of interest), or 31 percent. Of the state-owned enterprises that evaded or revoked their debts through restructuring, 86 percent were small and medium-size enterprises. The report also finds that most of the enterprises were from Beijing, Guangdong, Shandong, Hubei, Jiangsu, Liaoning, Shaanxi, and Qinghai; the provinces Guangdong, Shandong, Jiangsu, and Hubei involved the largest amount of debt evasion.[21] One reported cause of the typical debt evasion and rescission cases was the judicial system of the local governments. As the courts, procuratorates, and administrative and enforcement departments are constituted according to the levels of the various governments, judicial protection of local protectionism is prevalent. In the event of debt dispute between the banks and the local enterprises, the court often supports the enterprises. This support is given because these enterprises are owned by the local governments while the banks are nationally owned. In the event of any dispute between local enterprises and enterprises from other regions or central enterprises, the local governments or courts also tend to protect the interest of local enterprises.

In some debt evasion and rescission cases, the local governments play an important role. In one case involving RMB 500 million of debt, the local government had a direct liability.[22] In Guangdong Province, where the phenomenon was the most serious, the primary cause was also the vested interest of the local government.[23] The administrative and enforcement departments, as subordinate organizations under the government, are unable to supervise the government. In this existing institutional arrangement, the laws that express the will of the state are nullified to varying degrees owing to local protectionism.

There are at least three measures that can be taken to deal with the institutionalization of interests and the segmentation of the state's authoritative resources. The first is to further reform the vertical arrangement of administration, that is, the introduction of the system of superministries. This is an old problem that still remains unsolved.

The second is to change the practice of the planned economy era, which adopted an identical package of institutional arrangements in economic management departments at each local level, especially at the municipal and county levels. One reason is that there are few state-owned enterprises at the municipal and county levels, and therefore the industry- and product-based government departments serve no purpose. Another is that the economy is increasingly dependent on the state's macroeconomic policy. Therefore, the local government departments need to be streamlined. Regrettably, owing to traditional mind-sets, even some newly established systems, such as the China Development Bank, have also adopted traditional practices and have established county-level branches. This practice not only inflates the government system and increases the financial burden on local governments, but it also makes some local government departments into tools of local protectionism.

The third measure that can be taken is moderating both centralization and decentralization. The powers appropriate for decentralization should be decentralized, and those appropriate for centralization, such as the judicial and law enforcement system, should be centralized. China's reforms have been decentralization oriented, but in some fields a certain degree of centralization is necessary. In fact, the decentralization of the economic and administrative fields should be accompanied by centralization in the judicial and law enforcement fields. Administrative management is more locally based and therefore needs to be decentralized, while law is nationally unified and therefore should be centralized. Never mind the political unitary state of China; even in the typical federal state of the United States, judiciary power is centralized. As China's system is one in which executive power is strong and judiciary power is weak, national laws are easily manipulated by local governments in the existing judiciary and law enforcement system. Therefore, it is imperative to reorganize China's judiciary and law enforcement system. Such systems, including environmental protection, should be reorganized like the central bank. It is also beneficial to draw on the experience of other countries in this regard.

Several Discoveries

China's reforms began with decentralization and have come to change China's political structure and political process. The political unitary system based on CCP administration of government officials, or the strong government system, has remained unchanged. The strength of this unitary system is the CCP, the indispensable organizer of the national state's construction, which maintains national order and security and has its political legitimacy strengthened by being a development-oriented state. Yet the contest among the various government departments, each with its own vested interests, leads to the segmentation of state authority.

Under the political unitary system, the economic federalism formed through decentralization has actually strengthened fiscal extractive capacity. Several lessons may be drawn from this: The more the central government tries to centralize control over all social resources, the poorer its performance becomes; conversely, reforms that have institutionalized decentralization have eventually brought more benefits to the central government than expected. In other words, government performance or system competitiveness is dependent not on what the state directly controls but rather on what a country can eventually bring about through sound institutional arrangements. By extension, in the management of social, economic, and administrative affairs, direct control of the unitary system is not necessarily good, and the federalized economic management system is not necessarily bad; the unitary system and federalism are tools, not objectives, and have no ideological orientation of their own. The philosophical basis for decentralization is the ability to greatly stimulate both individuals and society at large, which are the ultimate driving forces of social progress. Therefore China's reforms have been pushing toward economic federalism, and institutionalized decentralization and cogovernance should thus lead the way for China's further reforms. Finally, the administrative monopoly formed through the protection of the unitary government system must be broken because it has become a malignant tumor triggering underlying social injustice.

Decentralization should not conflict with the state's judicial, administrative, and enforcement systems. Economic federalism should operate under a unified legal system. The existing judicial, administrative, and enforcement systems that are affiliated with the administrative system are not only detrimental to the development of economic federalism but may also lend federalism the air of traditional "fortified village politics" (土围子, *tu wei zi*). Therefore, the local judicial, administrative, and enforcement systems must be reformed. The judicial system should be reformed with a new structure like that of the central bank. The administrative and enforcement systems should both adopt the structure of superministries and draw on the structure of the central bank, as well. The judicial, administrative, and enforcement system should be nationally unified rather than locally segmented. A well-guaranteed judicial and institutional system will prevent any decentralization reform from distortion or deviation from the correct path.

The central government that maintains a stronger fiscal capacity should bear proportionally greater public service responsibilities and reduce the responsibilities of local governments accordingly, thus curtailing its obsession with GDP. Owing to the upward flow of fiscal power and the downward movement of administrative responsibility, local governments must meet the GDP growth targets set for them, but they bear more public service duties, which require more local revenue. This distorts the proper role of local governments, causing them to occupy themselves with land development–driven economic growth, which is detrimental to the interests of the citizens and inhibits the local governments from providing better public services. Therefore, the transfer payment system, which is an important element of the fiscal administration system, must be reformed to focus transfer payments on programs concerning local economic development and infrastructure as part of the public service–oriented fiscal system. The Chinese government is now financially strong enough to build a preliminary welfare state.

COMMENT
LYNN WHITE

Yang Guangbin's interesting chapter focuses primarily on the dangers of separation between central and local governments, which he sees as too great. It documents those problems and provides positive recommendations to solve them. In the West, separation of powers initially meant mutual horizontal constraints between agencies that have different roles. This was historically the first modern means of accountable governance.[24] And if a state separates legitimate powers to focus on domestic prosperity, efficiency, or equity, such divisions inevitably affect foreign policy, too.

Kinds of Power, Kinds of Division

Should powers be centralized or separated? Sometimes this is treated as a matter of political culture, an East-West issue, as if Asians always choose orderly centralization and Westerners always prefer wild strife among separated entities. But posing the case in that manner would be factually inaccurate. It is better to start with two more basic questions: First, what is power? Second, along what dimensions can analysis divide power?

Power can be exhibited in three ways: When a leader wants a follower to do something, and the follower complies but would otherwise not do it, that reveals an individual-behavioral kind of power. When procedural rules set agendas that determine what happens, that reveals institutional power. When actors receive no benefit from efforts to change established norms about the ways decisions are made, that is presumptive power.[25] None of these three types of power is exclusive to governments. Nonstate networks also display them.

The Confucian philosopher Mencius argued that the state can provide an example to other associations, especially families (which are arguably the most important polities for most people).[26] The Chinese word *guojia* (国家) conflates the meanings of "state" and "nation," suggestively linking it to "family" (家, *jia*).

The author thanks Professors Yu Keping, Li Cheng, Kenneth Lieberthal, Yang Guangbin, and Fu Hualing (head of the Law Department, Hong Kong University)—none of whom is responsible for any mistakes here.

Confucian concerns, which are now echoed in official mottos about harmony, are normative and ideological. They also begin to answer the second question raised above, which asks for the dimensions along which power can be divided.

The size-of-collectivity, or scalar spectrum (块块, *kuaikuai*), is perhaps the most important of these. It is often called vertical, although that word can be confusing if it conflates group sizes with actual influence, assuming larger networks are always more powerful than smaller networks (as they are not). Most discussions of vertical constraint center on elections. But it would be factually incorrect to imagine that such a vertical line were homogenous, as if intermediate-size groups had no effect on the constraints that voting or petitioning impose.

Study of China (or India, or other large nations) can contribute to general social science by showing the importance of this scalar "degree-of-zoom" dimension. Statistical norms of proof have led to overemphasis on small countries in studies of political development. When Yang Guangbin mentions the effects of the 1984 change in cadre appointment rules from "two levels up" to "one level up," he is addressing a scalar issue. Such variation can come in many scope sizes: global, national, local (for example, provinces or counties), associational, or individual. Power may also be separated in other ways.

Federal separations (or connections) are geographical. These are closely related to the scalar type but are tied to particular places that have differences beyond their similar size. In these comments, the scalar and geographical dimensions can be conflated.

Functional separations (or links) show another division. This kind became famous because of Montesquieu's influential misunderstanding of Britain's politics as divided into executive, legislative, and judicial roles.[27] Madison called for checks and balances between agencies that have different roles within government.[28] Functional divisions are already present in China's *tiaotiao* (条条) structures, and Yang is right to suggest that their roles could be more differentiated. Because those roles are in principle supposed to be equally effective within their functional spheres, this modern division of power has often been called horizontal, even though the internal structure of specialist *tiaotiao* bureaucracies is hierarchal.

Other kinds of power division (between state and nonstate, party and state, and so forth) are also important. Journalists and academics can be legitimated in nonstate monitoring and idea-spinning roles. The functional independence of defense lawyers is crucial in any rule-of-law system that aims to constrain authorities with evidence.

Leadership succession periods divide power along yet another dimension: time. Many democracies have fixed or flexible periods between elections. In China, as Cheng Li was early to point out, each "generation" of the Chinese

Communist Party has rightfully received ten years at the top, divided into two five-year terms.[29] This generation norm and policy balance between presidents and premiers within each generation suggests recent self-restraint.

Any divisions can overlap. They all become political. The main separations of power to be considered in this commentary are the functional-horizontal and electoral-vertical types. They are very different from each other. The purpose here is to suggest, on the basis of comparative politics, that China would serve itself by legitimating as separate the functions of its state institutions—and also by validating professional non-state functions such as reporters, academics, or lawyers exercise—before holding mass elections for national leadership. That would be one type of *decentralization,* a word that these dimensions help disambiguate.

For a Pragmatic Politics of Modern Power Separation

Hu Jintao has claimed that "there is no modernization without democracy."[30] Wen Jiabao has argued for political reform on many occasions, noting, for example, in 2010 that "the people's wishes for, and needs for, democracy and freedom are irresistible."[31] Wen favored Chinese political reform and encouraged Chinese to consider what form it should take.

Separation of powers (分权, *fenquan*) can involve both decentralization and professionalization. Two questions arise: Is *fenquan* bad? Is it un-Chinese? Yang rightly notes that the division of labor, leading to more complementary efficiency and raising production, is the logic of China's reforms. This process creates economic benefits but also administrative problems. For both domestic and foreign reasons, *fenquan* is not about to become the motto of the Chinese Communist Party. Professionalization (专业化, *zhuanyehua*) has been a politically more acceptable slogan because of old Chinese norms linking certified intelligence to rightful rule.

Any decision for separation of powers or democracy in China will be made solely by Chinese elites. Social conditions and national traditions naturally shape what they decide, but the wills of individual high leaders to undertake political reform—or not to do so—will determine what happens.

Yang begins his chapter by pointing out that market reforms divide social power. The new economy has changed the context of China's official politics. State-society relations have altered, as society (that is, networks other than the central party-state) has organized and disorganized itself. These changes often disadvantage the state.

Are these trends corrupting China's politics? The idea of corruption always implies at least two identifiable groups of different sizes. It usually asserts that benefits to the smaller group or individual should instead have gone to the larger. Yet sometimes this presumptive bias for larger groups leads to tragedy (as in the post–Great Leap Forward famine) or waste (as in the Great Third Front).[32] Ideas about social cleanliness or corruption change over time. It is possible to choose one or another size of collectivity, making an existential, a priori decision about which is rightful and inherently uncorrupt. It is more circumspect to look at results, not presuming that any one agency of influence (power) is for all purposes superior to others. It is wise, even if difficult, to try to judge consequences according to the viewpoints of multiple agencies together.

Links between local rent-seeking and development are particularly complex. Cadres try to lure investors into their jurisdictions by many means, including bribery and tax holidays. Such behavior, which is often predatory against larger community interests in the short run, may offset losses over longer periods by the tax revenues that the investments later bring. So there is a time dimension, as well as a scalar dimension, in the assessment of corruption.

Functional separations of power are natural in modernizing polities, because different kinds of knowledge and ethics are needed for running foreign affairs, courts, procuratorates, schools, armies, banks, and enterprises. Divided agencies with overlapping jurisdictions seek resources and often hide information from one another. Yang notes that at least four Chinese ministries are involved in transport, for example.

Rules for coordination are difficult to enforce, because the immediate heads of most legitimated agencies have an interest in not breaking ranks with one another. They keep secrets. If a regulator finds out about an anomalous decision that small-unit leaders have made, they can ordinarily justify it as following one or more of China's many diverse official rules. Such power is not just separated. From a centralist viewpoint, it is broken. Yang calls it an "India syndrome." (Actually, not all aspects of Indian governance have failed; but that is another big topic.)

The easiest modern way to talk about geographical (or scalar) separations is fiscal. Money is measurable, but actually the units being compared are groups and individuals. The units are existential entities, and the politics surrounding them involve symbols and meanings, not just money. Markets and money encourage social thinking that is abstracted from identifications. Local cultures, psychologies, resentments, and norms—not just accounts—exist in large, medium, and small networks.

Many scholars thus write about China's de facto federalism. Modern China practices federalism—while also delegitimizing it. Yang says that the ethnic autonomous regions do not differ from provinces, but actually, many of the provinces, municipalities, and regions have their own idiosyncratic relations with the central government. Our planet's limiting case of unacknowledged extreme federalism is Hong Kong, where just one of China's many laws, the Hong Kong Basic Law, applies. This structure works in the national context because Hong Kong tycoons, who are guaranteed low taxes under the substantive-policy local constitution, invest capital on the mainland, helping China grow.

The collapse of the Soviet federation intensified Chinese doubts about admitting to federalism, even while practicing it. But Chinese tend to forget that the Soviet Union's ethnic structure (only half the people were Russian) was very different from China's (where more than nine-tenths are Han). Some federal arrangements effectively prohibit secessions, even in electoral democracies.[33]

China (中国, *Zhongguo*) is the central state. So is it properly Chinese only as a centralized state? Should the name of the nation affect thinking, so that there might naturally be more bias for centralization in China than in other countries? Scalar arrangements of people, like functional ones, are not sealed off from one another. A pragmatic approach is to consider such various categories together, asking what uses each has for the people in them. This requires empirical research concerning what leads to order or disorder, prosperity or poverty, a sense of freedom or a sense of oppression. The modern division of labor brings a greater variety of groups and individuals. Trying to deal with all of them together requires subtler methods than any political rhetoric will accommodate.

Monitoring Money, Land, and Cadres

Yang writes vividly about local protectionism, a form of decentralization that harms both prosperity and governance. Debt evasion by state-owned local enterprises is rife, especially among medium-size enterprises in places that developed quickly, such as Guangdong, Beijing, Shandong, and Jiangsu. The big banks are relatively centralized national entities, and they are unable to stop the epidemic of debt evasion. When legal suits for nonpayment of debt are brought to courts, the latter tend to decide in favor of their local friends. Yet the amounts of money are so immense, central leaders with local connections probably approve these transfers to localities. Conspiracies between local judges and officials may not wholly explain them. Factions span the scalar spectrum.

Functional *tiaotiao* division of powers can also create problems, if the functions are not clearly differentiated. Yang blames such divisions for the bureaucratic tediousness that entrepreneurs face when they try to set up new companies. He is right; but professional state regulators, like independent judges who enforce contracts, can help the market function. The problem is not too much *tiaotiao* division. Difficulties come instead from contemporary continuation of the outmoded idea that, in a functionally nonspecific way, officials must supervise merchants, who merely manage their firms (an old imperial slogan was 官督商办, *guandu shangban*). That kind of official imposition on nonstate networks may not help political stability while it also hurts economic entrepreneurship.

Local government leaders want more money and engage in "land finance" (土地财政, *tudi caizheng*). Real estate developers connive with officials to buy land, and local budgets swell from the proceeds. Yang quotes startling figures, showing that such sales equaled half of the regular budgets of all local governments in 2007 (although revenues from land sales were just one-sixth of budgets in 2001). Dubious land transactions have been frequent cases of theft-by-semiprivatization. Raked-off revenues from investment projects, loans, and budgets in fields such as education and health are also frequent. Zhu Rongji reversed the tendency toward "dukedom economies" in the mid-1990s, especially because of tax reforms that raised central revenues.[34] These problems recur whenever central authorities cannot monitor them.

Yang calls for economic federalism under one political system. As he says, understanding party leadership is basic to any comprehension of China's politics, but new markets challenge party principles. China is becoming complex faster than the party is, and this difference creates governance problems.

Personnel departments approve important appointments, but the system was changed in 1984 in a way that Yang may disapprove of. Pierre Landry argues that the previous rule for cadre appointments, made by party organs two administrative levels higher than the posts to be filled, did not work well. Appointing committees lacked sufficient information about appointees and their localities.[35] Personnel departments two levels up could not effectively monitor or sanction them. Yang applauds 1990s norms that rotated cadres among jurisdictions and encouraged more postings of nonnatives. Along with taxation changes in the same decade, these measures were intended to counterbalance economic scalar decentralization.

As Yang says, informal politics is important. He wants to study every level of political life, informal as well as formal, things practiced as well as things written, behavior as well as laws. He emphasizes that meaningful aspects of politics cannot all be formalized. How far does one want to take this principle? What practices of institutional politics can never be subject to laws? When party nominees for provincial governorships were rejected by provincial legislatures in Zhejiang and Guizhou long ago (in cases to which Yang apparently alludes, though does not directly refer), the results were not disastrous for these provinces or for China. Rule of law requires actual laws—and assurance of their fairness.

Favoring Courts and Nonstate Overseers, Opposing Hasty Elections

Should China divide powers more than it has already done? If a Western academic may venture an answer, it is yes—so long as serious functional separations precede major electoral ones.[36] Scalar divisions generate most of the problems of misgovernment that Yang cites. More independent powers for role-specific functional managers can help correct these problems, so long as there is enough complementarity among these equally legitimated agents. Some but not all are within state institutions. Most journalists, academics, or lawyers are not; but their roles are also essential. The main point is that they must be able to do their jobs professionally, without fear or favor.

Yang says that when there is a conflict of laws and regulations in China—as there often is, because the nation has at least 30,000 different legal rules of various kinds—the courts cannot solve the problem. He says judges must legally refer such cases through higher courts to the State Council. But in practice, judges routinely decide cases on the basis of rules they consider right, without admitting there is any conflict of laws. This may violate China's administrative laws, but it is a common occurrence.

The system might be gradually reformed to accommodate more rightfully separated powers in the newly diverse elite. This would raise the variety of relevant information available to decisionmakers, thus raising the quality of decisions. That is liberal democracy. It is not mainly electoral democracy, although it would serve the people better. Western thinkers, like some scholars in China, have warned that elections can spur violence.[37] Having smart leaders may be as important as having mass-legitimated leaders.[38] Elections have often returned nationalist authoritarians (Hitler in 1933, Marcos in 1969, Thaksin in 2005, and many others; surely Bo Xilai would have won or bought electoral landslides in Chongqing if any mass vote had been held there before he was purged). Consultative institutions may arguably substitute for the participation that voting aims to achieve—and often misses achieving.[39] Vertical division of power in the form of all-China direct elections to national office might eventually be in the Chinese nation's future. (After a bumpy start, the Taiwanese have stabilized this procedure in their special Chinese context.)[40] Leaping to hold such elections for China's whole national government soon, however, would probably legitimate nondemocrats who could buy votes.

This would be a particular danger in a country that has recently enjoyed fast economic growth. Money presents problems for all democracies. Even though elections are the usual modern way to make a government seem rightful, no country with mass voting has fully answered the question of how to deal with the power of lucre. Chinese elites may want their country to help find solutions to this quandary, rather than to institute another example of it.

Democracy is not one good thing; it is two different and just potentially good things. The first is liberal, legitimated professionalization of power in different functions. Checks and balances between these can aid stability and fairness. They can reflect the growing specializations of economic and social networks outside the state. The second potentially good thing is elections, where individuals and small associations help to guide the government to serve the people. But elections can also cause instability and unfairness, even violence, if demagogues win.

Some may ask, doesn't democracy (民主, *minzhu*), rule by "the people," mean only elections? No, it does not. Who are these people, the *min* in *minzhu*? Are they just 51 percent, the majority? Yet the other 49 percent are also people. So democracy is not just about majorities deciding everything. It is equally about the task of defining—by constitutions, laws, constraints, and divisions—what the majority may not rightly do, so that the minority who are also people have appropriate protections. Only Chinese are qualified to create these definitions for China. But it is certain that democracy requires some divisions of power.

As Yang rightly notes, China's reforms are based on the logic of separation of powers, but that does not mean that the more separation, the better. He calls for more accumulation of power in economic management, legislation, and especially judicial work. He sees unitarism or federalism as tools, not ideologies. He wants stronger procurators and courts to fight turf localism. He is concerned by the money windfalls from which local leaders' networks have benefited at public expense (for example, in corrupt allocations of public land). But courts are even less centralized than banks, allowing such problems to fester.

China's polity will almost surely face resentment between rich and poor, especially between the controllers of capital and representatives of labor. Many comparativists in political science believe that workers' unions have been crucial in establishing welfare states such as Yang advocates in his very last sentence.[41] In any case, reform rather than revolution is now the maxim of the Chinese Communist Party. Fully harmonious change is unfeasible for any political elite to engineer, but contemporary China stands a good chance of success in creating more deliberative, fairer systems of governance.

Notes

1. Yang Guangbin, "Guojia jiegou lilun de jieshili yu shiyongxing wenti" [Explanatory power and applicability of state structure theories], *Jiaoxue yu yanjiu* [Teaching and research], no. 7 (2007).

2. Tong Zhiwei, "Danyizhi, lianbangzhi de qubie ji qi fenlei wenti" [The difference between the unitary system and the federal system and their classification], *Falü kexue* [Law science], no. 1 (1995); Tong Zhiwei, "Lun you Zhongguo tese de minzhu jizhong danyizhi" [On the democratically centralized unitary system of Chinese characteristics], *Jiangsu shehui kexue* [Jiangsu social sciences], no. 5 (1997); Ai Xiaojin, "Zhongyang yu difang guanxi de zai sikao: Cong guojia quanli kan wo guo guojia jiegou xingshi" [Thoughts on the central-local relationship: China's state structure from the perspective of the state power], *Zhejiang shehui kexue* [Zhejiang social sciences], no. 1 (2001); Yang Hongshan, *Fu ji guanxi lun* [Intergovernmental relationship theory] (Beijing: Social Sciences Press, 2005); Daniel J. Elazar, *Lianbangzhuyi tansuo* [Exploring federalism], translated by Peng Liping (Shanghai: Sanlian Publishing, 2004), p. 53.

3. For a focused discussion on China's nonformal politics, see *The Nature of Chinese Politics: From Mao to Jiang*, edited by Jonathan Ubger (Armonk, N.Y.: M. E. Sharpe, 2002).

4. Constitution of the People's Republic of China, chapter 1, article 3.

5. Ibid., chapter 3, article 89.

6. Constitution of the Communist Party of China.

7. For a detailed introduction to the functions of these systems, see Yang Guangbin, *Zhongguo zhengfu yu zhengzhi daolun* [Introduction to China's government and politics] (Beijing: Renmin University of China Press, 2003), pp. 24–43.

8. The list covers the secretaries, deputy secretaries, and standing committee members of the provinces, autonomous regions, and municipalities directly under the central government; secretaries and deputy secretaries of the commissions for discipline inspection of the provinces, autonomous regions, and municipalities directly under the central government; governors, deputy governors, chairmen, and vice chairmen of the provinces and autonomous regions; mayors and deputy mayors of the municipalities directly under the central government; directors and vice directors of the standing committees of the people's congresses of the provinces, autonomous regions, and municipalities directly under the central government; Chinese People's Political Consultative Conference chairmen and vice chairmen of the provinces, autonomous regions, and municipalities directly under the central government; chief justices of senior people's courts and chief procurators of senior people's procuratorates of the provinces, autonomous regions, and municipalities directly under the central government; secretaries, mayors, directors of the standing committees of people's congresses, and Chinese People's Political Consultative Conference chairmen of subprovincial cities (including Guangzhou, Wuhan, Harbin, Shenyang, Chengdu, Nanjing, Xi'an, Changchun, Jinan, Hangzhou, Dalian, Qingdao, Shenzhen, Xiamen, and Ningbo); and commander-in-chief, deputy commanders-in-chief, first political commissar, political commissars, and deputy political commissars of Xinjiang Production and Construction Corps. Hon S. Chan, "Cadre Personnel Management in China: The Nomenklatura System, 1990–98," *China Quarterly*, no. 179 (2004).

9. Data from *Zhongguo nianjian* [China yearbook], 1985, 1990, 1995, and 2000 (Beijing: Broadcasting and TV Press). Cited from Li Cheng, "Zhongguo shengji lingdao

de goucheng: Guojia zhenghe yu difang zizhu" [China's provincial leadership organs: National integration and local autonomy], *Zhongguo shehui kexue pinglun* [Chinese social sciences review], no. 2 (2002).

10. Charles E. Lindblom, *Zhengzhi yu shichang: Shijie de zhengzhi-jingji zhidu* [Politics and markets: The world's political-economic systems], translated by Wang Yizhou (Shanghai: Sanlian Publishing and Shanghai People's Publication House, 1991), p. 30.

11. For a detailed discussion of this issue, see Yang Guangbin, "Zhiduhua quanli de zhidu chengben" [Institutional cost of institutionalized power], *Tianjin shehui kexue* [Tianjin social sciences], no. 1 (2005).

12. CCTV, *"Xinwen hui ke ting"* [People in the news], dialogue with Li Zibin, deputy director of Western China Development Office of the State Council, April 1, 2005.

13. Editorial note: The Tieben incident refers to a 2004 case in China when a private company, Jiangsu Tieben Steel, began a high-value project with the blessing of the local government. The central government suspended the project, and several high-ranking local officials were punished.

14. Jonathan Rodden, "Comparative Federalism and Decentralization: On Meaning and Measurement," *Comparative Politics* 36, no. 4 (July 2004).

15. Barry R. Weingast, "The Economic Role of Political Institutions: Market-Preserving Federalism and Economic Development," *Journal of Law, Economics, and Organization* 11, no. 1 (April 1995); Qian Yinyi and Barry Weingast, "China's Transition to Markets: Market-Preserving Federalism, Chinese Style," *Journal of Policy Reform*, no. 2 (1996).

16. Zheng Yongnian, *De Facto Federalism in China* (Singapore: World Scientific Publishing, 2007).

17. An Tifu, "Zhongyang caizheng shouru zhan caizheng zong zhouru bizhong wenti yanjiu" [Research on the percentage of central fiscal revenue in the total fiscal revenue], *Caizheng yanjiu* [Public finance research], no. 1 (2006).

18. The conflict between citizens and the government as revealed in mass incidents is related to the central-local relationship. Yang Guangbin, "Wo guo xianxing zhongyang-difang guanxi xia de shehui gongzheng wenti yu zhili" [Social equality issues and governance under China's current central-local relationship], *Shehui kexue yanjiu* [Social sciences research], no. 3 (2007).

19. Yang Guangbin, "Zhongguo jingji zhuanxing shiqi de zhongyang-difang guanxi xin lun: Lilun, xianshi yu zhengce" [New thought on the central-local relationship in China's economic transformation period: Theory, reality, and policy], *Xuehai* [Academia bimestris], no. 1 (2007).

20. In their research on China's energy policy, Kenneth Lieberthal and Michel Oksenberg used "fragmented authority" among different government departments but in a slightly different context. Lieberthal and Oksenberg, *Policy Making in China: Leaders, Structures, and Processes* (Princeton University Press, 1988).

21. Data cited from Huang Ruiling, "Jiangsu qiye tao fei zhai wenti yanjiu" [Research on the debt evasion and rescission of Jiangsu Enterprises], *Zhexue shijie* [Philosophical horizon], no. 1 (2003).

22. Ke Lang, "Fujian wu yi tao fei zhai diaocha" [Investigation of a RMB 500 million debt evasion in Fujian], *Faren zazhi* [Faren magazine], no. 3 (2006).

23. Zhang Chi, "Guangdong qiye faren tao fei zhai xiongmeng" [Rampant debt evasion by enterprises in Guangdong], *Faren zazhi* [Faren magazine], no. 10 (2004).

24. Andreas Schedler and others, eds., *The Self-Restraining State* (Boulder, Colo.: Lynne Rienner, 1999).

25. Prominent analysts of these three types, respectively, are Robert Dahl, E. E. Schattschneider, and James Scott. See Steven Lukes, *Power: A Radical View* (London: Macmillan, 1974).

26. "Mencius," in *Sources of Chinese Tradition,* edited by Wm. Theodore de Bary (Columbia University Press, 1960), vol. 1, p. 92.

27. Montesquieu, *The Spirit of the Laws,* translated by Thomas Nugent (London: Bell, 1914; orig. 1748).

28. James Madison, *Federalist No. 51* (www.constitution.org/fed/federa51.htm).

29. Cheng Li, *China's Leaders: The New Generation* (Lanham, Md.: Rowman and Littlefield, 2001).

30. Quoted in Yu Keping, *Democracy Is a Good Thing* (Brookings Press, 2009), p. 5.

31. Wen Jiabao, "Zai hui Xinyi yi Yaobang" [Recalling Hu Yaobang when I return to Xingyi], *People's Daily,* April 15, 2010; Raymond Li, "Wen Vows to Keep on Pressing for Reform," *South China Morning Post,* October 4, 2010.

32. The Great Leap Forward of 1958 was an effort by political radicals under Mao Zedong to centralize, at least to higher-than-previous administrative levels, all agricultural and industrial activities, and it resulted in a tragic famine that killed tens of millions of Chinese (even according to PRC state sources). The Great Third Front was a similarly inefficient 1960s program for state investments for inland provinces, where economic returns were low but distances to then-threatening borders with the Soviet Union or America's East Asian allies were greater.

33. India's constitution is federal, assigning powers to states, but article 356 allows the president of India to take over any state's government in case of emergency, preventing secessions. The Soviet federal constitution's article 72 was in sharp contrast: "Each Union Republic shall retain the right freely to secede from the USSR."

34. See Shaun Breslin, "Paradigm Shifts and Time Lags? The Politics of Financial Reform in the People's Republic of China," *Asian Business and Management* 2, no. 1 (2003), pp. 143–66.

35. Pierre-François Landry, *Decentralized Authoritarianism in China* (Cambridge University Press, 2008).

36. See Robert Dahl, *Polyarchy* (Yale University Press, 1971); Samuel Huntington, *Political Order in Changing Societies* (Yale University Press, 1968).

37. Jack Snyder, *From Voting to Violence* (New York: W. W. Norton, 2000).

38. Daniel A. Bell, *Beyond Liberal Democracy* (Princeton University Press, 2006) moots the possibility of a Confucian upper legislative house, generated by examinations.

39. An abstract philosopher's argument is Stephen C. Angle, "Must We Choose Our Leaders? Human Rights and Political Participation in China," *Journal of Global Ethics*, no. 2 (2005).

40. Shelley Rigger, *Politics in Taiwan: Voting for Democracy* (New York: Routledge, 1999).

41. See Dietrich Rueschmeyer, Evelyne Huber Stephens, and John D. Stephens, *Capitalist Development and Democracy* (University of Chicago Press, 1992).

9

China's Grassroots Democracy

HUANG WEIPING

The institutional development of China's grassroots democracy is an important embodiment of Chinese-style democratic politics. Since the reform and opening-up period began, China's grassroots democracy has undergone a multifaceted transition from the countryside to the cities, from extraparty democracy to intraparty democracy, and from democratic elections to democratic governance. This trend has been spurred on in part by the central government's macro-level policymaking and the democratic space inherent in China's political system. It has also been closely related to citizens' initiatives for greater political participation.

Grassroots Democracy in the Chinese Context

The development of China's system of grassroots democracy is not only a political phenomenon that has attracted wide domestic and international attention but is also an embodiment of democratic politics with Chinese characteristics. Part of the national system, grassroots democracy has three main features: village autonomy based on village committees, the autonomy of urban residents based on residents committees, and worker autonomy based on workers' representative unions. According to the Constitution of 1982, "The residents committees and village committees established among urban and rural residents on the basis of their residence are mass organizations of self-management at the grassroots level."[1] At the 17th Chinese Communist Party (CCP) National Congress in 2007, the system of community-level self-governance was further elevated as an integral part of China's socialist political system. Scholars' notion of grassroots democracy in China is broader than those formerly defined in written documents. In addition to the village committee–based village autonomy and the residents committee–based residents' autonomy, such aspects as the directly elected people's congresses at the county and township levels, the reforms of township government elections, the open recommendation and election of grassroots officials, and even the establishment of homeowners committees also fall within the scope of research on China's grassroots democracy.

Although democracy as a basic political concept has been an object of dispute within Chinese political and academic circles, China's top leadership has always considered the development of democracy to be an important factor in advancing the country's reform and opening up. Deng Xiaoping observed that "at the third plenary session of the 11th Central Committee, our party, having reviewed our experience, laid down a series of new policies. There were two major domestic ones: to expand political democracy and to carry out economic reform and corresponding social reforms."[2] China's top decisionmakers have always emphasized that "without democracy there would be no socialism or socialist modernization."[3]

Admittedly, Deng often approached democracy from the perspective of political efficacy. He said, "Mobilizing initiative is the biggest aspect of democracy. As to how to put democracy into practice in different forms, that depends on specific conditions."[4] Deng's use of the term *initiative* referred to actions of the people who were building China into a modern socialist state, grounding this project in the legal basis of China's political system, active participation in the modernization cause, and support for the ruling party's leadership of the reform and opening up. The forms of democracy to be used to mobilize such initiative were to depend on China's national conditions. This is remarkably different from the Western understanding of democracy, which emphasizes free competitive political elections.

However, this does not mean that China's top decisionmakers have neglected the important value of achieving political democracy. In official CCP documents, democracy is broken down into four aspects: democratic election, democratic decisionmaking, democratic management, and democratic supervision, corresponding to the two dimensions of election and governance (the latter encompassing decisionmaking, management, and supervision).[5] The holding of democratic elections, in particular, is considered the first and most basic form of democracy because the degree to which a state accomplishes democratic elections determines or influences the level of development of democratic decisionmaking, management, and supervision. In other words, the status of democratic elections to a large extent constrains the degree of democratic governance.

The system of grassroots democracy in China discussed in this chapter centers on the development of democratic elections. It has two layers: grassroots society, made up of village committees and residents committees, and grassroots government, made up of party committees, people's congresses, and governments at the county and township levels. It has two dimensions: democratic elections and democratic governance. Statutory grassroots organizations, such as urban residents committees, did exist in the period before the reform and opening up, yet they had little autonomy within China's totalitarian system. Therefore, this chapter focuses on the development and evolution of the system of grassroots democracy since the reform and opening up in 1978.

Progress and Dimensions of China's Grassroots Democracy

There is some discrepancy between how China's system of grassroots democracy exists on paper and how the system has developed in practice. This is a result of a time lag between policy formulation and implementation. The formulation of a legal text is often followed by a long process of gradual implementation, which in this case represents the institutional space of development of China's political democracy. This trend of institutional development not only indicates the expansion of China's grassroots democracy in breadth and depth but also shows that China's democratization process is advancing steadily, making gradual progress in the realization of the rights of the citizens and CCP members as they appear on paper.

From Village Democracy to Community Democracy

The development of rural grassroots democracy is directly related to the change of the rural economic structure, the support of the state, and village participation. The rural system of household responsibility introduced in 1978 has not only restructured the rural collective economic system but also stimulated the reform of the existing power structure. The nature of village committees as grassroots autonomous organizations dictates that their members be elected by the villages themselves. Modern democratic elections thus first emerged in the rural areas, a segment of Chinese society that lacked any tradition of democratic elections.

The Election of Village Committees

The election of village committee members started in the rural areas nationwide in 1983 under the promotion of the Ministry of Civil Affairs. According to the Organic Law of the Village Committees of the People's Republic of China (for Trial Implementation), "The chairman, vice chairmen, and members of a village committee shall be elected directly by the villages. The term of office of a village committee is three years. Members of a village committee may continue to hold office when reelected."[6] The election of village committee members mostly followed the method used to elect people's congress members at the county and township levels in the early period.[7] After fifteen years of trial implementation, the Organic Law of the Village Committees of the People's Republic of China was formally implemented in 1998, bringing further improvement to the standardization and democratization of elections for village committees. To ensure equality and fairness, various methods of election have been introduced, including popular election, the one-step method, and group election.[8] The governments at various levels have also established election supervision organizations, a legal relief system, and an election observer system.

From 2005 to 2007, a total of 623,690 villages nationwide, 99.53 percent of the total, have elected village committees; 95.85 percent of these villages set up rooms for secret balloting, and 85.35 percent finalized their election systems. The average participation rate in village committee elections nationwide has reached 90.97 percent. The method of popular election, whereby village committee members are directly elected by the villages, was piloted or implemented on a large scale in seventeen provinces.[9] The village committee election has become the most widely used practice in China's grassroots democracy and the most important form of village political participation.

With the increasing competitiveness of township-level elections, there has been a growing trend of power flowing to the advantaged. According to investigations undertaken by the Ministry of Civil Affairs in such provinces as Shandong, Hebei, and Henan, village elites make up a majority of village committees.[10] In affluent Zhejiang province, more than two-thirds of village committee directors or party branch secretaries are entrepreneurs, private business owners, or large poultry farmers.[11] That village cadre positions are so monopolized by elites indicates that the competitiveness of elections requires candidates to have not only ability but also resources. This has given rise to worries that election bribery and the intervention of clan forces in the election process will become major challenges to the development of village-level democracy.

Another factor that affects the development of village-level elections is the rural tax and fee reform. In an effort to reduce the burden on farmers and prevent grassroots cadres from making gains at their expense, the central government promulgated the Rules on Transfer Payments from the Central Government to the Local Governments on Rural Tax and Fee Reform, a direct consequence of which was the cancelation of the agricultural tax. This policy has had a mixed effect on rural elections. On one hand, the cancelation of taxes and fees has not only soothed tension between cadres and villages but has also reduced the phenomenon of local governments imposing sundry tasks on village cadres, allowing them to focus on the needs and interests of the villages and the related autonomous activities of the village. On the other hand, the cancelation of taxes and fees has led to the upward centralization of fiscal powers and the trend of "the county administering township finance" and "the township administering village finance."[12] As a result, village-level finance is being put into the hands of townships, and even the salaries and subsidies of village cadres, rather than being supported by the farmers, are financed by the township governments. This is leading to the bureaucratization of village cadres, weakened interests that link them and villages, and the gradual waning of village interest in village-level elections and autonomous activities.[13]

Institutional Design of Residents Committee Elections

Resident autonomy in the cities and villager autonomy in the countryside are considered to be the two cornerstones of China's system of grassroots democracy. Residents committees are mass organizations that implement "self-management, self-service, self-education, and self-oversight" under the leadership of the CCP.[14] As of 2007, there were 81,372 residents committees nationwide. However, the development of grassroots democracy in the cities lagged behind that in the countryside. In 1982 the residents committee system was written into China's Constitution as an organization of grassroots autonomy. The Organic Law of the Urban Residents Committees promulgated in 1989 explicitly provided for the election of residents committees, stating that members shall be elected from local residents, household representatives, or village group representatives. However, direct election of residents committee members rarely occurred before 2000; members were usually appointed by local governments. During that period, residents committees were autonomous organizations only in name, not in substance. Residents committees were more at the service of grassroots governments than of the residents. Their main function was to implement government orders and manage and control grassroots society on behalf of the government through civil welfare, dispute mediation, statistics collection, and reporting on local sentiment. Interest articulation at the grassroots level was never as well developed as it was with the village committees in the countryside.

Grassroots democracy in cities began developing gradually with the progress of China's reform and opening up and economic marketization. With the gradual loosening and disintegration of the unit system that marked the era of the planned economy and the constant expansion of residential property, the market and society began to expand. As a result, residents committees began to include more and more citizens who fell outside the traditional unit system. In the mid and late 1990s, when it became imperative to implement urban community development and grassroots governance reforms, the residents who used to live in houses provided by their work units and the residents committees constituted on this basis began to be restructured into residents committees of communities of privately owned houses. Not surprisingly, the functions of residents committees began to change. As the residents under their management became more diverse, the committees increased their number of employees and improved both the work environment and equipment.

More important, the civil affairs government departments in charge of urban construction also began to introduce election mechanisms used in village committee elections to the election of residents committees. Nationwide, although the direct election of residents committee members occurred later than that of village committee members, it was promoted faster in the cities. Starting in 2000, the election of residents committees was promoted in provinces and municipalities such as Shanghai, Beijing, Guangdong, Liaoning, Guangxi, and Zhejiang. At the end of 2004, there were 71,375 residents committees nationwide, more than half of which had completed turnovers through elections—9,715 used direct elections, 12,975 used household representative elections, and 22,078 used residents group representative elections. Residents committees that used direct elections accounted for 22 percent of the total.[15]

The direct election of residents committees both drew on and improved on the election of village committees. In 2006 the Ministry of Civil Affairs began to encourage activities related to competitive elections, such as making public speeches, meeting with supporters, posting wall posters, broadcasting, and community-based campaigning online. It also released specific rules regarding vote count and on-site declaration of results. Although urban elections of residents committee members have an advantage over those in rural villages in terms of voter educational attainment, transportation infrastructure, and information technology, they do lag behind in participation, competitiveness, equality, and fairness. As of 2009, only one-third of all provinces nationwide directly elected at least 25 percent of their residents committees, and there were only ten provinces in which participation in household representative elections reached more than 20 percent.[16] Two major factors account for this situation. First, grassroots governments are concerned about the direct election of residents committees because they have been accustomed to appointing residents committee members who are familiar or trusted. The local governments thus take various measures to control elections, and this tends to discount the will of residents. Second, in comparison with village committees, residents committees lack collective assets and therefore are not closely linked to the interests of the residents. Urban residents, especially young people and office workers, generally lack interest in residents committee elections.

From Grassroots Society to Grassroots Government

In the late 1990s, after twenty years of development of village autonomy, direct election of township mayors began. The foundation of this change was the improved general awareness of elections and the relevant training that had occurred in connection with the village committee elections.

Direct Election of Township Mayors

Judging from the experience of Buyun Township, in Sichuan Province, which held the first direct election of a township mayor in China, the primary reasons behind election reform were the slow pace of local economic development, the fiscal difficulties facing the township governments, and the resulting dissatisfaction among local people. As the township mayors appointed by the higher-level government were able to neither reduce the various contradictions nor win the trust of the people, the local government began to reform township mayor elections.

The direct election of the mayor of Buyun Township followed this procedure: First, candidates were selected through self-recommendation or recommendation by villages or the local party committee. The names of these candidates were then submitted to a meeting attended by village committee members, village group leaders, and village representatives, where two formal candidates were chosen. These two formal candidates and one candidate recommended by the local party committee then ran for the post of township mayor. The position was determined by the votes of all villages. The candidate that received the most votes was approved at the local township-level people's congress before formally assuming the position.[17]

Similar elections have since been carried out in such provinces as Guangdong, Henan, Guangxi, Jiangsu, Hubei, Yunnan, and Chongqing. The advancement of the election of township mayors is considered both an expansion of electoral democracy from grassroots organizations to grassroots governments and the beginning of democratization of state organs, thus constituting the second wave of the development of China's grassroots democracy after the direct election of village committees.[18]

In comparison with village committee elections, the development of township mayoral elections has been less smooth. This reform has faced a number of almost insurmountable legal, systematic, and even political obstacles. By law, the township mayors shall be elected at the local people's congress rather than being directly elected by the villages. Immediately after the direct election of the mayor of Buyun Township, criticism appeared in the media that the practice was a violation of the Constitution. From the perspective of the socialist state of China, where the Chinese Communist Party administers the cadres, the township mayors are cadres of the grassroots governments and therefore should be selected within that framework of the party administering the cadres. The candidates for township mayor must be subject to the recommendation or determination of the party committee at a higher level, rather than being chosen by popular election. Politically, the direct election of township mayors will lead to a relative decrease of the authority of the township party committees. With the direct election of township mayors, the legitimacy of the township party secretaries appointed by the party committee at the higher level will also lessen.

The reform of the township mayoral election, then, faces three major obstacles. The first is that such a change would most likely shake the absolute political authority of the ruling party. A second is concern that the township mayoral election may be used to legalize the influence of clans and other illegal or malignant forces. The third obstacle is institutional constraint: reform of township mayoral elections conflicts with the existing system of cadre management and the principle of democratic centralism.

Such reform efforts occurred mainly from 1999 to 2004 and have stagnated since. Even so, the positive response to these pilot election reforms, both in the press and from the public, has strengthened the top leadership's confidence in advancing grassroots democracy. What has occurred since is only that the reform's direction has shifted from the election of township mayors to the election of township party committees, for which the method of election changed from direct election or de facto direct election to direct election based on public recommendation. The approach signals the gradual expansion of intraparty democracy, which in turn helps bring about people's democracy.

Competitive Election of Grassroots People's Congress Deputies

The people's congress system is the fundamental political system of China. According to the Constitution of the People's Republic of China, "All power in the People's Republic of China belongs to the people. The [National People's Congress] and the local people's congresses at various levels are the organs through which the people exercise state power." The people's congresses at the county, district, and township levels are grassroots organizations of the National People's Congress and grassroots organs of state power. The Electoral Law for the NPC and Local People's Congresses and the Organic Law of the Local People's Congresses and Local People's Governments promulgated in 1979 stipulate that the deputies to the people's congresses at the county level or below shall be generated through direct election. The Electoral Law for the NPC and Local People's Congresses also provides for the principles of multicandidate election and preliminary election, which are beneficial to the people's exercise of their rights.

In view of the significant differences between the cities and the countryside in economic and social development and in the educational level of voters, however, the law also provided for different ratios of representation of local people's congress deputies at the city and countryside level. The population representation ratio of county-level people's congress deputies in the cities and in the countryside is one to four. This ratio is increased to one to five at the provincial people's congresses and one to eight at the National People's Congress. In 2010 the law was revised at the National People's Congress to eventually achieve equal representation of the people's congress deputies in cities and the countryside.

The regulations governing the election of grassroots people's congress deputies promulgated in 1979 greatly stimulated the enthusiasm of the people for political participation. From 1979 to 1981, direct election of local people's congresses was achieved in 2,368 county governments, or 85.82 percent of the nationwide total, and the rate of voter participation was as high as 96.56 percent.[19] The electoral law, under which a person may run for election after receiving nominations from three individuals, also provided an institutional space for citizens to run for election at the people's congress deputy level, thus increasing the competitiveness of those elections. At the time, many college students were active in running for election in the contests for people's congress deputy in such regions as Shanghai, Beijing, and Hunan. These students promoted their own political slogans, made their own election platforms, and made campaign speeches.[20] Their campaigns were harmful to political stability and ran counter to the ruling party's focus on economic development.

For a long time the election of people's congress deputies had been an arranged affair in which candidates were determined by the ruling party; most positions went to party and government officials at various levels, and the remaining positions were assigned to outstanding figures and social elites as a token of political prestige. Such elections lacked openness and competitiveness. Even so, the direct election of grassroots people's congress deputies still demonstrates citizens' desire to express their interests and exercise their democratic rights through the people's congress system. Zeng Jianyu, a people's congress deputy of Luzhou in Sichuan Province who was elected in 1992, and Yao Lifa, a people's congress deputy of Tijiang in Hubei Province who was elected in 1995, were both elected as "self-recommended candidates."[21] In 2003, during the elections for people's congress deputies in some districts and counties in Beijing and Guangzhou, many ordinary citizens competed with candidates recommended by party committees. These independent candidates generally lacked financial and social mobilization resources. Their main methods of campaigning were holding press conferences, setting up their own election offices and support teams, posting election posters, distributing election pamphlets, and mobilizing voters.[22] Similar campaigns launched by independent candidates occurred elsewhere, including Qianjiang in Hubei and Quanzhou in Fujian.

What was unique to the campaigns by independent candidates in 2003, besides specific political convictions, was a strong expression of economic interests. These candidates were mostly private homeowners who ran for election to elevate their political status and magnify their political influence. They desired to better defend their interests in economic disputes with real estate developers, property management companies, and government departments in charge of urban planning. Their campaigns were more mature, more diversified than the typical election of party-selected candidates. For example, they were careful to carry out their campaigns within the scope permitted by law and even resorted to the law to resolve election-related disputes. They also tried to establish their own election organizations and offices. The phenomenon of independent candidates in the election of people's congress deputies has provided momentum outside the established system to develop China's grassroots democracy, improve the competitiveness of such elections, and gradually realize the citizen's right to vote.

From Extraparty to Intraparty Elections

As China's ruling party, the CCP organizes party committees at various levels of state organizational power from the central government down to the local governments, a network that plays the leading role in "making overall plans and coordinating all parties."[23] The ruling party also organizes party committees within the grassroots government departments and grassroots autonomous organizations to enforce political leadership. According to the Constitution of the CCP and the Interim Rules on the Election of Grassroots CCP Organizations, the leaders of these grassroots organizations shall be generated through multicandidate elections at the meetings of party members or the people's congresses, and candidates nominated by the existing party committees shall be subject to the examination and approval of the party committees at the higher level or the presiders over the meetings. In actual implementation, however, ordinary CCP members and people outside the party have no chance to participate in the nomination of candidates for grassroots party leadership. Intraparty elections, an integral part of the cadre selection system, are elections in name only because there is no competition involved.

With the promotion of village autonomy and election reforms at the township level, external pressure has been brought to bear on the mechanisms for selection of grassroots party leaders. If the development of village autonomy and the election of township mayors are not accompanied by democratization in the selection of grassroots party leaders, the political authority of these leaders will be weakened. To improve popular support for grassroots party organizations, a series of reforms featuring the two-ballot system for election of village party branch members and the system of direct election of township-level party committee members based on public recommendation have been introduced.

Two-Ballot System for Selection of Rural Party Branch Members

The introduction of the two-ballot system is related to the erosion of the authority of village party branches that resulted from the direct election of village committees. Village committees constituted through direct election have greater and wider support from the villages than do the village party branch members, who are elected only from local party members. In the face of the village committees that enjoy popular support, the village party branches are at risk of having their political authority marginalized.[24] Reports have come to light about violent conflict between village party branches and village committees, suggesting the degree of tension that has built up between the two.[25]

In response to such tension, local party committees began to explore measures to improve popular support for village party branches. This was the environment in which the two-ballot system was gradually introduced. Under the two-ballot system, village party branch members are determined by two rounds of voting. The first vote is for a list of preliminary candidates chosen by all villagers, rather than by only village party members, though the candidates are subject to the examination and approval of the party committees. The second vote is for final determination of the village party branch members by the village party members through the casting of secret ballots.

Direct Election of Township Leaders Based on Public Recommendation

When the direct election of township mayors was first attempted, a similar conflict occurred between the township governments and the party committees at their corresponding levels. Direct election may strengthen the legitimacy of township government and township mayors, it but may also cause a decline in the authority of the township party committees. When township governments carry out their work according to the instructions of the township mayors rather than those of the corresponding party committees, tensions build up and power struggles between the two can occur.[26] The democratic election of grassroots government thus began to pose a challenge to the leadership of the party at the grassroots level. It was against this backdrop that the election of township mayors gradually evolved into the direct election of township party committee members based on public recommendation.

The mechanism of direct election based on public recommendation (公推直选, *gongtui zhixuan*) is a development grounded in the two-ballot system (两票制, *liang piao zhi*). The system has such variations as two recommendations and one election, direct recommendation and direct election, and popular recommendation and direct election (海推直选, *haitui zhixuan*). All these practices, in essence, consist of three procedures. The preliminary candidates for township party committee members are chosen through public recommendation and self-recommendation in addition to the recommendation of the party committee. The election organizer, led by the ruling party, performs a comprehensive evaluation of the candidates, one based largely on their degree of popularity, before finalizing the candidate pool. Finally, direct elections are held at the party congress or the meeting of party member representatives of the township to determine the members of the township party committee.

Under the traditional procedure, the township party committee members were appointed by the party committee at the higher level and then subjected to a routine perfunctory election. Direct election based on public recommendation has expanded the scope of candidacy by changing the appointment by the party committee at the higher level to recommendation through various methods and a final determination of candidates on the basis of popular support by the higher-level party committee before the final election by party members. This expansion of public participation in choosing candidates constitutes a major step forward in the CCP's intraparty democracy.

The direct election of township party committee members based on public recommendation strikes the best balance between the CCP's leadership and the advancement of grassroots democracy. As the election of township party committee members fully represents both public opinion and opinion inside the party, it stands to reason that the higher-level party committee recommends the township party committee members as candidates for township mayors and standing committee directors of township people's congresses. This procedure—of generating township party committee members through direct election based on public recommendation and then recommending some for the election of township mayors at the people's congresses—ensures the political legitimacy of the township party committees and secretaries and their leadership and authority over the township governments and people's congresses. This reform of township party committees via direct election based on public recommendation reflects the CCP's commitment to advancing popular democracy on the basis of expanding intraparty democracy.

Because it adheres to CCP leadership while advancing grassroots democracy, the public recommendation–based direct election at the grassroots level got the nod from China's top leadership and has since seen rapid development. First being implemented in Nancheng Township in Qingshen County in Sichuan in 1999, it has since been piloted in such provinces as Hubei, Jiangsu, Yunnan, Jilin, and Chongqing. Before 2007, the public recommendation–based direct election was mainly confined to the election of township and town party committees and was most widely piloted in Sichuan and Jiangsu. In 2007 the report to the 17th CCP National Congress stated explicitly, "We will spread the practice in which candidates for leading positions in primary Party organizations are recommended both by Party members and the public in an open manner and by the Party organization at the next higher level, will gradually extend direct election of leading members in primary Party organizations to more places, and will explore various ways to expand intraparty democracy at the primary level."[27] Since then, the practice has been widely adopted for all kinds of elections of grassroots CCP organizations, including those of some private enterprises. There are signs that the public recommendation–based direct election may be adopted at higher levels. This practice was used, for instance, in the election of district and county party secretaries in Guiyang in 2008 and of some party congress deputies and members of the Chinese People's Political Consultative Conference in Shenzhen in 2010. This mechanism is quickly becoming the mainstream grassroots democratic election method in China.

From Democratic Election to Democratic Governance

The development of grassroots democracy includes not only the establishment of a written system and specific practices but also the development of democratic governance, which is made up of democratic supervision, democratic decision-making, and democratic management. Along with the advancement of grassroots democracy, grassroots democratic governance has also been widely explored.

Since the reform of village committee elections, various mechanisms of democratic participation have been introduced in the rural areas to strengthen the supervision of village cadres, including village councils, village meetings, village boards of supervisors, and transparency of the village administrative and financial affairs. In some places, a system of deciding important public affairs by public vote has been introduced, especially on such issues as the management and allocation of village collective economy, charity causes, and the use of residential real estate.

In many cities, the rise of homeowner committees has filled the functional gap of residents committees and further strengthened urban grassroots democracy. Owing to the low confluence of interest between residents committees and residents, especially after the marketization of residential housing, it is homeowners, with their property assets, who are the most concerned members in a community. In the event of a conflict of interest with developers, property management companies, and even government departments in charge of urban planning, residents committees usually cannot represent homeowner interests. As a result, there are a growing number of homeowner committees in large and medium-size Chinese cities. At the end of 2007, according to Ministry of Civil Affairs statistics, 22 percent of urban communities in China had established homeowners committees.[28]

In rural townships, democratic consultation is considered a form of grassroots democracy that is not relevant to elections but is instead concerned with village participation in the village's democratic decisionmaking, management, and supervision. The practice of democratic consultation started in Wenling, in Zhejiang Province. The practice is essentially a system of holding open hearings for decisionmaking on a wide variety of issues, including important plans of the village party committee and government, adjustments to township planning, important projects, problems brought up by the public, and other important matters of immediate interest to the public.[29] With the practice of democratic consultation have come changes in form and scope. In some Wenling townships, such as Xinhe and Zeguo, democratic consultation has been expanded to include the supervision of town people's congresses over the budget of the town government, where the deputies of the town people's congress and town voters deliberate on the government budget and then submit the results of the meeting to the town people's congress for further deliberation. This democratic consultation is considered a form of democracy outside elections and a force for the promotion of grassroots democracy.

Impetus and Impediment of China's Grassroots Democracy

Over the past thirty years China's grassroots democracy has shown itself to be an experimental field of direct elections, a main channel for fostering democratic awareness and skills in the populace, and an important symbol of China's democratic progress. Grassroots democracy is both pushed from the ground up and responsive to the strategic deployments of the ruling party and the state and the innovations of local officials. In comparison with the enthusiastic discussion of grassroots democracy that occurred ten years ago, however, China's current development of grassroots democracy is facing a dilemma. Owing to the growing gap between expectations for and the actual practice of democracy, enthusiasm for democracy is waning from the top leadership to the local governments, from political to academic circles, and from officials to private citizens. Some people have even lost confidence in grassroots democracy.

Grassroots Democracy under the Drive of Government and Private Society

The development of grassroots democracy in China has benefited from both government and private society. The CCP views the development of grassroots democracy as an important means to improve its political legitimacy. While still dedicated to the maintenance of overall social stability, high economic growth, and its ruling position, the ruling party has been exploring and reforming China's system of grassroots elections to strengthen its popularity among the people. From the perspective of the public, participation in grassroots elections and democratic governance is driven by a new awareness, following the reform and opening up, of their own interests—a development further strengthened by the marketization process. Out of the need to safeguard their own interests, the people have gradually come to realize the need to exercise their political rights to protect their lawful rights and, as a result, have increasing enthusiasm for political participation. Second, with the dissemination of modern political culture, the popularity of social scientific knowledge, and China's increasing participation in the international community, the citizens have become increasingly aware of such concepts as democracy, rule of law, human rights, competition, and equality, which have awakened in them a sense of their own rights. Additionally, the expansion of civil society in China has added fuel to the development of grassroots development. The spread of urban homeowner committees and various civic organizations shows that under the market economy, citizens have begun to join together to safeguard their common interests. With this budding of civil society, people's concerns have gradually expanded from private affairs to public affairs and from personal efforts to collective efforts to protect their rights.

Challenges to the Development of China's Grassroots Democracy

Grassroots democracy has also faced growing pains during its thirty years of development. China's social conditions are not yet ripe for democratic general elections. Civil society and the rule of law in the country are still immature, and effective solutions to bribery and coercion in village committee elections are not yet available. There is also low participation, less than one-third of those eligible to vote, in the direct elections of urban residents committee members, and most of the elections are controlled or influenced by the government. As a result, ordinary residents do not bother with the results of the elections. The public recommendation–based direct election of township and town party committees remains in experimental stages and is marked by a low degree of standardiza- tion and institutionalization. Although there are laws concerning the direct elec- tion of the deputies of grassroots people's congresses, ordinary citizens still face obstacles in running for election as independent candidates. This situation has resulted from a variety of factors.

First, the development of grassroots democracy is not matched at the macro level of the political system; yet its development, ultimately, is dependent on the existing macro level political system. Without reform of the latter, the former cannot go far. After thirty years of experimentation, direct elections are still con- fined to the level of grassroots society and grassroots governments, and indirect elections are still used for local government organs at the county level and above. Under the system of the party administering the cadres and the organizational principles of democratic centralism, the leaders of governments and party com- mittees are appointed by the organization at the higher level. If this system is not reformed, the experiment of direct grassroots election will always be limited.

Second, the way democratization brought about a change in ruling party, economic recession, and political instability in the former Soviet Union, Eastern European countries, and Taiwan also caused worry in China about expanded use of democratic elections. Additionally, rushed implementation of democratic elections without the presence of well-developed civil society can easily lead to the trap of populism. To maintain economic growth and political stability, the Chinese government must strike a balance between national interests, economic development, social order, civil freedom, and political democracy. Against this backdrop, countries like Singapore have become the main models for China. Worries about the democratic election system are also reflected in academic cir- cles. Whether the topic is universal values, the embrace of the rule of law and the rejection of democracy, or electoral democracy, many scholars are suspicious of Western-style democracy or electoral democracy.[30]

Third, some local officials lack confidence and motivation to develop grassroots democracy. Under China's current official performance evaluation system, eco- nomic growth and social stability are the two most important indicators, the for- mer determining their future promotion and the latter determining whether they can even continue to occupy their existing post. As democratic elections increase the dependence of grassroots officials on the masses rather than on the leaders at the higher level, tension will invariably develop between local officials appointed by higher authorities and the grassroots cadres elected by the masses. Many local officials therefore have a negative attitude toward grassroots democracy.

Fourth, grassroots democracy in China has not yet shown prominent effects. The development of grassroots democracy can increase the realization of citizens' democratic rights and strengthen trust between cadres and the masses, thus improving grassroots cadres' sense of responsibility. Owing to the overall low developmental level of the rule of law and the long tradition of the rule of man in China, however, competitive elections often lead to various negative phenomena, such as bribery, clan conflicts, and the rising influence of illegal social forces.[31] Even if not the by-product of electoral politics, bribery in electoral politics is no different from buying and selling government appointments under the existing system of official selection. Such bribery has shaken the confidence in grassroots democracy held by quite a few cadres and citizens. After all, for the great number of grassroots citizens in China, still a developing country, economic benefits are more practically important than the exercise of democratic rights.

Finally, there is a contradiction between constructed democracy and inborn democracy. Inborn democracy includes village self-governance, independent participation in elections for grassroots people's congress, property owners committees, and the people's congress representative workstation. All of these institutions have strong support from the public and are led by effective local opinion leaders. Constructed democracy includes residents committee elections, township elections, and others. These are democratic reforms initiated under the direction of the ruling party and the government. The people's participation in constructed democracy is weak and passive. At the urban community level, the contradiction between inborn democracy and constructed democracy is especially obvious. On one hand, community residents are generally indifferent to government-guided elections of residents committee members; on the other hand, resident property owners actively participate in property owners committees, which face various restrictions imposed by local authorities. Such trends reveal the contradictory attitude of the government and the party toward developing grassroots democracy: they want the development of grassroots democracy to be under their effective control so that people's demands and appeals for participation can be brought into established institutionalized channels, yet they worry that independent political participation of the people will result in social instability and threaten the authority of the ruling party.

Overall Assessment of China's Grassroots Democracy

The development of China's grassroots democracy has been a major area of democratic progress in China in the era of reform. Its institutional evolution can be seen from the countryside to the city, from grassroots society to grassroots government, from outside the ruling party to within the ruling party, and from democratic election to democratic governance. Grassroots democracy is encouraged by both the central leadership and the wide participation of the people. The democratic progress of China's macro-level political system is manifested in the democratic values found in official texts and government exhortations; democratic progress at the grassroots level is concretely expressed in the actual level and degree of development of grassroots political participation by the people.

China's grassroots democracy has strategic importance for CCP legitimacy. It also has great room for development under the existing system. Characterized by the model of public recommendation–based direct election, China's grassroots democracy will undergo a long process of interaction of various political forces. China's decisionmakers, by means of the current practice of grassroots democracy and intraparty democracy, have been seeking to lay a solid foundation, win wide support, and build more consensus for the gradual development of democratic politics. In a sense, it can be said that huge pressure stemming from the various problems and challenges in the modernization process are the real driving force behind the development of democratic politics, just as China's reform and opening up itself was originally brought about by crisis.

COMMENT
JEAN C. OI

Huang Weiping's chapter on China's grassroots democracy assesses the possibility for future democratic governance and politics in China's one-party authoritarian system through an insightful review of the evolution of local elections in China. He systematically examines the evolution of elections in China from their start in villages and experiments in townships to their use in urban districts and in people's congresses. He details the different types of democratic elections and their different development paths to show that elections can take diverse forms and yield different results for the electorate. Huang notes the different approaches the state took in establishing elections in villages and in urban districts. In doing so he astutely highlights that the existence of codified laws does not always indicate the degree of enthusiasm for elections. In the case of urban district elections, the state first created a law and then tried to promote elections. Yet in the case of village elections, which have been much more successful, the law was not ratified until more than a decade after it was first introduced as a draft and implemented on a trial basis.

Political change in China is like a drawn-out chess game. It is slow and, at times, tedious, and dependent on the response of the other player. The moves in the game—the type and direction of change in electoral forms—are dependent on interests. The interests of the electorate play a role, but most important are the interests of the ruling party state. Huang traces the twists and turns of the evolution of elections by examining how the various forms affected the interests of those in power—thus explaining why some forms continued and why others were forced to change or were blocked.

One of the strongest parts of Huang's chapter is his discussion of the evolution of township elections. It provides an extremely insightful analysis of why direct elections in townships were thwarted—they threatened party power and authority—and why they are now widely implemented across the country and even being tried at higher levels of government in some localities. The reformed township leader election process, which is similar to the two-ballot system for village elections, is called public nomination with direct election by the party (公推直选, *gongtui zhixuan*). This revised election form allows nominations from outside the party, but the decisionmaking is kept within the party. In this way it provides a feasible electoral option that allows popular participation but does not threaten the ruling party. Huang effectively uses such examples to underline his point that all forms of election must be in line with the interests of those in power.

The ruling party holds power and determines when and how elections can be held, but in the end, elections have become a useful tool. It is this that allows Huang to conclude somewhat optimistically that the prospects for an expansion of democratic politics are good. He argues that the driving force that will push the ruling party down a more democratic path is the need for elections to deal with the increasing challenges of development. He points to *gongtui zhixuan* as the way to such reform. Huang argues that interparty democracy will move forward people's democracy.

Participation in Authoritarian Systems

Elections often are seen as the essence of democratic rule, as the measure of good governance and decisionmaking by the people. Assessment often centers on whether there are elections at the national level and on the electoral process itself—are there more candidates than offices, is there a secret ballot, is there transparency in vote count, and are there any signs of vote buying or fraud? However, a host of other questions, including those addressed in Huang's chapter, need to be asked when trying to understand the evolution of democratic governance and elections, especially in one-party authoritarian states that are just beginning to allow more citizen participation.

Democratic multiparty and one-party authoritarian systems stand on opposite ends of the political spectrum. However, authoritarian regimes differ in the degree to which the ruling party allows diverse voices to be heard within the system. The literature on authoritarian regimes has begun to distinguish between those that allow other parties to compete through formal elections at the national level, even if the chances that other parties will win are slim, and those that do not. While one can argue that such elections are relatively meaningless in bringing about real political change, there is evidence that the process of holding elections alters the strategies of the ruling party and its interactions with its people. Within the one-party states with no national elections there also is variation in the degree to which participation is allowed.

Although China remains in the category of one-party authoritarian states in which there are no national elections, the Chinese party state surprised many in the late 1980s by initiating village elections, which allowed the majority of China's population the right to have competitive, direct elections. Granted, these direct elections were only for a portion of the village leaders—the village committee and not the party committee within the village. However, this was a positive institutional step forward from the days of the Mao period, when elections at the production team level were simply a rubber stamp of appointments made at higher levels. Village elections granted those at the grassroots an element of choice.

Local Elections as a Window on Democratic Development

Huang seeks to answer the question that many American scholars have asked since village elections were first instituted—whether such local elections will pave the way for an increase in democratic politics both at the local and eventually the national levels. Like many scholars he realizes that national elections will most likely remain an elusive goal in China's foreseeable future. Nonetheless, he shows that elections over the past two decades have spread, if in a limited way, up from the villages through a good portion of the larger political system—from outside the ruling party to inside the party. As such, China offers an interesting case, an opportunity to explore a set of questions about when and why a one-party authoritarian system promotes and allows elections and when it does not. Such an understanding may be the best lens through which to assess the chances of future change at higher levels of the political system.

In thinking about the general lack of participation in authoritarian systems, some might assume that people would immediately jump at the chance to participate in elections. Huang's study shows that elections in China have demonstrated that such participation cannot be assumed. One cannot take for granted citizen interest in participating in elections when they are endowed with that right. To understand the evolution of elections, Huang carefully examines the interests of those who have the right to participate in them and those whose power will be affected by them. With regard to this first group—those who have the right to vote but who have little interest in voting—he provides a very apt example of urban district elections, wherein apathy exists because elections are not linked to the routine interests of the electorate. He suggests that urban districts decide little of vital importance to the interests of the electorate.

Huang should fully explore the same question of interests for village elections. What explains the variation in the implementation of village elections over time and the ability of those who are elected to exercise power? We know from recent empirical work that village elections are now widely implemented. However, we also need to know whether the universal implementation of village elections also means that villagers are interested in these elections as China's economy booms and many villagers migrate toward cities. How have interests changed, if at all, in these village elections, since they first came into being in the late 1980s?

The effectiveness of elections depends on whether they will further the interests of the voters. The electorate must be stakeholders in the outcome of elections, and those elected must control the resources to serve the interests of the electorate. Often missed in studies of village elections is that when village elections were first introduced in 1987, there was no rush to embrace the democratic right to vote. Moreover, contrary to comparative theories about the link between demands for participatory rights and development, it was the poor, less developed villages that embraced village elections, not the rich, industrialized villages. Elections only became universal when an actual law in 1998 required all villages to hold elections. A significant point is that the decision to have village elections was a top-down initiative, not the result of a groundswell of demand from the grassroots. Moreover, the Chinese Communist Party turned to village elections as a means to solve problems in rural areas. Village elections were used as a safety valve and as a means to strengthen CCP rule. Huang seems to echo a similar argument when he writes that the party-state will turn to more participatory politics to solve new problems that are appearing in the course of rapid development. Certainly the CCP has used elections as other authoritarian regimes have, but recent developments raise questions as to whether other policy solutions may dilute elections that have already been put in place. The existence of elections and popular participation in the selection process are necessary but not sufficient to ensure effective democratic governance.

The Uncertain Road Ahead for Elections

Beginning in the late 1990s the state started to adopt two sets of policies in the countryside. The first involved the ratification of the Organic Law of the Village Committees and led to experimentation with the two-ballot system, extending popular participation in the selection of party leaders to the village level. But concurrently, the CCP also shifted its policies in the countryside and began to recentralize administrative and fiscal control, a new policy known in Chinese as *shuangdai guan* (双代管). This included the much-welcomed end of fees and the eventual end of all taxes on peasants. However, these moves were accompanied by a hollowing out of cadre power at the village and township levels. The *shuangdai guan* policy took control of village accounts, and funds from the village into the hands of township officials. The stationing of upper-level cadres helps oversee village cadres. The salaries of elected village officials are now paid by these supervisory cadres. These policies were adopted to improve accountability, and they do so in a number of respects. Yes, they cut down corruption, but are such policies necessarily good for strengthening the interest in and impact of local elections?

The recentralization of cadre control also signals that the upper levels of the party-state have grown more wary of, rather than more supportive of, increased local self-governance. This recentralization of power, I would argue, was a reaction to the inability of earlier policies, including village elections, to ensure stability and solve the peasant burden problems. Increasingly, the solution seems to be to simply step back and once again take more direct control over solving problems, even if it costs the state more in fiscal revenues. Upper levels of the party-state now have the funds to assume increased fiscal responsibility. Such patterns bode less well for the conclusion that increasing challenges of development may push the regime to adopt more democratic electoral forms. Moreover, such patterns may also undermine the elections that the regime has already instituted. They create negative incentives for those who are elected to support entrepreneurial activity and to put the interests of the villagers first, regardless of the precise process through which candidates are selected.

We not only should be concerned about the method and the degree of popular participation in the selection process, but we also need to ask what elected officials have the power to do. Moreover, we need to ask how powers are changing over time at the different levels at which elections have been instituted. While it is important to consider whether the methods by which candidates are selected threaten local power holders, we also need to know whether those who are elected, regardless of the process of election, have the resources and authority to further the interests of those who elected them. These questions are more relevant than ever because of the recentralization of administrative and fiscal control in the rural areas. How much can elected village officials do after they are elected? What powers do township officials have? What can people's congresses do? How have these polices affected the incentives for developing strong, entrepreneurial leaders? What will happen to village elections when villages are merged into new multivillage *shequ* (社区, rural communities)?

Huang rightly notes the ambiguous impact of abolishing the agricultural tax and taking over the payment of village cadre salaries by higher-level supervisors. Without question, these changes ease the tensions between cadres and peasants. But do they also loosen the tie between villagers and their leaders? An even greater problem is that village finances are now controlled by the township. Will this reduce the incentives to hold elected office? Will cadres—as well as villagers—lose interest in village elections?

The effort to relocate villages into new rural communities in the face of a rapid migration that has emptied some villages of able-bodied laborers creates particular dilemmas and questions about the fate of village elections. The creation of *shequ* is part of the current regime's efforts to create a new socialist countryside and improve the provision of public goods. But it also is fraught with many potential points of conflict and, at least in the short term, leaves open whether elections will still determine leadership at the grassroots level. In some *shequ* the leadership has been appointed, not elected. China faces great new challenges in governance, but we must wait and see whether the regime will once again turn to elections as a means to help solve its problems. Currently, the recentralization polices may be eroding the effectiveness of electoral forms that have already been implemented.

Notes

1. *Zhongguo Renmin Gongheguo xianfa* [Constitution of the People's Republic of China] (Beijing: People's Publishing House, 1982), p. 40.

2. Deng Xiaoping, "Zhengzhi shang fazhan minzhu, jinji shang shixing gaige" [Develop democracy in politics, implement reform in the economy], in *Deng Xiaoping wenxuan* [Selected works of Deng Xiaoping], vol. 3 (Beijing: People's Publishing House, 1993), p. 116.

3. Deng Xiaoping, "Jianchi si xiang jiben yuanze" [Uphold the four cardinal principles], in *Deng Xiaoping wenxuan*, vol. 2 (Beijing: People's Publishing House, 1994), p. 168.

4. Deng Xiaoping, "Gaige de buzi yao jia kuai" [The pace of reform must increase], in *Deng Xiaoping wenxuan*, vol. 2, p. 242.

5. Hu Jintao, *Gaoju Zhongguo tese shehuizhuyi weida qizhi, wei duoqu quanmian jianshe xiaokang shehui xin shengli er fendou* [Hold high the great banner of socialism with Chinese characteristics and strive for new victories in building a moderately prosperous society in all respects], report to the 17th CCP National Congress, October 15, 2007, *Qiushi* [Seek truth] 11.

6. *Zhongguo Renmin Gongheguo cunmin we'yuanhui zuzhi fa, shixing* [Trial version of PRC law for organization of village committees] (Beijing: Falü chubanshe [Law Press], 1988), p. 4.

7. Shi Weimin and Lei Jingxuan, *Zhijie xuanju: zhidu yu guocheng* [Direct elections: System and process] (Beijing: Zhongguo shehui kexue chubanshe [China Social Sciences Press], 1999), pp. 201–34.

8. Popular election, or *haixuan* (海选) in Chinese, is a form of preliminary election in which villagers who are eligible to vote may nominate themselves as candidates, with all voters then choosing among the nominees. Under the one-step method, the candidate who receives the greatest number of ballots wins the election. In a group election, the candidate chosen by the village committee director is determined by a majority vote of the villages, and the candidate then chooses the candidates of other village committee members, thus forming a campaign group to run for the election in two stages.

9. Wu Jing, "Zhongguo cunguan xuanju zouxiang 'changtaihua'" [China's village cadre election goes regular], *People's Daily,* January 9, 2008.

10. Shi Weimin and others, *Zhongguo jiceng minzhu zhengzhi jianshe fazhan baogao* [Report on the development of China's grassroots democratic political construction] (Beijing: Zhongguo shehui kexue chubanshe [China Social Sciences Press], 2008), pp. 98–99.

11. Shang Yiying and others, "Fu ren zhi cun: 'Laoban cunguan' de huise zhiyi" [Villages managed by the rich: Doubts on "former bosses-turned-village cadres"], Xinhua wang Zhejiang pindao [Xinhua Zhejiang TV], September 16, 2009 (news.xinhuanet.com/focus/2009-09/16/content_12022093.htm).

12. Zhou Feizhou, "Cong jiuxing zhengquan dao 'xuanfuxing' zhengquan: Shuifei gaige dui guojia yu nongmin guanxi zhi yingxiang" [From extracting government to "suspension" government: The impacts of tax-fee reforms on the relationship between the state and peasants], *Shehuixue yanjiu* [Sociology research], no. 3 (2006), pp. 1–37.

13. Zhang Xinguang, "Qian yi 'xiang zhen kong chao hua, cunguan xingzheng hua' xianxiang de shehui weihai" [On the social consequences of "empty nests and village cadre bureaucratization" in townships and towns], *Zhongguo shehui bao* [China society report], January 18, 2010; Ren Zhongping, "Dangqian cunmin zizhi mianlin de kunjing, guiyin yu chulu: Hou shuifei shidai Sichuan sheng bufen nongcun cunmin zizhi zhuangkuang de diaocha baogao" [The current predicament, causes, and solutions of village self-governance: An investigation report of the status of village self-governance in selected villages in Sichuan after the tax-fee reforms], *Ruan kexue* [Soft science], no. 6 (2007).

14. *Zhong ban fa,* no. 23 (2000), (circular forwarded by the General Office of the CCP Central Committee and the State Council of the Opinion of Ministry of Civil Affairs on the all-round advancement of urban community construction), *Fujian zhengbao* [Gazette of Fujian provincial people's government], no. 12 (2000).

15. Zheng Quan, "Zhongguo shequ jiben qingkuang diaocha baogao" [Investigation report on the basic situation of China's communities], *Shequ* [Communities], no. 11 (2005), pp. 26–29.

16. Shi Weimin and others, *Zhongguo shequ juweihui xuanju yanjiu* [Research on China's residents' committee elections] (Beijing: China Social Sciences Press, 2009), p. 358.

17. Zhang Jinming, "Buyun xiangzhang zhixuan de beijing, guocheng yu xiaoguo" [The background, process, and effects of the direct election in Buyun township], *Zhongguo xuanju yu zhili wang* [China elections and governance], October 14 (www.political-china.org/NewsInfo.asp?NewsID=78930).

18. He Baogang and Lang Youxing, "China's First Direct Election of the Township Head: A Case Study of Buyun," *Japanese Journal of Political Science*, no. 1 (2002).

19. Cheng Zihua, *Guanyu quanguo xianji zhijie xuanju gongzuo de zongjie baogao* [Summary report on county-level direct elections nationwide], *People's Daily*, September 12, 1981.

20. Xiao Donglian, *Lishi de zhuanzhe: Cong ba luan fan zheng dao gaige kaifang (1979–81)* [A historic turn: From the correction of past mistakes to the reform and opening up, 1979–81] (Hong Kong: Chinese University of Hong Kong Press, 2008), pp. 410–13.

21. Min Jie, "Zeng Jianyu: Jingxuan chu lai de daibiao" [Zeng Jianyu: The self-made representative], *Zhongguo qingnian bao* [China youth daily], January 14, 2002.

22. Tang Juan and Zou Shubin, eds., *2003 nian Shenzhen jingxuan shilu* [Actual records of elections in Shenzhen in 2003] (Xi'an: Northwest University Press, 2003).

23. Jiang Zemin, *Quanmian jianshe xiaokang shehui, kaichuang Zhongguo tese shehuizhuyi shiye xin jumian* [Build a well-off society in an all-round way and create a new situation in building socialism with Chinese characteristics] (Beijing: People's Publishing House, 2002), p. 34.

24. Li Lianjiang, "The Two-Ballot System in Shanxi Province: Subjecting Village Party Secretaries to a Popular Vote," *China Journal*, no. 42 (1999), pp. 103–18.

25. Jing Yuejin, *Dangdai Zhongguo nongcun "liang wei guanxi" de weiguan jiexi yu hongguan toushi* [Micro-level explanation and macro-level assessment of the "two-committee relationship" in the countryside] (Beijing: Zhongyang wenxian chubanshe [Central Party Literature Press], 2004).

26. CCP Sichuan Provincial Organizational Department Task Force, "Conflict and Coordination of Interest in the Process of the Advancement of Rural Grassroots Democracy," *Marxism and Reality*, no. 2 (2003).

27. Hu, *Gaoju Zhongguo tese shehuizhuyi weida qizhi, wei duoqu quanmian jianshe xiaokang shehui xin shengli er fendou.*

28. Li Xueju, "Wo guo jiceng qunzhong zizhi zhidu diwei de zhongda tisheng" [Major elevation of China's self-governance system at the grassroots level], *Qiushi* [Seek truth], no. 3 (2008), pp. 18–20.

29. CCP Wenqiao Town Committee and Wenqiao Town People's Government, *Jiceng minzhu zhengzhi jianshe tansuo yu chuangxin—Wenqiao zhen shenhua "minzhu kentan" huodong ziliao huibian* [Exploration and innovation in grassroots democratic

politics: compilation of materials on "democratic consultations" in Wenqiao Township], August 2002, pp. 44–45.

30. Zhou Xincheng, "Yixie ren guchui de pushi jiazhi shiji jiushi xifang de jiazhi" [The universal values preached by some are actually Western values], *Guangming ribao* [Guangming daily], September 16, 2008; Pan Wei, *Fazhi yu "minzhu mixin"* [The rule of law and "democracy superstition"] (Hong Kong: Hong Kong Social Sciences Publishing, 2003); Wang Shaoguang, "Fansi xiandai minzhu zhidu" [Reflection on the modern system of democracy], *Shehui kexue bao* [Journal of social sciences], no. 1221 (July 29, 2010).

31. Lu Fuying, "Cunweihui xuanju zhong siying qiyezhu de jingxuan xingwei" [Campaign behaviors of private entrepreneurs in village committee elections], *Xuexi yu tansuo* [Study and exploration], no. 2 (2009).

10

China's Interest Coordination Mechanism

JING YUEJIN

Since the reform and opening-up period began, both China's social structure and interest structure have undergone major and profound changes, and contradictions and conflicts of interest have since become a constant of social life. How to view this phenomenon, and how to coordinate these conflicts of interest, is an important subject in the study of contemporary Chinese politics.

Scholars and policy advisers in China frequently refer to reconstructing "the interest coordination mechanism."[1] The interest coordination mechanism established in the era of the planned economy has proved unable to cope with the complicated interest structure in the new open environment, and it is thus imperative to replace it with a new interest coordination mechanism that is compatible with the market economy.

Both Chinese and foreign scholars are drawn to this subject because of two important empirical facts: China is facing growing social tension, including an increase in petitioning activities and mass disturbances; and industrial and commercial enterprises that have emerged during China's transition to a market economy are increasingly active in using their economic power to influence the governmental policies in order to maximize their own interests.[2] The former relates to the struggle of the weak to seek redress of their damaged interests, and the latter is an endeavor of the strong to maximize their profits or avoid being washed away by market tides. The struggle of the weak is directly related to social stability and the political order and has therefore become the focus of the media, the public, and academia. In contrast, the activities of the business elite, which often occur at hotel banquets, golf courses, and tourist resorts, have largely remained out of public view. Owing to various limiting factors, this chapter focuses primarily on China's increasing social tension.

Contradiction and Conflicts of Interest in Contemporary China

Since the socialist transformation of the 1950s, Chinese society has been composed of the working class, the peasant class, and the cadres (including intellectuals). This social structure, largely a by-product of the national political structure, assumed the characteristics of a totalitarian society under a planned economy imposed by the government.[3]

Major Changes in China's Social and Interest Structures

Chinese society experienced drastic change following China's introduction of market-oriented economic reforms. The reform and opening up greatly changed the social landscape within a very short time. There was a dizzying array of profound changes in many areas, including the disintegration of the work-unit system, the reorganization of government departments, the emergence of new social strata, the creation of new social spaces, the expansion of both interest differentiation and the income gap, and the increasing self-interest of local governments in response to decentralization reforms. In light of traditional class theory and the theory of social stratification, China's social structure had assumed an unprecedented level of complexity.

The evolution of the social structure has been accompanied by major changes in the interest structure. According to the *People's Daily Online,* the income gap among China's various social groups has been growing since the reform and opening up began. The income ratio of urban to rural residents expanded from 2.36 in 1978 to 3.33 in 2009. There is now a remarkable gap between the eastern and western regions in China in the incomes of both urban and rural residents: in 2009 the per capita disposable income of urban and rural residents in Zhejiang reached RMB 24,611 and RMB 10,007, respectively, while that in Guizhou stood at only RMB 12,862 and a little more than RMB 3,000, respectively. There has been rapid growth in the wealth and consumption capacity of the highest social strata, which has made China the second-largest luxury market in the world. On the other hand, China has more than 40 million people living below the absolute poverty line, with an additional 270 million characterized as low income. One important measure of income inequality is the Gini coefficient. Generally, a Gini coefficient between 0.4 and 0.5 indicates an excessive income gap and anything exceeding 0.5 expresses a serious social polarization. China's Gini coefficient currently stands at approximately 0.47.[4]

All these changes have altered the macro-level structure of China's interest politics. Now that the traditional structure of interest politics is a thing of the past, there is a need for a recoordination and a rebalancing of interests. The Decision of the CCP Central Committee Regarding Several Major Issues on

Building a Harmonious Socialist Society adopted at the sixth plenary session of the 16th CCP Central Committee in October 2006 used four "profound" changes to describe these historic changes: "profound changes in the economic system, profound changes in the social structure, profound adjustment of the interest structure, and profound changes in people's ideology and outlook."[5]

Heightened Contraction and Conflict of Interest

Social transformation, interest differentiation, and a governance crisis have combined to throw China into a period of intense conflicts of interest. As Zeng Qinghong, then vice president, expressed frankly in 2004, "As China enters a key period in which we will see our per capita GDP increase from USD 1,000 to USD 3,000, we face a period of both 'golden development' and 'heightened contradiction.'"[6] Although this expression has not appeared in important party documents, it has been widely quoted by government officials and the media.

There are two meanings associated with this expression, "the period of heightened contradiction." First, it establishes a connection between a specific stage of China's economic development (per capita GDP growing from USD 1,000 to USD 3,000) and contradictory social problems. Second, it is also a reminder that China has entered a new stage.[7] The underlying assumption is that social conflict is an objective phenomenon independent of people's subjective will. There is thus a theoretical basis on which to establish a corresponding stability-maintenance mechanism and increase government spending on maintaining stability.

According to relevant resources, the number of petitions nationwide has been growing over the past ten years since its rebound in 1993.[8] The year 2003 had been called the "year of the petition flood" by Chinese media.[9] The situation became even more serious in 2004, with an increase over 2003 of 11.7 percent, 58.4 percent, and 52.9 percent, respectively, in the number of letters, groups, and petitioning individuals received.[10]

Things began to change for the better in 2005, with a decrease in the total number of overall petitions, collective petitions, and first-time letters and calls.[11] This was the first time in fifteen years that the number of petitions declined. This positive trend continued in 2006, which saw a further 15.5 percent decrease in the number of petitions.[12] However, Wang Xuejun, director of the State Bureau for Letters and Calls, noted that "although there have been good changes in the petition situation, the total amount of petitions has remained at a high level."[13]

Corresponding to the objective data are people's subjective understanding and social reception of conflicts of interest in China. According to the *Research Report on China's Social Harmony and Stability* released by the Chinese Academy of Social Sciences, only 16.3 percent of respondents stated that "there is no conflict among the various social groups in China," while 67.9 percent held the opposite view. This shows that conflicts of interest among different social groups have been increasingly recognized by people and has become an important topic among the public.[14] The resentment toward the rich as shown in the various high-profile mass disturbances in recent years reflects to a considerable degree the tension and confrontation among different interest groups.

Complexity of Conflicts of Interest

Social conflicts have centered on material interest. In an interview in 2003, Zhou Zhanshun, the director of the State Bureau for Letters and Calls, said, "Of the many problems reflected in the petitions, especially collective petitions, more than 80 percent have arisen during the process of the country's reform and development; more than 80 percent are reasonable or involve certain practical problems and difficulties to be resolved; more than 80 percent can be solved by the efforts of the Party committees and governments at the various levels; more than 80 percent are problems that can be solved even at the grassroots level."[15]

Contradiction among the People

This "depoliticized" judgment has great significance for China's good governance because it has a direct bearing on how governments at various levels address the contradictions.[16] For reasons that are known to all, after the Tiananmen Square protests in 1989, many officials sought to eliminate problems as soon as they appeared. Understanding that there are real contradictions among the people helps address problems through reasonable and lawful means rather than by armed force.

Recognizing that there are legitimate conflicts among the people is not enough, however, to construct a new interest coordination mechanism. The construction of such a coordination mechanism falls within the distinct domain of governance. The new social environment requires, in part, an understanding of the differences between the conflicts of interest that occur between officials and citizens and those between labor and capital. Although both fall within the scope of the contradictions among the people and are not mutually exclusive, their solutions require different approaches.

Official-Citizen Contradictions and Labor-Capital Contradictions

Experience shows that most petitions and mass disturbances are directed at governments and officials at the grassroots, or local, level.[17] Contradictions between officials and citizens are not a product of modern society; rather, they have a long tradition in Chinese history. Of course, conflict in contemporary China does have a number of unique characteristics.

Officials profiting at the people's expense is a major cause of a large number of mass disturbances. As a result of decentralization reforms, local governments have formed independent interests; in many cases, these interests are intertwined with the private interests of government officials. Accordingly, local governments often not only fail to perform their obligations to provide public services for their citizens but also actively abuse their power by infringing on citizen interests. For example, some local governments advancing urbanization bluntly infringe on the interests of ordinary people by embezzling compensation related to relocation and land acquisition and lowering the standards of compensation for relocation under the pretext of development and the public interest. In the event of any open opposition, local officials stand by the developers and even use police power to settle disputes. Arbitrary government charges are yet another comparable example.

The bureaucracy of government departments is another major cause of conflict between officials and citizens. The accumulation of various administration-related misdeeds—including power abuse, negligence, omission, indifference to people's concerns, oversimplification in handling things, arrogance toward the people, violent law enforcement, and lack of transparency—has kept the relationship between these two groups in a constant state of tension. The people's dissatisfaction is further fueled by rampant corruption of government officials, often pushing them to angrily vent their suppressed dissatisfaction in protests against the government.

The contradictions between officials and citizens are also related to institutional arrangement. China's economic transformation has been carried out under the control of the governments at various levels. Many local governments use administrative means to shape the market economy, where the government not only plays the role of the referee but is also a rule-defying player. This contradictory arrangement clearly leads to abuses of power.

Conflict between officials and citizens can also be seen in a more optimistic light by interpreting some of the problems, such as the layoffs and unemployment that have resulted from the reform of the economic system. With social progress and the country's continued economic development, these problems will begin to change and, eventually, fade away. For example, the petitions in 2003 focused on eight major areas, including enterprise restructuring, labor and social security, "agricultural, rural, and farmer" (三农, *sannong*) problems, legal disputes, urbanization-related dismantling and relocation, official malpractice, reform of grassroots organs, environmental pollution, and settlement of

Figure 10-1. *Labor Dispute Cases Accepted by Labor Dispute Arbitration Committees, 1996–2008*

Number

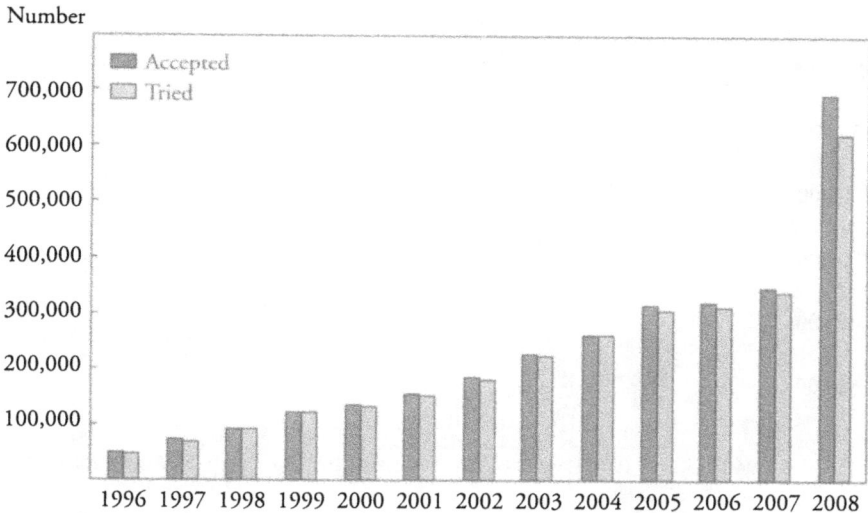

Source: *Zhongguo laodong tongji nianjian* [China labor statistical yearbook] (Beijing: Zhongguo tongji chubanshe [China Statistics Press], 2009).

demobilized army cadres. By 2007 these issues had given way to land acquisition, urban construction–related relocation, environmental protection, restructuring and bankruptcy of enterprises, and legal disputes. This shows that the causes of contradiction between officials and citizens and the nature of interest conflicts cannot be described in sweeping terms but should be analyzed on a case-by-case basis. It also means that this contradiction both can be solved and will constantly take on new forms.

Compared with the contradictions between officials and citizens, those between labor and capital have their own peculiar logic. The biggest change brought about by China's social structure has been the formation of new social strata and the corresponding labor-capital relationship. For a considerable period of time, many local governments obsessed with GDP growth have focused their efforts on attracting investments and thus have lacked commitment to the protection of the lawful rights and interests of laborers.[18] Under a dual urban-rural structure and the restrictive household registration system, the migrant workers are often in an even worse situation. The increasingly intensified labor-capital relationship is shown in figures 10-1 and 10-2.

Figure 10-2. *Labor Dispute Cases Tried by Courts, 1994–2009*

Number

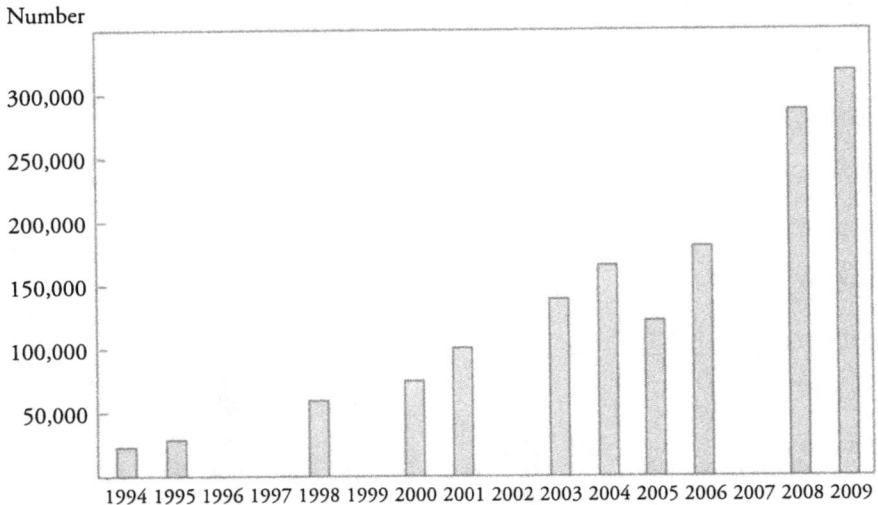

Source: Work reports [gongzuo baogao] of the Supreme People's Court from 1995 to 2010; data for 1996, 1997, 1999, 2002, and 2007 omitted.

The formation of the labor-capital relationship illuminates two enduring issues related to conflicts of interest that must be faced. First, owing to the economic logic of modern society, the relationship between the government and the business world has become increasingly important. In this situation, how does the government maintain its independence in making public policy? Second, workers are in a disadvantageous position when negotiating with employers over such terms of employment as salary, welfare, and working conditions. This is a general phenomenon globally, and China is no exception. Against this backdrop, how does China, with socialism as its official ideology, protect the interests of this disadvantaged group?

Institutional Bottlenecks and the Pressure for Transformation

Interest contradictions existed before the reform and opening up, but the mechanisms for handling them were markedly different. Under the system of state monopoly and allocation of resources, "the coordination and integration of different interests was based on a state-centered top-down 'determinative' relationship and set of mechanisms."[19] These mechanisms faced unprecedented challenges after China's transition to a market economy. The sharp increase in petitions and mass disturbances means that the original mechanisms of interest coordination have lost their utility.

Pressure to Reform the Petition System

The system of public letters and calls is illustrative. From a political perspective, three factors make the existence of this system necessary. First, the centralized system does not have an independent judiciary or a more general mechanism for the separation of powers. In the event of any conflict of interest between officials and citizens, citizens, including citizen groups, can only rely on administrative channels. In this sense, the system of letters and calls serves as a substitute for the judicial function. Second, these letters and calls from the people have the function of information dissemination, a means by which the central government can overcome or reduce the information asymmetry inherent in a centralized system, thereby imposing strong political control over grassroots and local governments and officials. Third, the system of letters and calls provides an opportunity for the citizens to petition, thus reinforcing the people's perception that the policies of the central government are good and that the problem is that local government goes against the spirit of the central government when implementing policies. In this sense, the system of letters and calls helps safeguard the legitimacy of the central government.

Therefore, that petitions are encouraged (actively or passively) by this system is not hypocrisy. This is only the first half of the story. To listen to the second half, one must turn an ear to the citizens. From their perspective, there are two factors to consider about petitions. First, it is often difficult for officials to rectify their mistakes (doing so is not in their interests under the existing system); it is absolutely impossible if there is indeed corruption involved. Second, there is a network of various relationships among officials, which tends to make them help and protect one another. Therefore, to overcome these two obstacles citizens feel they can only petition higher authorities. The assumption behind their actions is often that small disturbances bring about small solutions, big disturbances bring about big solutions, and no disturbances bring about no solution.

As a result of the great number of petitions being sent to higher authorities, new problems have emerged. The handling capacity of the system, for instance, has limits. When the number of petitions reaches a certain point, the government feels a need to limit the number of petitions to avoid system paralysis. In response, suppressive measures are taken, including "zero target," "veto system," and petitioner repatriation (often implemented under cover).[20] This accountability imposed by the central government on local governments is conveyed level by level with increasing sternness. By the time accountability reaches the grassroots level, local officials feel great pressure to resort to any means, even illegal ones, to suppress petitioning activities.

There are contradicting incentives within the petition system. Petitioners are motivated to create disturbances (believing that a greater disturbance leads to a higher probability of problem resolution), but local officials are motivated to suppress petitioning activities (to protect their career development). However, a considerable percentage of the petitioners not only do not yield to attempts by local officials to suppress them but have also become full-time petitioners (in many cases, the original cause of their petitions has become less important than the subsequent suffering they have experienced while having their petitioning activities suppressed). As a result, for a country whose bureaucratic machine relies on the smooth functioning of a system of letters and calls, there is now the widespread phenomenon of local officials' intercepting petitioners who make petitions according to the system and a succession of cat-and-mouse games between petitioners and officials.

This institutional paradox is largely logical. Whether it occurs, when it occurs, and to what extent it occurs are empirical questions. The judgment about the "period of heightened contradiction" means that we have reached this bottleneck, and that the theoretical paradox has become a paradox in real life.

Growing Pressure to Maintain Stability

Although the existing interest coordination mechanism has faced unprecedented challenges and has experienced many symptoms of imbalance, China is socially stable overall. Most mass disturbances are isolated events lacking organization (with industrial actions being the exception), and their claims are nonpolitical and therefore not difficult to handle. Moreover, the existing system still has a strong mobilization capacity, and when necessary, some governments take a campaign approach to address interest contradictions and conflicts. The local governments have also been improving their competence in dealing with mass disturbances. The existing system faces various problems, but it still is not completely ineffective.

Meanwhile, it should be noted that the Chinese government is facing increasing pressure, and the cost of maintaining stability is growing. Under the veto system, local governments give top priority and dedicate huge resources to maintaining stability, and in addition to setting up various government agencies (such as offices for stability maintenance, social security control, and emergency response), they also contract for many services to maintain social stability. According to one estimate, from 1996 to 2006 the Jinshan District of Shanghai spent a total of RMB 1.25 billion on stability maintenance, accounting for 5 percent of its total fiscal spending and representing an annual growth of 17.34 percent. Spending

Figure 10-3. *China's Public Security Expenditures, 2000–09*

RMB 100 million

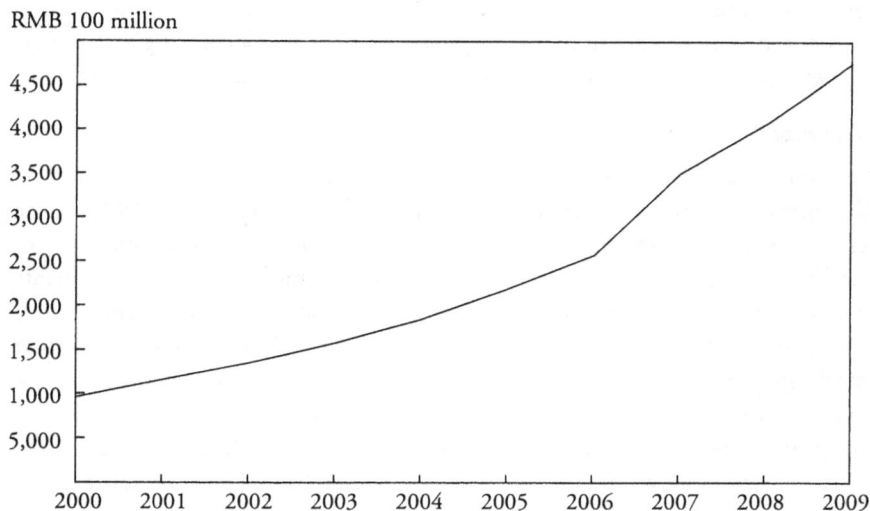

Source: Consolidated sheets of fiscal spending in various years, released by the Chinese Ministry of Finance on its official website (www.mof.gov.cn); *Zhongguo caizheng nianjian* [China fiscal yearbook], *Caizheng* (magazine), 2001–05.

on stability maintenance in Guangzhou topped RMB 4.4 billion in 2007, far exceeding the province's spending on social security and employment, which stood at RMB 3.52 billion.[21] Guangzhou's experience is not atypical.

China's public security spending from 2000 to 2009, as shown in figure 10-3, exhibits a trend of significant growth. Although 2005 was deemed by the central government as the year that saw an inflection point in the occurrence of petitions, China's spending on social stability maintenance and public security has actually increased. This indicates considerable rigidity in how social stability is handled. Given the present situation, it may be possible to maintain overall social stability, but there is no way the country can build a truly harmonious society. Therefore, the construction of a new interest coordination mechanism is not only a major challenge that must be faced but is also a natural step in China's ongoing social transformation.

An Interest Coordination Mechanism with Chinese Characteristics in the Making

Any organization or system has a process of adaptation, and the political system is no exception. Since the reform and opening up, China's has undergone a political evolution involving many layers and processes. In the construction of an interest coordination mechanism compatible with the market economy and an open environment, two aspects are important: optimizing public policymaking and exploring new approaches and methods of coordination between labor and capital.

Optimizing Public Policymaking

The optimization of public policymaking involves two dimensions. The first dimension concerns optimization of documentary politics. In the 1990s some scholars set about describing the process of China's top-level "documentary politics."[22] Although the process of drafting official documents continues to operate in a black box, there have been signs that some subtle yet significant changes are emerging. A review of the process for drafting party congress reports and other important documents since the 15th CCP National Congress shows that the political process is increasingly institutionalized. Once preliminary surveys and the establishment of a number of major issue areas have been completed, the process usually follows the following steps: the establishment of a leading group for report drafting; the taking of extensive opinion poll surveys on the major issue areas; consultation with various CCP departments and other governmental institutions as well as grassroots party organizations; the determination of the themes of the report; circulation of the report drafting plan among high-level leaders for comments; further surveys; circulation of the draft report for comments and approval among the high-level leaders; circulation of the draft report for comments both within the lower levels of CCP leadership and among key non-CCP elite; circulation of the draft report at the party congress or the plenum for discussion; and the delivery and approval of the report.

There are two features of the optimization of top-level documentary politics: the scientific determination and research of major issue areas and the expansion of the scope of hearing or comment solicitation. This decisionmaking process helps the ruling party draw on the wisdom of a wider array of people when making major policies so as to take into account different interests and reduce the risk of arbitrary policymaking.

The second dimension centers on increasingly open public policies. Although the optimization of the documentary politics has a strong elitist color, openness characterizes the changes in the middle and lower layers of China's political system, because they are the result of a synthesis of pressures from the top down and from the bottom up. The pressure from the bottom mainly stems from the people's growing awareness of their rights as citizens; an expanded space for expression provided by technological advances, especially communication technologies; the means of lawful confrontation and flexibility of interest articulation; the public sphere based on the modern media; and rapidly changing political culture and concepts (including the recognition of personal interests and confirmation of interest politics).

Top-down stress mainly comes from the active efforts of the central government. Through a series of documents, the central government has ordered the governments at various levels to advance scientific and democratic decisionmaking; improve their decisionmaking information and intelligence support system; strengthen the openness of government; safeguard citizens' rights to know, to participate, to express, and to supervise; solicit public opinion when adopting laws, regulations, and public policies that are closely related to the immediate interests of the people; and expand the channels for expression of social sentiment and public opinion and construct a platform supporting all forms of communication.

Pressure from the top and pressure from the bottom combine to help create many institutional innovations and promote their institutionalization. These include the practices of public hearing, democratic consultation, consultative dialogue, opinion pooling, information disclosure, administration transparency, and open-door decisionmaking. Indeed, the traditional model of public policymaking is undergoing changes that, though gradual, are both irreversible and significant.

The significance of the openness of public policymaking is the shift in the focus of interest politics from the end to the preliminary period of the policymaking process and from the passive response to complainants to the government's active participation in interest balancing. This change will have a far-reaching impact on China's political process.

Coordinating Labor and Capital Interests

The Decision of the CCP Central Committee Regarding Several Major Issues on Building a Harmonious Socialist Society adopted at the sixth plenary session of the 16th CCP National Congress in October 2006 was the first document of its kind to highlight the importance of labor relations, with an emphasis on developing harmonious labor relations and improving the existing labor relation coordination mechanism. The policy changes at the state level have caused a turning point in the development of relations between labor and capital.

Labor-capital relations involve many factors. It is generally understood that the labor contract system and the collective wage-negotiation system are two basic systems for coordinating labor-capital relations. In the presence of a labor contract, the core of labor-capital relations is the allocation of wealth. This means income to workers and labor cost to enterprises. In a given situation, there is a zero-sum relationship between the two—where one wanes, the other waxes. For example, when there is an adequate labor supply, the enterprises are in an advantageous position and the workers are in competition for the existing jobs. When the labor supply is tight, enterprises must compete for workers. It is thus easy to see why labor-capital relations can require the intervention of the government.

A tripartite mechanism—integrating the government, enterprises, and the trade unions (representing the workers)—serves both as a basic framework for the government to address issues in labor-capital relations and as a platform for trade unions to negotiate with enterprises on an equal footing. As the mediator in coordinating labor-capital relations, the government encourages enterprises to implement the collective wage-negotiation system and emphasizes that the trade union and the enterprise are equal in these negotiations. This system poses a serious challenge to the trade unions. China's trade unions served as a welfare organization in the planned economy era. Following China's economic transformation, however, when it comes to labor disputes, trade unions, regardless of the nature of the enterprises involved, usually do not represent the interests of the workers but instead speak for the enterprises. Obviously, China's trade unions must undergo an overhaul, and only after such problems as "puppet" trade unions, "crony" trade unions, and "ghost" trade unions (unions that exist only in name) are solved can the trade unions become capable of playing the role assigned to them in the tripartite mechanism.[23]

Despite the unsatisfactory nature of the situation, substantial improvements have already occurred. A number of innovative and effective methods have been introduced, including the following practices:

—The government now sends an offer for negotiation to enterprises that have not established or refuse to establish the collective wage-negotiation system or whose existing wage agreements are expected to expire soon, as well as to those that directly or in effect refuse to respond to the offer or issue an order of rectification.

—The trade union at the higher level performs part of the rights-defending obligations of enterprise-level trade unions, in which case the trade union at the higher level may, at the request of the labor union at the lower level, send personnel to negotiate with the enterprise on collective wage negotiation as its representatives.

—The core role of the presidents of trade unions has been strengthened, so that in some circumstances the president is democratically elected, and it is stipulated that enterprise managerial personnel shall not serve as the president or vice president of trade unions and that the termination of the labor contracts of trade union leaders shall consider the opinion of the trade union at the higher level.

—Trade union management has been increasingly professionalized.

—Efforts have been stepped up to strengthen the technical competence, particularly negotiation skills, of the staff representatives and their mentors participating in collective wage negotiations in order to solve the problems commonly seen in wage negotiations such as inequality, power imbalance, mismatch of competences, and information asymmetry.

—Efforts have been made to expand the awareness of labor rights and the legal means for their protection, as attested by the establishment of the official trade-union lawyer system by the All-China Federation of Trade Unions in 2006 and the first voluntary labor-related legal service group in Guangzhou in 2010.[24]

—The government has granted full scope to the role of the press, in directives such as the Regulations on Democratic Management of Enterprises in Guangdong Province, whose draft has the provision that "a collective wage negotiation may be initiated at the request of at least 20 percent of the total staff" and which puts the enterprises within the scope of the supervision of the media.[25]

At present, China is facing the challenge of economic transformation. The transition from export reliance to domestic consumption provides a beneficial environment in which ordinary workers can protect and advance their own rights and interests. In the economically developed coastal region, the role of some local governments has also been undergoing subtle changes. There is good cause to expect China's labor-capital relations to develop in the direction of benign interaction.

Open Discussion

As a late-starting developing country undergoing modernization and facing a shortage of domestic resources and also international pressures, China must concentrate its limited resources on key areas. To strive for long-term balance while accepting temporary imbalance and to accept partial sacrifices to strive for overall development is the basic spirit of this development strategy. This spirit has a remarkable influence on the landscape of China's interest politics.

Development Model and Institutional Adaptability

In the era of the planned economy, China's urban and industrial development came at the expense of the interests of the countryside and the farmers. The resulting dual urban-rural structure and the interest structure surrounding the household registration system have remained solid to this day. The reform and opening up has not changed this development logic. The concept of allowing a segment of the population to get rich first, in essence, is to have other people or regions bear a certain cost for jumpstarting the economy. In this sense, the allocation of resources among different strata of Chinese society and the existing interest structure are largely determined by China's development strategy. In different periods, there are different interest structures among different social strata owing to differences in the state's policy focus and resource allocation strategies.

The problem related to agriculture, the countryside, and the farmer problem is one example. After the implementation of the system of tax sharing between the central and local governments in 1994, the financially strained local and grassroots governments were forced to strengthen their fiscal revenues through excessive exploitation of rural resources, which directly led to an increased burden on farmers (though this was not an intended consequence). Conversely, the tax and fee reforms started in 2002 and the complete ending of taxes on farmers in 2004 thoroughly removed the root cause of a series of petitions and mass disturbances. At present, China's development strategy is at a critical period of transformation, as reflected in the growing frequency of use in government documents and in the public sphere of such expressions as public finance, service-oriented government, equal access to public services, social security, welfare policy, and civil rights. The new discourses and the related practices will have a deep influence on China's interest politics.

This has three implications for China's current interest politics and its future evolution. First, the imbalance of interests is an inevitable product of an imbalanced development strategy of modernization. Second, this problem, created by the development strategy, can be solved through the adjustment of public policies. Third, the period of heightened contradiction suggests that the party-state system faces serious challenges but also that it may eventually pass through this rough period. This author believes that China is undergoing a crisis in three realms—social, governance, and political—each with its own distinctive logic and, when combined, a greatly increased likelihood of political disorder.

There is a dynamic process where relative balance is achieved through overcoming difficulties and imbalances. This can occur when the preliminary success of this development strategy brings more economic resources, which are then used to supplement or reduce the interest imbalance caused by the development strategy. Indeed, many believe that only through maintaining economic growth can conflicts of interest caused by tension over resources be lessened. With the increase of public resources available to the government, there will be fewer situations where economic development is pursued at the expense of the interests of the people or where the government benefits itself at the expense of the people. As a result, there will be fewer mass disturbances caused by contradictions between officials and citizens. Many conflicts that used to seem unsolvable now can be ameliorated through the adjustment of public policies. The goal is to implement a benign mechanism of interaction. Such a system would both enable the government to allocate more resources for interest coordination and spur the transition of the country's development strategy, making the imbalanced development strategy gradually lose its reason for being. In this dynamic process, how

Figure 10-4. *The Transformation of China's Interest Politics*

Number of mass disturbances

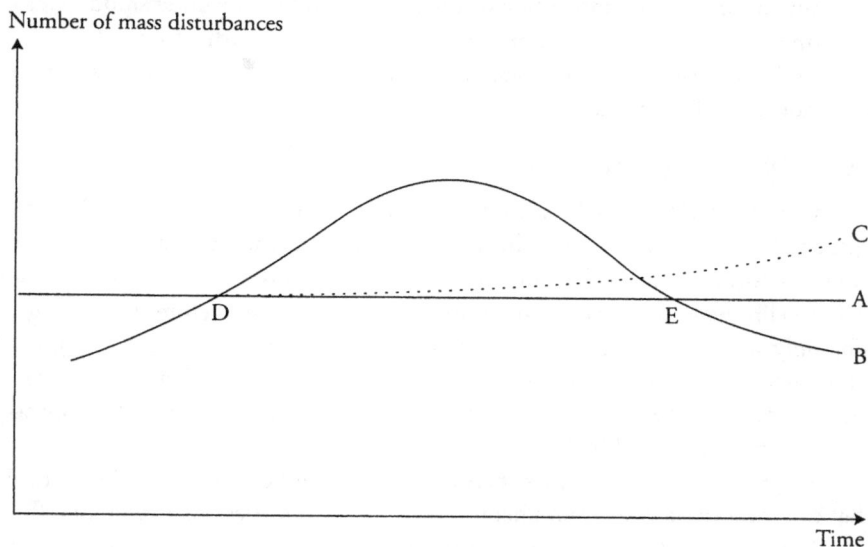

Time

Source: Author.

the state strikes a balance between the pressure of development and the need for benevolent paternalism will require extraordinary political wisdom.

If the three aspects of the dynamic transformation—the government's development strategy, the optimization of the public policymaking process, and the construction of a new labor-capital relationship—are combined with the top-down and bottom-up processes, one may expect the emergence of a relatively stable and elastic interest articulation and coordination mechanism and a subsequent transition from the existing situation of rigid social stability to one of soft or elastic social stability. The logical structure of this vision is shown in figure 10-4.

In figure 10-4, curve B denotes the number of interest conflict–related events, which will increase over a period of time before decreasing. The straight line A denotes the institutional capacity of the traditional interest coordination mechanism (the system of letters and calls, the mediation system, and so on), which will lose its normal functions when its institutional capacity is breached by line D, accompanied by the remarkable phenomenon of "disturbance paradox" and "petition cycle."[26] When point E is reached, the system's efficacy and functions gradually resume, and the negative effects begin to decline. The space between D and E represents the period of heightened contradiction. The curve C represents the expansionary capacity of the existing system through optimization of the government process and institutional construction and can be understood as representing the new methods and mechanisms of interest coordination.

Even if this vision cannot be ascertained empirically, it is a possible scenario that should not be excluded.

Institutionalized Space of Choice

A basic characteristic of China's reform and opening up is institutional development (institutionalization). This is also reflected in the development of new interest coordination mechanisms. In the words of Sun Liping, "It is not possible to eliminate interest contradictions and conflicts even before they emerge. The only way is institutionalization, which implies two things: first, it implies strengthening the system's accommodating capacity for contradictions and conflicts of interest; and second, it implies strengthening the ability to solve contradictions and conflicts of interests institutionally."[27]

The question now is whether there is only one kind of institutional structure that can meet these two requirements. Developing countries are inevitably influenced by their predecessors in modernization. It is only natural to consider the prior methods used to solve the problems arising from the modernization process to be universally effective. The historical experience of modernization, however, has shown that theoretical universality is always tested by reality. Our understanding of what does and does not work is far from complete.

Academically speaking, *institutional development* (or *institutionalization*) is a neutral term.[28] It means that the direction of institutional development is not fixed. When it comes to constructing a new interest coordination mechanism, China can draw on the systems and practices of Western countries but not necessarily copy them. With this understanding in mind, the CCP's practices in the new era might be seen as an exploration of the relationship between universality and peculiarity. An empirical model has perhaps already taken shape. Figures 10-5 and 10-6 contrast China's emerging interest politics model with the Western interest politics model of pluralism (using the United States as an example).

China's emerging interest politics model, which is structured within the party-state system, takes on markedly different characteristics, as shown in figure 10-6. The challenge of this model is whether it can eventually fully take shape and grow sustainably. To evaluate this question, we must move on to yet another question.

Unitarism and Pluralism

The term *unitarism* as used here means the long-term exclusive rule of a single entity, which by definition precludes the existence of political opposition. This is

Figure 10-5. *Interest Politics Model in the West*

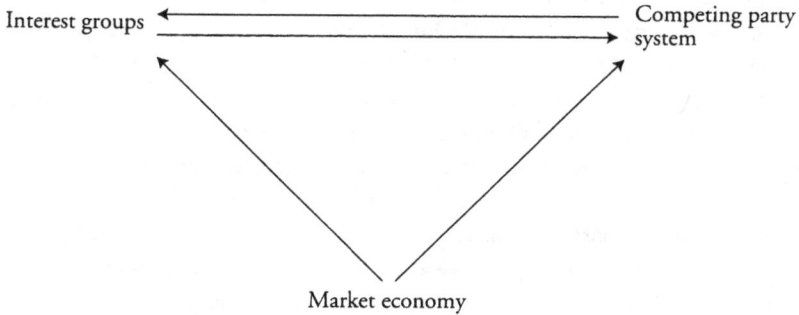

Interest groups ←————————————————— Competing party
                 ————————————————→ system

Market economy

Figure 10-6. *China's Interest Politics Model in the Making*

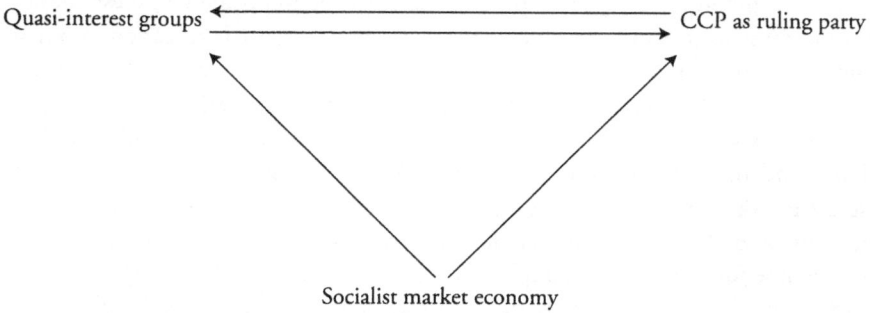

Quasi-interest groups ←————————————— CCP as ruling party

Socialist market economy

Source: Jing Yuejin, "Dangdai Zhongguo liyi chuanshu jizhi de zhuanhuan: Guanyu goujian 'hexie shehui' zhengzhi luoji de chubu sikao" [The transformation of the contemporary Chinese interest transmission mechanism: Preliminary thoughts on building the political logic of a "harmonious society"], in *Quanli, zeren, yu guojia*. [Power, responsibility, and the state], *Fudan zhengzhixue pinglun* [Fudan University political science review], no 4 (2006), p. 30.

what the CCP dictatorship of the proletariat or the people's democratic dictatorship means. Unitarism is both a political reality and a political aspiration of the ruling party, which aims to improve its ruling capacity and maintain its long-term ruling position by adapting to the changing environment.

The term *pluralism* as used here does not mean political pluralism (that is, a multiparty system) but refers instead to a pluralistic social structure and interest structure in the market economy. While opinions vary on other issues, people have reached a high degree of consensus that the harmonious society China is building is a pluralistic society.

The relationship between unitarism and pluralism in China poses a question: Can political unitarism be maintained alongside a pluralistic economic foundation and social interest structure? Our current understanding is mainly based on the developmental experiences of Western society, wherein social pluralism is matched with political pluralism. China's experience may point to another possibility. If the integration of a Leninist party and the market economy is a great but unprecedented miracle in the history of human society, then how to coordinate the relationship between the pluralistic interest structure and the unitary political system within the existing political framework represents a huge challenge facing the CCP. Some such attempts have already been made or are ongoing, including the transition from a revolutionary party to a ruling party and the wide variety of measures that have subsequently been adopted, including administrative skill building, administrative method transformation, the Three Represents theory, the building of a harmonious society, the absorption of emerging social strata, the scientific outlook on development, the construction of new interest coordination mechanisms and social-governance mechanisms, the permeation into new organizations and other new social spheres, and the cadre system reforms characterized by public selection, open government, and information transparency.

One view holds that there is an inherent conflict between the Communist Party and the market economy society. "With the pluralization of the social structure, the original simple political and social structure of 'the party, the proletariat, and the people' in fact no longer exists. And at the same time, it is impossible for the existing complicated interest structure to be fully reflected by the Party." "In an increasingly pluralistic society, the complicated and varying social interests cannot be expressed through a singular party. It is impossible for the CCP to represent the fundamental interests of the whole society (the people) as it did in the past. It can only represent the interests of one portion of the people and lose the chance to represent the interests of the rest of the people. This is an unsolvable dilemma."[29]

In reality, deductive theory tends to oversimplify things. With respect to the representation of interests, the Three Represents theory has two basic assumptions. The first is exclusiveness in the representation of fundamental interests, and the second is holistic representation. The former embodies political unitarism, and the latter stresses the long-term and fundamental interests of the nation and the country. Together, they provide an institutional and ethical basis for state autonomy (whether government autonomy or party autonomy) from different angles. Therefore, logistically, the Three Represents theory neither excludes other representatives of social interests nor denies the various specific interest articulation mechanisms. The practical challenge faced by the Chinese government is how to integrate the Three Represents theory with the changing social reality and maintain the inherent balance between government autonomy and the full articulation of interests in a new interest structure.

Conclusion

Whether a sound institutionalized method to handle interest contradictions and conflicts can be put in place has a bearing not only on the sustainability of China's economic growth and the maintenance of social stability but also on the basic direction of China's political development. If this bottleneck cannot be resolved, China's modernization may be hurt or even aborted.

If the focus on the conflicts of interest in the period of transformation is the basis of our thinking of the interest coordination mechanism, then a correct understanding of these conflicts is the methodological precondition for discussing the interest coordination mechanism. Accordingly, this chapter differentiates between two types of interest conflicts: that between officials and citizens and that between labor and capital. The former is caused by a variety of complex factors. In this chapter, prominence is given to the characteristics of the process of transformation, emphasizing that the creation and forms of contradictions between officials and citizens are closely related to the specific development strategies, resource allocation methods, and policy implementation processes adopted by the state. In this sense, many of these contradictions can be understood as problems of development that one hopes will lessen over the process of continued development. The labor-capital relationship, in contrast, has its own complexity. In addition to the factors mentioned above, it also has a structural dimension. In comparison with the interest conflicts between officials and citizens, the potential conflicts in labor-capital relations are inevitable and more enduring.

To deal with these two types of contradictions, interest coordination in the period of transformation must be sensitive to their differences. Within the existing system, contradictions between citizens and officials can be adjusted through such means as the opportune adjustment of the development strategy (that is, changes of resource allocation methods), the optimization of the public policymaking process, and the improvement of the governance mechanism. In the absence of interest organization, more effort can be made to develop the public sphere and encourage public participation in different ways. The goals would be to ensure that the policies of the governments at various levels are in the best interest of the people, thus reducing the opportunities for officials to benefit at the expense of the people. As for the handling of labor-capital relations, it is necessary to introduce new governance methods. The government should assume adequate independence and autonomy in this respect and develop a new tripartite interest coordination mechanism based on labor-capital consultation.

Although the reform and opening up has substantially changed China's political process, it has not fundamentally changed the institutional structure and basic mechanisms of Chinese politics. The continuity of the party-state system before and after the reform and opening up is clear. Both the reality of interest conflicts and the construction of the interest coordination mechanism take place within this framework. It provides a strong and highly restrictive module for China's emerging new interest coordination mechanism. In the words of the scholar Li Lulu, "Different institutional backgrounds lead to different systems and mechanisms for coordinating and integrating interest conflicts."[30]

During this period of transformation, it is necessary to maintain an open mind, both in terms of theoretical imagination and perceiving the empirical world. Practice is both the criterion for testing truth and the ruler by which to determine whether existing political theories (most of which are Western in origin) have universal applicability. In this respect, the construction of an interest coordination mechanism compatible with the market economy is an important field of practice.

COMMENT
CHENG LI

While assessments of China's political development are often remarkably divergent, there is considerable convergence in the recognition of the critical importance of Chinese interest groups. Scholars both in China and abroad agree that dynamic interest groups will help determine China's future political trajectory. Opinions on the nature of Chinese interest group politics, however, vary widely, especially regarding their scale and scope, their coordinating mechanisms and effective institutional responses, and their role in China's democratic transformation.

Jing Yuejin's chapter represents the sophisticated thinking of the mainstream Chinese scholarly community on the ever-growing role of interest groups in the country. His discussion of China's emerging interest groups is well grounded in empirical evidence, links closely to existing debates (both theoretical and policy based) in the field, and sheds valuable light on the necessity of major initiatives to reform China's political system. The author is candid and straightforward in acknowledging the daunting political challenges that China faces. Jing also offers a set of comprehensive coordinating mechanisms with which the Chinese leadership may be able to reconcile or even resolve the tensions and conflicts caused by competing interest groups.

For foreign students of Chinese politics, Jing's chapter also provides many data-rich observations and thought-provoking ideas to facilitate a better-structured intellectual dialogue. Such an exchange may not only reveal the areas in which Chinese scholars and their American colleagues agree or disagree but also help clarify deficiencies in research and analysis on both sides, such as prevalent misperceptions, blind spots, topical obsessions or inadequacies, and methodological missteps. A cross-country comparison may also be able to turn a deep-rooted fear of interest group politics into a cause for hope: that interest groups can foster a more institutionalized, orderly, peaceful, and democratic transition in China. Inspired by Jing's analysis, I would like to address the following two questions: What is the scale and scope of interest group politics in present-day China? In what direction and with what mechanisms should China institutionalize its interest group politics?

Scale and Scope of Interest Group Politics

Never in the six-decade history of the People's Republic of China have the Chinese leadership and the general public paid as much attention to interest groups as they have in recent years. Jing notes that in contrast to the early years of communist rule, when the concept of interest groups was politically taboo, China's current leadership has come to recognize the validity of individual and group interests. At the same time, the Chinese people have become conscious of their own rights and interests. Thus interest group politics have gained legitimacy in the eyes of both the Chinese political establishment and the general public.

As Jing observes, Chinese market reforms, particularly the rapid growth of the private sector since the 1990s, have been the primary source for the emergence of interest groups. As a result of market reforms over the past two decades, every major social class—peasants, workers, intellectuals, entrepreneurs, and cadres—has undergone profound changes. Additionally, substantially different subgroups have emerged from each of these classes. For example, within the traditional category of peasants, some are now peasants-turned-rural entrepreneurs and others have become migrant workers.

Jing highlights two important aspects of Chinese interest group politics: the role of vulnerable social groups (弱势群体, *ruoshi qunti*) and the growing role of corporate and industrial interest groups (工商企业利益集团, *gongshang qiye liyi jituan*). In Jing's words, "the former relates to the struggle of the weak to seek redress of their damaged interests, and the latter is an endeavor of the strong to maximize their profits" through the power-capital nexus. The way in which these two groups protect or advance their individual interests is profoundly different.

As Jing describes, the vulnerable social groups exert their grievances through petition letters, group appeals, and street protests. These types of activities often receive much media coverage, may cause social unrest, and can result in serious government crackdowns.

In contrast, corporate and industrial interest groups often exchange favors and make deals at such occasions or places as "hotel banquets, golf courses, and tourist resorts." Not surprisingly, a new term, "black-collar stratum" (黑领阶层, *heiling jieceng*) was recently created in China to refer to the increasing number of the rich and powerful who dress in black, drive black cars, have hidden incomes, live secret lives with concubines, have ties to the criminal underground (黑社会 *heishehui*, black society), and, most important, operate their businesses and wield their economic power in an opaque manner. The coinage of this new term reflects widespread resentment at the increasingly close associations between government officials and the business executives of large corporate and industrial firms.

Jing's focus on these two aspects of Chinese interest group politics is analytically appropriate. The growing prominence of these two groups not only reflects the two predominant tensions in present-day China—between officials and the masses (官民, *guanmin*) and between laborers and capitalists (劳资, *laozi*)—but also represents what are arguably the two most formidable political challenges to the legitimacy of the Chinese Communist regime. Jing is ambiguous, however, about whether these tensions constitute two long-term challenges or rather are simply temporary problems that have arisen as a result of immediate issues. He believes that as the Chinese government obtains more financial resources and uses them for social welfare, social protests will gradually decline. In my view, resources will remain limited as China faces serious demographic challenges in the years to come. These tensions reflect some of the major deficiencies of the Chinese political structure and its system of resource allocation, which will not be relieved through policy adjustments but rather will require systematic changes. Without a more representative and more institutionalized political framework, problems of distributive injustice will become increasingly acute.

As for the vulnerable social groups, their resentment and protests derive from a number of factors, such as growing economic disparity, inflation, social dislocation, political repression, environmental degradation, lack of work safety or job security, inadequacy of consumer rights, problems of internal migration, ethnic tensions, and official corruption. It would be naive to believe that the Chinese government will come up with an easy solution for any of these problems in the foreseeable future. On the contrary, the financial cost of maintaining social stability (维稳, *weiwen*), primarily through the police force, has become astonishingly high. As Jing notes, in 2007 Guangzhou spent as much as RMB 4.4 billion on its police force, a figure that exceeded the total cost of social welfare spending (RMB 3.5 billion) in the city that year. Nationwide, according to a recent Tsinghua University study, the total amount of money spent to maintain social stability in 2009 was RMB 514 billion, almost identical to China's total national defense budget (RMB 532 billion) in the same year.[31]

As for the corporate and industrial interest groups, they have exacerbated social injustice and public resentment. China's most active business interest groups consist mainly of two clusters. The first includes economic elites who work in state monopolized industries such as banking, oil, electricity, coal, telecommunications, aviation, and shipping; and the second consists of the lobby groups who work for state, foreign, or private firms in sectors such as real estate. It has been widely reported in the Chinese media that business interest groups have routinely bribed local officials and formed a "wicked coalition" with local governments.[32] The oligopoly of state-owned enterprises hurts the Chinese private enterprises and small business. This explains the wide use of a new Chinese concept, "the state advances and private companies retreat" (国进民退, *guojin mintui*) to criticize the growing trend toward a strong government with a weak society."

The various players associated with property development have emerged as one of the most powerful special interest groups in present-day China. According to Sun Liping, a sociology professor at Tsinghua University, the real estate interest group has accumulated tremendous economic and social capital during the past decade.[33] The group includes not only property developers, real estate agents, bankers, and housing market speculators but also some local officials and public intellectuals (economists and journalists) who promote the interests of that group. The power of this group explains why it took China thirteen years to pass the antimonopoly law, why the macroeconomic control policy in the mid 1990s was largely ineffective, and why the widely perceived property bubble in coastal cities has continued to grow. In each of these cases, corporate and industrial interest groups have encroached on the governmental decisionmaking process, either by creating government policy deadlock or manipulating policies in their own favor.

While the vulnerable social groups and the corporate and industrial interest groups are both crucial players in Chinese interest group politics, there are still many other major actors that are not adequately discussed or even mentioned in Jing's chapter. They include, for example, geographic regions, various bureaucratic institutions, the military, the increasingly commercialized media, nongovernmental organizations, and local governments. Local governments in the coastal and inland regions are political interest groups that exert strong influence in Beijing and work to ensure that the central government adopts policies that advance their regional interests. By way of background: in 2012, among China's 100 wealthiest counties, 93, including all of the top 40, are located in the coastal provinces.[34]

According to one recent study, nearly 90 percent of China's exports still come from the coastal provinces.[35] In the past few years, provincial and local governments' liaison offices in Beijing (驻京办, *zhujingban*), the region-based Chinese lobbying groups, have rapidly increased in number. In January 2010 the central government had to issue new regulations to substantially reduce the permitted number of these offices representing local interests and to require financial auditing of the remaining lobbying groups at the province and municipality levels.[36]

I take issue with Jing's argument that a majority of mass protests by vulnerable social groups in present-day China are nonpolitical. Although the specific demands of some of these mass protests might be economic or financial rather than political, interest group politics are by nature essentially political. Jing may reasonably argue that none of the major socioeconomic groups in China intend to challenge Chinese Communist Party rule, but it is not difficult to imagine that the party leadership may lose its mandate if it fails to address public resentments and concerns in this new domestic environment.

The most important interest group that determines China's political future, I would argue, is neither the black-collar stratum nor blue-collar workers but rather the white-collar members of China's emerging middle class. This important interest group is noticeably absent in Jing's analysis. China's new middle class has been a political ally for the Chinese Communist Party in its formative years, largely owing to their shared interest in maintaining social and political stability.[37] More recently, however, middle-class grievances directed at rampant official corruption and government policies that favor state-owned enterprise monopolies in several industrial sections have become increasingly evident.[38] The growing unemployment rate among recent college graduates (who usually come from middle-class families and are presumed to be members of China's future middle class) should also send an alarm to the Chinese government.

A recent study conducted by a Chinese scholar at the Chinese Academy of Social Sciences has found that if a large number of middle-class members feel that their voices are suppressed, that their access to information is blocked, or that their space for social action is confined, a political uprising will likely take place.[39] This study implies that what happened in South Korea and Brazil, in terms of middle classes' demand for direct elections, could also occur in China. Just as yesterday's political target could be today's political ally, so too could today's political ally become tomorrow's political rabble-rouser.

Mechanisms for Institutionalizing Interest Group Politics

Challenges arising from angry vulnerable social groups and greedy bureaucratic-corporate interest groups are not unique to reform-era China. Democracies in the West (and the East) are certainly not immune to these problems, and in fact, public petitions for social justice and protests against governments' domestic or foreign policies are often seen as part of normal socioeconomic and political life in many countries.

As for the corporate and industrial interest groups, they are probably equally powerful and influential in some Western countries than they are in China— if not more so. In the United States, for example, hundreds of lobby groups have flooded Washington, D.C., constituting an essential feature of American politics. From time to time, some powerful business lobby groups have been caught manipulating the democratic system for a company's commercial gain. As Theodore Lowi, a distinguished political science professor at Cornell University, observes, the U.S. government "expanded by responding to the demands of all major organized interests, by assuming responsibility for programs sought by those interests. . . . This in turn led to the formulation of new policies which tightened the grip of interest groups on the machinery of government."[40] Despite the apparent deficiencies of money politics in American democracy, *interest politics liberalism,* a term that Lowi has created, reflects the pluralistic competition that results from the broad expansion of public programs in the United States.

Lowi's notion of pluralistic competition has been further developed by Robert Dahl, a political science professor at Yale University, who argues that the development of Western democracies is a process dominated by many different sets of leaders, each having access to a different combination of political resources and representing the interests of different sectors and groups in society.[41] The democratic pluralistic system disperses power, influence, authority, and control away from any single group of power elites sharing the same social background toward a variety of individuals, groups, associations, and organizations.[42] In a sense, democracy is a matter of establishing rules for mediating conflicting interests among social groups in a given society. Yao Yang, a professor at Peking University, argues along the same lines: "An open and inclusive political process has generally checked the power of interest groups in advanced democracies such as the United States. Indeed, this is precisely the mandate of a disinterested government—to balance the demands of different social groups."[43]

In democracies, interest group politics are seen as neither a threat to sociopolitical stability nor a challenge to the legitimacy of the government Rather, they are regarded as necessary components for democratic governance. The key to coordinating interest group politics—as Lowi, Dahl, and Yao all seem to agree— is to establish institutional and democratic mechanisms. Various interest groups can exert their influence over presidential and congressional elections, bureaucratic decisionmaking, and judicial processes. In response, the independence of the media and the supremacy of the Constitution supervise and safeguard the democratic process. Although political crises do occur from time to time, democratic institutions in general and interest group politics in particular are not the source of sociopolitical instability but rather the foundation of long-term stability in a given country.

As the title of his chapter indicates, Jing wisely emphasizes the necessity of establishing a Chinese coordinating mechanism to institutionalize interest group politics. In particular, he recommends two sets of mechanisms. The first is the incremental opening of the public policymaking process, which could involve public hearings, democratic consultation and dialogue, opinion polls, and information disclosure. The second set, what Jing calls "tripartite mechanisms," involves consultation and negotiation among government, business groups, and trade unions representing workers. While these mechanisms can be helpful, they are perhaps not strong enough to respond effectively to pressures from either the vulnerable social groups or the corporate and industrial interest groups. The ineffectiveness of the first set of mechanisms has actually driven dissatisfied citizens to make louder noises in the public sphere.

Jing is apparently not enthusiastic about adopting the Western democratic system of a three-branch government and multiparty elections. This is, of course, a reasonable scholarly position, as each country's political development should be based on its own historical, cultural, and socioeconomic environment. But it seems to me that Jing goes too far in endorsing traditional paternalism for the political system in present-day China, arguing as he does that the Chinese leadership should search for a "balance between the pressure of development and the need for benevolent paternalism." In my view, paternalism associated with strongman politics is a bygone political idea for today's China. The country is now in fact led by a collective leadership with competing factions and coalitions.

I agree with Jing that it is not feasible for China to develop a multiparty political system in the near future. The defining characteristic of the Chinese political system at present is perhaps what Jing candidly calls a "party-state system," the one-party rule by the Chinese Communist Party. But this does not necessarily mean that the party leadership is a monolithic group of elites with the same socioeconomic backgrounds, professional careers, policy initiatives, and worldviews. I believe that the leadership consists of two informal and almost equally powerful competing political coalitions. These two groups can be identified as the populist coalition and the elitist coalition. Chinese leaders have begun using the term *intraparty democracy* to describe a party-state that has institutionalized checks and balances within its leadership.

These two coalitions represent two different socioeconomic classes and geographical regions. The elitist group represents the interest of the coastal region (by analogy, China's "blue states"), while the populist coalition often voices the concerns of the inland region (China's "red states"). The elitist coalition consists of princelings (太子党, *taizidang*), the Shanghai gang, entrepreneurs, and foreign-educated returnees. The populist coalition consists of Chinese Communist Youth league officials (团派, *tuanpai*) and often claims to represent the interests of farmers, migrant workers, and the urban poor. These two coalitions have contrasting policy initiatives and priorities. The elitist coalition emphasizes GDP growth, while the populist coalition advocates social justice and social cohesion. I call this new dynamic "one party, two coalitions."[44]

These two leadership groups have their own political resources and leadership expertise and together can represent different interest groups in the country, thus maintaining a healthy, constructive, and effective coordinating mechanism in the Chinese political system. The relationship between these two groups is both competitive and cooperative. A dynamic intraparty bipartisanship can help prevent the situation that Shen Mingmin (as quoted in Jing's chapter) describes: the Chinese Communist Party representing only one group of people (presumably the rich and powerful) in Chinese society.

That the competing coalitions in the party leadership can represent different socioeconomic groups and political constituencies may also make Jiang Zemin's theory of Three Represents more meaningful, as Jing suggests in his chapter. Most important, only in such an increasingly representative political system can Hu Jintao's notion of a harmonious socialist society become intellectually persuasive and practically concrete. One of the most important and urgent tasks for the Chinese leadership, therefore, is to make factional politics more transparent, representative, and legitimate in the Chinese political system.

Notes

1. Sun Liping, "Liyi shidai de chongtu yu hexie" [Conflict and harmony in the era of interest], *Nanfang zhoumo* [Southern weekly], December 30, 2004.

2. For detailed research on China's government-enterprise relationship, see Scott Kennedy, *The Business of Lobbying in China* (Harvard University Press, 2005).

3. Zou Dang, *Ershi shiji Zhongguo zhengzhi: Cong hongguan lishi yu weiguan xingdong jiaodu* [China politics in the twentieth century: From the perspective of history and action], Chinese ed. (Hong Kong: Oxford University Press, 1994); Sun Liping, "Guojia yu shehui de jiegou fenhua" [Structural differentiation of the state and the society], *Chinese Social Sciences Quarterly* (Hong Kong), no. 1 (1992).

4. "Tan xian jieduan fenpei bu gong: Putong laodongzhe shouru piandi" [Inequality of allocation in the current stage: Low income of ordinary laborers], *People's Daily Online,* July 9, 2011 (news.sina.com.cn/c/sd/2010-07-09/072020642618.shtml).

5. CCP Central Committee, *Zhonggong zhongyang guanyu goujian shehuizhuyi hexie shehui ruogan zhongda wenti de jueding* [Certain major decisions on the construction of a socialist harmonious society], October 18, 2006 (news.xinhuanet.com/politics/2006-10/18/content_5218639.htm).

6. Zeng Qinghong, "Jiaqiang dang de zhizheng nengli jianshe de ganglingxing wenxian" [A programmatic document on strengthening the ruling party's governance capacity], *People's Daily,* October 8, 2004.

7. The following data are particularly important: China's Gini coefficient breached the warning line of 0.4 in 2000, when it reached 0.417; China's GDP topped RMB 10 trillion for the first time in 2002; and China's per capita GDP topped USD 1,000 in 2003.

8. Wang Yongqian, "Guojia xinfang ju juzhang cheng: 80% shangfang you daoli" [SBLC chief: 80% of petitions reasonable], CCTV International News channel, November 20, 2003 (www.cctv.com/news/china/20031120/100764.shtml).

9. Hu Kui and Jiang Shu, "2003 nian Zhongguo zaoyu xinfang hongfeng, xin lingdaoren mianlin feichang kaoyan" [China encounters petition flood in 2003, new leaders face serious challenges], *Liaowang dongfang zhoukan* [Oriental outlook], no. 4 (2003).

10. Shao Daosheng, "Xinfang gongzuo: Jiang 'quntixing shijian' xiaomi yu wei mengqi" [SBLC: Eliminate the causes of mass disturbances], *Lianzheng liaowang* [Clean government watch], September 2005, p. 12.

11. Data from "Guojia xinfang ju fuzeren tan 'xinfang tiaolie' de guanche shishi qingkuang" [SBLC chief on the implementation of the regulations on complaint letters and petitions], *People's Daily Online,* April 29, 2006 (news.163.com/06/0429/13/2FSNTO6Q0001124J.html).

12. Wang Xuejun, "Jin yi bu jiaqiang he gaijin xin shiqi xinfang gongzuo" [Further strengthen and improve petition administration in the new period], *Qiushi* [Seek truth] no. 17 (2007). Whether the decrease in the number of petitions is related to the interception of petitions has yet to be ascertained. For reports about interception of petitioners, see "Waidi ganbu jin Jing jiefang xingcheng huise chanye lian" [Interception of petitioners as a grey industry chain], *Sina Online,* November 25, 2009 (news.163.com/09/1125/03/5OUG576D000120GR.html).

13. Wang Xuejun, "Jin yi bu jiaqiang he gaijin xin shiqi xinfang gongzuo."

14. This report was compiled by the Institute of Sociology of the Chinese Academy of Social Sciences, using data from research carried out from March to May 2006. The research covered 7,100 households, including 7,061 valid samples, in 520 villages or villager committees in 130 counties in 28 provinces, municipalities, and regions in the eastern, central, and western regions. Li Peilin and others, *Zhongguo shehui hexie wending baogao* [Social harmony and stability in China today] (Beijing: Social Sciences Academic Press, 2008)

15. Wang Yongqian, "Guojia xinfang ju juzhang cheng."

16. *Depoliticization* as used here does not mean that contradictions among the people are not political but rather that the existing system has been particularly sensitive to mass events after the 1989 protests. In this sense, *depoliticization* means a return to the normal state.

17. Yu Jianrong, "Quntixing shijian zhengjie zai yu guanmin maodun" [The official-citizen contradiction behind mass disturbances], *Zhongguo baodao* [China report], no. 1 (2010) (www.china.com.cn/book/zhuanti/qkjc/txt/2010-01/13/content_19228539.htm).

18. Yang Jingyu, chairman of the Legal Committee of the National People's Congress, has acknowledged the problems that resulted from sacrificing the lawful rights and interests of laborers in the rush to attract investments in some places. "Laodong hetongfa jiang yange zhuijiu laodong bumen bu zuowei" [Labor contract law to punish dereliction of duty of labor departments], *China Business News,* July 24, 2007.

19. Li Lulu, "Hexie shehui: Liyi maodun yu chongtu de xietiao" [Harmonious society: Coordination of interest contradictions and conflicts], *Tansuo yu zhengming* [Exploration and free views], no. 5 (2005), p. 2.

20. Under China's centralized system, the upper-level governments determine the allocation of honors, benefits, and promotions among lower-level officials by referring to their performance on various evaluation "indicators." In this process, some indicators were prioritized. For instance, *zero target* referred to certain events that the upper-level government deemed should not take place in the areas governed by lower-level governments. Under a *veto system,* if some important tasks were not met or serious accidents occurred in a given locality, the upper-level government would negate all the work of the lower-level government, even though the latter might perform well in terms of other indicators.

21. Xiao Shu, "Gao'ang weiwen chengben weihe nan jiang" [Why is it difficult for the expensive stability maintenance cost to go down?], *Dongfang zaobao* [Oriental morning post], June 26, 2009, p. A23.

22. The concept of documentary politics was put forward by Guoguang Wu, "Documentary Politics: Hypotheses, Process, and Case Studies," in *Decisionmaking in Deng's China,* edited by Carol Lee Hamrin and Suisheng Zhao (Armonk, N.Y.: M. E. Sharpe, 1995), pp. 24–38.

23. Xu Deming, "Shenru guanche luoshi 'qiye gonghui gongzuo tiaolie' nuli tigao qiye gonghui gongzuo shuiping" [Implement the provisions on the work of enterprise trade unions and improve the trade union work of enterprises], speech delivered to the class on the implementation of the provisions on the work of enterprise trade unions, May 10, 2007 (www.acftu.org/template/10004/file.jsp?cid=318&aid=72556).

24. Since the 1990s, China has been piloting an "official lawyer system" by encouraging state organs and government organizations to hire professional lawyers, who are tasked with providing legal consultancy as well as engaging in administrative suits on behalf of the government. In 2005 the National Federation of Trade Unions started to pilot an official lawyer system, which was later implemented in all trade unions in China. Official lawyers in China's trade unions are tasked with engaging in the drafting of certain laws and regulations, providing legal suggestions, engaging in the investigation on trade union–related illegal activities, and providing legal assistance to trade union members, among other things.

25. "Guangdong ni guiding gonghui ke gongkai qianze bu zuowei qiye" [Guangdong plans to authorize trade unions to condemn enterprises for dereliction of duty], Dayoo.com and *Guangzhou ribao* [Guangzhou daily], August 5, 2010 (news.sina.com.cn/c/2010-08-05/040420828472.shtml).

26. *Disturbance paradox* refers to the phenomenon in China whereby the petitioners tend to purposely confront the government in hope of achieving a better solution. Designed to alleviate or resolve conflicts, China's petition system actually tends to intensify some disputes and conflicts. *Petition cycle* refers to an imbalanced cycle in China's government process: on one hand, the government needs to know about people's appeals and concerns through the petition system; on the other hand, however, when such appeals become too vehement, the upper-level government feels uneasy and then transfers the pressure to the lower-level governments.

27. Sun Liping, "Jianli shichang jingji tiaojian xia de liyi junheng jizhi" [Establish an interest coordination mechanism compatible with the market economy], *Nanfang dushi bao pinglun zhoukan* [Southern metropolis weekly], December 28, 2008.

28. Samuel P. Huntington demarcates "institutionalization" as follows: "Institutionalization is the process by which organizations and procedures acquire value and stability. Its level may be defined by the complexity and coherence of organizations and procedures as they lead to adaptability and autonomy." Huntington, *Biange shehui zhong de zhengzhi chengxu* [Political order in changing societies], translated by Li Shengping (Beijing: Huaxia Publishing House, 1988), pp. 12–13.

29. Shen Mingmin, "Zhengzhi zhuanbian zhong de Zhongguo gongchangdang" [The CCP in political transformation], *Ershiyi shiji (wangluo ban)* [Twenty-first century, online edition], no. 38 (May 31, 2005).

30. Li, "Hexie shehui," p. 2.

31. Qinghua daxue shehuixuexi shehui fazhan yanjiu ketizu [Research team of social development of the Department of Sociology at Tsinghua University], "Weiwen xinsilu" [New idea about maintaining social stability], *Nanfang Zhoumo* [Southern weekend], April 15, 2010. Also *Shijie ribao* [World journal], October 15, 2010, p. A3.

32. *Zhongguo xinwen zhoukan* [China newsweek], January 13, 2006; *Liaowang xinwen zhoukan* [Outlook newsweek], December 5, 2005; also see Chinese Newsnet (www.chinesenewsnet.com), December 12, 2005.

33. Sun Liping, "Zhongguo jinru liyi boyi de shidai" [China is entering the era of the conflict of interests], February 6, 2006 (http://chinesenewsnet.com).

34. See www.360doc.com/content/13/0629/21/1542087_296426923.shtml.

35. Yao Yang, "The End of the Beijing Consensus: Can China's Model of Authoritarian Growth Survive?" *Foreign Affairs*, February 2, 2010 (www.foreignaffairs.com/articles/65947/the-end-of-the-beijing-consensus).

36. *Liaowang xinwen zhoukan* [Outlook newsweek], January 23, 2010.

37. Jie Chen and Bruce J. Dickson, *Allies of the State: China's Private Entrepreneurs and Democratic Change* (Harvard University Press, 2010).

38. Zhang Yi, "Dangdai Zhongguo zhongchan jieceng de zhengzhi taidu" [Political attitudes of the middle stratum in contemporary China], *Zhongguo shehui kexue* [Chinese social sciences], no. 2 (Summer 2008).

39. Ibid.

40. Theodore Lowi, *The End of Liberalism: The Second Republic of the United States* (New York: W.W. Norton, 1979), dust jacket.

41. Robert Dahl, *Who Governs? Democracy and Power in an American City* (Yale University Press, 1961), p. 68.

42. Ibid., pp. 252, 270.

43. Yao, "The End of the Beijing Consensus."

44. For a more detailed discussion of this formulation, see Cheng Li, "The New Bipartisanship within the Chinese Communist Party," *Orbis* 49, no. 3 (summer 2005), pp. 387–400.

11

Contemporary China's Decisionmaking System

ZHOU GUANGHUI

lthough the reform and opening up has brought extensive and profound
changes to Chinese society, the basic pattern of state-led social development has not changed. The state's leadership is basically realized through public policy formulation and implementation. To better understand China's development, therefore, we must look at the decisionmaking system that determines and influences contemporary Chinese policy. As noted by Carol Lee Hamrin, "Reform of the Chinese system in the 1980s proceeded in cycles or waves, rather than a straight linear fashion."[1] Each cycle began with a new policy initiated by reform leaders. The main purpose of this chapter is not to explore how China's decisionmaking system has influenced the country's development but rather to discuss the formation of this decisionmaking system and its basic characteristics, rationality, problems and crises, and changes and trends. The analysis of these variables draws on the historical institutional analytical method as well as political development theory.

The Formation of China's Decisionmaking System

Political decisions have a strong bearing on the direction of national and social development, the authoritative allocation of social resources, and the expression of volition and the balance of interests for different political participants and interest groups that seek to influence the decisionmaking process. In this sense, the political decisionmaking process is essentially a course of interest compromise, game playing, and balance of interests. Modern political theories take evaluation of the actual decisionmaking process as an important method of political analysis. A historical institutional analysis analyzes the political process from the perspective of the institutional system. The institutional system is a set of rules or norms that governs interpersonal interaction and cooperation.

Owing to constant changes in the preferences of decisionmakers, subjectivity of motivations, the information available, and the situations faced, it is often difficult to understand the specific process of and the real motives behind major decisions. However, the actual context of policy formation can be explored by analyzing the causal relationships among the major variables of the decisionmaking system. It is in this sense that Douglass North has noted that "the past can be understood only as a process of institutional evolution."[2] According to Sven Steinmo, "Institutions structure politics because they: 1) define who is able to participate in the particular political arena, (2) shape the various actors' political strategies, and (3) influence what these actors believe to be both possible and desirable (i.e., their preferences)."[3] National policies are the core content of political decisionmaking, which is a process whereby individuals, political organizations (parties), or governments formulate and choose action plans concerning the direction, goals, principles, methods, and procedures of national and social development; the important issues in social and public life; and the adjustment of important interest relations. Practically speaking, the leadership of a ruling party is conceived by making and implementing political decisions.

Generally, decisionmaking refers to "the process by which a solution is chosen to be implemented. The formation of a decision usually requires a decisionmaker (the person who makes the final choice) and a decisionmaking body (a group, organization, or government composed of all persons participating in the decisionmaking process), who analyze information, establish goals, put forward and assess various solutions, and arrive at a conclusion for responding to a problem or a series of problems."[4] The decisionmaking structure, mode, and mechanisms are three major interrelated parts of the decisionmaking system.

These elements have changed considerably with the reform and opening up, though the Chinese Communist Party's leading role in the decisionmaking system has remained unchanged. This paradox has resulted in controversies over the course of China's political reforms.

Formation of China's Decisionmaking System

Elements of China's present decisionmaking system were in place before 1949 but took formal shape in the early years of the People's Republic of China (PRC). At the top level, it consists of five constituent parts: the party, government, army, law, and people. *Party* refers to the ruling party and other parties participating in the management of state affairs. *Government* encompasses the National People's Congress (NPC) and its standing committee and the State Council. *Army* refers to the Central Military Commission. *Law* comprises the Supreme People's Court and the Supreme People's Procuratorate. *People,* in its narrow sense, stands for citizens and social groups without official duties. These five bodies have a center and four relationships.

At the center is the Chinese Communist Party (CCP), the core of the decisionmaking system. Article 15 of the CCP constitution states that "only the CCP Central Committee reserves the power to make decisions on national policies; departments and local Party organizations may make proposals but shall not make decisions or make announcements."[5] The Politburo of the CCP Central Committee and its standing committee exercise the powers of the CCP Central Committee when the latter is not in session. This means the Politburo and its standing committee, whose administration office is the Secretariat of the CCP Central Committee, are the de facto decisionmaking bodies.

The four relationships in the decisionmaking system are those between party and government, party and army, ruling party and parties participating in the management of state affairs, and party and the people or the masses. This last relationship is a noninstitutionalized one in the decisionmaking process. Since the Central Committee previously would release documents on major decisions formally in the names of the Central Committee, the State Council, and the Central Military Commission, foreign scholars termed it a "party-government-army" decisionmaking system (*government* is used hereafter as broad term that incorporates regime, the government, political laws, and so forth).[6]

From the perspective of the allocation of decisionmaking powers, the party-government relationship is the most fundamental and complex of all. The CCP Central Committee, especially the Politburo of the CCP Central Committee, has long worked closely with the State Council, and they developed the practice of cosigning documents on important decisions. Since the late 1990s, with the standardized division of duties between the party and the government, such forms of cooperation have been less frequent, but the practice of cosigning documents has continued. The Outline of China's National Plan for Medium and Long-Term Education Reform and Development (2010–20), for example, was jointly issued by the CCP Central Committee and the State Council on July 8, 2010. According to the principle of CCP leadership and other long-standing norms, at its full or executive meetings the State Council discusses and makes decisions on national economic and social development plans, national budgets, major macroeconomic policies, important state and social management affairs,

legislative proposals, and administrative regulations. It then must submit its findings to the Politburo for discussion and approval.[7]

There is no provision for the establishment of the leading groups of the CCP
Central Committee in chapter 3 (Central Committee Organizations) of the CCP
constitution. However, the notice on the CCP Central Committee's decision to
establish five leading groups (finance and economics, politics and law, foreign
affairs, science, and culture and education) on June 10, 1958, stated that "these
teams are affiliated organizations of the Politburo of the CCP Central Committee and the Secretariat of the Central Committee and report directly to them.
The Politburo deals with overall policies and the Secretariat deals with deployment."[8] These leading groups have not only played a vital role in the Politburo's
decisionmaking but also extended the functions of the CCP Central Committee's departments from managing cadres to the work conducted by the State
Council's departments. They play the important role of coordinating the party-
government relationship to some extent.

The leadership of the CCP in China's decisionmaking system is neither self-
appointed nor imposed by force. Rather, it is a result of the long historical process by which the CCP led the Chinese people to seek national independence
and national unification. On September 15, 1954, the first session of the 1st
National People's Congress of the PRC was held, during which the Constitution
and related laws were passed. Based on these laws, the chairman of the PRC, the
NPC Standing Committee, the State Council, the Supreme People's Court, and
the Supreme People's Procuratorate were first elected. This was the official start
of the CCP-centered decisionmaking system.

Historical Rationality of China's Decisionmaking System

The formation of China's decisionmaking system shows that the position and
role of the CCP in the decisionmaking system evolved over a long revolutionary history. At the time of the founding of the PRC, China was still a backward
agricultural country dominated by a small-scale peasant economy and facing the
arduous task of industrialization. In addition, not only was China internally seriously divided but on the international stage it was an insignificant developing
country that had just achieved national independence. The Chinese now faced
the important tasks of putting an end to internal division, achieving political
integration, and maintaining the country's sovereignty and unification; putting
an end to social disorder and reestablishing political order; and changing China
from a weak and poor country to a strong industrial country. The accomplishment of these tasks required the strong authority of the CCP Central Committee.
The decisionmaking system established in the early years following the founding

of the PRC played a vital role in asserting the CCP Central Committee's authority, integrating society, and rebuilding social order. According to historical institutional analysis, the effectiveness and adaptability of a system can be understood from the historical process of the interaction of its political and economic spheres.

From a political perspective, Chinese society had long been polarized and stratified, leaving it in severe disarray throughout the beginning of the modern era. One reason was intervention by external forces. Internally, the collapse of central authority posed a huge challenge to political integration, and because decisions could not be implemented effectively at the grassroots level, anarchy spread across society. The decisionmaking system established in the early years of the PRC had three major characteristics. First, decisionmaking powers were centralized in the CCP, specifically in the Politburo. Second, once a decision was made, no other state organ or individual could change or oppose it but instead had to implement it resolutely. Third, decisions made by the Central Committee were implemented by organizations at all levels, from the Central Committee to grassroots bodies across the country. Such a system guaranteed the CCP's political leadership and promoted political integration among the central and local governments, grassroots organizations, and individuals. As long as decisions could be implemented effectively at the grass roots, the people would gradually accept the CCP's decisions.

This centralized system put in place in the early period of the PRC solved the problem of differentiation of political power and weak leadership of the central government and effectively safeguarded the political authority of the CCP Central Committee. At the same time, party organizations at all levels were able to convey the CCP's decisions to grassroots units, ensuring that central policies would be implemented effectively on a national scale. Yes, China did have the problem of going to extremes—such as what occurred in the Suppression of Counterrevolutionaries movement and the Three-Anti and Five-Anti Campaigns. But without a unified and centralized decisionmaking system and its timely, decisive, and effective responses to various crises, the new government would have been unable to survive the complicated situation of the early PRC period.

China was an agricultural country that had been dominated by a small-scale peasant economy for thousands of years. Despite facing the twin pressures of modernization and bullying by world powers, however, China still firmly pursued industrialization. If the achievement of national independence and unification was the political theme in the first stage of China's modernization, then the accomplishment of industrialization was to be the economic theme in the next stage. Industrialization necessitates the pooling of all social resources, which in turn requires a powerful central authority. With efficient administrative intervention and resource-pooling capabilities, the decisionmaking system that developed in China created the ideal political conditions for the rebuilding of the economy and social order.

The period from the founding of the People's Republic in 1949 to completion of the 1st Five-Year Plan in 1957 was marked by an exceptionally rapid pace of both reform and economic development. Within only three years, China restored its national economy and laid a solid foundation for industrialization by initiating 156 major construction projects. For a large economically backward country with an 80 percent illiteracy rate, complex ethnic divisions, and distinct regional disparities, such political integration, resource integration, and modernization could not have occurred without a centralized and authoritative decisionmaking system.

Characteristics, Problems, and Crises of China's Decisionmaking System

Given that China's historical experience and political party system are different from those of the West, the governing CCP has played a different role in the decisionmaking system from that of its Western contemporaries. Western countries have adopted a competitive party system. In general, any party that wins the general election becomes the ruling party and recommends party members to represent the people, indirectly, in government. In contrast, China has not implemented such a competitive multiparty system. This means first and foremost that the CCP has a leading position in China's decisionmaking system. It does not parallel, but rather leads, all other decisionmaking bodies. Every state organ performs its duties under the CCP's direct leadership, which is accomplished mainly by drawing up legislation, itineraries, guidelines, and policies. The expression "The party commands the gun" vividly captures the relationship between the party and the military. The relationship between the CCP and the various democratic parties is one between the ruling party and the participatory parties in the state power system. It is firmly reflected in the multiparty cooperation that occurs under the leadership of the CCP and political consultation on major decisions. Second, the CCP maintains its leading role in the decisionmaking system on a permanent basis. One has to bear in mind these two characteristics to understand the fundamental difference between the decisionmaking systems of China and the West.

Major Problems of the Decisionmaking System in the Early Period of the PRC

The decisionmaking system formed in the early period of the PRC experienced three main problems regarding, respectively, the decisionmaking structure, mode, and mechanisms. First, the decisionmaking structure stressed vertical allocation of decisionmaking power but overlooked the horizontal functional division of labor. In the early years of its founding, the CCP basically copied the model of the Communist Party of the Soviet Union by establishing strictly disciplined hierarchical organizations and centralizing power in the hands of the Central Committee. During prolonged revolutionary wars, the party's major task was to lead armed struggle; party organizations were thus deeply influenced by military activities. As a result, the party's organizational structure bears some resemblance to the army. At the same time, the CCP's centralized leadership was reinforced in the army, so that the army became used to giving orders in the name of the CCP.

After the founding of the PRC, a campaign against decentralism and localism was launched nationwide. This campaign neglected the horizontal development of the decisionmaking system, which led to a lack of division of responsibilities between the party and government, and power became largely concentrated in the party, especially in the CCP Central Committee. Consequently, the decisionmaking functions of other state organs could not operate as they were designed; in some cases they were even replaced outright by the party.

With decisionmaking power highly concentrated in the CCP Central Committee in a manner that lacked both an institutional arrangement for public participation and transparency, it was difficult for citizens to take part in the formulation of public policies. In spite of strong organization and mobilization capabilities, this decisionmaking system proved very weak in reflecting the needs of the grassroots masses. This lack of public participation and articulation of different interests discouraged innovation. With decisions largely dependent on the decisionmakers' understanding of the interests of the people, any major mistake in that understanding would have a direct impact on the credibility of decisions and could result in a legitimacy crisis of the decisionmaking system. Although in the initial period of the PRC the party's Central Committee sought out the opinions of the representatives of people's organizations and democratic parties in making the major decisions, the participants in these people's organization and democratic parties were themselves elites and clearly reflected the particular characteristics of elite decisionmaking.

Second, the method of decisionmaking was problematic in a couple of ways. It lacked a strong scientific basis. Those decisionmakers who managed to survive the war were accustomed to making decisions by virtue of their rich experience rather than by the use of scientific methods. Experience-based decisionmaking, being characterized by convenience, low cost, flexibility, and quick response, is helpful in times of war. This approach is, however, out of place in a period of peace, especially for a country pursuing large-scale economic construction.

Moreover, the decisionmaking method lacked transparency, a problem that can be traced to three factors: the legacy of confidentiality from the war; a lack of scientific classification of decisions involving national security and military issues that should be kept confidential versus those involving the public interest that should be made public; and a tendency for decisionmaking disagreements to be linked with class antagonism. In this opaque decisionmaking process disagreements were concealed lest they be misinterpreted as a split within the party.

Third, and finally, the mechanisms of decisionmaking had other major problems. Decisionmaking in China was characterized by a low level of institutionalization, and decisionmaking procedures had no rigid constraints. These issues undermined the stability, predictability, standardization, objectivity, and continuity of the decisionmaking process. The decisionmaking mechanisms were inefficient and could not function normally; channels for communication of information were rough, and there was a limited role for expert consultations and supervisory bodies. The feedback and coordination mechanisms and the accountability systems, which are integral to a complete decisionmaking mechanism, were nonexistent. And, under the life-tenure cadre system, decisionmakers had no term limits. As a result, the decisionmaking system had no self-corrective function, and erroneous decisions, which could bring serious consequences, could not be suspended in a timely fashion.

Crises of the Decisionmaking System before the Reform and Opening-Up Period

According to historical institutionalism, a system develops under certain social, economic, and cultural conditions. A particular historical background translates into a particular path dependence for future evolution. Douglass North has pointed out that "the choices people made in the past will determine what choices they may make now."[9] Immediately after seizing political power, the CCP was active in promoting democracy within the party. At the 8th CCP National Congress, convened in September 1956, major decisions were made to improve the system of democratic centralism, establish the CCP Standing Committee and the tenure system of party leaders, and expand intraparty democracy at all levels of party organization.[10]

These decisions were not implemented immediately after the meeting, however, or translated into specific binding organizational systems and mechanisms. The success of the Central Committee's decisionmaking process in its early years only served to nourish conceit and complacency among major CCP leaders as time went on. The CCP was accustomed to working under the banner of revolutionary wars, political campaigns, and large-scale mass movements, just as it had built its authority through political revolution. In this period, the highly central-ized structure of the CCP's decisionmaking system was only reinforced. Under the slogan of strengthening the party's absolute unitary leadership and through the struggle between different political factions within the party, decisionmaking power became increasingly centralized. When the Cultural Revolution began, the decisionmaking powers of the CCP Central Committee were centralized within the party's core leadership.

Such a highly centralized decisionmaking system had several disadvantages. First, when power is centralized in the hands of individuals, other decisionmak-ing organs cannot perform their functions normally. Individuals, of course, have their shortcomings and can often make wrong decisions. The Great Leap For-ward, for instance, caused staggering losses for the country.

Second, with no tenure limits for decisionmakers, the decisionmaking system had no mechanism to correct decisions, even in the case of major errors. The Cultural Revolution took place and was allowed to last close to ten years not only because of Mao Zedong's leadership but also, and most important, because of how the system was institutionalized at that time. If what triggered the Cul-tural Revolution was the highly centralized decisionmaking system, then what sustained it for so long was the lifelong tenure of the top leadership.

Third, without institutionalized procedures, the decisionmaking process was subject to change and hard to predict. Since the founding of the PRC, the nation had spent so much effort on large-scale mass movements that it had overlooked institutional construction, thus further centralizing decisionmaking power and making the existing policies and procedures a mere formality. Conferences of the Politburo, and even the NPC and the CCP National Congress, could not be held as scheduled. There was a gap of ten years between the third and fourth national people's congresses, and one of thirteen years between the eighth and ninth CCP national congresses.

In spite of its emphasis on the path dependence of a system, historical insti-tutionalism also admits that when the cost of maintaining the system becomes unsustainable, the system will inevitably change. Deng Xiaoping once observed, "The lessons of the Cultural Revolution tell us that there will be no way out if we do not reform or formulate new political, economic, and social policies."[11] In this regard, the institutional crisis helped a consensus form between the CCP and the people that only reform could extricate the nation from its predicament.

Changes in Contemporary China's Decisionmaking System

The reform of contemporary China's decisionmaking system initiated at the end of 1978 is a primary focus of China's reform and opening-up policy. According to the political theory of new institutionalism, institutional change can be either spontaneously induced or initiated by government coercion. The reform of China's decisionmaking system belongs to the latter type and was led by the CCP.

The third plenary session of the 11th CCP Central Committee held in 1978 not only realized a strategic shift in the party's central task from class struggle to economic development but also began the process of reform of China's decisionmaking system. On August 18, 1980, at an expanded meeting of the Politburo, Deng Xiaoping delivered a speech entitled "On the Reform of the System of Party and State Leadership," proposing the task of reforming the party and state's political decisionmaking system. On July 31, 1986, in a speech entitled "Democratic and Scientific Decisionmaking Is an Important Topic of Political Reform," Vice Premier Wan Li clearly stated that the basic objective of reform of the decisionmaking system was to realize democratic and scientific decisionmaking.[12] This speech represented the collective will of the CCP Central Committee.

In 1987, in its political report to the 13th National Congress of the CCP, the party raised the issue of democratic and scientific decisionmaking. This was the first time in the CCP's history that a proposal on the issue was made in an official document. This meant that the promotion of democratic and scientific decisionmaking had become the will of the party. In November 2002, in his political report to the 16th National Congress of the CCP, Jiang Zemin remarked that "correct decisionmaking is an important prerequisite for success in all work" and proposed general requirements for reform and improvement of the decisionmaking mechanism.[13] In October 2007, in the political report to the 17th National Congress of the CCP, Hu Jintao stressed the need to "expand the citizens' orderly participation in political affairs at each level and in every field," and he pointed out that the focus of scientific and democratic decisionmaking was "to increase transparency and expand public participation."[14] Four aspects of the reform of China's decisionmaking system—its objectives, structure, modes, and mechanisms—are discussed below.

Objectives of Decisionmaking Reform

Placing decisionmaking on a more scientific, democratic, and rule-of-law basis is a manifestation of the inner logic of the process of the CCP's transition from a revolutionary to a ruling party and is also an objective requirement for implementing a modern decisionmaking system. If we say that democratic decisionmaking reflects value rationality, then scientific decisionmaking governed by the rule of law reflects instrumental rationality. The objective of reform is searching for democratic, scientific, and law-based decisionmaking, which was one of the painful lessons of the Cultural Revolution. It also expressed a renewed understanding of the laws of building socialism and the correct comprehension of the

CCP's style of governance, as well as a deep understanding of the laws of decisionmaking. A correctly defined objective not only indicates the direction for reform of decisionmaking structures, mechanisms, and modes but also provides a path for the reform of the specific contents of the decisionmaking system.

Structure of Decisionmaking

Reforming the highly centralized structure of decisionmaking power is an objective requirement for realizing democratic and scientific decisionmaking. After years of reform, China has developed a six-part decisionmaking structure of unified leadership and pluralistic participation.

—Under the prerequisite of maintaining the leadership of the CCP, attention has been paid to the horizontal division of decisionmaking power whereby public power has been rationally divided, legalized, and institutionalized according to the different functions of the ruling party and state organs. This is a significant change from the past, when there was no distinction between the responsibilities of the party and those of the government, when the former was substituted for the latter, and when the party decided everything. The CCP constitution adopted at the 12th CCP National Congress states that "the Party must conduct its activities within the framework of the Constitution and other laws. It must ensure that the legislative, judicial, and administrative organs of the state . . . work with initiative and independent responsibility and in harmony."[15] This provided the legal basis for clarifying the relationship between the CCP and organs of the state. First, it makes clear that the party's decisionmaking must be completed in accordance with the law and that it is only after statutory procedures that the guidelines and policies formulated by the party can be raised to the level of national will and thence become laws or public policies. Second, the CCP must ensure that the state legislative, administrative, and judiciary organs exercise their respective powers and function independently in accordance with the constitution and the law. The statement above is the first time in the history of the CCP that the party has been placed under the constraints of the law. This disallows the previous practice of party members and leaders putting personal views above the law and substituting policy for law. This also indicates that China has started a historical transition from the rule of man to the rule of law.

To adapt to this change in the party's style of leadership, all organizational forms and organs of the CCP from the central to the local level have been adjusted. Party secretaries or members of the party's standing committee are no longer specially appointed to take charge of government affairs without a government post. Agencies that overlap with government departments have been removed, leaving the management of administrative affairs to the relevant government department. In general, decisions on affairs within the sphere of responsibility and authority of the State Council are no longer made in the party's name. For example, to deal with the global financial crisis, the State Council held an executive meeting on November 8, 2008, to discuss and then formally announce measures to further expand domestic demand and promote stable and rapid economic growth—what has since become known as the four trillion (RMB) investment plan.

—To stop the concentration of decisionmaking power in the hands of individuals, the party's collective decisionmaking system has been improved at all levels from the central to the local. Three main approaches have been taken. First, there is no longer a chairman of the CCP Central Committee. Rather, there is now a secretary general who is responsible for convening the meetings of the Politburo and its standing committee and presiding over the work of the Secretariat. Second, relationships between the plenary session of the CCP Central Committee and the Politburo, its standing committee, and the CCP Secretariat have been clarified, and a system has been established whereby the members of the standing committee must report on their work regularly to the Politburo and the Politburo must report to the plenary session, giving full play to the active collective decisionmaking role of the CCP Central Committee. It is clearly prescribed that the Secretariat does not have a decisionmaking function but is just an administrative office of the Politburo and its standing committee.

Finally, a system has been established by which collective decisions are made at formal meetings. Depending on their importance, major decisions concerning national and social development are made by meetings of the Politburo, its standing committee, the Central Economic Work Conference, or the plenary session of the CCP Central Committee or the National Congress. Decisions on major issues that fall within the responsibilities of the State Council must be discussed at plenary meetings or executive meetings of the State Council; work rules, procedural rules, and a system of "democratic life" meetings have been established in the Politburo and its standing committee to institutionalize collective decisionmaking; and a system has been established to solicit opinions concerning major policy decisions. In the latter, before any major decision is collectively made, intraparty democracy must first be given full play, in-depth investigations and research must be undertaken, and the opinions of all localities, departments, and democratic parties must be solicited. For instance, the scope for comments on the report to the party's 17th National Congress and the amendment to the constitution of the CCP extended from the provincial-level leadership to the party delegates from the 16th Congress and the newly elected delegates of the party's 17th Congress.

—To change what was in practice lifelong tenure for leading posts, both a strict tenure system and systems for the resignation and retirement of leading cadres have been established. At the CCP 16th Congress, normalized, standardized, and institutionalized succession of the older by the younger generation was realized at the top level. The profound significance of the implementation of this tenure system is that through the peaceful and standardized replacement of veteran cadres with younger ones, the decisionmaking process now contains a self-correction and adjustment mechanism. The establishment of a retirement system for leading cadres means society has the ability to reduce a political leader to an ordinary citizen, which is one of the important benchmarks of a society's political civilization.

—The system of political consultation between the CCP and the democratic parties has been improved to expand the power of the latter in major decisionmaking. In 1989 the CCP issued the View of the CCP on Persisting in and Perfecting the System of Multiparty Cooperation and Political Consultation under the Leadership of the Communist Party, which confirmed the democratic parties as parties participating in state affairs. At the first session of the 8th National People's Congress, held in 1993, the following statement was added to the PRC Constitution so that the system of multiparty cooperation and political consultation would have a constitutional basis: "The system of multiparty cooperation and political consultation led by the CCP will continue to exist and develop."

Currently, the democratic parties' main participation in political decisionmaking takes two institutional forms. First, they can make direct policy recommendations or proposals. For instance, in March 1986 some members of the Jiu San Society presented to the CCP Central Committee its Proposal for Tracking the Development of World Strategic High Technology. Based on this proposal, the CCP Central Committee and the State Council drafted the High-Tech Research and Development Program (known as the 863 Program), which is a significant milestone in the history of China's scientific and technological development. Another example is the important decision made by the CCP Central Committee on the development of the Shanghai Pudong Economic Development Zone, which was based on a proposal submitted by the central committee of the China Democratic League entitled A Preliminary Idea for Establishing the Yangtze River Delta Economic Development Zone. Second, the democratic parties consult with the CCP before the party makes major decisions. From 1990 to 2009, as many as 287 consultations, seminars, or briefings were held by the CCP Central Committee, the State Council, or relevant departments. Of these, 85 were hosted or attended by the secretary general of the CCP Central Committee.[16] The participation of the democratic parties in political decisionmaking is not only an important form of democratic decisionmaking but is also an important part of scientific decisionmaking.

—Relatively independent advisory bodies have also been established to improve the scientific quality of the decisionmaking structure. Their relative independence means that, organizationally, they are not policy research agencies within the power system, nor is their style of work administrative; their advisory activities, especially the research processes that provide support for decisionmaking, must be independent. In recent years the participation of experts and scholars has progressed significantly in terms of both breadth and depth. For example, more than 4,000 experts from various fields have taken part in the formulation of the mid- and long-range plans for development of science and technology.

—Mass media have become an important part of the decisionmaking structure. With the deepening of reform in this area, China's mass media have taken on an industry and market orientation that has greatly changed the identification of their role and functions. To both survive and prosper, mass media must increase their income from advertising by increasing audience ratings; to that end, media groups have sought to establish credibility by taking into account the needs of the people. This has fundamentally changed the media from their previous status as a mere party and government mouthpiece into an important communication platform for the expression of public opinion, thereby forming a bridge between the government and the public by becoming an important window into state decisionmaking. Especially with the spread of the Internet, various interest groups now have a convenient platform for interaction and participation, which highlights the role played by the mass media in influencing decisionmaking.

Modes of Decisionmaking

The recent democratic and scientific reforms have changed the decisionmaking process in two profound ways. Decisionmaking is now based not simply on experience but on a combination of experience and scientific methods, with the latter playing the primary role. A modern society is a risk society marked by high complexity, high mobility, fast-flowing information, and close connections among different factors. It is now difficult for individual leaders to make correct decisions by relying solely on their own experience and wisdom. In the past there was both an abundance of simplistic thinking and a lack of scientific techniques; the national accounting system, for example, emphasized accounting for economic output and the growth rate, failing to take into account the importance of our ecological resources and environmental conditions on which the development of the national economy depends. Since reform and opening up, the CCP

Central Committee has therefore introduced a number of practices to boost scientific decisionmaking through the use of modern scientific technologies, tools, methods of analysis, and operating procedures in the decisionmaking process.

One of these practices has been the establishment of a democratic and scientific decisionmaking evaluation system. Under this system, whether formulating major national development strategies and planning, constructing major projects, or formulating policy concerning the livelihood of the people, all plans must first go through a process of democratic assessment, expert scientific evaluation, and the production of a report before being submitted to the decisionmaking body for discussion. Yet another practice is the use of scientific decisionmaking methods. For example, for decisionmaking regarding overall and long-term national and social development goals, the methods of setting an overall objective, conducting systems analysis, achieving overall balance and strategic planning, and the like are usually used. For major issues in a specific area, methods such as summing up experience, drawing logical inference, and investigating exemplary cases are often used. Yet another practice is the introduction of scientific and technological means and tools into the decisionmaking process to improve accuracy. With some complex issues that require accurate analytical conclusions, ordinary decisionmaking methods, such as forecasts of economic development trends, are insufficient to meet the requirements. In such cases, some modern methods and tools are needed. These include tools of mathematical analysis, which quantify the relevant variables and establish corresponding mathematical models. Mathematical operations and deduction based on the models are then undertaken to obtain accurate results, and finally an educated decision can be made. Another tool of analysis is the computer. Several simulation models targeting the issues to be resolved are established on the basis of detailed data. Once empirical data confirm that the requirements of the situation have been met, formal decisions can be made on the basis of the simulations. Of course, the emphasis on scientific decisionmaking does not deny human experience or the distinctive role played by experience in decisionmaking.

Scientific and democratic reform has also made an impact on the modes of decisionmaking. To meet the requirements of democratic decisionmaking and to uphold the rights of the citizenry to be informed, to participate, to be heard, and to oversee, decisionmaking by the government has changed over the past three decades from a closed to an open format. This has occurred through continuous progress in the reform of the decisionmaking system and through a process that draws on local and primary-level decisionmaking experience, such as the system of openness in village affairs. This change has been gradual and has been mainly reflected in the following ways.

Openness in Party Affairs

Over time, the openness in government affairs spread to openness in party affairs. After the 13th CCP National Congress announced that it was "enhancing the openness of the activities of leading organs so that the people are informed of major issues and discuss them," open decisionmaking was launched. This started with openness in government affairs—that is, the implementation of a system to keep the public informed of what the government was doing. Openness had a positive effect on society, particularly among the general population, which in turn contributed to openness in party affairs. The fourth plenary session of the 16th CCP Central Committee clearly stated, "We should establish and improve intraparty information sharing and reporting systems and the system of soliciting opinions concerning major policy decisions, gradually implement the openness of Party affairs, and increase transparency in Party affairs."[17] This was the first time in history that the CCP proposed openness in party affairs, and it marked an important step in intraparty democracy.

Dynamic Openness

The partial openness in government affairs has developed into a dynamic openness of the entire process. The first step in increasing openness in government affairs was to make public what the government was doing in some sectors; the practice was then extended to the entire process of the exercise of administrative power. To prevent some government departments from making incomplete and unclear information disclosures, the General Office of the State Council required governments at all levels to compile a catalogue of government information disclosures and to draw up and publish flowcharts of administrative power, in accordance with the published operational procedures of administrative powers.

Disclosure

Yet another aspect of the change involves gradually extending the practice of government information disclosure to the legal system. To solve the problem of the nonstandard, casual, and capricious manner in which some local governments and central departments implemented open government, the state sped up the process of bringing open government under the legal system. In March 2005 the CCP Central Committee and the State Council jointly issued Opinions on Further Promoting Open Government, which proposed that laws and regulations on open government be formulated and improved. After two years of work, the Regulations on Open Government Information was formally promulgated and took effect on May 1, 2008. The implementation of these regulations provides effective legal protection for lawful access to government information for citizens, legal persons, and other organizations and has increased the transparency of government work.

Complete Openness in Decisionmaking

The purpose of open decisionmaking is to uphold citizens' rights to be informed and to make it easier for people from all walks of life to exercise their right of oversight, so that decisionmaking power can operate in the open. In soliciting citizens' opinions and pooling their wisdom, open decisionmaking fulfills citizens' right to participate and expresses the value of public involvement. In recent years, the state has accelerated the process of open decisionmaking, which has taken increasingly diverse forms, including the widely implemented system of press releases, the system of keeping the public informed on major issues, vigorous promotion of e-government, and building networked platforms for government information disclosure. The report to the 17th National Congress of the CCP clearly commits the state to open decisionmaking: "To ensure scientific and democratic decisionmaking, we will improve the information and intellectual support for it, increase transparency, and expand public participation. In principle, public hearings must be held for the formulation of laws, regulations, and policies that bear closely on the interests of the masses."[18] On April 15, 2008, the second chairman's meeting of the Standing Committee of the 11th National People's Congress decided that henceforth all draft laws submitted to the NPC will generally be published to facilitate obtaining the views of the public. Since 2005, following the publication of the draft Property Law for public comments, the full texts of thirty-five draft laws have been released for public consideration.

From August 2008, when the Outline of China's National Plan for Medium and Long-Term Education Reform and Development (2010–20) was released for public consideration, until May 5, 2010, when the State Council executive meeting examined and approved it in principle, the formulation of the outline took twenty-one months. More than 500 experts and scholars participated in eleven major strategic special groups, more than 1,800 seminars were held at home and abroad with more than 35,000 people taking part in the discussions and forty rounds of major revision undertaken. The public was twice invited to comment and responded with more than 2.1 million suggestions and opinions and more than 14,000 letters during the first round and more than 27,900 suggestions and opinions during the second, not to mention 2.49 million opinions and suggestions expressed via the mass media and the Internet. The complete openness of major decisionmaking in terms of form constitutes an important component of the reform of the decisionmaking system of the CCP; it is an important means of enhancing the credibility of the ruling party, a display of confidence, and, in particular, a demonstration of respect for the rights of citizens.

Mechanism Reforms

In the past the CCP stressed the need to promote democracy and took democratic centralism as the guiding principle of decisionmaking; yet when problems came up, especially when different views were voiced on problems, this principle was often replaced by arbitrary decisions and peremptory action. One main reason was the stress placed on the principle of democratic decisionmaking to the neglect of decisionmaking mechanisms and procedures. A procedural decisionmaking mechanism is a prerequisite to democratic and scientific decisionmaking, for democratic decisionmaking will be nothing but an empty slogan if it exists only at the level of principle without corresponding implementation mechanisms and strict procedures and specific procedural arrangements. In this sense, the construction of decisionmaking mechanisms is indispensable to democratic and scientific decisionmaking. Since reform and opening up, China has made great efforts in the reform of decisionmaking mechanisms, efforts that have played an important role in promoting democratic and scientific decisionmaking.

The establishment of a sound decisionmaking procedure includes interrelated stages and steps arranged in a clear sequence to form an orderly process. The second is the change from non-institutional to institutional decisionmaking mechanisms. To change the old practice, whereby leaders made decisions on the basis of personal experience or feelings, and instead ensure decisionmaking procedures are subject to hard constraints, the government has in recent years strengthened the institutionalization of decisionmaking mechanisms. The fourth plenary session of the 16th CCP Central Committee further proposed the establishment of systems for the extensive solicitation of comments, decisionmaking consultation and coordination, expert verification, technical advice, decisionmaking evaluation, publication and hearings, accountability for decisionmaking mistakes, and so on. To further improve the quality of legislation, in 2000 the government adopted the Legislation Law to standardize legislative procedures. The law clearly stipulates that a bill must go through three deliberations, thereby changing the previous practice of simply requiring that it be deliberated on without specifying clearly how many times this should occur.

Major Problems

There remain four main problems. First, the division of functions between the CCP and state organs is not yet sufficiently standardized, and the relationship between the CCP and the democratic parties is not yet highly institutionalized; the NPC and Chinese People's Political Consultative Conference, in particular, do not have fully developed roles. Second, decisionmaking power in some areas is still too centralized. Third, decisionmaking procedures should be improved as some hearings and consultations are mere formalities, channels for citizens to participate in the public decisionmaking process are limited, and institutionalized interest-expressing mechanisms are lacking. Finally, the decisionmaking supervision system needs to be improved; there is no system for assessing decisions or for examining the legitimacy of decisionmaking.

Suggestions for Further Reforms

China has instituted its decisionmaking system to ensure smooth information communication, quick response to public opinion, transparency, and scientific analysis—a system led by the CCP, joined by many participants, and based on rule of law. Guided by this objective, I propose the following five suggestions to further the reform of the decisionmaking system:

—Further standardize the relationship between the CCP and various state organs in the decisionmaking system and, in particular, reinforce and prioritize the roles of the NPC and Chinese People's Political Consultative Conference (CPPCC) as systems that function to realize democratic consultation, implement public opinion, and supervise decisionmaking.

—Further advance the openness of party and government affairs and increase decisionmaking transparency so that the decisionmaking process is visible and accessible to the public.

—Establish a complete set of decisionmaking procedures, build diverse mechanisms through which citizens can express their opinions and participate in the decisionmaking process, and allow the representatives of various interest groups to attend hearings and expert consultancy meetings so that the decisionmaking system can better accommodate the demands of pluralistic interests.

—Advance institutionalized law-based decisionmaking and establish a judicial review system for major decisions to avoid unauthorized or illegal decisionmaking.

—Implement a sound feedback and assessment system for major decisions and a sound decisionmaking accountability system.

Further reforms are needed to allow China's decisionmaking system to operate on a democratic, scientific, and legal basis. This may entail taking some risks, but such risk-taking is the only way to prevent more serious consequences.

COMMENT
DAVID M. LAMPTON

Zhou Guanghui has written a profoundly important piece on the "democratization of decisionmaking." In the few pages allocated to me for this critical review of his complex and subtle chapter, I address the following four issues: What are Zhou's key points? How do Zhou's points on "democratic" and "scientific" decisionmaking fit within a larger developmental perspective? What are some of the conceptual challenges that the notions of democratic and scientific present to the analyst? What are the challenges to moving gradually toward not only just and effective decisionmaking but just, effective, and durable governance as well? In the final analysis, there is no singular pathway or optimum balance between effective and just governance; we all are looking for those ever-changing balances between effectiveness and justice, between equity and efficiency. Each nation must find its own way forward, on its own schedule. And once found, it is not easy to maintain those precarious balances.

Overview of the Main Points

Zhou starts off noting that public policy is not simply a result of economic determinism, but rather it also reflects the structure and operation of the decisionmaking system, the central nervous system of China. He argues persuasively that China's decisionmaking system reflects historical conditions and circumstances and that since 1978 that system has dramatically improved, in terms of both its participatory (democratic) character and its scientific (appropriate, predictable, and fact-based) operation. Charges that China's political system has remained largely unchanged in the past three decades do not strike me as balanced for many of the reasons that Zhou gives.

Zhou locates his decisionmaking system reforms along the spectrum of comprehensive political system reform. Decisionmaking reform is not coterminous with political system reform, the latter being broader than the former. The latter is broader than the former inasmuch as political system reform also addresses the fundamental processes of selecting those authorized to participate and be key actors in the process, and it includes the basic composition and interrelationships among political institutions (the rules of the game). Although decisionmaking is important, it is not the totality of political reform. Decisionmaking reform concerns the central nervous system, but it is not the whole body politic. Zhou traces the origins of China's present decisionmaking system to 1949, when China earned its independence and needed to establish basic order, effectively delineate and enforce national borders, restore basic economic functions, and begin to industrialize society. All these considerations pushed in the direction of building a powerfully centralized decisionmaking system. This was so even though many of the prerequisites for making such a system efficient (for example, effective national communications, statistical, and education infrastructure) were lacking. This centralized system, while understandable in light of the exigencies of the postliberation moment, showed increasing disabilities over time.

Among those weaknesses and disabilities were a system subject to catastrophic leader misjudgments, fuzzy separation of powers between the Chinese Communist Party and state, problems in getting initiative in the state apparatus and accountability in the structure as a whole, overconcentration of power in the party, stove-piped organizations with weak horizontal coordination, little citizen participation in decisions and sometimes excessive citizen involvement in implementation (mass campaigns), little capacity to respond to mass citizen complaints and aspirations, "experience-based" rather than "scientific" decisionmaking, poor information on which to base decisions, lack of binding rules and procedures, system dysfunction and little room for expertise, few feedback loops so that when policy went awry at lower levels it took considerable time for higher-level authorities to respond appropriately, and a system that did not reward innovation. These flaws became increasingly apparent from 1957 onward, culminating in the Cultural Revolution decade of 1966-76. Indeed, this decade set the predicate for Deng Xiaoping's reform era, the opening-up and reform policy, and Zhou's suggested reforms of the decisionmaking system. In sum, by 1978–79, this decisionmaking system had become the biggest institutional obstacle in pushing forward China's modernization process.

Since 1978–79 the changes in the decisionmaking system have been important, and part of the overall political reform process that began with various Deng Xiaoping speeches shortly after his return to power in 1977, at the 13th National Congress of the Chinese Communist Party in 1987, and extending through the 16th Congress in 2002 and onto the present era of the 17th Congress, which called for "orderly participation in political affairs."[19]

The most notable dimension of reform in the decisionmaking system has been to introduce "instrumental rationality" through a number of steps: having clear reform goals, the most important of which is the democratization of decisionmaking as an intrinsic requirement of a democracy of the people; incorporating the interests and demands of more actors into the process; taking account of public opinion (in multiple ways, including opinion polls, public hearings, straw polls, and local elections); using scientific evidence and data to make decisions; more clearly defining the respective roles of party and government organs (including the party's Politburo and Secretariat, the State Council, and myriad other organs and bodies); defining the interrelations and zones of competence among individual organs in both the state and party hierarchies; specifying the role of law and asserting that law and constitutional principles apply to the party as they do to all other agencies and individuals in China; taking account of the growing importance of interest groups in the policy process; and consulting more meaningfully with other actors, including the democratic parties. All this is vital, because to implement democratization and scientific method into decisionmaking, it is necessary to maintain the legitimacy of the ruling party. I was struck by Premier Wen Jiabao's remarks in Shenzhen, in August 2010, in which he made a similar point and went on to say, "We must not only encourage institutional reform in economic life but also institutional reform in political life. Without the safeguard of political reform, the fruits of economic reform would be lost and the goal of modernization would not materialize."[20]

Looking Down the Development Road

Zhou places emphasis on the use of "mathematical analysis tools . . . to quantify the relevant variables and establish corresponding mathematical models" so that accurate results can be obtained and educated policy decisions can be made. He also calls for transparency ("the right to be informed") in party affairs and more publicizing of which government organs are responsible for which decisions. Most important, Zhou notes that the people's awareness of their rights is growing and that profound changes in the pattern of interests and values in society are occurring. The decisionmaking system, therefore, must evolve to accommodate these changes. The party's continued legitimacy rests on accommodating these changes.

In my view, Zhou has focused on one (albeit very important) part of a complicated and protracted political development process. I draw on Samuel Huntington's concept from *Political Order in Changing Societies* that development is a process in which a society strives to keep balance between enlarging volumes of popular participation and increasing institutional capacity. If there is excess participation (mass mobilization) in the absence of sufficient institutional capacity to regulate and channel that participation in productive directions, society moves into a zone of disorder, tumult, and potential chaos—the zone above the line in figure 11-1. If there is excessive institutional capacity to regulate society without corresponding levels of popular participation (in fact, repressing the expression of societal interests), the society becomes subject to various degrees of authoritarian and repressive control. The trick of development in these terms, therefore, is to keep an approximate balance between popular capacity for expression and

Figure 11-1. *Political Participation and Institutional Capacity*

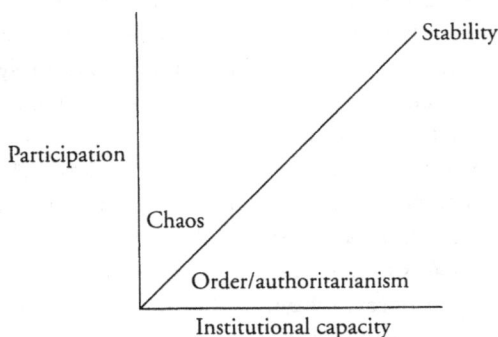

Source: Adapted from Samuel P. Huntington, *Political Order in Changing Societies* (Yale University Press, 1968), p. 79.

society's capacity to responsibly and productively regulate such participation. Rule of the mob is not to be preferred to rule of the few. Political development in these terms is the ever-larger empowerment of citizens within the framework of ever more capable and representative institutions, institutions capable of maintaining reasonable stability. It seems to me that the "democratic" and "scientific" decisionmaking process that is the focus of Zhou's chapter is in the middle stages of institutional development—building the channels and institutions that allow decisionmakers to intelligently analyze and hear an increasingly broad range of inputs. This is absolutely essential, but it is not the end of political development.

Other institutional capacities are required, as Zhou says or implies. Among these are the participatory capacities that permit the broader and more effective articulation of the varied interests of an increasingly pluralized system (for example, intraparty or interparty development, legislative development, and associational and civic society development); institutional capacities that ensure a more representative and predictable peaceful transfer of power; and institutions that resolve conflicts among parties under a rule of law and with reference to widely shared norms (for example, independent courts and other adjudication mechanisms). In short, improving the decisionmaking system is important, but it is only part of a much more protracted, complex, and sensitive undertaking. Democratic and scientific decisionmaking is a way station along a journey of great length; indeed, it is a journey that countries like the United States are still on as well. As China becomes more pluralized and complex, its interest groups and diversity will become progressively more difficult to contain within the existing framework. The question is, then, what new structures and processes can move toward a stable and productive future?

A Few Thoughts on Science and Democracy

When one talks of democracy that is stable, one must talk about more than simply participation, institutionalization, supervision, and feedback, important as they are. One needs to talk first about the things government does not have the right to decide—what Robert Dahl calls the "mutual guarantees": some "things are too precious to be at the disposal of majorities."[21] So democracy is not simply about decisionmaking by majorities, it also is about deciding what majorities cannot do.

Second, it is not enough to speak of the decision process in terms of participants, data, and procedures. There is the larger question of who chooses the participants, empowers certain actors, and designs the structure in which the decisionmaking process occurs.

With respect to "science," this is a method, not an end. Politics is the means by which societies define and specify ends. Science cannot tell us what we should want normatively. Science cannot answer the most fundamental questions of life and society. For example, science cannot tell us what balance should be struck between equity and efficiency, between environmental values and economic growth, between traditional social values and those of global urban culture, between the collective and the individual, between the center and the locality, or between Chinese national interests and human global interests. Only politics can address these balance issues, and democracy is one system that is designed to do so in a stable way in a highly heterogeneous social setting. The rules are popular sovereignty, elite circulation through open contest, and leaders and citizens who are subject to the same rules, impartially determined and limited to certain spheres. Democracy is built on compromise; science is not.

Conclusions

I am reminded of the basic problem that confronted the framers of the U.S. constitutional system as they deliberated how to build a new system in the United States after the first American constitutional construct, the Articles of Confederation, was found wanting. Put succinctly, the problem (as articulated in the *Federalist Papers*) was how to build a government strong enough to protect the people from both internal and external predators and create a framework for economic development, without creating a government so strong that it could oppress the people. This is the dilemma facing all people, albeit people in different circumstances. Development is a balance between expression and order. There is no perfect balance. There is no permanent balance.

Zhou's paper on decisionmaking addresses a very important facet of political change—making better decisions. Much progress has been made to date. Each nation needs to find its own path forward from there.

Notes

1. Carol Lee Hamrin, *China and the Challenge of the Future: Changing Political Patterns* (Boulder, Colo.: Westview Press, 1990), p. 3.

2. Douglass North, *Zhidu, zhidu bianqian yu jingji jixiao* [Institutions, institutional change, and economic performance], translated by Liu Shouying (Shanghai: Shanghai Sanlian Bookstore, People's Press, 1994), p. 1.

3. Sven Steinmo, "The New Institutionalism," in *The Encyclopedia of Democratic Thought*, edited by Barry Clark and Joe Foweraker (London: Routledge, 2001).

4. David Miller and others, eds., *Bulaikewei'er zhengzhixue baike quanshu* [Blackwell encyclopaedia of political thought], translated by Deng Zhenglai (Beijing: Chinese University of Political Science and Law Press, 2002), p. 196.

5. *Zhongguo gongchandang zhangcheng* [Constitution of the Chinese Communist Party] (Beijing: People's Publishing House, 2006), p. 13.

6. Kenneth Lieberthal, *Zhili Zhongguo: Cong geming dao gaige* [Governing China: From revolution to reform], translated by Hu Guocheng and Zhao Mei (Beijing: Chinese Social Science Press, 2010).

7. *Jianguo yi lai zhongyao wenxian xuanbian* [Selected important documents since the founding of the PRC], compiled by the Archive Office of the Chinese Communist Party Central Committee, vol. 4 (Beijing: Zhongyang wenxian chubanshe [Central Party Literature Press], 1992), pp. 67–72.

8. *Jianguo yi lai Mao Zedong wengao* [Selected writings of Mao Zedong since the founding of the PRC], compiled by the Archive Office of the Chinese Communist Party Central Committee, vol. 7 (Beijing: Zhongyang wenxian chubanshe [Central Party Literature Press], 1992), p. 268.

9. Douglass North, *Jingjishi zhong de jiegou yu bianqian* [Structure and change in economic history] (New York: W. W. Norton, 1982), p. 1. Chinese edition (Shanghai: Shanghai People's Publishing House, 1994).

10. *Jianguo yi lai zhongyao wenxian xuanbian*, vol. 9 (Beijing: Zhongyang wenxian chubanshe [Central Party Literature Press], 1994), pp. 79–89, 111–12, 135–37.

11. Deng Xiaoping, "Dang he guojia lingdao zhidu de gaige" [On the reform of the system of party and state leadership], in *Deng Xiaoping wenxuan* [Selected works of Deng Xiaoping] (Beijing: People's Publishing House, 1993), vol. 2, p. 266.

12. Wan Li, *Wan Li wenxuan* [Selected works of Wan Li] (Beijing: People's Publishing House, 1995), pp. 514–32.

13. Jiang Zemin, *Quanmian jianshe xiaokang shehui, kaichuang Zhongguo tese shehui-zhuyi shiye xin jumian* [Build a well-off society in an all-around way and work hard to create a new situation in building socialism with Chinese characteristics], in *Zhongguo gongchandang di shiliu ci quanguo daibiao dahui shang de baogao,* report to the 16th CCP National Congress, *People's Daily,* November 8, 2002, p. 1.

14. Hu Jintao, *Gaoju Zhongguo tese shehuizhuyi weida qizhi wei duoqu quanmian jianshe xiaokang shehui xin shengli er fendou* [Hold high the great banner of socialism with Chinese characteristics and strive for new victories in building a moderately prosperous society in all respects], in *Zhongguo gongchandang di shiqi ci quanguo daibiao dahui shang de baogao* [Report to the 17th CCP National Congress], *People's Daily,* October 25, 2007, p. 1.

15. *Zhongguo gongchandang zhangcheng.*

16. Zhang Xiansheng, "Zhongguo canzhengdang de lilun jiazhi he shijian yiyi [The theoretical value and practical significance of the Chinese political parties], *Zhengzhixue yanjiu* [Political science studies], no. 2 (2010).

17. *Zhonggong zhongyang guanyu jiaqiang dang de zhizheng nengli jianshe de jueding* [Decision of the CCP Central Committee on strengthening the party's power building], in *Zhongguo gongchandang lici quanguo daibiao dahui shujuku* [Complete database of CCP National Congress], *People's Daily,* September 19, 2004 (cpc.people.com.cn/GB/64162/64168/64569/65412/6348330.html).

18. Hu, *Gaoju Zhongguo tese shehuizhuyi weida qizhi,* p. 1.

19. Though a development occurring after this comment was written, the 18th Party Congress in 2012 and its Third Plenum the following year pushed further ahead trying to refine the bureaucratic and decisionmaking systems through bureaucratic consolidation and the creation of more cross-system integrating bodies to coordinate policy.

20. Justin Li, "Political Reform in China: Wen Will It Happen and Hu Will Lead It?," East Asian Forum, September 19, 2010 (www.eastasiaforum.org/2010/09/19/political-reform-in-china-wen-would-it-happen-and-hu-will-lead-it/).

21. Robert Dahl, *After the Revolution?* (Yale University Press, 1970), p. 16.

12

Building a Modern National Integrity System: Anticorruption and Checks and Balance of Power in China

HE ZENGKE

orruption is the abuse of entrusted power for private gain. The possibility of the abuse of power for private gain exists as long as the principal and the entrusted agent are kept separate. The prevention of abuse of public power cannot go without supervision of power and restrictions on that power. The supervision of power is the process by which the principal uses various means to supervise the agent to ensure that power is used as intended. The restriction of power is the process by which agents are entrusted with powers in such a way that they remain subordinate and subject to rigorous checks and balances to prevent the abuse of power.

In the face of the corruption that has arisen during the process of China's marketization and modernization since 1978, the Chinese Communist Party (CCP) and the Chinese government have sought to combat corruption by putting forward an anticorruption strategy that combats corruption from "six channels" (六管齐下, *liuguan qixia*) and by building a corruption punishment and prevention system that attaches equal importance to education, supervision, and institutionalization. Put differently, the country has been constructing a national integrity system with Chinese characteristics. These efforts have met with some successes, but overall the successes have been limited owing in large part to the inherent defects of the existing "clean-government" system. Deepening political reform and giving full scope to the role of electoral accountability, the separation of powers, and checks and balances will substantially improve the effectiveness of China's anticorruption efforts.

366

Anticorruption since the Reform and Opening Up

Over the more than sixty years since the founding of the People's Republic of China, the anticorruption strategy of the CCP has gone through three stages. In the first thirty years of the People's Republic, up until the reform and opening up began in 1978, the CCP combated corruption mainly by launching anticorruption mass movements. From 1949 until the eve of the 8th CCP National Congress in 1956, the CCP used three approaches: an ideological and educational campaign characterized by the rectification of the party and its work style, an anticorruption and antiwaste mass movement, and severe punishment of corrupt officials, especially those in high positions. From the convening of this congress until the Cultural Revolution was set into motion in 1966, tackling corruption by rectifying the party and its work style continued with the expansion of class struggle. From 1966 until the third plenary session of the 11th CCP National Congress in 1978, anticorruption efforts were guided by a leftist ideology and mainly took the form of mass political movements.

From the beginning of the reform and opening up in 1978 to the 16th CCP National Congress in 2002, the party adopted the approach of institutionalization to combat corruption. Reflecting on the Cultural Revolution, Deng Xiaoping has said that although moral degradation is an important reason for corruption, an effective system plays a more fundamental role in determining whether corruption is curbed. He brought reform to the leadership system of the party and the state and favored anticorruption efforts that were based on the rule of law rather than mass movements. Jiang Zemin proposed anticorruption guidelines that featured the "treatment of both symptoms and root causes," "integrated regulation," "reliance on institutional reforms," and "institutional innovation."[1] He also put in place the three major requirements of "cleanness and self-discipline of officials," "prosecution of corrupt officials," and "rectification of unwholesome tendencies." Institutional reforms and innovation, ideological education, and moral self-discipline became China's new important corruption prevention measures. Equal importance was also attached to corruption prevention and punishment.

Since the 16th CCP National Congress, the CCP's anticorruption strategy has gone a step further toward the establishment of a full-featured anticorruption system. Under Hu Jintao the CCP Central Committee adopted the clean government guideline of "fighting corruption in a comprehensive way, addressing both its symptoms and root causes, and combining punishment with prevention, with emphasis placed on prevention."[2] The committee also made the strategic decision to establish a corruption punishment and prevention system integrating education, supervision, and regulation, which extended the previous three-point approach to encompass the six points of education, institutionalization, supervision, reform, rectification, and punishment, known as the "six channels" to fight against corruption.[3] It was at this point that the party and the government made a conscious decision to establish a national integrity system with Chinese characteristics, one that integrates punishment and prevention to curb corruption. A series of major measures in education, supervision, institutionalization, and reform were specifically designed to prevent corruption. In addition to institutional innovation and institutional reforms, greater emphasis was placed on the position and role of both education and supervision in preventing corruption.

Since the reform period began, a series of breakthroughs and innovations have been made in China's anticorruption policy. For one, emphasis has been placed on the self-discipline of officials at various levels so they may serve as exemplars of clean government. The Chinese Communist Party stresses the importance of the moral caliber of all officials and the exemplary role they should play in terms of self-esteem, self-warning, self-reflection, self-encouragement, and strict self-discipline. As the Chinese saying goes, "If a leader sets a bad example, it will be followed by his subordinates."

Ideological and moral education plays an underlying role in anticorruption and clean government development. The state governance concept of the "combination of propriety and law, with education supplemented by punishment" is deep rooted in China.[4] Edification has priority in official management. In its efforts to combat corruption and build a clean government, the CCP also emphasizes the fundamental role of ideological and moral education. What is different is that the abrupt centralized educational campaigns commonly practiced following the reform and opening up have gradually given way to regular and more targeted educational and cultural measures regarding clean government construction.

Supervision has also been highlighted as an important link in corruption prevention. To separate supervisory power from other powers and to set up supervisory organs to oversee the exercise of administrative power is an important anticorruption tradition in China. Since the reform and opening-up period began, the CCP has carried on this tradition and placed strong emphasis on the role of supervision in corruption prevention by strengthening both the powers of the supervisory organs and top-down accountability.

Yet another prominent characteristic of China's anticorruption strategy after the reform and opening up has been the combination of corruption prevention and anticorruption system reform, especially the establishment of a corruption prevention system. The CCP has gradually come to realize that morality and self-discipline are not enough to prevent corruption and that the institutionaliza-tion of corruption prevention is a more effective approach. It emphasizes reform and innovation in anticorruption efforts and incorporates institutional develop-ment and reform in the scope of the six-point anticorruption guidelines.

Another prominent characteristic of China's anticorruption strategy of late has been the combination of conventional law-based punishment of corrup-tion and special anticorruption campaigns. Up until the commencement of the reform and opening up, the CCP would combat corruption through special campaigns. Since the late 1970s, however, law-based punishment of corruption has received great weight, though the practice of special campaigns is also used to address corruption that is particularly prominent and has caused concern from the public.

One final characteristic of China's anticorruption efforts during this period has been the meting out of severe punishment for those convicted of corruption. The application of penal codes in China has always stressed the practice of "exe-cuting one as a warning to others." Since the founding of the People's Republic, the CCP has continued this approach in its anticorruption efforts, with crimi-nal law punishing corrupt elements either by depriving them of freedom or by outright execution. In special anticorruption campaigns, punishments are both more severe and enforced more quickly than in regular cases.

The main achievement China has made toward combating corruption dur-ing the past three decades has been the preliminary establishment of a corrup-tion punishment and prevention system, that is, a national integrity system with Chinese characteristics.[5] This system includes the goals of the CCP and the state in building a clean government, establishing the institutional pillars of a clean government, and educating the public and public servants of the value of a clean government by fostering of a clean government culture.

The theoretical concept of socialism with Chinese characteristics is used to educate the whole party and gradually establish the three major goals for the development of China's national integrity system—namely, scientific devel-opment, social harmony, and general prosperity (小康社会, *xiaokang shehui*). Through the efforts of the three generations of collective leadership represented by Deng Xiaoping, Jiang Zemin, and Hu Jintao, the CCP has gradually imple-mented socialism with Chinese characteristics, including the overall goals of China's socialist modernization.

Meanwhile, the various institutional pillars of the national integrity system have been established, and the positions and roles of the various institutional actors have been defined. The establishment of anticorruption bureaus of procu-ratorates and the National Bureau of Corruption Prevention marked a substantial step forward in the professionalization of China's corruption prevention and punishment efforts. Since the reform and opening up, the private economic sector—made up mainly of individually owned businesses, private enterprises, and foreign enterprises—has grown to become an important force in China's social and political life. With the separation of state and society, civil organizations and the online public sphere have been quietly growing. Civil society has come to play an increasing role in supervising the exercise of public power and the speeches and behavior of government officials. In the process of marketization and commercialization, the press has become increasingly independent and critical and has gradually developed into an important anticorruption force. There has also been further progress in bilateral and multilateral international cooperation to fight corruption.

As the various institutional actors within and outside the state power system have become increasingly active, the CCP has sought to clarify both the leadership and the workings of China's anticorruption system, which is characterized by the unified leadership of party committees, the joint administration of party and government organizations, the coordination of commissions of discipline inspection, the accountability of various competent departments, and the reliance on the support and participation of the masses to achieve synergy in anticorruption efforts. These developments are combining to form an anticorruption structure led by major party and government officials. In this structure the professional anticorruption organizations are playing the major role, the responsibilities are being divided among the various competent departments, and institutional actors, including civil society, are actively participating.

In addition, a set of core rules has been put in place. These rules—on intraparty democracy and supervision—ensure that the ruling party can function normally. In an effort to promote intraparty democracy, party organizations at the grassroots level are piloting public recommendation–based direct elections. The Procedural Rules of Local Party Committees provide a procedural guarantee for democratic decisionmaking within the party committees. The Regulations of the CCP on Protecting the Rights of Party Members provide an intraparty legal basis for party members to exercise their rights and seek redress for grievances. A series of intraparty regulations have been released, including the Regulations of the CCP on Intra-Party Supervision (Trial), Supervisory Measures for the Selection and Appointment of Leading Party and Government Cadres (Trial), Regulations of the Commission of Discipline Inspection and the Organizational Department of the CCP Central Committee on Inspection Work (Trial), and Rules for Intra-Party Question and Inquiry by Members of Local Party Committees and Local Commissions of Discipline Inspection, which provide regulatory and procedural guarantees for party members and party organizations to carry out intraparty supervision.

Discipline inspection and supervisory organs are the most important intraparty supervision and administrative supervision organizations and professional anticorruption organs in contemporary China. These organs have taken a full range of measures to ensure the relative independence and authority needed to perform their duties and rights, including changing the constitutional method (from election at the plenary session of the party committee to direct election at the party congresses at the various levels), adopting a dual leadership system, implementing unified management of their branches, and using inspection-based supervision.

With their independence strengthened through the implementation of a dual administration system, the supervisory and auditing organs also release auditing reports on a regular basis, which further strengthen the effect of their supervision and auditing. The establishment of the Anticorruption and Antibribery Bureau and organizations for prevention of duty-related crimes has improved the professionalization of the procuratorial system in terms of corruption punishment and prevention. The adoption of the Judges Law and Procurators Law has promoted the professionalization of the judicial system. The promulgation of the Anti-Money Laundering Law has granted anti–money laundering organizations the power to track and investigate money-laundering behavior, which has been a significant boon to anticorruption efforts. The Administrative Procedural Law grants the courts the power to have a judicial review of administrative actions. The Civil Servant Law has improved the professionalization of the civil servant system. The Law of the People's Republic of China on the Supervision of Standing Committees of People's Congresses at All Levels provides the legal basis for the standing committees of the people's congresses at all levels to supervise the governments, courts, and procuratorates at their respective levels.

Under the efforts of the CCP, the functions of the democratic parties and the Chinese People's Political Consultative Conference (CPPCC) in the deliberation and administration of state affairs, democratic consultation, and political supervision are all being strengthened. The promulgation of the Anti-Unfair Competition Law and the Antimonopoly Law provides a legal framework that encourages the private sector to compete and thereby serves to break monopolies. The promulgation of three administrative regulations—the Regulation on Registration and Administration of Social Organizations, the Provisional Regulations for the Registration Administration of People-Run Non-enterprise Units, and the Regulations on Foundation Administration—has achieved law-based management of private organizations, which to a certain extent helps ensure the freedom of association. The Regulations of the People's Republic of China on Making Public Government Information, which perpetuates China's achievements in government transparency in legal form, provides a legal basis for the media and the public to access government information and to supervise officials. At the time of this writing, China has entered into 106 judicial assistance treaties with sixty-eight countries and regions and acceded to the United Nations Convention against Corruption, which increases the cooperation and assistance China receives from international actors in such aspects as the extradition of corrupt officials, the return of embezzled assets, and joint investigations.

Finally, efforts to promote anticorruption education and a culture of clean government have heightened anticorruption awareness by both the public and officials, thereby laying a solid foundation for China's national integrity system. From 1978 to 1992, the discipline inspection and supervisory organs mainly focused on party character and party style education to ensure the purity of the ruling party. From 1992 to 2002, the focus was on the advancement of anticorruption education and public diplomacy, which integrated legal and moral education and achieved close cross-department coordination. From 2002 to the present, China has highlighted educational efforts to combat corruption and has advocated clean government as a fundamental task, efforts that have received great attention from party committees and governments at various levels. A social environment that "takes cleanness as glory and corruption as a shame" is taking shape.[6]

Since the reform and opening-up period began, China has achieved substantial success in corruption prevention and punishment. Over these thirty years, the discipline inspection and supervisory organs at various levels have duly performed their duties and put great effort into supervision and anticorruption, making an important contribution to China's clean government building in the process. According to statistics, in the period from the beginning of the reform and opening up to November 2009, the discipline inspection and supervisory organs registered 2,945,844 cases, as many as 2,706,223 of which received party or government disciplinary action. In the twelve years for which accurate data are available, as many as 78,631 cadres at the county or division level or above were punished.[7] According to other statistics, from the beginning of the reform and opening up to late 2009, the procuratorial organs at various levels investigated 1,095,297 cases of embezzlement and bribery and punished 667,113 persons, including 46,420 at the county or division level or above.[8] The corruption perceptions index released by Transparency International reflects the changes of corruption in China over the past thirty years, as shown in table 12-1.

These changes in the corruption scores illustrate how corruption in China grew steadily worse (its score of 2.43 in 1993–96 places China among the most

Table 12-1. *China's Public Perception of Corruption Index, 1980–2009*[a]

Year	CPI	Year	CPI
1980–85	5.13	2002	3.5
1988–92	4.73	2003	3.4
1993–96	2.43	2004	3.4
1997	2.88	2005	3.2
1998	3.5	2006	3.3
1999	3.4	2007	3.5
2000	3.1	2008	3.6
2001	3.5	2009	3.6

Source: Transparency International, "Corruption Perceptions Index" (www.transparency.org/policy_research/surveys_indices/cpi/2009/cpi).

a. CPI = corruption perceptions index.

corrupt countries in the world during that period) before changing for the better in the mid-1990s thanks to the country's process of modernization, marketization, and globalization. According to a public opinion survey taken by the State Statistics Bureau, the Chinese public's satisfaction with the country's corruption situation increased from 60.5 percent in 2005 to 69.2 percent in 2009, and the percentage of the public who agreed that corruption in the country had been somewhat curtailed increased from 75.2 percent in 2005 to 82.6 percent in 2009. These figures indicate a certain degree of growing public satisfaction with China's anticorruption performance.

Effectiveness of China's Existing Clean-Government System

At the present stage, China faces a number of prominent problems regarding anticorruption. First, checks on the corruption of leading party and government officials are weak. The rampancy of corruption among top leaders, which has gone virtually unchecked, has set a bad example and seriously discredited the government's anticorruption efforts.

Second, serious corruption, such as that in the appointment system or judiciary, has grown increasingly worse. Corruption within official appointments is both a hotbed of other forms of corruption and an important form of corruption among top leaders. Judicial corruption causes irreparable damage and takes away the last defense of social justice. The spread of judicial corruption has weakened and undermined public trust in and support of the Constitution, the legal system, the party, and the government.

Third, unhealthy tendencies and government extravagance have also gone unchecked. The unhealthy tendencies within the party and among government departments and industries in benefiting at the expense of the public, especially abuses of power for private gain and the waste of public funds, have not been effectively checked in spite of repeated orders and instructions from the party and the government.

Fourth, there has been a trend of legalizing exclusive privileges of civil servants, especially leading officials, in such areas as housing, medical care, vehicles, and other benefits. The legalization and expansion of these special privileges make fighting corruption more difficult.[9]

Fifth, punishing those found to be corrupt has resulted in problems. For example, there is now excessive judicial discretion in sentencing and a low probability that corruption will be discovered in the first place, let alone punished. There is remarkable variation from period to period and from region to region in the severity of punishment and the standards applied in the sentencing of corruption cases. In cases where special campaigns against corruption are conducted, the punishments tend to be more severe, while in other periods the anticorruption efforts tend to slacken and the government even turns a blind eye to corruption. The anticorruption organs often act on the orders of the leaders or the cases of injustices brought forward by the masses rather than by actively tracking and investigating corruption cases. This results in a low probability that corruption cases will be discovered and thus punished and gives the impression that cases of corruption are punished selectively.

Sixth, punishment largely takes the form of party and government disciplinary sanctions and monetary penalties rather than legal persecution, the former often taking precedence over the latter. Of the cases of prevention and punishment of corruption noted earlier, only approximately one-third of those that were subject to party discipline sanctions, and a quarter of those subject to government sanctions were actually prosecuted—a low percentage of prosecution, indeed.

Overall, China now faces serious difficulties in its anticorruption efforts. From 1998 to 2009, China's corruption perceptions index scores swung between 3.1 and 3.6 (see table 12-1), placing the People's Republic of China among the countries with the most serious corruption during that period. China's corruption situation has not seen any substantial improvement and has remained at a high level ever since. According to a Horizon China survey, the urban public's concern for clean government and anticorruption issues ranked seventh among all social concerns in 2001, eleventh in 2005, and fifth in 2010.[10] This shows that the public still has great expectations that the country will improve its anticorruption performance.

Table 12-2. *Criteria for the Effectiveness of a Clean-Government System*

Criterion	Organizational effectiveness	Effectiveness of rules
Balanced institutional pillars	Independence Coordination	Completeness Authoritativeness
Universal establishment of core rules	Specialization Matching	Operability Desirability
Closed supervision and restriction of power	Appropriateness Transparency Accountability	Sustainability Zero sum or positive sum Compatibility

The rampant corruption and unsatisfactory anticorruption performance are closely related to the lack of effectiveness of China's national integrity system in terms of power supervision and restriction as well as corruption prevention and punishment. The criteria for effective corruption efforts—power supervision and restriction and corruption prevention and punishment—include criteria for overall effectiveness and for organizational category-based effectiveness (see table 12-2). There are three criteria for overall effectiveness: the national integrity system has well-balanced institutional pillars that support and restrain each other and jointly prop up the system; institutional pillars each have a set of core operating rules and fully perform their respective duties; and there is a closed structure of power supervision and restriction where the vertical and horizontal accountability mechanism with the electoral system and the system of separation of powers at the core operates throughout both the organizational system and all governing rules so that all public powers and civil servants are under effective supervision and restriction. The effectiveness of the organizations and the governing rules that are covered by each pillar of the clean-government system can be evaluated according to several categories. The organizational effectiveness mainly measures whether full scope is given to the responsibilities, functions, or roles of the institutional actors. The criteria for organizational effectiveness include the following:

—independence: whether the legal position and external relations of the institutional actor can ensure the independent performance of its duties

—coordination: whether there is any conflict among the different roles assumed by the institutional actor that prevents it from performing its main duties

—specialization: whether the knowledge, skills, and information possessed by the institutional actor can ensure the effective performance of its duties

—matching: whether the power and resources of the institutional actor match its responsibilities

—appropriateness: whether the organizational structure and working model of the institutional actor are appropriate for the performance of its duties

—transparency: whether the process of the institutional actor performing its duties or functions is transparent and under effective supervision

—accountability: whether there is an effective external evaluation and accountability system for the institutional actor's performance of its duties

The criteria for rule effectiveness include the following:

—completeness: whether there are any important rules missing or material omissions

—authoritativeness: whether there is an appropriate level of authority for the rules

—operability: whether the rules are enforceable and operable

—desirability: whether the process of rule formulation and implementation complies with the principles of transparency, participation, and fairness

—sustainability: whether the rules are stable and predictable

—zero sum or positive sum: whether the interests of the parties affected by the rules are affected on an equal basis

—compatibility: whether the rules are compatible rather than contradictory

Over the more than thirty years since reform and opening up, China has implemented a national integrity system, but its institutional pillars have failed to fully play their intended roles owing to the lack or incompleteness of their core rules. An overall assessment of China's existing clean-government system is provided in table 12-3. The fifteen institutional pillars of China's clean-government system have been universally established, but some of the core rules for ensuring that these institutional pillars are effective are missing. There is an imbalance among the fifteen institutional pillars.

The seven criteria of organizational effectiveness can be used to assess the effectiveness of the various institutional pillars in light of the actual conditions of their institutional development. Table 12-4 rates the effectiveness of the fifteen institutions on a three-grade scale, where 1 denotes low, 2 denotes medium, and 3 denotes high effectiveness. Within the state power framework, the institution that is the most effective in supervision and accountability enforcement is the top-down CCP committee system, followed by the administrative organs, the CCP discipline inspection system, then the auditing organs, procuratorates, and courts, followed by the people's congresses and the civil service system. Outside the state power framework, the most effective social supervision and accountability institution is the private economic sector, followed by the media and

Table 12-3. *The Overall Performance of China's National Integrity System*

Institution	Institutional pillar present?	Core rules	Core rules present?
CCP committees at various levels as the core of leadership	Yes	Electoral accountability	No
People's congresses at the various levels and their standing committees as the legislative and supervisory organs	Yes	Guarantee of the exercise of veto power	No
Democratic parties and CPPCC organizations as political supervision organizations	Yes	Guarantee of participation in major decisionmaking and ability to speak openly without fearing repression	No
Administrative organs	Yes	Conflict of interests	Yes for some
Auditing organs	Yes	Independence	No
Discipline inspection and supervisory organizations as supervisory organizations	Yes	Independence from the objects of supervision	No
Procuratorates and corruption prevention bureaus as professional anti-corruption organs	Yes	Enforceability and strict enforcement of anticorruption laws	Yes for some
Courts as judicial organs	Yes	Independence	Yes for some
Civil servant system	Yes	Moral standards on public services inherent in the cadre personnel system	Yes for some
Local governments in the vertical and horizontal structure	Yes	Reflective of the principle of aid	No
Public sector	Yes	Transparency, participation, and accountability in governance structure	Yes for some
Private economic sector	Yes	Pro-competition policy	Yes for some
Media, including online media	Yes	Freedom of expression	Yes for some
Civil society	Yes	Guarantee of free speech	Yes for some
International community	Yes	Effective mutual legal or judicial assistance	Yes for some

Table 12-4. *Effectiveness of the Institutional Pillars of China's Existing National Integrity System*[a]

Institution	(1)	(2)	(3)	(4)	(5)	(6)	(7)	(8)
CCP committees	3	3	1	3	3	1	1	15
People's congresses	1	2	2	1	2	2	1	11
Democratic parties and CPPCC organizations	1	1	3	1	1	1	1	9
Administrative organs	1	3	2	3	1	2	2	14
Auditing organs	1	2	3	1	1	2	2	12
Discipline inspection and supervisory organizations	1	3	3	3	2	1	1	14
Procuratorates and corruption prevention bureaus	1	2	3	2	2	2	2	14
Courts	1	2	3	2	1	2	1	12
Civil service system	1	1	2	2	1	2	2	11
Local governments	1	1	2	1	1	2	1	9
Public sector	2	1	2	2	1	2	1	11
Private economic sector	3	1	2	2	2	1	1	12
Media, including online media	1	1	2	1	1	2	1	9
Civil society	1	2	1	1	1	1	1	8
International community	3	1	3	1	1	3	2	14

a. Numbered column headings are as follows: (1) independence; (2) coordination; (3) professionalization; (4) matching; (5) appropriateness; (6) transparency; (7) accountability; (8) total. For numbers in cells, 1 = low, 2 = medium, and 3 = high.

civil society, the public sector, local governments, democratic parties and the CPPCC. The lack of independence of the professional supervision organs—such as the discipline inspection commissions, the auditing organs, the procuratorates, and the courts—has prevented them from effectively performing their duties.

Figure 12-1 illustrates the effectiveness gap among the various institutions of the national integrity system.

In recent years, China has made much progress in building a regulatory system for clean government in spite of serious omissions in its core rule structure. A number of important clean government–related laws and regulations have been promulgated, including the Law on the Supervision of Standing Committees of People's Congresses at All Levels, the Regulations of the Communist Party of China on Intra-Party Supervision, the CCP Regulations on Disciplinary Sanctions, and the Civil Servant Law. According to incomplete statistics, since the

Figure 12-1. *Effectiveness Evaluation of Institutional Pillars*[a]

Effectiveness score

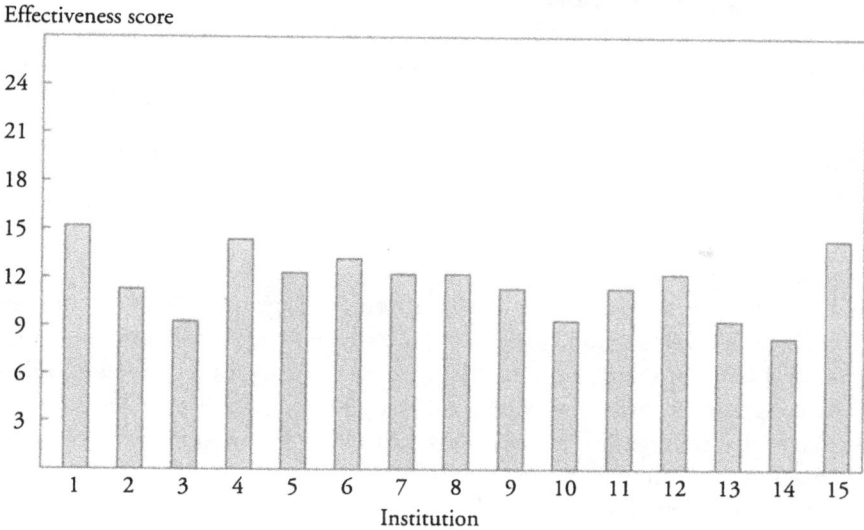

Source: Data and design from author's studies

a. The numbers 1 through 15 on the horizontal axis denote (1) party committees, (2) people's congresses, (3) democratic parties and the CPPCC, (4) government, (5) auditing organs, (6) discipline inspection commissions, (7) procuratorates and the bureau of corruption prevention, (8) courts, (9) civil servants, (10) local governments, (11) public sectors, (12) private economic sector, (13) press, including online media, (14) civil society, and (15) international actors. On the vertical axis, the numbers 1 through 27 denote the effectiveness scores of the representative institutional pillars.

16th CCP National Congress, the Central Commission of Discipline Inspection and the Ministry of Supervision have formulated or amended more than 160 regulations and rules, in addition to the more than 40 regulations drafted along with other departments. Moreover, the local governments and competent departments have drafted more than 1,000 regulations.[11] According to the effectiveness criteria established above, it is possible to conduct a preliminary assessment of the overall effectiveness of China's existing regulatory system of clean government. As shown in table 12-5, China ranks at the medium level in terms of the completeness of its regulatory system of clean government but ranks low in terms of such criteria as authoritativeness, operability, desirability, sustainability, positive-sum, and compatibility, with an overall performance of "less than satisfactory."

China has also made great progress in establishing a vertical and horizontal accountability mechanism featuring closed power supervision, though there are still some obvious shortcomings. The direct election of villager committees

Table 12-5. *Assessment of the Effectiveness of China's Existing*
Clean-Government Rule System

Criterion	Rating	Criterion	Rating
Completeness	Medium	Sustainability	Low
Authoritativeness	Low	Positive sum	Low
Operability	Low	Compatibility	Medium
Desirability	Low		

and the public recommendation–based election of villager party branches started China's democratic election system and have strengthened accountability at the grassroots level. In some places, the delegates to the people's congresses and the party congresses at the county level are directly elected, which provides a means of electoral accountability to the voters. However, these electoral reforms are confined to a very limited number of places.

For the selection of delegates to the people's congresses and party's congresses at higher levels, owing to the absence of direct and competitive elections, the voters and party members lack the means to hold these delegates accountable. Furthermore, because the people's congresses and the party's congresses have very short sessions, there is a lack of adequate deliberation on and review of the matters on the agenda, which, coupled with the lack of veto power and no-confidence motions, weakens the power of delegates to the people's congresses and of delegates to the party's congresses to make party and government leaders accountable. With respect to the construction of the supervision and account-ability system, there has been a significant strengthening of supervision provided by the professional supervisory organs and the people's congresses and their standing committees. Meanwhile, online public opinion is playing an increas-ingly large role in supervision. However, supervision by the democratic parties, CPPCC organizations, the media, and civil society is hardly satisfactory. Overall, the supervision of and restrictions placed on the ruling party and top govern-ment and party leaders at the various levels are still weak, and a closed power-supervision and restriction system has yet to be established.

In the sixty years since the founding of the People's Republic, particularly during the more than thirty years that have passed since the reform and opening-up period began, China has made great progress in building its national integ-rity system with well-structured institutional pillars. China's achievement in combating corruption and promoting clean government is closely related to its clean-government system. It should be noted, however, that the development of institutional pillars of the clean-government system has not been balanced. The few institutional pillars in the party committee, government, and special supervision branches have played an effective role while the majority of pillars throughout the system have more or less failed to function as intended. This failure has come about because of the absence of core rules needed to support some institutional pillars and the lack of either a vertical electoral accountability mechanism or a horizontal "separation of powers" accountability mechanism. These shortcomings have prevented the formation of a closed power-supervision and restriction mechanism.[12] Taken together, these factors have seriously undermined the national integrity system as a whole and have bottlenecked China's anticorruption efforts.

National Integrity System: Modern Transformation, Power Supervision, and Anticorruption Efforts

China's existing national integrity system has the major features of both a modern national integrity system and a traditional centralized clean-government system, thus assuming the characteristics of transition and hybridization. The major institutional actors of the existing clean-government system—including the people's congresses, the democratic parties, CPPCC organizations, the market economy, the private sector, the media (including new media), and civil society—have grown rapidly since the reform and opening up and are playing some role in restricting power and preventing corruption. Owing to serious stagnation in the reforms of some core areas of the political system, however, the existing national integrity system has come to face a number of insurmountable institutional barriers from the centralized political system in terms of both power supervision and restriction as well as in corruption prevention and punishment.

First, excessive concentration of power inhibits effective supervision and restriction of government heads and party chiefs at various levels. The separation of the functions of the party and the government met huge resistance and encountered many problems, resulting in the shelving of relevant reforms. Top party and government leaders at various levels continue to hold personnel and fiscal powers, and it is difficult for their deputies to supervise them. Furthermore, the people's congresses and CPPCC organizations, which are subordinate to the party committees at their own respective levels and are also subject to the governments at their own respective levels in terms of staffing and budget, also find it difficult to impose effective supervision. By having the top leaders assume overall responsibility, the accountability system leads to the concentration of various powers in the hands of the top leaders of various departments at various levels. As a result, how to effectively supervise these top leaders has become a long-standing problem, and corruption among top leaders has become rampant.

Second, the administration system, which puts supervision organs under the leadership of the objects of supervision, restricts the performance of the supervision system. At present, China's local professional supervisory organs at the various levels—such as party discipline inspection commissions, audit bureaus, and procuratorates—are all subject to a dual leadership system. Party discipline inspection commissions at the various levels, as professional intraparty supervision organs, are generated at the party congresses at their respective levels and yet are subject to the leadership of the party committees at their own levels, which are generated at the same time as party congresses and which should be subject to the supervision of the former. As a result, with the discipline inspection commissions lacking independence from the party committees at their own levels and with the discipline inspection commissions at the superior level playing a leading role only in terms of supervisory functions, it is difficult for the discipline inspection commissions to supervise the party committees at their own levels, especially members who are major party leaders.

The administrative supervision and audit organs, which are responsible for supervising and auditing the administrative organs and their officials and should have been subordinate to the people's congresses at their own levels, in fact are actually subordinate to the governments at their own levels and answer to the government heads at their own levels. Even guidance from the supervisory organs at a superior level is unable to resolve this problem of administrative organs supervising themselves. The procuratorates, which serve as statutory supervisory organs, are not only subject to the leadership of both the people's congresses and the party committees at their respective levels but also have their staffing and budget controlled by the local governments at those levels as well. This lack of independence remains unresolved in spite of the powers of guidance and personnel review held by the procuratorial organs at the superior level. As the existing administration system of professional supervisory organs subordinates the supervisors to the supervised, supervisory bodies often either dare not or cannot supervise party and government leaders at their own levels.[13]

Third, by integrating deliberation and execution, the system lacks separation and a system of checks and balances among the powers of decisionmaking, execution, and supervision. The party committees and people's congresses at various levels implement a leadership system that integrates deliberation and execution, with the decisionmaking, executive, and supervisory powers concentrated in the same organization, thereby rendering impossible either reasonable separation of powers or checks and balances. The standing committees of the party committees of the various levels are generally composed of the main leaders from the party administration, people's congress, the CPPCC, and government systems. The standing party committees, as the leadership core, are responsible for collective decisionmaking, with the standing committee members responsible for the implementation of the decisions. The standing committee is also responsible for the supervision of the implementation of the decisions.

In reality, intraparty supervision, people's congress–based supervision, and CPPCC supervision are all under the leadership of the party standing committees. The people's congresses also implement the deliberation and execution in one type of leadership system. By law, the National People's Congress is the highest organ of legislative power, enjoying the power to appoint or remove officials, the power to make resolutions on important issues, and supervisory power. It serves as both the legislature and supervisor with its own enforcement organs. In terms of institutional design and according to judicial logic, it has extensive, unlimited, and unchallengeable powers.[14] The three-in-one power structure makes it impossible, or at least very difficult, to ensure the soundness of decisionmaking through supervision from the outside, and the same can be said of outside supervision of executive power. The practice of concentrating all powers either in the same organization or individual inevitably leads to power that is both unchecked and arbitrary and thus ultimately leads to the abuse of power.

Fourth, supervision by the press and public opinion lacks effective legal protection. China's present press administration system focuses on pre-event review rather than post-event punishment, with the emphasis on positive reporting and "guided" public opinion rather than on critical supervision. It relies largely on policy documents, administrative intervention, and personnel appointment and removal, with the media experiencing more prohibitions than protections. Owing to the absence of basic laws to protect the survival and development of the press (such as a press law and press tort liability law), freedom of the press is not guaranteed, and the lawful rights of supervision by the press are not protected.[15] In such a press environment, to what degree the supervision by public opinion can be effective is mainly dependent on the support and attitude of the leaders at various levels. And the efficacy of the supervisory power of online opinion is mainly dependent on whether the leaders and professional supervisory organs respond to the issues in question.

Fifth, with democracy and rule of law both underdeveloped, the use of electoral accountability, separation of powers, and checks and balances is limited. In China—with its 2,000-year history of feudal autocracy and a highly centralized political system borrowed from the former Soviet Union—the development of democracy and the rule of law will inevitably be a long process. In spite of the more than thirty years of efforts China has taken to promote democracy and the rule of law, both remain grossly underdeveloped. Free competitive direct elections are the cornerstone of democratic politics. However, with one exception (for the direct election of the deputies to the people's congresses, which has been elevated to the county, municipal or district level), direct election of party and government leaders has been confined to the village level. The multicandidate election mechanism applies only to deputy positions and is largely perfunctory, lacking necessary competition and thus leaving little room for choice. Top-down appointment remains the main method of delegation of power, and top-down accountability remains the most powerful means of accountability.

The supervisory function of the people's congresses at the various levels is ineffective owing to the large number of deputies, a lack of professionalization, and short meeting sessions. There is a lack of checks and balances among the legislature, the judiciary, and the executive. The localization and administration of the judiciary also hinder justice. There is not yet a judicial review system for laws and regulations. There is also a serious lack of external supervision of the ruling party. These problems in the development of democracy and the rule of law have limited the potential of growth of mechanisms for accountability, separation of powers, and checks and balances.[16]

The national integrity system is a generic term for a full range of organizations and rules featuring vertical electoral accountability and horizontal separation of powers based on checks and balances. Building a modern clean-government system is the inevitable path for countries seeking to effectively manage corruption, improve its powers of supervision, and check power. China's existing national integrity system mainly relies on the top-down accountability of the party committees and governments at the various levels and the supervision of the professional supervisory organs for supervision and corruption prevention and punishment. This clean-government system, burdened with characteristics of the traditional centralized political system, has been plagued by bottlenecks. Supervising and restricting the power of party and government leaders has been difficult, given information asymmetry and the phenomenon of officials at higher levels providing a "protective shield" for those under investigation. The professional supervisory organs, moreover, also face the problems of institutional and power expansion and the conundrum of determining who supervises the supervisors. Deepening the reforms of the political system and achieving the modern transformation of the national integrity system have become a matter of urgency for China.

The core task in building a modern national integrity system is to implement rigorous vertical and horizontal accountability systems by deepening political reforms and removing barriers to supervision and checks on power. As long as there exists power above and beyond supervision, corruption will be a political cancer and eventually spell the ruin of the regime. Therefore, supervision is a key link in effectively preventing and punishing corruption.

Fostering civil society and strengthening the supervision of state power is a basic approach to preventing state power from going unchecked and overriding civil society. Civil society's most effective means of checking the political state is its right to vote. Through free and regular competitive elections, citizens can peacefully oust corrupt or power-abusing leaders, thus establishing an effective vertical accountability mechanism that holds the government and national leaders accountable to the public. This electoral accountability cannot be replaced by any other means. It is important therefore to advance electoral democracy and achieve the transition from selection politics to electoral politics and from indirect elections to direct elections.

Implementing checks and balances among various powers within government organs is an effective method to prevent the abuse of power. At the 17th CCP National Congress, it was decided to "establish a sound power structure and enforcement mechanism featuring both restraint and coordination among decision-making power, executive power, and supervisory power,"[17] which is indicative of the direction of the institutional development of the separation of powers with Chinese characteristics. The party committees, governments, people's congresses, democratic parties, and CPPCC organizations at all levels need soundly divided and clearly defined responsibilities in such areas as proposition, participation, deliberation, execution, appraisal, review, and adjustment concerning personnel affairs and policies, thereby ensuring checks and balances among the various organs.

The party committees have the powers in personnel and policy proposition and adjustment to ensure their leadership position as decisionmakers and coordinators. As a check on the party committees' decisionmaking power, the democratic parties and the CPPCC should have the power to participate in and appraise the decisionmaking of the party committees, and the people's congresses should have the power to review and veto the policies and bills submitted by the party committees via the governments. This is indispensable for ensuring the soundness of decisionmaking and for preventing the abuse of power.

The government, as the main body that exercises public power, has the power to execute policies. As a check on the government's executive power, the democratic parties and CPPCC organizations need the power to appraise the implementation of policies, and the results of their appraisal should serve as an important reference for the government in terms of policy revision and personnel adjustment.

Figure 12-2. *Proposed Separation of Decisionmaking, Executive,*
and Supervisory Powers

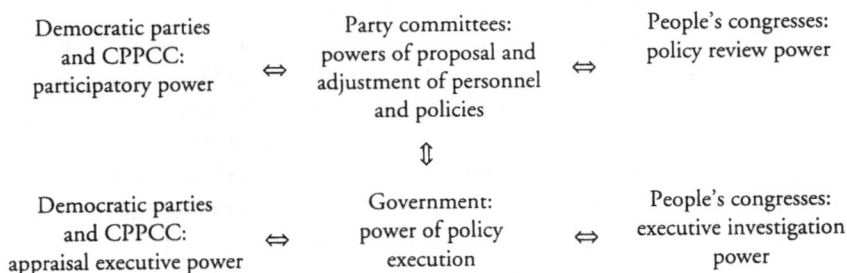

Democratic parties and CPPCC: participatory power	⟺	Party committees: powers of proposal and adjustment of personnel and policies	⟺	People's congresses: policy review power

⇕

Democratic parties and CPPCC: appraisal executive power	⟺	Government: power of policy execution	⟺	People's congresses: executive investigation power

The people's congresses should have the power to supervise policies and budgets. At the same time, to improve the expertise and effectiveness of supervisory power, it is necessary to put the administrative supervisory and audit organs under the people's congress system, where the administrative supervisory organs accept complaints from the citizens and handle improper administrative actions under the leadership of the people's congresses while the audit organs perform independent audits on behalf of the people's congresses and other public power organs and directly submit the audit results to the people's congresses.

This mechanism of checks and balances is illustrated in figure 12-2. People's congresses need to wield veto power during deliberation and review to effectively exercise their supervisory power. Ensuring the protection of speech of CPPCC members during deliberation and appraisal is the core rule for those leaders to effectively exercise their supervisory power.

This institutional design based on checks and balances both ensures the party committees' leadership position and strengthens the supervisory power of the people's congresses and the CPPCC over the decisionmaking and executive powers. At the same time, it does not weaken the executive power of the government. It is an institutional arrangement that faces the least resistance, one that all parties should be ready to accept. With the effective operation of the mechanism of checks and balances based on separation of powers, there will be a significant decrease in the need to rely on the professional supervisory organs, and the powers of the professional supervisory organs will be strong enough to effectively fight corruption.

Since the reform and opening up, China has made great strides in building a modern national integrity system. The existing system has played a definitive role in power supervision and restriction, as well as in corruption prevention and punishment, and has achieved some progress in combating corruption. Because of the centralized political system, however, this system has been unable to achieve full scope in terms of its anticorruption functions. Looking forward, China's efforts toward anticorruption and power supervision should focus on deepening reforms of the political system, overcoming the institutional barriers that prevent the existing national integrity system from playing its full role, and improving the vertical electoral accountability and horizontal checks-and-balances mechanisms.

COMMENT
MELANIE MANION

Professor He Zengke's stimulating chapter on the design of clean governance for China meticulously assesses the status quo of corruption in China and proposes a comprehensive design for new structural relationships to control corruption and constrain power in that country. His design takes as its point of departure a number of fundamental institutional features that, in his analysis, contribute to a situation of persistently widespread and increasingly serious corruption, despite a Chinese anticorruption effort of more than thirty years.

Symptoms

He records indexes of some success in anticorruption efforts over the past three decades, but his overall assessment of the Chinese anticorruption system is generally critical, appropriately so in my view.[18] Among the particularly troubling features of corruption in contemporary China that have emerged in recent years, he notes the following: corruption by top generalist leaders (一把手, *yiba shou*) in positions of executive (mainly Communist Party) power at all levels, corruption in personnel appointments and judicial corruption, and legalization of special privileges (in housing and health care, for example) for leading officials. As to anticorruption enforcement, he criticizes the great unevenness of enforcement priorities over the years and the substitution of party penalties for criminal punishments for officials.

My own work analyzes at length these two flaws of Chinese anticorruption enforcement.[19] The Communist Party discipline inspection system, with its broader jurisdiction, stronger monitoring capacity, and advantaged investigatory and sanction position (compared with the procuracy) is supposed to hold public officials to a higher ethical standard as party members. As He shows, it has instead routinely kept a great deal of official crime out of the criminal justice system, so that milder party disciplinary action substitutes for harsher criminal punishments—turning on its head the ostensibly higher standard for party members. The periodic turn over the past three decades to short bursts of intensified enforcement through anticorruption campaigns to solve fundamental problems of structure and authority in routine enforcement produces cycles of routine and campaign anticorruption enforcement. Ironically, punishment according to law is most strongly emphasized in campaign periods, when enforcement is most highly politicized—a situation that obstructs development of routine expectations of the relevance of law (or rules more generally) in controlling corruption. We know from innovative field and natural experiments that an expectation of enforcement of rules is a necessary tool for successful corruption control,[20] that it can occasionally work on its own at high levels of intensity, but that a sustained intermediate level of enforcement combined with reduced incentives for corrupt acts is more effective.

Diagnosis

The chapter identifies excessive concentration of power in the political system (集权政治体制, *jiquan zhengzhi tizhi*) as the core obstacle to significant anticorruption progress. In a nutshell, according to He's diagnoses, the existing system works against both horizontal and vertical accountability (问责, *wenze*) because of its lack of checks and balances (制衡, *zhiheng*) or appropriate distribution of powers (分权, *fenquan*).

As to horizontal accountability, at each level, major powers (such as personnel and budgetary powers) are concentrated in the hands of top generalist leaders in the leading agencies of the party-state.[21] Furthermore, functionally different sorts of powers (such as executive and legislative power) are merged in small leading agencies: for example, at each level, party committee standing committees bring together main leaders of the party, government, and congress; these small party-led agencies formulate policies executed by the separate agencies and then monitor policy outcomes—that is, the same agency formulates policies and evaluates their outcomes.[22] He also points to a problem specific to anticorruption that has received wide criticism from Western scholars: namely, discipline inspection committees are under the leadership of party committees at their respective levels; they lack the requisite independence and authority to monitor their superiors, a problem that the professional guidance (业务指导, *yewu zhidao*) relationship in the discipline inspection committee hierarchy does not solve.

As to vertical accountability, the chapter points to a lack of legal protection for press freedoms. In those infrequent situations (or localities) where the press has played a significant role in exposing corruption, it has relied on the goodwill of particular relevant leaders for support in this role. Indeed, Aymo Brunetti and Beatrice Weder demonstrate a robust, substantively large (and statistically significant) inverse relationship between press freedoms and corruption around the world, even when only developing countries are taken into account; moreover, the key feature of press freedom that impacts corruption is lack of censorship.[23] Second and especially, He is critical of the weakness of legal provisions for significant electoral accountability: direct, contested elections currently are in place only for township and county congress delegates; as to government leaders, electoral contestation is required in China's quasi-parliamentary system only for deputy leaders.

Overall, the political system He describes has failed to control corruption because the agency relationship is structured as a closed bureaucratic hierarchy: lower-level agents (including state agencies, formally elected officials, and the press) answer to principals who are their political superiors; essentially, all monitoring is self-monitoring by small circles of generalist (especially party) leaders or individual top leaders at each level.

This diagnosis of the sources of persistently widespread and increasingly serious corruption in mainland China is essentially institutional. By this, I refer to a perspective in an extensive literature that privileges incentives in defining institutions.[24] It defines institutions as relatively stable patterns of action sustained by a structure of incentives and beliefs. Incentives that bind players to act in particular ways create credibility; in particular, we look within structures for incentives that "tie the hands" of powerful players so they cannot renege on their commitments, even if they prefer in some instances to do so.[25]

Returning to He's chapter, the diagnosis of the problem is institutional in its recognition that all monitoring in the Chinese political system is essentially self-monitoring. Obviously, not all top generalist party leaders in contemporary China abuse their powers to advance private gain separately from public gain, but little other than reputational concerns and their bosses constrains them from doing so. Nothing ties their hands.

Prescription

Yet if the diagnosis of the problem is institutional, the prescriptive policy design is only partly so. The first part of He's prescription aims to address the horizontal lack of accountability. It proposes to restructure governance arrangements so as to separate powers and introduce checks and balances.[26] At the policymaking level, Communist Party committees would have authority over personnel and the power to propose and make changes to policies; people's congresses would formulate policies; the democratic parties and consultative congresses would advise party committees.[27] As to policy execution, the governments would execute policy, the people's congresses would oversee its execution (that is, monitor the government), and the democratic parties and political consultative congress would evaluate it. This design does indeed reallocate responsibilities to break up concentration (or monopoly) of functional authority in the hands of top leaders or party committees, for example. Why, however, should we expect such a design (if adopted) to matter? Institutionally, I argue, nothing has changed.

Specifically, rules or structural arrangements matter when they constrain powerful players (party committee secretaries, for example) to act in ways that are not always consistent with their preferences in each and every circumstance. That is, when we say the design matters, we must mean that powerful players would have chosen a different outcome in at least some circumstances that fall under their jurisdiction. Do we expect this from the proposed design for the Chinese party-state? It seems that the design, if adopted, is, however clever, fundamentally a "parchment institution."[28] That is, even if codified in law, regulations, or the constitution, nothing about the new design necessarily constrains the powerful players identified in them to act differently from before. Nothing "ties their hands." And if nothing ties the hands of powerful players, then there is no reason for less powerful players (discipline inspection committees and democratic parties, for example) to expect a different pattern of action. The design does not solve the fundamental problem of credibility: if the design were adopted, why would any of the players (especially the less powerful ones) believe it is more than authoritarian "cheap talk."[29]

How can Chinese leaders credibly commit to He's design for clean governance? Here, the second part of He's prescription, which addresses the vertical lack of accountability, may be more relevant. The chapter directs our attention from the powerful to the most powerless players. It argues that the way forward is the development of social checks on state power; the most effective mechanism for this is direct, free, competitive elections so that voters can throw corrupt leaders out of office. The transformation from a "selectoral to a truly electoral politics" (从选拔政治向选举政治, *cong xuanba zhengzhi xiang xuanju zhengzhi*) in He's design is the necessary foundation of vertical accountability. Certainly, in the Chinese quasi-parliamentary system, direct, free, competitive election of people's congresses by ordinary Chinese and free, competitive elections of governments by people's congresses do go some way toward changing the fundamental design—by linking government policy outcomes to mass public preferences through congressional election. This does not seem to address the role of the powerful party committees, however.[30] In this sense, the design seems only partly institutional and partly (merely) structural.

Even direct, free, competitive elections are not fully an institutional solution in the sense of the term used here. This has most to do with the problem of information, which limits the degree to which ordinary voters can truly act as principals of their elected congresses. In China, as in traditional Leninist polities, a single communist party prohibits independent political organizations outside the party and political factions within it. Without competitive interest aggregation along some lines—in liberal democracies, this occurs through political parties—the ordinary mass public simply cannot sort through candidates (or elected delegates) and assign, through votes in elections, credit (or blame) for government outcomes. That is, without informational labels that at the same time impose policy discipline on their members, the agency relationship between congress delegates and their constituents is, for practical purposes, severed. Competitive multiparty elections are not the only institutional mechanism that can cut through this knot: if the "nonparty" label or intraparty policy groups acquired such meaning as an informational shorthand, this problem could be addressed. In short, a truly institutional solution to the problem of credible commitment need not be the Western liberal democratic solution of a multiparty system.

Why would Chinese leaders choose to credibly commit to He's design for clean governance? That is, why would powerful players choose to tie their own hands? He cautions that absent fundamental change in constraints on power, the Chinese state risks collapse from the burdens accompanying growing corruption. Comparatively and historically, we know that single-party authoritarian states survive longer than do other authoritarian states.[31] At the same time, we also know that economic crisis poses a challenge to all regimes, democratic or authoritarian, and that economic crisis in a situation of low per capita incomes is the most common cause of regime collapse, whether democratic or authoritarian. The preponderance of econometric evidence indicates that corruption has high political and economic costs;[32] and neither China's spectacular economic growth nor the high level of direct foreign investment in China suggest that China is immune to these costs.[33] In short, He's bold design for vertical accountability is the start of a way forward for Chinese leaders because it cuts to the core of the anticorruption reform problem and, in controlling corruption, establishes a sounder basis for governance and political legitimacy.

Conclusion

Evidence abounds that Chinese leaders already recognize that building regime support only upon the scaffolding of economic growth entails risks. He's comprehensive clean-governance design surely also entails risks, but it offers an opportunity for Chinese leaders to invest strategically for their longer survival in an infrastructure that goes well beyond observed political reform to date. As I have argued, for the design to be successful this investment involves not only a commitment to new political arrangements (structures) but also and necessarily a commitment to new institutions to demonstrate the government's credibility.

Notes

1. Jiang Zemin, *Lun dang jianshe* [On the construction of the CCP] (Beijing: Zhongyang wenxian chubanshe [Central Party Literature Press], 2001), pp. 475–80.

2. Hu Jintao, *Gaoju Zhongguo tese shehuizhuyi weida qizhi wei duoqu quanmian jianshe xiaokang shehui xin shengli er fendou* [Hold high the great banner of socialism with Chinese characteristics and strive for new victories in building a moderately prosperous society in all respects], report to the 17th CCP National Congress, October 15, 2007 (Beijing: People's Publishing House, 2007), p. 33.

3. For further details, see He Yong, ed., *Huihuang licheng: Dang de jilü jiancha gongzuo sanshi nian* [A glorious process: The CCP's discipline inspection work in thirty years] (Beijing: China Fangzheng Press, 2008).

4. For further details, see Dai Zhechun, "Shilun wo guo gudai 'li fa bing yong, de zhu xing fu' de zhiguo fanlue" [On China's traditional state governance approach of "combining law and discipline rite, with education supplemented by punishment"], *Heilongjiang shehui kexue* [Heilongjiang social sciences], no. 5 (2001).

5. The concept of the national integrity system was put forward by Jeremy Pope. The national integrity system can be likened to a Greek temple, with the three major goals of sustainable development, rule of law, and quality of life as its roof, the institutional actors and their governing rules as its pillars, and public awareness and social values as its foundation. Only when the institutional pillars are balanced and the public awareness and social values are firm can the mansion of the national integrity system stand and can the three major goals be attained. On the basis of this concept, Pope derives the concept of the institutional system of national integrity, which is the generic term for the institutional actors and their corresponding core rules that make up the national integrity system. Under the modern institutional system of national integrity, institutions and their operating rules are girded not only by electoral accountability but also by vertical and horizontal accountability mechanisms based on separation of powers and checks and balances within state power. For more on the concept of the national integrity system, see Jeremy Pope, *Zhiyue fubai: Jiangou guojia lianzheng tixi* [Confronting corruption: The elements of a national integrity system], translated by the Public Integrity Research Institute, School of Public Policy and Management, Tsinghua University (Beijing: China Fangzheng Publishing House, 2003).

6. He, *Huihuang licheng*, pp. 250–61.

7. The data in this paragraph are the author's calculations based on work reports delivered to the plenary sessions of the Central Commission of Discipline Inspection over the years. Interested readers may refer to the relevant contents at the website of the Ministry of Supervision and the archive column at www.xinhuanet.com.

8. These data are the author's calculations based on the work reports of the Supreme People's Procuratorate for the years 1983, 1988, 1993, 1998, 2003, 2008, 2009, and 2010. Further information is available on the website of the Supreme People's Procuratorate (www.spp.gov.cn/gzbg/). The work report for 2010 may be retrieved at *People's Daily Online* (www.people.com.cn.)

9. Yu Keping, "Yu Keping cheng fan fubai cuzai wuqu zui danxin fubai xiang tequan zhuanhua" [Anticorruption the wrong way: The worrying blurring between corruption and privilege], *China News,* December 9, 2008 (www.chinanews.com.cn/gn/news/2008/12-09/1478674.shtml).

10. The data for 2001-09 are cited from Horizon Research Consultancy Group, *Zhongguo jumin shenghuo zhiliang diaocha baogao* [Research report on the quality of life of Chinese residents]. The data for 2010 are cited from *Zhongguo gongzhong he zaihua waiguorenshi yan zhong de Zhongguo guojia diweiguan diaocha* [China's international position in the eyes of the Chinese public and foreign expats in China], a research project conducted by Horizon Research Consultancy Group for the China Development Research Foundation (www.horizonkey.com/cn/ourfruit/zhuangao.html).

11. Li Yifan, "Shiliuda yilai Zhongguo tese fanfu chang lian jianshe qude xianzhu chengxiao" [Fruitful anticorruption with Chinese characteristics since the 16th CCP National Congress], September 10, 2007 (news.xinhuanet.com/lianzheng/2007-09/10/content_6697188.html).

12. Interested readers may refer to He Zengke, "Zhongguo muqian lianzheng zhidu tixi zongti zhuangkuang ji qi youxiaoxing pinggu" [Assessment of the overall status and effectiveness of China's existing institutional system of national integrity," *Xuexi yu shijian* [Study and practice], no. 5 (2009).

13. Wang Yanjun, "Wo guo xianxing quanli jiandu zhiyue jizhi de zhuyao biduan yu quexian fenxi" [Analysis of the main setbacks and defects of China's existing power supervision and restriction mechanism], *Lilun daokan* [Journal of socialist theory guide], no. 9 (2003); Gao Xuedong and others, "Dangqian wo guo quanli jiandu yu zhiyue jizhi boruo de jili fenxi" [Analysis of the weaknesses of China's existing power supervision and restriction mechanism], *Shandong xingzheng xueyuan Shandong sheng jingji guanli ganbu xueyuan xuebao* [Journal of Shandong Administration Institute, Shandong Economic Management Personnel Institute], no. 5 (2005).

14. Li Shiyong and Ma Yan, "Lun wanshan wo guo quanli jiandu tixi de ji dian shexiang: jian lun wo guo de wei xian shencha zhidu" [Several suggestions on improving China's power supervision system, also on China's judicial review system], *Yunnan xingzheng xueyuan xuebao* [Journal of Yunnan Administration College], no. 3 (2004), p. 80.

15. Fu Ning and Wang Yongliang, "Yulun jiandu he zhengzhi wenming: Zhong Mei bijiao yanjiu" [Supervision by public opinion and political civilization: Comparative

research between China and the United States," *Shiyou daxue xuebao* [Journal of China University of Petroleum], no. 3 (2003), pp. 78–82.

16. A detailed analysis of the problems of China's power supervision system can be found in He Zengke, "Shixi wo guo xianxing quanli jiandu cunzai de wenti ji yuanyin" [Preliminary analysis of the problems of China's existing power supervision system and the causes], *Xuexi yu tansuo* [Study and exploration], no. 4 (2008).

17. Hu, *Gaoju Zhongguo tese shehuizhuyi weida qizhi wei duoqu quanmian jianshe xiaokang shehui xin shengli er fendou*, p. 33.

18. He's line of analysis presents a perspective that is analytically similar to (although substantively different from) that of Patrick Meagher, who also undertook to create a rigorous "scorecard" by which to assess performance of the organization of anticorruption efforts. Meagher focuses on anticorruption agencies only; He's perspective is broader. See Patrick Meagher, "Anti-Corruption Agencies: Rhetoric versus Reality," *Journal of Policy Reform* 8, no. 1 (2005).

19. Melanie Manion, *Corruption by Design: Building Clean Government in Mainland China and Hong Kong* (Harvard University Press, 2004).

20. Ray Fisman and Edward Miguel, "Cultures of Corruption: Evidence from Diplomatic Parking Tickets," Working Paper 122 (Durham, N.C.: Bureau for Research in Economic Analysis of Development, 2006); Rafael Di Tella and Ernesto Schargrodsky, "The Role of Wages and Auditing during a Crackdown on Corruption in the City of Buenos Aires," *Journal of Law and Economics* 46 (2003).

21. The idea that some new norm of collective decisionmaking operates widely in party committees is rejected here: even deputy leaders are effectively shut out of substantive power.

22. In this framework, coordination through overlapping directorships is a structural problem, not a solution.

23. Aymo Brunetti and Beatrice Weder, "A Free Press Is Bad News for Corruption," *Journal of Public Economics,* nos. 7–8 (2003).

24. See, for example, Robert H. Bates and others, *Analytic Narratives* (Princeton University Press, 1998); Randall Calvert, "The Rational Choice Theory of Social Institutions: Cooperation, Coordination, and Communication," in *Modern Political Economy: Old Topics, New Directions,* edited by Jeffrey S. Banks and Eric A. Hanushek (Cambridge University Press, 1995), pp. 216–67; Douglass C. North and Barry R. Weingast, "Constitutions and Commitment: The Evolution of Institutions Governing Public Choice in Seventeenth-Century England," *Journal of Economic History,* no. 4 (1989); Kenneth A. Shepsle and Barry R. Weingast, "When Do Rules of Procedure Matter?," *Journal of Politics,* no. 1 (1984).

25. For example, North and Weingast ("Constitutions and Commitment") analyze the institutional arrangements that emerged out of the 1688 Glorious Revolution and find them stably "self-enforcing," that is, characterized by incentives constraining both sovereign and parliament from reneging to engage in confiscatory actions. They point to evidence of a capital market response consistent with a change in beliefs that, they argue, is the result of the changed incentive structure.

26. It is sketched out in figure 12-2 of the chapter.

27. By this, it seems that the *nomenklatura* system (that is, cadre management by party committees) remains unchanged. This seems to be a sina qua non of feasible political reform.

28. John M. Carey, "Parchment, Equilibria, and Institutions," *Comparative Political Studies*, nos. 6–7 (2000).

29. *Cheap talk* is a game theoretic term for communication that does not affect the payoffs of the players in a game.

30. For example, despite changes since 1995, Communist Party committees at all levels continue to control "elections" by congresses of main government leaders, through their recommendations to congress presidiums and precongress meetings of party-member congress delegates, for example (see Melanie Manion, "When Communist Party Candidates Can Lose, Who Wins? Assessing the Role of Local People's Congresses in the Selection of Leaders in China," *China Quarterly*, no. 195 (2008). If, as in He's design, party committees are to retain authority over personnel, does this change?

31. Barbara Geddes, *Paradigms and Sand Castles: Theory Building and Research Design in Comparative Politics* (University of Michigan Press, 2003); Beatriz Magaloni, "Credible Power-Sharing and the Longevity of Authoritarian Rule," *Comparative Political Studies*, nos. 4-5 (2008).

32. Paolo Mauro, "The Effects of Corruption on Growth, Investment, and Government Expenditure: A Cross-Country Analysis," in *Corruption and the Global Economy*, edited by Kimberly Ann Elliott (Washington, D.C.: Institute for International Economics, 1997), pp. 83–107; Mitchell A. Seligson, "The Impact of Corruption on Regime Legitimacy: A Comparative Study of Four Latin American Countries," *Journal of Politics*, no. 2 (2002); Daniel Treisman, "The Causes of Corruption: A Cross-National Study," *Journal of Public Economics*, no. 3 (2000).

33. Shang-Jin Wei, "Why Does China Attract So Little Foreign Direct Investment?," in *The Role of Foreign Direct Investment in East Asian Economic Development*, edited by Takatoshi Ito and Anne O. Krueger (University of Chicago Press, 2000), pp. 239–61.

Contributors

JACQUES DELISLE is the Stephen A. Cozen Professor of Law and professor of political science at the University of Pennsylvania, director of the university's Center for East Asian Studies, deputy director of the university's Center for the Study of Contemporary China, and director of the Asia Program at the Foreign Policy Research Institute.

LARRY DIAMOND is a senior fellow at the Hoover Institution and at the Freeman Spogli Institute for International Studies, where he directs the Center for Democracy, Development, and the Rule of Law.

JOSEPH FEWSMITH is professor of international relations and political science and director of the Boston University Center for the Study of Asia. He is also a research associate of the Pardee Center for the Study of the Longer Range Future at Boston University and of the John King Fairbank Center for East Asian Studies at Harvard University.

MARY GALLAGHER is an associate professor of political science at the University of Michigan where she is also the director of the Center for Chinese Studies. In addition, she is a faculty associate at the Center for Comparative Political Studies at the Institute for Social Research.

HE ZENGKE is the director of the China Institute of Global Development Strategies, affiliated with the Central Compilation and Translation Bureau of the CCP.

HUANG WEIPING is a professor and the director of the Institute for Contemporary China Politics at Shenzhen University.

JING YUEJIN is professor of political science at Tsinghua University.

DAVID M. LAMPTON is George and Sadie Hyman Professor and director of China Studies at the Johns Hopkins School of Advanced International Studies.

CHENG LI is senior fellow and director of research at the Brookings Institution's John L. Thornton China Center. He also serves as a director of the National Committee on U.S.-China Relations and as a member of the Academic Advisory Team of the Congressional U.S.-China Working Group, of the Council on Foreign Relations, and of the Committee of 100.

KENNETH LIEBERTHAL is senior fellow at Brookings Institution's John L. Thornton China Center and Global Economy and Development program. He is professor emeritus at the University of Michigan.

LIN SHANGLI is a professor of international relations and public affairs at Fudan University and also serves as vice president.

MELANIE MANION is Vilas-Jordan Distinguished Achievement Professor of political science and public affairs at the University of Wisconsin–Madison.

JEAN C. OI is the William Haas Professor in Chinese Politics in the Department of Political Science and a senior fellow of the Freeman Spogli Institute for International Studies at Stanford University.

ANTHONY J. SAICH is the director of the Ash Center for Democratic Governance and Innovation (Harvard), the Daewoo Professor of International Affairs, the director of the Rajawali Foundation Institute for Asia, and faculty chair of the Asia and China Public Policy programs at Harvard University's Kennedy School of Government.

SHI HEXING is a professor of political science and deputy director-general in the Department of Public Administration and Policy at the Chinese Academy of Governance.

ANDREW WALDER is at Stanford University where he is the Denise O'Leary and Kent Thiry Professor and chair of the Department of Sociology, a senior fellow in the Freeman Spogli Institute for International Studies, and director of the Division of International, Comparative, and Area Studies (School of Humanities and Sciences).

WANG CHANGJIANG is a professor and the director of the Center of Comparative Party Studies at the Central Party School of the CCP.

WANG MING is a professor of public management at Tsinghua University. He is also the director of the NGO Research Center at Tsinghua University and chief editor of *China Nonprofit Review*.

LYNN T. WHITE III is professor emeritus at Princeton University's Department of Politics and Woodrow Wilson School.

YAN JIRONG is a professor of political science and deputy director of the Institute of Political Development and Governance at Peking University.

YANG GUANGBIN is the Cheung Kong Professor of Political Science and the director of the Institute of Comparative Politics at Renmin University of China.

YU KEPING is professor and director of the China Center for Comparative Politics and Economics (CCCPE) and also professor and director, Center for Chinese Government Innovations, at Peking University.

YU JIANXING is a professor of political science and the vice dean of the College of Public Administration at Zhejiang University. He is also the director of the Center for Civil Society Studies at Zhejiang University.

ZHOU GUANGHUI is a professor and the director of the Department of Administration at Jilin University, vice chairman of the Chinese Association of Political Science, and deputy director of the College Politics Discipline–Teaching and Direction Committee of the Ministry of Education. He is also a research associate at the Center of Political Development and Government at Peking University.

Index

Academic exchange between China and
United States, x, 36–37
Accountability, 7, 29, 37, 60, 98, 100, 246,
249, 251; of CPPCC, 381, 383; of deci-
sionmaking mechanism, 347, 357, 358;
of election process, 303, 366; of NGOs,
182; of petition process, 315–16; vertical
and horizontal system of, 32, 375, 379,
381, 384–91. *See also* Integrity system;
Rule of law; Separation of powers
ACFTU. *See* All-China Federation of Trade
Unions
Administrative Procedural Law, 259, 371
Affluence, effect of, 58, 309
Agricultural Bank of China, 266
AIDS prevention, 169
All-China Federation of Trade Unions
(ACFTU), 170, 172, 186, 321
All-China Women's Federation, 170, 172
Amnesty International, 179
Anhui Province, 201
Anticorruption. *See* Integrity system
Anticorruption and Antibribery Bureau, 371
Anti-Japanese demonstrations (Beijing), 176
Anti-Japanese War, 138–39, 141
Anti-Money Laundering Law, 371
Antimonopoly Law, 331, 371

Anti-Rightist Movement of 1957–58, 40,
41, 45
Anti-Unfair Competition Law, 371
Asian Barometer, 94
Associational life, 167, 168–71, 187, 188.
See also Civil society
Association for the Handicapped, 80
Authoritarian systems: and CCP, 79; and
defiance of law, 49; elections in, 300–01;
fragmented authoritarianism, 123; and
institution building, 96; moderation of,
99; single-party autocratic system, 11,
24; suppression of dissent, 48
Autonomy. *See* Social autonomy

Bank of Communications, 266
Beijing, 176, 194, 204, 231, 267, 274, 287,
290
Berman, Sheri, 187
Biliang Hu, 251
Black-collar stratum, 330, 332
Boston Consulting Group, 173
Bo Xilai, 276
Brezhnev, Leonid, 18, 215
Bribery. *See* Corruption; Integrity system
Brookings forum on China's governance
(May 2011), x

Brunetti, Aymo, 389
Budgeting and finance, 13, 120–21, 158–59, 161, 234, 286, 295. *See also* Tax-sharing system
Business. *See* Trade associations
Business Association, 80
Buyun Township (Sichuan Province), 288, 289

Cadre management. *See* Chinese Communist Party (CCP); Decentralization
Campaign to Suppress Counterrevolutionaries (1953), 40
Cao Dewang, 174
CCP. *See* Chinese Communist Party
CCP Central Committee: 11th, 3, 42, 43, 46, 50, 52, 124, 223, 283, 349; 13th, 57; 14th, 53; 16th, 46–47, 56, 205, 226, 310, 355, 357; 17th, 87, 88, 177, 200, 233; 18th, 244; chairmanship abolished, 351; decisionmaking authority of, 342, 343–44, 346, 347, 348, 357–58; Opinions on Further Promoting Open Government (2005), 355; Opinions on Strengthening the Work of the CPPCC (2006), 153; organization of five leading groups, 343; in party organization, 79; scientific decisionmaking practices of, 353–54; Secretariat, 342, 343, 351, 360; Secretary General, 351, 352; on social organizations, 177. *See also topics of Central Committee decisions*
CCP National Congress, 89–90; 8th, 78, 347, 367; 11th, 367; 12th, 52–53, 198, 350; 13th, 349, 355, 360; 14th, 198, 224; 15th, 51, 198, 318; 16th, 46, 49, 51, 82, 87, 116, 199, 226, 227, 319, 349, 351, 352, 360, 367, 379; 17th, 49, 53, 57, 87, 177, 199, 227, 282, 294, 349, 351, 356, 360, 385
Central Economic Work Conference, 351
Centralization: democratic centralism after revolution, 347, 357; evolving to decentralization, 20–22, 51–54; of political power in CCP, 79; relationship of central and local governments, 34, 61, 254. *See also* Decentralization

Chambers, Simone, 188
Chambers of commerce, 13, 170
Charitable donations, 172, 173
Charter 08, 93–94, 129
Checks and balances. *See* Separation of powers
Chiang Kai-shek, 142
China Association for Science and Technology, 170, 172
China Children and Teenagers Foundation, 172
China Construction Bank, 266
China Democratic League, 55, 352
China Development Bank, 267
China Disabled Persons Federation, 170, 172, 186
China Light Industry Association, 53
China Textile Industry Association, 54
China Welfare Foundation for the Handicapped, 172
Chinese Academy of Social Sciences, 310–11, 332
"Chinese Civil Society: Concept, Classification, and Institutional Environment" (Yu Keping), 167
Chinese Communist Party (CCP): cadres, administration of, 21, 257–58, 271, 274–75, 289, 303, 347; Central Committee, 153, 257; centralized authority of, 54; competition with and fighting against Kuomintang, 140–42; constitution of, 49, 88, 199, 257, 291, 342, 343, 350, 351; decisionmaking authority of, 341–42, 344, 350; Decisions on Some Important Issues to Strengthen and Improve the Leadership of the Party (2009), 87; Decisions on Strengthening the Governing Capacity of the Party (2008), 88; Diamond on future path of, 93–100; functions of, 84; goals of, 61, 138; grassroots-level party cells, transformation of, 90–91; ideological changes, 59, 87–88; influences on, 6, 40, 48, 73–78, 97, 138–39; leadership succession, 271–72, 352; legitimacy of, 83–84; liberal-minded intellectuals within, ix; Long March, 138; membership,

broadening of, 88–89; military nature of, 75; and morality of officials, 368; organization and operation of, 6, 78–81; political consultation system strengthened by, 136, 137, 156; reforms within, 6, 7, 28–29, 87–91, 92, 98; relationship with government, 115–17, 254, 257; Resolution on Certain Questions in the History of Our Party since the Founding of the PRC, 46; from revolutionary party to ruling party, 5–8, 39–44, 58, 73–102, 140; ruling style of, 8, 84–85, 95; Secretariat, 351; and social autonomy, 198–200; and society, 86–87, 249, 326, 335; and state power, 8, 80, 85–86; and supervision in corruption prevention, 368–69, 385; tenure of party leaders, 347; and term limits, 95–96; variables shaping, 74–78; vested interests as threat to, 92–93; and village elections, 302. *See also* CCP Central Committee; CCP National Congress; Intraparty democracy

Chinese Communist Youth League, 172, 193, 335

Chinese People's Political Consultative Conference (CPPCC): 1st, 142; 2nd, 145; 8th, 145; 11th, 145; Common Program of, 103, 106, 143, 156, 161; constitution of, 148, 151, 152–53; decisionmaking role not fully developed, 358; entrepreneurs appointed to, 160; functions of, 152–53; Interim Provisions on Political Consultation and Democratic Supervision, 152; lack of actual power held by, 13, 151, 161; local party committees working with, 154; multiparty cooperation and political consultation through, 12, 137, 147–56; National Committee, 152–54; near-term goals for, 62; number of proposals submitted by, 154, 161; Opinions on Strengthening the Work of the CPPCC (2006), 153; Provisions of the CPPCC National Committee on Political Consultation, Democratic Supervision, and Participation in the Administration and Discussion of Government Affairs (1995), 152, 153; public

recommendation-based direct election of members of, 294; reform and strengthening of, 4, 162; restoration after Mao's death, 161; supervision of members and accountability, 381, 383

Chinese Social Sciences Quarterly, 166

Chinese Soviet Republic (Jiangxi), 137–38

Chongqing Province, 276, 288, 294

Circular on Implementing the Separation of Government and Society and Establishing Township Governments (1983), 201

Civil servants. *See* Government officials

Civil society, 13–14, 165–91; associational life, 167, 168–71, 187; as check on state power, 385; and constitutional development, 121; constraints on development of, 15, 177–78; definition of, 167–68; development trends, 15, 181–83, 296; encroachment of market mechanism, 180–81; evolution from political state to, 13–15, 54–57, 86; Gallagher's comment on, 183–88; ideological restriction on, 178–79; inadequate professional competency, 179–80; lack of social supervision, 180; micro and macro structures of, 168; Nu River dam, campaign against, 175, 176, 180, 186; official attitude toward, 176–77; Opinions on Deepening the Administrative System Reform (2009), 177; privatization of public services, 20, 175–76; and public sphere, 167–68, 174; pursuit of good society, 15, 167, 171–74; scholarship on state-society relations, 195–97; stages of development of, 168–69; theory, 194–95; Wenzhou Lighter Association, 174–75. *See also* Nongovernmental organizations (NGOs)

Civil Society (Edwards), 167

"Civil Society, Grow Together" (Shenzhen slogan), 13, 165, 183

Class struggle, 44–47, 63

Class theory, 309

Clean-government system, 31, 367, 372, 373–81

Collective wage negotiation system, 320

Comintern (Communist International), 74

Commune system, 16
Communist neo-traditionalism, 245
Communist Party of Russia, 137–38
Communist Party of the Soviet Union
   (CPSU), 6, 73–74, 79, 88, 95, 97, 156,
   346
Communist Youth League, 80
Community-based organizations, 169–70,
   251
Company Law, article 8, 260
Compulsory Education Law (2006), 228–29
Conflicts of interest, 25–27, 120, 259, 273,
   295, 309–14
Confucianism, 77–78, 98, 99, 270–71
Constitutionalism, 9–11, 105–08, 112,
   117–21, 126–28
Constitution of the People's Republic of
   China: 1954, 103, 107, 112, 118; 1975,
   107–08, 115; 1978, 107–08, 113, 204;
   1982, 103, 108–12, 114, 115, 118, 147,
   282, 286; 1986, 109; 1995, 109; 2004,
   109; 2009, 109; administrative power
   placed in National People's Congress,
   80, 103; adoption of, 107, 343; as basis
   for standard of conduct, 9; centralist
   approach of, 255, 256; constitutional
   review system, need for, 121; CPPCC
   not vested with power under, 151;
   enumeration of fundamental rights and
   duties of citizens, 111; on ethnic autonomy, 256; government system established
   by, 9, 103, 110–11, 114; human rights,
   protection of, 111; multiparty cooperation and political consultation as tenet
   of, 151, 352; private property ownership,
   right to, 111; subdistrict office system
   restored under, 204; voting rights and
   electoral system established by, 112
Consultative politics, 136–64. See also Political consultation system
Cooperation, multiparty. See Political consultation system
Corporate social responsibility, 173, 174
Corruption, 68, 212–13, 260, 272–73, 285,
   298, 330, 366. See also Integrity system
CPPCC. See Chinese People's Political Consultative Conference

CPSU. See Communist Party of the Soviet
   Union
Cultural Revolution: anticorruption efforts
   of, 367; class factions involved in, 45;
   CPPCC role during, 151, 154, 161;
   decisionmaking authority at time of, 348;
   end of, 42; evolution of CCP during, 78;
   lessons from, 349, 360; multiparty system ceasing during, 81, 157; and orderly
   political participation, 113; part of Mao's
   continuous revolution ideology, 40; and
   politicization of all social life, 55; rule of
   law as legal principle during, 50; seizure
   of subdistrict offices, 204; suffering and
   disaster of, 3, 5, 28, 41–42
Custody and Repatriation Regulations, 128

Dahl, Robert, 333, 363
Debt evasion and rescission phenomenon,
   266–67, 274
Decentralization, xi, 254–81; and administration system, 258–61, 269; cadres,
   administration of, 21, 257–58, 271,
   274–75, 303; from centralization to
   decentralization, 20–22, 51–54, 225;
   fiscal federalism, 261–65; kinds of power
   and kinds of divisions, 270–72; monitoring money, land, and cadres, 274–75;
   more division as part of reform, 276–77;
   reforms accompanying, xi, 268–70;
   and separation of powers, 272–74; unitary system, 255–61, 265–68; White's
   comment on, 270–77. See also Fiscal
   federalism
Decisionmaking system, 28–30, 340–65;
   characteristics, problems, and crises of,
   60, 345–48; contemporary changes
   in, 348–57; crises prior to reform and
   opening-up period, 347–48; definition
   of decisionmaking, 341; deliberative
   decisionmaking, 98; democratization of
   decisionmaking, 30, 295, 363; disclosure, 355–56; and documentary politics,
   318–19; dynamic openness, 355; in early
   period of PRC, 345–47; experience-
   based, 346–47; formation of, 340–45;
   "garbage can model" of, 117; historical

rationality of, 343–45; instrumental rationality of, 360; and interest groups, 331; Lampton's comment on, 359–64; and mass media, 353; mechanism reforms for, 357, 358; modes of, 353–55; objectives of decisionmaking reform, 349–50; openness in, 356–57; Opinions on Further Promoting Open Government (2005), 355; and political participation, 361–62; problems in, 357–58; and public opinion, 358; Regulations on Open Government Information (2008), 355–56; relationship with CPPCC, 153; scientific approach to, 349, 353, 360, 362; structure of, 350–53; vertical allocation of power in, 346. *See also* Political consultation system

Decisions. *See topic of decision*

Decree 319, 259

Deliberative democracy vs. consultative democracy, 12, 98, 155, 157–58

deLisle, Jacques, 10–11, 121

Democracy: aspects of Chinese democracy, xii, 8, 11, 60, 99, 119, 128–30, 283; within CCP, 98; Chinese public view of, 128–30; and constitutional government, 9–11; democratic centralism, 52, 60, 68; from dictatorship to democratic system, 3–4, 8–11, 47–49, 64–65; direct democracy, 74; effect of democratic systems, xii, 276; inborn vs. constructed democracy, 298; indirect democracy, 74; modernization's need for, 272, 283; and mutual guarantees, 363; need for transition to fundamentally democratic political system, 64–65; and rule of law, 41, 50; variations illustrated by other countries, 118, 130, 276. *See also* Deliberative democracy; Grassroots democracy; Intraparty democracy

"Democratic and Scientific Decisionmaking Is an Important Topic of Political Reform" (Wan Li), 349

Democratic legitimacy, 111, 116, 117, 119, 122, 126, 296

Deng Xiaoping: on CCP reorganization, 78, 87; combining party and state leadership,

140; criticizing party as governing organ, 76; on Cultural Revolution, 348, 367; decentralization of authority by, 21; on democracy and modernization's relationship, 89, 283; on dictatorship, 48; on feudalism and tradition, 78; market economy established by, 55–56; on multiparty cooperation, 152; reform policy and opening-up period under, ix, 2, 3, 30, 42–44, 59, 349, 360; on relationship between party and state as key to political reform, 92, 115; and rule of law, 50; socialism with Chinese characteristics implemented by, 369; stability as important precept for, 108; as successful leader and visionary, 4–5, 63, 65–66

Deng Zhenglai, 166

de Tocqueville, Alexis, 167, 187, 216

Diamond, Larry, 7–8, 33, 93

Dictatorships. *See* Authoritarian systems

Documentary politics, 318–19

"Doing Well in the Work of the Special Committees of the People's Congress" (Wan), 110

Earthquake. *See* Wenchuan earthquake (2008)

East Asian democratization, 126

Eastern European countries, democratization of, 297

Easton, David, 25

Economic development zones, 235, 261, 352; A Preliminary Idea for Establishing the Yangtze River Delta Economic Development Zone (China Democratic League), 352

Economic federalism. *See* Fiscal federalism

Economy: Decision of the CCP Central Committee on Issues Regarding the Establishment of the Socialist Market Economic System (1993), 53; Decision on Several Issues to Improve the Socialist Market Economic System, 199; economic development as primary focus of government, 42, 223, 269; examination and approval economy, 260; macroeconomic control, 261–62, 263, 331;

planned economy, 82, 84, 222, 267, 321; political economy, importance of, 66–67; post-revolution gains in, 40–41; rapid economic development from 1978 to 2008, 43–44, 57; rural economic change under Deng, 43; socialist system, 40, 41, 54–55, 60, 82. *See also* Fiscal federalism

Education: college student increase from 1978 to 2008, 44; Compulsory Education Law (2006), 228–29; lunch subsidy, 229; narrowing gap between urban and rural education, 229; Outline of China's National Plan for Medium and Long-Term Education Reform and Development (2010–20), 342, 356; post-revolution increases in literacy, 41; rural compulsory education, 223, 228–29; School Bus Safety Regulations (2012), 229; transition from free to paid system, 224

Edwards, Michael, 167

Elderly, basic old-age security and senior services, 230–31, 250; Opinions on Accelerating the Development of the Elderly Services Industry (2006), 231; Social Care Service System Building Plan for Old Age (2011–2015), 231

Elections: in authoritarian systems, 300–01; citizen participation in, 301–02; constitutional provision on, 112; in consultative system, 160–61; direct election based on public recommendation, 293, 297, 381; evolution of Electoral Law (1972, 1979, 2009), 109, 112; first general election in PRC (1953–54), 106–07; local elections as window on democracy, 301–02; at national level, 97; one-fourth clause, 112; positive aspects of, 277; of township mayors, 23, 285, 288–89, 292–94, 300; two-ballot system, 23; uncertain future of, 303–04; and vertical division of power, 276; village elections, 23–25, 97, 122, 129, 284–86, 292, 302; violence as result of, 276, 277; voting rights, 112, 120

Electoral Law (1953), 112

Electoral Law (1972), 109

Electoral Law (1979), 112, 289–90

Electoral Law (2009), 112

Embezzlement. *See* Integrity system

Employment Promotion Law (2007), 228

Employment security and service, 227–29

Engels, Friedrich, ix, 39–40, 75, 179

Enterprise Bankruptcy Law, 123

Enterprise Income Tax Law (2008), 173

Entrepreneurship, 5, 228, 274

Environmental protection, 166, 169, 175, 176

Ethnic groups. *See* Minorities

Evolution of China's political development, xi; from anticorruption to supervision of power, 30–32; from centralization to decentralization, 20–22, 51–54; from class struggle to harmony, 44–47; from conflicts of interest to coordination of interests, 25–27; from control to service, 18–20; from dictatorship to democratic system, 8–11, 47–49, 64–65; from government rule to societal autonomy, 15–18; from grassroots democracy to national democracy, 22–25; Lieberthal's comment on, 62–69; from political consultation to deliberative politics, 11–13; from political state to civil society, 13–15, 54–57; prior catastrophic failure as prerequisite for major reform, 66; progress in political development, 33–37, 67–68; from revolutionary party to ruling party, 5–8, 39–44, 73–102; from revolution to reform, 2–5, 39–44, 68, 122; from rule of man to rule of law, 49–51; from traditional decisionmaking to modern decisionmaking, 28–30. *See also* Chinese Communist Party (CCP)

Family and hierarchical order, 77–78

Federalism. *See* Fiscal federalism

Fei Xiaotong, 193

Fewsmith, Joseph, 12–13, 156

Fiscal federalism, 21, 255–56, 261–65; tension from dual political-economic structure of, 265–68; trends, 269

Fishkin, James, 158

Five-Anti Campaign, 344
Five Black Categories, 45
Five-Year Plans: 1st, 345; 11th, 226, 235, 237; 12th, 68, 233
Former Soviet states: comparison of China to, 215; lessons from, 97, 297; multiparty systems of, 212; as new struggling democracies, 15, 126, 184
Foundations, 170–71, 172; development trends, 182; Measures for the Management of Foundations (1988), 172; Regulations on Foundation Administration (2004), 170, 172, 173, 180, 371–72
Four Cardinal Principles, 48, 49
Fujian Province, 237, 291

Galbraith, John Kenneth, 167
Gallagher, Mary, 14–15, 165, 183
Gang of Four, 42, 46
The General Rules of the Revolutionary Party of China (Sun), 75–76
Globalization, 59–60, 296, 351
Good governance: Chinese assumptions about, xi; and elections, 24; goal of, 67–68; perspectives on China's evolution toward, 1–38. *See also* Evolution of China's political development
Good society, 15, 167, 171–74
Gorbachev, Mikhail, 18, 95, 214, 215
Governance. *See* Good governance
Government officials: competition to evaluate performance of local officials, 225; number of, 144–45; public opinion of, 249–50, 380; Rules on Official Rotation (1999), 258; self-discipline of, 368; special privileges for civil servants, 374; top-down appointment and accountability, 384. *See also* Conflicts of interest; Corruption; Integrity system; Interest-coordination mechanism
Grassroots democracy, 22–25, 119, 282–307; assessment of, 5, 298–99; challenges to development of, 296–98; from democratic election to democratic governance, 294–95; election of local people's congress deputies, 289–91; election of town mayors, 23, 288–89; election of

village committees, 284–86; from extraparty to intraparty elections, 62, 291–94; from grassroots society to grassroots government, 22–25, 288–91; impetus and impediment of, 295–98; institutional design of residents committee elections, 286–88; Interim Rules on the Election of Grassroots CCP Organizations, 291; misconstruction of, 92; near-term goals for, 62; Oi's comment on, 299–304; overview of Chinese context, 282–84; progress and dimensions of, 4, 23–24, 284–95; social autonomy in urban areas, 203; from village democracy to community democracy, 23–25, 284–88. *See also* Elections
Great Leap Forward, 157, 273, 348
Great Third Front, 273
Green Earth Volunteers, 175
Greenpeace, 179
Guangdong Province, 186, 232, 237, 267, 274, 287, 288; Regulations on Democratic Management of Enterprises in Guangdong Province, 321
Guangxi Province, 201, 287, 288
Guangzhou, 290, 317, 321, 330–31
Guiyang, 294
Guizhou, 246, 275, 309

Habermas, Jürgen, 167, 188
Hamrin, Carol Lee, 340
Hardin, Russell, 105, 119
Harmonious society, 44–47, 221, 226, 245, 249, 271, 325, 335; Decision of the CCP Central Committee Regarding Several Major Issues on Building a Harmonious Socialist Society (2006), 199, 226, 309–10, 319
Health services. *See* Public health; Public service system
He Baogang, 158
Hegelian theory and model, 195–96
He Long, 42
Henan Province, 285, 288
Henan Seeds case, 127
He Zengke, 31–32, 366, 387–91
Hezhai Village, 201

Hobbes, Thomas, 105
Homeowner associations, 129, 204, 205, 295, 296
Hong Kong, 213, 245, 255, 256, 274
Horizon China survey, 374
Horizontal structures. *See* Accountability; Political system
Household registration system, 228, 245, 248, 313, 321
Household responsibility system, 43, 84–85, 200, 223, 284
Housing: and economic federalism, 263; low-income housing, 232–33; Notice on Resolutely Curbing the Soaring of Housing Prices in Some Cities (2010), 232; Several Opinions of the State Council on Solving the Housing Difficulties of Urban Low-Income Families (2007), 232; transition from public housing allocation to commercial housing, 224
Huang Weiping, 23–25, 282, 299–304
Huang Zhezhen, 193
Hubei Province, 237, 267, 288, 290, 291, 294
Hu Jintao: on citizen participation in political affairs, 349; clean government guidelines of, 367; on fair and democratic society, 47; on harmonious society, 335; on modernization's link to democracy, 272; and public service supply system, 20, 245, 247, 248–49; socialism with Chinese characteristics implemented by, 369; on upholding law and Constitution, 124, 128
Hukou reforms, 248
Human rights, protection of, 111, 166, 169
Hunan, 290
Huntington, Samuel, 361
Hurun Wealth Report, 173

Ideological change, 59, 78–79, 87–88, 178–79. *See also* Chinese Communist Party (CCP); Marxism; Socialism
Income gap, growth of, 309
India syndrome, 260, 273
Industrial and Commercial Bank of China, 266

Industrialization, 344
Industry associations, 170, 208
Institution building, 92, 96, 122, 153, 260, 324; neglect of, after revolution, 347, 348
Integrity system, 30–32, 366–92; from anticorruption to supervision of power, 30–32; Antimonopoly Law, 371; Anti-Unfair Competition Law, 371; Civil Servant Law, 371, 378; conflicts of interest among government offices and officials, 120, 259, 273; Corruption Perception Index, 372–73; corruption since reform and opening-up period, 3, 31, 367–73; criteria for organizational effectiveness, 375–76; criticism from Western scholars, 388; diagnosis of corruption, 388–89; effectiveness of existing clean-government system, 31, 367, 372, 373–81; Judges Law, 371; Manion's comment on, 387–92; modern characteristics of, 381–87; National Bureau of Corruption Prevention, 369–70; overall performance of, 377–78; prescription of corruption, 389–91; Procedural Rules of Local Party Committees, 370; Procurators Law, 371; Provisional Regulations for the Registration Administration of People-Run Non-enterprise Units, 371–72; and public opinion, 380, 383; punishment of corrupt officials, 31; Regulations of the CCP on Protecting the Rights of Party Members, 370; Regulations of the Commission of Discipline Inspection and the Organizational Department of the CCP Central Committee on Inspection Work (Trial), 370–71; Regulations of the People's Republic of China on Making Public Government Information, 372; Regulations on Disciplinary Sanctions, 378; Rules for Intra-Party Question and Inquiry by Members of Local Party Committees and Local Commissions of Discipline Inspection, 370–71; and supervision in corruption prevention, 368–69, 371; Supervisory Measures for the Selection and Appointment of Leading Party and Government Cadres

(Trial), 370–71; symptoms of corruption, 387–88. *See also* Separation of powers
Interest coordination mechanism, 25–27, 308–39; Li's comment on, 328–35; with Chinese characteristics in the making, 317–19; conflicts of interest, 25–27, 309–14; contradiction among the people, 311; coordinating labor and capital interests, 319–21; development model and institutional adaptability, 321–24; and imbalance of interests, 322; institutional bottlenecks and pressure for transformation, 7, 314–17; institutionalization mechanisms, 332–35; and institutionalized space of choice, 324; labor-capital contradictions, 311–14, 319, 330; major changes in social and interest structures, 309–10; and mass disturbances, 322–23; need for reform, 308; official-citizen contradictions, 311–14; optimizing public policymaking, 318–19; petition system, 315–16; pressure to maintain stability, 316–17; scale and scope of interest group politics, 5, 329–32; and transformation strategy, 323–24, 328; unitarism and pluralism, 277, 324–27
Interest politics liberalism, 333
Internet, 176, 186, 214, 353, 356
Intraparty democracy, 291–94; development of, 89–90, 347; forms of, 160–61; future role of, 4, 6–7, 62, 63, 92, 119; Jiang Zemin on, 115–16; Regulations of the CCP on Intra-Party Supervision (Trial), 370–71, 378; Some Norms Concerning Intra-Party Political Life (1980), 52; use of term, 334
Investment projects under control of central government, 261

Japanese invasion, 138–39
Jiangsu Province, 205, 231, 262, 267, 274, 288, 294
Jiangxi Province, 137–38, 237
Jiang Zemin, 113, 115–16, 124, 247, 349, 367, 369
Jilin Province, 294

Jing Yuejin, 25–27, 308, 328–34
Jinshan District (Shanghai), 316
Jiu San Society, 55, 352
Journalists Association, 80
Jowitt, Kenneth, 157
Judicial assistance treaties, 372

Kopstein, Jeffrey, 188
Korea, 99, 157
Kuomintang: competition with and fighting against CCP, 140–42; corporatist framework of, 162; Long March of CCP in reaction to, 138; as one-party dictatorship, 76, 137, 142; political parties in opposition to, 81; revolutionary overthrow of (1949), 3, 39, 86; in Taiwan, 97

Labor-capital relationship, 313–14, 319, 330
Labor Contract Law (2007), 228
Lampton, David M., 29–30, 359
Land Administration Law, 261
Landry, Pierre, 275
Land transfer to private ownership. *See* Property ownership
Law on ___. *See topic of law*
Leadership succession, 271–72, 352
Legal system, 49–51; Administrative Procedural Law, 259, 371; conflict of laws, 259, 276; and decisionmaking system, 358; development of socialist system of laws with Chinese characteristics, 108, 114–15, 120; Directive of the CCP Central Committee on Resolutely Implementing the Criminal Law and the Criminal Procedural Law, 50–51; goals for, 67; judicial corruption, 373; Organic Law of the People's Courts (1954), 107; professionalization of judicial system, 371; rule of man as guiding principle, 49–51, 130. *See also* National People's Congress (NPC); Rule of law
Legislation, Law on (2002), 109–10, 125, 126, 128, 129
Legitimacy. *See* Democratic legitimacy
Leninist theory and influences, ix, 47, 48, 68, 75, 139, 157, 326

"Let some people get rich first," 173, 183
Liaoning Province, 201, 237, 267, 287
Li Cheng, ix, 26–27, 271–72, 328
Lieberthal, Kenneth, ix, 4–5, 62
Li Huijuan, 127
Li Lulu, 328
Lin Biao, 46
Lindblom, Charles Edward, 260
Lin Shangli, 11–12, 13, 136, 156–59, 161–62
Lin Yutang, 77
Li Peng, 122–23
Liu Shaoqi, 42
Lobbyists and interest groups, 331. *See also* Interest coordination mechanism
Local people's congresses, 104, 110, 129, 158–59, 289; Law of the People's Republic of China on Deputies to the National People's Congress and Deputies to Local People's Congresses (1992), 109; Law of the People's Republic of China on Deputies to the National People's Congress and to the Local People's Congresses at Various Levels, 112; Organic Law of the Local People's Congresses and Local People's Governments (1954), 107; Organic Law of the Local People's Congresses and Local People's Governments (1979), 289–90; Organic Law of the Local People's Congresses and Local People's Governments (1979, amended 1982, 1986, 1995, 2004), 109. *See also* People's congress system (PCS)
Lockean theory and model, 195–96
Long March, 138
Lowi, Theodore, 333
Lucheng District Shoe Association, 159
Lu Zhiqiang, 174

MacFarquhar, Roderick, 104
Macroeconomic control, 261–62, 263, 331
Madison, James, 271
Manin, Bernard, 119
Manion, Melanie, 32–33, 387
Mao Zedong: analysis of types of state systems by, 138–39; on CCP's victory in Chinese revolution, 138; on class struggle, 44–45, 47, 63; on constitutional government, 10, 117; and democratic centralism, 52; Deng righting the course of, 65; design of state system by, 139; on desirability of permanent revolution, 3, 40, 42, 45; on development of Chinese Communist Party, 74, 75; on formation of new democratic republic, 139; leadership and tenure of, 348; political mechanisms of, ix, 2; supreme directives of, 50; on violent suppression of enemies, 48. *See also* Cultural Revolution
Market economy, effect of introduction of, 13, 16, 43, 58, 82
Marshall, T. H., 248
Martial law, 123
Marxism, ix, 40, 44, 46, 47–48, 74–75, 78, 88, 139, 179
Mass protests, 129
Mencius, 270
Mexico's one-party-dominant authoritarian regime, 96–97
Middle class, 27, 332
Migrants: and public service provision, 224, 225, 226, 227, 228, 230, 245, 248; and social structure, 313
Mineral resources, 235, 261
Ministry of Civil Affairs: classification of NGOs, 206; corruption investigations by, 285; election of village committee members promoted by, 284; Guiding Principles on Conducting Rural Autonomy Demonstrations Nationwide (1994), 201; homeowners committees statistics, 295; old-age pension system, 231; pilot village autonomy programs, 201; registration of and rules on foundations, 172; registration of community-based organizations, 170; residents committees, election of, 287; socially based social welfare instituted by, 224; Wenchuan earthquake (2008) relief, 209
Ministry of Finance's Accounting Rules for Nonprofit Organizations, 172
Ministry of Housing and Urban-Rural Development, 233
Ministry of Light Industry, 53–54

Ministry of Textile Industry, 53–54
Minorities: constitutional rights of, 255; Han ethnicity as dominant, 215; minority autonomous regions, 104
Modernization theory, 8, 94, 272
Montesquieu, 271
Multiparty system, 81, 93, 95, 97, 99, 136–64, 212–13, 301, 352. *See also* Political consultation system

Nancheng Township (Sichuan Province), 294
Nanjing, 186, 204, 205
Narada Foundation, 170–71
National Congress. *See* CCP National Congress
National Development and Reform Commission, 258, 261
National People's Congress (NPC): 1st, 107, 343; 2nd, 49; 5th, 108–09, 110, 113; 6th, 115; 7th, 109, 115; 8th, 147–48, 352; 9th, 109, 116; 10th, 109, 111, 226; 11th, 356; administrative power of, 80, 103, 115; budgeting and fiscal system, improvement of, 120–21; chairman's role and leader-centered model, 122–24; constitutional power of, 10–11; democratization, role in, 128–30; entrepreneurs appointed to, 160; future of, 98, 120; grassroots organizations of, 289; Law of the People's Republic of China on Deputies to the National People's Congress and Deputies to Local People's Congresses (1992), 109; Law of the People's Republic of China on Deputies to the National People's Congress and to the Local People's Congresses at Various Levels, 112; law-related powers of, 125; Legal Development Committee of the NPC Standing Committee, 113; near-term goals for, 62; Organic Law of the National People's Congress, 107, 108–09; as organ of state power, 9, 10, 49, 103, 114; part of people's congress systems (PCS), 103; power of, 103, 107, 123; as prime organ of state, 143; promulgation of laws by, 51, 120, 259;

relationship with CCP, 115–17, 257; Rules of Procedure for, 110–11; Several Opinions on Giving Full Scope to the Role of Special Committees (General Office of NPC Standing Committee), 110; special committees (standing committees), 110, 120; Standing Committee, 109, 116, 123, 128, 198, 343
National Rural Work Conference (1982), 43
National Working Meeting on Harmonious Neighborhood Building (2009), 205
Nazi Party, 187
Neighborhood associations, 160, 205–06
NGO Forum on Women (1995), 166
Nongovernmental organizations (NGOs), 14, 165–91; Accounting Rules for Nonprofit Organizations, 172; advice from, 159; city models, 170, 186; dissolution at time of CCP taking power, 55; for human rights and environmental protection, 166, 169; number of, 56, 86, 169, 171, 206–07; registration system for, 170, 172, 178; Regulations on Registration and Administration of Social Organizations, 371–72; role in society, 53–54, 168. *See also* Civil society
North, Douglass, 341, 347
NPC. *See* National People's Congress
Nu River dam, campaign against, 175, 176, 180, 186, 261

O'Brien, Kevin, 104
Oi, Jean C., 24–25, 299
"On the Reform of the System of Party and State Leadership" (Deng), 78, 140, 349
Opium Wars (1840), 106
Organic Law. *See topic of law*
Outline of Local Autonomy (Huang Zhezhen), 193
Oxfam International, 179

Panyu waste incinerator protest, 176
"Party and State Leadership System Reform" (Deng), 78
Paternalism, 334
PCS. *See* People's Congress System
Peng Dehuai, 42

Peng Zhen, 110, 115, 122, 198

Pension system, 230–31

People's congress system (PCS), 103–30; constitutionalism and reform of, 117–21, 126–28; creation of, 139; deLisle comment on, 121–30; democratic legitimacy of, 126; democratization, role in, 104, 128–30; development of, 108–10; establishment of, 103, 105–08; Law of the People's Republic of China on the Supervision of Standing Committees of People's Congresses at All Levels, 371, 378; Law on the Supervision of Standing Committees of People's Congresses at Various Levels (2006), 109, 115; law-related powers of, 125; organization of, 103–04, 108–17; previous research on, 105; relationship and coordination with other state organs, 104, 113–15; relationship with CCP, 115–17; relationship with minority autonomous regions, 104; relationship with the people, 103, 110–13, 120, 139; stability, importance of, 108, 118–19, 130; supervision of members and accountability, 381. *See also* Local people's congresses; National People's Congress (NPC)

People's Daily, 113, 309

Petition system, need to reform, 315–16

Philanthropy, 173–74

Politburo, 66, 342, 343, 344, 348, 349, 351, 361

Political centralism and economic federalism, 21. *See also* Fiscal federalism

Political consultation system, 11–12, 136–64, 352; contribution to China's political development, 67, 119, 154–55, 276; deliberative democracy vs., 12, 98, 155, 157–58; experiments in Zeguo and Xinhe townships, 158–59, 161; Fewsmith's comment on, 156–62; forms of, 148; foundation of, 137–39; leadership, cooperation, and consultation, 12, 143–47, 155–56; mechanics of, 147–50; number and relationships of actors in, 144–45; Opinions on Further Strengthening the Building of the System

of Multiparty Cooperation and Political Consultation Led by the CCP (2005), 149; political orientation of, 6, 139–43; View of the CCP on Persisting in and Perfecting the System of Multiparty Cooperation and Political Consultation under the Leadership of the Communist Party (1989), 352. *See also* Chinese People's Political Consultative Conference (CPPCC)

Political disorder, likelihood of, 322

Political economy, importance of, 66–67

Political Order in Changing Societies (Huntington), 361

Political parties, 73–76, 81, 84. *See also* Chinese Communist Party (CCP); Multiparty system; Political consultation system

Political reform: cycles of reform, 340; incremental reform leading to innovation and transformation, 61; lagging behind economic development and social changes, xi, 61, 93, 99; measures taken by CCP, xi, 7; near-term goals for, 62; prior catastrophic failure as prerequisite for major reform, 66; resistance to, 5, 68; slow pace of, 299–300; transition to fundamentally democratic political system, 64–65; types needed, 64–68. *See also* Evolution of China's political development

Political system: building of nation-state envisioned by Sun Yat-sen, 106; formal and informal nature of, 256, 275; grand unity of political centralization, 13; horizontal organization of government departments, 265, 266; horizontal triangular framework of constitutional branches of government, 114; and modernization, 322, 327; paternalism in, 334; progress in political development, 33–37, 67–68; public service provision's effect on, 247–51; scholarship on, 35–36; traditional political culture, 6, 77–78, 192; triangular structure of party, state, and society, 114, 144, 146, 155; unitary, 255–61, 265–68; vertical and horizontal power of central government,

34, 61, 254; vertical organization of government departments, 258–60, 265, 266, 271; vertical triangular framework of power structure, 114. *See also* Authoritarian systems; Constitutionalism; Fiscal federalism; People's congress system (PCS); Political consultation system
Power, exhibition of, 270–72
PRI. *See* Revolutionary Institutional Party
Professionalism, 98
Property Law, 123
Property ownership: constitutional right to, 111; conversion costs and real estate development, 263–64, 275
Provisional Regulations. *See topic of regulation*
Public choice theory, 259
Public health, 224, 229–30, 242; Guiding Opinions on Establishing and Standardizing the Essential Drug Procurement Mechanism for Government-Sponsored Medical and Health Institutions at the Grassroots Level (2010), 230; Implementing Opinion on the Establishment of an Essential Drug System (2009), 230; National List of Essential Drugs for Primary Healthcare Facilities (2009), 230; Opinions on Deepening the Reform of the Medical and Health Care System (2009), 230; Provisional Regulations on the Administration of a National List of Essential Drugs (2009), 230; Work Plan on Five Major Issues Concerning the Medical and Health Care System Reform (2011), 230
Public policymaking, 318–19, 322
Public security expenditures, 316–17, 330–31
Public service system, 18–20, 221–53; basic medical security, 229–30; basic old-age security and senior services, 230–31, 250; development and reform of, 221–27, 246–51; employment security and service, 227–29; fiscal support system for, 233–38, 240–41; impact on political development, 247–51; localization of, 224–25, 239; low-income

housing, 232–33; marketization of, 224, 227; minimum living security and social assistance, 231–32, 246, 264, 265; pilot programs, 223, 242; privatization of, 175–76; problems and prospect of, 221–22, 238–44; "province administering the county" system, 236–37; Regulations on Securing Minimum Living Standards for Urban Residents (1999), 231–32; Saich's comment on, 244–51; self-reliance as principle for, 245–46; social changes necessitating, 171; Social Insurance Law of the People's Republic of China (2010), 227; social policy system as government focus, 227–33; and tax-sharing system, 225; transition to equal access approach, 226–27, 234–35, 240; urban-rural duality model, 222, 223–24, 240, 246
Public sphere and civil society, 167–68, 174
Pudong Economic Development Zone, 352
Pudong New District, 175, 251
Putnam, Robert, 121, 167
PX factory protests (Xiamen), 176
Pye, Lucian, 107, 118, 126

Qianjiang (Hubei Province), 291
Qiao Shi, 123
Qing dynasty, 193
Qinghai, 267
Qi Yuling, 127
Quanzhou (Fujian Province), 291

Red Cross Society of China, 170
Reform. *See* Evolution of China's political development; Political reform
Regulations. *See topic of regulation*
Regulatory governance, 51, 108–17, 259
Report to the 17th National Congress of the CCP, 87, 89, 177, 351, 356
Research Report on China's Social Harmony and Stability (Chinese Academy of Social Sciences), 310–11
Residents committees, election of, 286–88
Revolutionary Institutional Party (PRI, Mexico), 96–97
Revolution as continuous goal under Mao Zedong, 3, 40, 42, 45

Revolution of 1911, 137
Revolution of 1949, 3
Rule of law: promotion of, 6, 9, 67, 91, 99, 108, 125; relationship to CCP and democracy, 119–20; revolutionary neglect of, 8; from rule of man to rule of law, 49–51, 130; and separation of powers, 271; socialist approach to, 9; underdevelopment of, 296, 298, 383
Rule of man as legal principle, 49–51, 130
Rules of Shanghai Municipality on Subdistrict Offices (1997), 204
Ruling party. *See* Chinese Communist Party (CCP)
Rural China. *See* Villages
Russia. *See* Former Soviet states; Soviet influences; Soviet Union

Saich, Tony, 19–20, 210, 244
Scalapino, Robert, 99
Schmidt, Carl, 121
Scientific and technological development: and decisionmaking process, 354; High-Tech Research and Development Program (863 Program), 352; political openness fostering, xii; productivity gains from, 25; Proposal for Tracking the Development of World Strategic High Technology, 352; social pressures of, 89, 318
Scientific outlook on development, 29, 30, 35, 49, 59, 221, 222, 226, 242, 296
Self-government, 192, 199, 211. *See also* Social autonomy
Separation of powers, 34, 60, 86, 254, 271, 272–74, 277, 381, 382, 386
Shandong Province, 201, 267, 274, 285
Shanghai, 204, 205, 231, 232, 246, 251, 287, 290, 316
Shanghai Pudong Economic Development Zone, 352
Shanghai Young Men's Christian Association, 251
Shen Mingmin, 335
Shenzhen, 165, 175–76, 186, 204, 294
Shenzhen Special Economic Zone, 262
Shi Hexing, 9–10, 11, 103, 121–22, 126, 128–30

Sichuan Province, 209, 294
Singapore, 7, 8, 17, 94–95, 99, 213, 245, 297
Single-party system. *See* Authoritarian systems
Size-of-collectivity, 271
Social autonomy, 15–17, 192–220; defined, 15; development of social organizations and industry autonomy, 82, 206–08; evolution of district-level governments, 203–06; government efforts toward, 15–18, 198–200; Guiding Principles on Conducting Rural Autonomy Demonstrations Nationwide (1994), 201; Organic Law of Urban Neighborhood Committees (1954), 204; Organic Law of Urban Subdistrict Offices (1954), 204; reconstructing state-society relations, 193–98; resident autonomy in cities and villages, 286–88; tradition of, 192–93; urban grassroots communities, 203; village autonomy, 200–03; Walder's comment on, 211–16. *See also* Grassroots democracy
Social enterprise, 174
Social Insurance Law of the People's Republic of China (2010), 227
Socialism, 40, 41, 44–45, 47, 49, 54, 82, 249, 369
Social organizations, 80, 177, 206–07, 224; Regulations on Registration and Administration of Social Organizations, 371–72. *See also* Civil society; Nongovernmental organizations (NGOs)
Social safety nets, 68. *See also* Public service system
Social structure: black-collar stratum, 330, 332; CPPCC attitude toward changes in, 146; elitists, 334–35; labor-capital relationship, 313–14, 319, 330; pluralism of, 326–27; populists, 334, 335; post-reform and opening up changes, 309; post-revolution changes, 309; of pre-communist China, 139; scholarship on state-society relations, 195–97; and social injustice, 331
Song Ching Ling Foundation, 172

South Korea, 245, 247, 332

Soviet influences, 76, 79, 141, 215, 346, 383

Soviet Union: collapse of, 18, 95, 126, 214–15, 274; comparison to China, 215–16, 247; democratization of, 297. *See also* Communist Party of the Soviet Union (CPSU); Former Soviet states

Special economic zones, 60, 65, 262

Stability, importance of, 108, 118–19, 130, 316–17, 330–31. *See also* Public security expenditures

Stalin, Joseph, ix

State Council: constitutional powers of, 256; departments and state offices under, 144; disclosures report to, 355; enactment of regulations, 51, 128, 259; first election of, 343; General Office, 230, 355; health care initiatives, 229–30; land under control of, 261; low-income housing provision, 232; NPC relationship with, 123, 124, 256; Organic Law of the State Council, 107; relationship with CCP, 342, 351; rural education meeting, 228; social pension insurance, adoption of, 230, 231; social security system for rural residents, 232; tax-sharing reform, adoption of, 53, 234, 235. *See also specific subjects of regulations promulgated by State Council*

State-owned enterprises: CCP power from, 85; contribution to gross industrial output, 55; corporate social responsibility of, 174; debt revocation or evasion by, 267, 274; economic restructuring of, 223, 224, 231, 245; effect on private enterprises, 331; foundations established by, 173; monopoly of, 261; policies favoring, 332; as recipients of wealth, 68; in socialist economic scheme, 54

State-private joint ownership of industries and business, 54

State Statistics Bureau, 373

Steinmo, Sven, 341

Sun Liping, 324, 331

Sun Yat-sen, 6, 74, 75–76, 106, 139

Sun Zhe, 120

Sun Zhigang, 128

Suppression of Counterrevolutionaries, 344

Supreme People's Court, 256, 259, 342, 343

Supreme People's Procuratorate, 256, 342, 343; Organic Law of the People's Procuratorates (1954), 107; Procurators Law, 371

Taiwan, 97, 99, 157, 245, 297

Tanner, Murray Scot, 104, 117

Tax-sharing system: adoption of, 53, 234; and central-local relationship, 262–64; and public service system, 225, 234–36; Rules on Transfer Payments from the Central Government to the Local Governments on Rural Tax and Fee Reform, 285

Technology. *See* Scientific and technological development

Thornton, John, 33

Three-Anti Campaign, 344

"Three awards and one subsidy" policy, 235

Three Represents theory, 6, 59, 88, 89, 95, 117, 124, 326–27, 335

"Three-three" governance system, 141

Tiananmen Square protests (1989), 122, 172, 311

Tianjin, 205, 231, 246

Tieben Incident (2004), 262

Totalitarian politics, 195

Townships: Circular on Implementing the Separation of Government and Society and Establishing Township Governments (1983), 201; mayors, election of, 23, 285, 288–89, 292–94, 300

Trade associations, 159–60, 193, 320

Trade Union Federation, 80

Transparency, need for, 7, 67, 98, 246, 249, 251, 300, 356

Transparency International, 372–73

Tsai, Lily, 251

Tsinghua University, 331

Unemployment rate, 332

Unitarism and pluralism, 324–27

United Nations: Convention against Corruption, 372; Development Program, 94; Fourth World Conference on Women, 166, 169

United States: dilemma facing framers of U.S. constitutional system, 363; expansion of federal powers in, 213; lobbyists and organized interests in, 333; political corruption in, 212–13; scientific approach to decisionmaking in, 362. *See also* Western democracies

Urban administration, 204; medical care system, 229; National Working Meeting on Harmonious Neighborhood Building (2009), 205; Organic Law of the Urban Residents Committees (1989), 286; Organic Law of Urban Neighborhood Committees (1954), 204; Organic Law of Urban Subdistrict Offices, 204; Regulations on Securing Minimum Living Standards for Urban Residents, 231–32; Regulations on Securing Minimum Living Standards for Urban Residents (1999), 231–32; Rules of Shanghai Municipality on Subdistrict Offices (1997), 204; Several Opinions of the State Council on Solving the Housing Difficulties of Urban Low-Income Families, 232; social autonomy of, 203; work-unit welfare, 222

Urban-rural duality: continuance of, 321; and public service system, 222, 223–24, 240

Vargas Llosa, Mario, 96, 97

Vertical networks, 271. *See also* Accountability; Political system

Villages: agricultural tradition of pre-communist China, 139, 343; autonomy of, 200–03; collective welfare in, 222; compulsory education, 223, 228; elections, 23–25, 97, 122, 129, 284–86, 292, 302; medical cooperative scheme, 229; Organic Law of the Village Committees of the People's Republic of China (1987), 201, 202, 203, 284–85, 303; pilot social pension system in, 223; social security system for rural residents, 232; two-ballot system and direct election method, 292, 380–81; Village Elections Law, 122

Voting. *See* Elections

Walder, Andrew, 17, 211, 245
Wang Changjiang, 5–6, 73, 93, 95, 99
Wang Jianlin, 173–74
Wang Ming, 13–14, 165, 183–88
Wang Shengjun, 127–28
Wang Xuejun, 310
Wan Li, 110, 115, 122–23, 349
Wealthy class, growth of, 58, 309
Weder, Beatrice, 389
Weimar Germany, 187–88
Welfare system. *See* Public service system
Wenchuan earthquake (2008), 14, 173–74, 209
Wen Jiabao: on democracy as critical, 272; on institutional reform, 361; on lag between socioeconomic growth and political development, xi; and Nu River Dam project, 175; and public service supply system, 20, 226, 245, 247, 248–49; rule of law endorsed by, 124; on social organizations, 177
Wenling (Zhejiang Province), 295
Wenzhou Lighter Association, 174–75, 186, 208
Western ability to visit China and gather information, 34
Western democracies: and civil society, 179; comparative constitutional democratic systems in, 121; compared to Chinese system, 283, 325; and emergence of political parties, 74; and interest coordination mechanism, 324, 325; and lobbyists and organized interests, 333; multiparty systems in, 213, 345. *See also* Deliberative democracy; United States
White, Lynn, 22, 254, 270
Women's Federation, 80, 186
Workers' unions, role in welfare states, 277
World Bank, 234
World Conference on Women (Beijing 1995), 166, 169
World Trade Organization, 43, 60, 174, 259
World Values Survey, 94
World Vision International, 179
Writers Association, 80
Wu Bangguo, 113, 114–15, 123

Xiamen PX factory protests, 176
Xia Ming, 104
Xiao Yang, 128
Xi Jinping, 124, 128
Xi Mei Dong Song program, 261
Xinhe township, 158–59, 161, 295

Yang Guangbin, 21–22, 254, 270–77
Yangtze River Delta Development Zone, 352
Yan Jirong, 16–17, 192, 211–12, 214, 216
Yao Lifa, 290
Yao Yang, 333
Youth Federation, 80
Yu Jianxing, 18–19, 221, 244, 246
Yu Keping, xi, xii, 1, 39, 62–63, 66, 68, 167

Yunnan Province, 288, 294
Yushu earthquake (2010), 174

Zedillo, Ernesto, 97
Zeguo township, 158, 295
Zeng Jianyu, 290
Zeng Qinghong, 310
Zhang Youyu, 10, 117–18
Zhao Baoxu, 121
Zhao Ziyang, 122
Zhejiang Province, 158, 231, 232, 237, 251, 285, 287, 309
Zhou Enlai, 142
Zhou Guanghui, 28–29, 340, 359–64
Zhou Qiang, 128
Zhou Zhanshun, 311
Zhu Rongji, 247, 248, 262, 275

www.ingramcontent.com/pod-product-compliance
Lightning Source LLC
Chambersburg PA
CBHW021806270326
41932CB00007B/78